M000218457

god is green

God is Green

An Eco-Spirituality of Incarnate Compassion

ROBERT E. SHORE-GOSS

CASCADE *Books* · Eugene, Oregon

GOD IS GREEN
An Eco-Spirituality of Incarnate Compassion

Copyright © 2016 Robert E. Shore-Goss. All rights reserved. Except for brief quotations in critical publications or reviews, no part of this book may be reproduced in any manner without prior written permission from the publisher. Write: Permissions, Wipf and Stock Publishers, 199 W. 8th Ave., Suite 3, Eugene, OR 97401.

Cascade Books
An imprint of Wipf and Stock Publishers
199 W. 8th Ave., Suite 3
Eugene, OR 97401

www.wipfandstock.com

paperback ISBN 13: 987-1-4982-9919-0
hardcover ISBN 13: 987-1-4982-9921-3
ebook ISBN 13: 987-1-4982-9920-6

Cataloging-in-Publication data:

Names: Goss, Robert Everett.

Title: God is green : an eco-spirituality of incarnate compassion / Robert E. Shore-Goss.

Description: Eugene, OR: Cascade Books, 2016. | Includes bibliographic references.

Identifiers: 987-1-4982-9919-0 (paperback). | 987-1-4982-9921-3 (hardcover). | 987-1-4982-9920-6 (ebook).

Subjects: LCSH: Ecotheology. | Environmental ethics. | Nature—Religious aspects. | Deep ecology.

Classification: BT695.5 G67 2016 (print). | BT695.5 (ebook).

Manufactured in the U.S.A.

Dedicated to Rev. Joseph Shore-Goss,
G. T. Glander our Church Gardener
Allis Druffel an Earth Companion
the Valley Church in North Hollywood,
and to Earth-centered Heroes and Heroines in this book

If we fall in love with God's Earth,
we will fight to save the Earth.

Contents

Introduction

God is a life that bestows life, root of the world-tree and wind in its branches. She is glistening life alluring all praise, all awakening, all resurrecting.

—Hildegard of Bingen[1]

There is no such thing as 'human community' without the earth and the soil and the air and the water and all the living forms. Without these, humans do not exist. In my view, the human community and the natural world will go into the future as a single sacred community or we will both perish in the desert . . .

—Thomas Berry[2]

There are three symbols that together describe my project. They are interrelated and indelibly impressed in my consciousness: It is Jesus' "Parable of the Wicked Tenants" (Mark 12:1–12; Matt 21:33–45; Luke 20:9–19, Thomas 65–66); the other is "The Green Christ of Breton Cavalry" painted by French Paul Gauguin; and finally, the notion of *viriditas* or "greening energy" in the visionary writings of the 12th century mystic and Benedictine abbess Hildegard of Bingen. These three shape my ecospirituality

1. Hildegard of Bingen, *Smyposia: A Critical Edition of the Symphonia Armonie Celestium Revelationum*, 140–41.
2. Berry, *The Dream of the Earth*, 43.

1

and a response to the challenges of climate change. The three combined articulate my journey of faith in the last eight years, but the seeds were sown years before in my spiritual formation through Ignatian spirituality, ordination as a Jesuit priest, Buddhist studies, and as an AIDS activist/theologian. This text is about my falling in love with God's Earth and a journey to envisioning God's Incarnated Christ in the world.

The Parable

The context of the "Parable of the Wicked Tenants" is set by Mark in Jerusalem after Jesus' provocative demonstration in the Temple and several challenges to the Jewish leadership. Jesus' original parable does not include the Markan edition of vs. 10–12 with the cornerstone saying function as a passion and passion prediction. The original parable, notes Steve Patterson, is not about the reign of God: "This is a parable about the world—the world as it really is when we dare to peak behind the carefully erected mythic façade, designed to protect our sensibilities from its brutalities."[3] The parable stripped of its Christological interpretation offers a scenario building on the allegorical verses in Isaiah 5:1–5, where God plants a vineyard, it does not bear fruit, and God destroys it. The Isaiah poem is applied to an unruly Jerusalem resulting from social oppression, revolt, and devastation brought about the politics of the Roman Empire and the co-opted Temple theocracy. This parable is told during the last days of Jesus in an escalating conflict with the Temple authorities and directed against "the chief priests, Pharisees, and scribes."

What if in our imagined reading, we understand God's Earth as the vineyard and humans as the tenants. It is a bleak vision of the brutal dynamics of Empire, resistance, religion, and destruction in first-century CE Palestine. The leading tenants are prosperous amidst the poor subsistence of the other tenants around them. It is a safe to assume that many tenants are poor or perhaps day laborers. For today, the comparable elites consisting of the 1% and fossil fuel billionaires whose greed for profit at all cost ravage the Earth, compliant politicians and church folks denying climate change, unbridled consuermism, and globalized capitalism seeking to expand. The vineyard owner sends slaves to collect his share of the harvest. The tenants at behest of their leaders take those sent from Greenpeace, Sierra Club, Environmental Defense Fund, and Interfaith

---

3. Patterson, *The God of Jesus*, 140.

Power & Light beat them and/or kill them. Then the owner sends his own beloved child, saying "they will respect my heir."[4] But the leaders seize the heir, murder him, and throw him out of the vineyard. This parable has become all too real to mysef when two environmentalists in the Amazon were recently murdered, and the numbers of murdered environmental-ists between 2002 -2013 in Brazil total four-hundred forty-eight.[5] They were killed by loggers, prompted by elite corporate interests, for their work for conservation of the Amazon rainforest, and they are martyrs for God's Earth.

Steve Patterson's conclusion about Jesus' glum parable seems still applicable to us today:

> One needs only play by the rules, accept your assigned role and everything will work out fine . . . Jesus lived among persons for whom the world never worked. He knew that the justice and fairness of the workday was an illusion. The nihilistic parable exposes it as such. In it, no one errs . . . Can a world so hierarchi-cal in assumptions as to accept without question the existence of landlords and tenants ever offer more than this? Jesus' parables were not just a visionary glimpse of the Empire of God. They represent an all-out offensive against the world as it was conven-tionally conceived. Before the Empire of God can capture the imagination and become a reality, the old world of conventional assumptions must be undermined to the point of collapse.[6]

Jesus uses a readily understood social metaphor of the oppressive dynam-ics of tenant farming to delineate the counter-forces to God's reign. At the end of the parable, the owner destroys the tenants and gives the vineyard to others. Our planet has evolved into a globalized plutarchical Empire of the 1% of the population that own 40% of the world's wealth, and they continue to inflict violence against the Earth through reckless exploita-tion of resources, ruthlessly horizontal fracking the Earth, mountain top harvesting of coal, polluting the soil, air, and water. We live in world dominated by human greed, globalized over-consumption of the earth's resources, short-term profit over long-term harmful consequences to the

4. A good summary of a wide range of interpretations of this parable. See Paul Y. Chang," Listening to the Listeners," 165–86.

5. These are saints and martyrs for the Earth. Sister Dorothy Stang, a 73-year-old nun, was assassinated by two gunmen because of her advocacy for small scale farm-ers in conflict with large corporate interests and cattle ranch owners. Michael Miller, "Why are Brazil's Environmentalists Being Murdered?"

6. Patterson, *The God of Jesus*, 141.

Earth, humanity, and other life. Everything is for their benefit, profit, and rule. Those poor residents in the vineyard continue at their subsistent levels, but they do not matter. It mirrors our own world addicted to fossil fuels, driven without regard to the consequences to the ravages of the Earth, the poor and vulnerable other life. Millions, if not hundreds of millions of humanity along with other, will be sacrificed for greed.

There is, however, a Christological reference in the parable of the vineyard to the owner's son. Mark further attempts to salvage the parable by adding a Christological affirmation of hope: "The stone that the builders rejected has become the cornerstone; this was the Lord's doing, and it is amazing in our eyes" (vv. 10–11). The addition is a sword with a twofold edge, for it heightens the Christological reference of the owner's son; secondly, it places the conflict of Jesus within the sequence of conflictive encounters with the Temple—starting with Mark 11:38, where Jesus angers the Temple authorities and ends with his arrest, the legal proceedings against him, and handing him over to Pilate. Pilate then offers the crowds in Jerusalem a choice between Jesus and Barabbas, and the Temple leaders incite the crowds to choose Barabbas.

I have heard too many times from both Christian environmentalists, despondent about our current climate crisis: "Humanity may not survive, but the Earth will survive!" Some environmentalists candidly speak of the possibility of an impending sixth extinction. These comments of friends and activists draw me to this glum parable of Jesus and the last line of story: "The owner will come and destroy the tenants and give the vineyard to others." When I ask myself, "where do I see myself in this troublesome story?" The dynamics of Empire and oppression in early first century CE Jerusalem have been recycled over the two millennia to human apartheid from nature, the industrial domination of the Earth, an addiction to fossil fuels and economic over-consumption of resources disproportionate to the seven billion people and project rapid growth of population to fifteen billion by the end of the century. If I follow my usual practices of exegetical unpacking a scriptural text and contemplative placement within the text, I envision myself as a tenant in the vineyard or other times a slave sent by the owner to claim a share of the produce struggling against an overwhelmingly oppressive system with two billion or more people with inadequate food or clean water or little water, species extinction accelerating, and the possibility that life in the oceans may come to an end this century. The Earth may have her last say in judging humanity for its crimes against life.

What gives me hope is my faith in Mark's addendum to the parable of the cornerstone saying. It transforms the parable from a fourth passion prediction with the addition of the allusion to the resurrection in the cornerstone saying. The message of the cornerstone is God's reign. Mark's solution to this parable is to choose to follow Jesus' non-violent ministry of challenge and co-empowering disciples to resist the power dynamics of Empire in a time of crisis and Jesus' trust in Abba.

The Painting of the Green Christ

Now we turn to the portrayal of "The Green Christ of Breton Cavalry" painted by French impressionist Paul Gauguin in 1889. Gauguin's painting opens me emotionally and contemplatively beyond the gloominess of Jesus' parable, and visualization of the painting in meditative practice creates new dimensions of hope in our climate change crisis. Gauguin portrays the women at the foot of the cross, tenderly carrying the body of Jesus, the vineyard heir down from the cross. The crucified Jesus is contextualized in the wild Breton landscape of France. Christ's body is green, prophetically signifying for myself that his death was green—bringing life to all. Three women are colored the same shade of green as Christ's dead body, while the vertical timber of cross remains a dark brown color. There is a woman in typical Breton dress with a sheep in the foreground of three women holding the body of Christ. The green shading from women and the body of Christ appear to be spilling green from themselves to the grass or ground. There is some green shading of the hills in the background with the shore line.

I have found this painting profoundly symbolic of the ecological Christ, crucified and interwoven within "this-worldly" Breton landscape. His body's green coloring signifies growth and life and the women and the Earth herself accept the murdered and ravaged body of Christ. The eventual entombment of Christ into the Earth evokes the second creation of Adam, for the Genesis 2 creation account associates the earthling (*adamah*) or soil creature. Daniel Hillman writes,

> The ancient Hebrew association of (hu) man with soil is echoed
> in the Latin name for man, *homo*, derived from *humus*, the stuff
> of life in the soil. This powerful metaphor suggests an early

realization of a profound truth that humanity has since disregarded to its own detriment.[7]

Hillman associates the Latin word for humanity, *homo* with humus soil,
the organic matter formed from the decayed leaves or plant material. It
is hard not to associate humus further with the cognitive derived Latin
word "humble" or "humility" as well as the early Christian hymn in Philippians 2:6–11, where Christ empties himself of equality with God to
take on the form of a slave. This kenotic aspect is correlated with the
"humus" dimensions of Christ and his entombment provides me with
intimations of resurrected life, a second Adam created from the humus of
the Earth. The Christian hymn celebrates a divine kenosis self-emptying
relationship with Earth and provides hope.[8]

For myself, Gauguin's Green Christ incorporates the multiple levels
of notion of green grace and its greening consequences, and it highlights
Christ death for healing and life—with a clear assertion that the cross of
death is transformed into the tree of life. There are shades of greening
in the background landscape, and the greening emerges from the green
Christ. I identify myself contemplatively with one of three women who
tenderly hold the body of the green Christ taken down from the cross. As
I place myself in the painting, I imagine myself touching the dead body
of Christ, but it spills greening life to those holding on to him, greening
the foreground and background. I imagined an embodied greening pulse
of energy streaming into myself and generating sparks of hope and faith
in the green Christ's cross into the Tree of Life. Greening energy pulses
with hope inspite of death.

Greening Grace

But there is an additional theo-spiritual and contemplative trajectory
woven into Jesus' parable and Gauguin's Green Christ, for I turn to the
twelfth century Benedictine mystic visionary, poet, musician, and theologian, Hildegard of Bingen. She wrote of about the green power of God's
Spirit, coining the word *viriditas* from "greening" and "truth." It was
for her a divine attribute, the divine greening power or life force that
animates creation's fecundity from the beginning, planting, nourishing,
and flourishing. She envisioned God's gracious energy as a green fire or

7. Hillel, *Out of the Earth*, 14.
8. See McFague, *Blessed are the Consumers*.

energy spilling out from the triune community of love. Greening was her metaphorical language for speaking of the green presence God's Spirit in humanity and creation. Christian theologian Veli-Matti Karkkainen writes, "For this spiritual mystic, *viriditas* was a key component of spirituality that expressed and connected the bounty of God, the fertility of nature, and the enlivening, fresh presence of the Spirit."[19] The Spirit's greening presence sustains and transforms all creation towards the incarnational transformation and flourishing intended by the triune God.

Hildegard was a uniquely gifted mystic and prophet, and she envisioned the inner life of the Trinitarian God as pouring out grace to the world. She calls this gracious love and energy *viriditas*, greening power. *Viriditas* represents the principle of life, growth, and fertility flowing from the life-creating power of God into Earth and life. Grace is green for me, and it leads us to see God as greening energy of love. The life of God as Creator, Christ, and Spirit expresses the heart of *viriditas* as creative interrelatedness, mutuality and fecundity. God births *viriditas* as interrelatedness, Christ incarnates as *viriditas*, and the Spirit germinates as the greening power of life. For Hildegard, *viriditas* emerged from her bodily experience as a woman and imaginative engagement with the land as a Benedictine nun committed to a vow of stability and a member of the soil community. It also evokes a woman's ability to bear life in the womb as a wonderful metaphor for grace. Hildegard understood God's Incarnation as the green source of flesly life, and she drew her inspiration of *viriditas* from her interactions with the rural countryside. God's greening power shapes, nourishes, and confronts us. It is God's inner interrelatedness, interrelated with us, and all life. Hildegard states, "everything exists to respond to the other."[10] For Hildegard, "to be green was to be more receptive to the Divine Presence in humanity and in creation."[11]

Viriditas is Hildegard's description of God's grace as greening power, profound interrelatedness, and fecundity. Renate Craine explains *viriditas*,

> This intense stirring calls us to wake up to its presence and to become conscious participants in the interrelated web of life that reveals the mystery of Trinitarian God. Her theological

9. Karkkainen, *Pneumatology*, 51.

10. Craine, *Hildegard*, 41,

11. Kujawa-Holbrook, *Hidegard of Bingen*, Loc. 1737.

term for this profound interrelatedness is *viriditas*, a mutuality
and fecundity that is the work of Christ and the human task.[12]

The greening power of God interrelates with our lives and all fleshly life,
and we become connected to the green web of life. It reveals something of
the mothering nature of God, in whose image we are made green. It taps
the reservoir of greening power within ourselves, for when we engage it,
we are, in turn, changed and find ourselves in love with God and all life.
There is a birthing of this greening life and fecundity within the "wombs"
of our lives. And it spills out into awareness of interrelatedness.

Viriditas is the interpretative lens through which I experience
Gauguin's "The Green Christ" with hope. There is an added agency, the
greening death of Christ and the greening interrelatedness of Christ that
counters greed and self-centeredness of the tenant leaders' move towards
annihilation. Christ becomes God's "green word" and "greening energy"
interwoven with all fleshly life. Gauguin's green Christ and Hildegard's
notion of *viriditas* draw fleshly or incarnational interconnectedness between the Earth as the Body of Christ.[13]

Many of us have lost a reverence for life and for the Earth, and we
have collectively created cultural-spiritual apartheid between ourselves
and the Earth. And we are all paying for this apartheid from nature. Hildegard would be quick to point out that such self-centeredness short-cir-
cuits or disrupts the flow of *viriditas*. She would be the first to understand
that our Earth crisis has closed us to the web of divine interrelatedness
in creation and ourselves. And Gauguin's painting in "The Green Christ
of Breton Cavalry" furthers my dream that God's greening of Easter will
triumph over the Wicked Tenants. Theologian Jay McDaniel looks to
God's green grace:

> Green grace is the healing that comes to us when we enjoy rich
> bonds with other people, plants and animals, and the Earth. It is
> a kind of grace celebrated by ecofeminists, native peoples, deep
> ecologists, and sacramentalists. It is green because as the green
> color suggests, it engenders within us healing and wholeness, a
> freshness and renewal that lead us into the very fullness of life
> . . . In a world torn asunder by violence, forgiveness is a most
> precious form of green grace.[14]

12. Craine, *Hildegard*, 39.

13. I also acknowledge McFague's identification of the Earth as God's Body.
McFague, *The Body of God*.

14. McDaniel, *With Roots and Wings*, 44.

A similar notion of hope is expressed by Mark Wallace when he writes,

> The cross is green. It is green because Jesus' witness on the cross
> is to a planet where all of God's children are bearers of life-giv-
> ing Spirit. It is green because the goodness of creation is God's
> here-and-now dwelling place where everyday life is charged
> with sacred presence and power.[15]

Mark Wallace involves the green cross in planetary healing, for we face
a self-inflicted theodicy that may result in extinction of life, but God's
power of resurrection will harness the greenness of the cross and unleash
its resurrection power of divine compassion through the Spirit.

Ecological Location

Ethicist Daniel Spencer insists that we include "ecological location" to
rethink theology:

> By ecological location, I mean enlarging the term social loca-
> tion to include . . . where human and non-human creatures
> and communities are situated with respect to other members of
> the biotic community as within human society and within the
> broader biotic community as well as conceiving other members
> of the biotic community and the biotic community itself as lo-
> catable active agents that historically interact with and shape the
> other members of the ecological community, including human
> beings.[16]

Here Spencer de-centers the anthropocentric context of most theologies
by providing an ecological location, comprehensive of the interactive reality of ourselves in a web of interrelated environmental relations, including other life and the biotic processes of the Earth herself. He takes the
theological notion of the social context for particular theologies to widen
it to include ecological location: how the particular geographies, environmental factors, local wildlife and planted life, and local environmental
processes shape us and how we shape the local environment. Spencer
underscores five elements of ecological location:

---

15. Wallace, *Green Christianity*, 38.
16. Spencer, *Gay and Gaia*, 295–296.

1. Nature's agency and humanity's unique agency within nature;

2. Both differences within human communities and between humanity and other parts of nature;

3. The variation and particularity of human power and privilege vis-à-vis nature;

4. The historical dimension of ecology and nature;

5. Recognizing the spiritual dimension of human interactions and histories with particular places, habitats, and geographies.

Eco-theology starts with these specific features of eco-location just as a variety of contextual theologies start with personal social context. Take a moment and be mindful of your eco-location as you start to read. I will likewise describe my own in the next section. Eco-location forces us first to look at our interrelationships with nature and make us less the center but focus on the network of ecological interrelationships. This remains the greatest challenge to move our ego-centric priorities over the environment and other life. Thus, Daniel Spencer provides a wider and interactive theological framework for an eco-theological spirituality. Spencer invites us to listen to our ecological backdrop as expressed by John Muir's words: "When we try to pick out anything by itself, we find it hitched to everything in the universe."[17] Listening to the backdrop of nature hearkens to what Buddhists call mindfulness. For example, Buddhist environmentalist Stephanie Kaza points out that trees and animals can be wisdom teachers; they can teach us much if we attempt to listen:[18] She notes,

> Trees, plants, animals, places—I am naming these possibilities to illustrate the many options for green mentoring within the streaming field of wisdom in the great web of life . . . there is an arresting garden of seven stones placed in a raked sand field, sixty feet wide and forty feet deep. Every time I visit, I want to stop and stay with these stones, listening, sensing: *What are they saying? What is it about how they are placed? Why is it so compelling?*[19]

17. Muir, *My First Summer in the Sierra,* 110
18. Kaza, *The Attentive Heart,* 1993.
19. Kaza, *Mindfully Green,* 91.

Mindfulness is listening to the many voices of nature. In Job 12:7, we read, "Ask the animals, and they will teach you, ask the birds, and they will teach you; ask the plants of the earth, and they will teach you." Job asks us to expand our perspective by listening to the text of nature. By listening to nature, Celtic and Orthodox Christians, Francis of Assisi and his successors led them to deep contemplative and incarnational experiences of Christ and the Spirit. By the time of Galileo, some Christians spoke of two books of revelation: the Bible and the Book of Nature. Contemplative strands of Christianity—Celtic and Orthodox Christianities, Francis of Assisi, Hildegard of Bingen, Ignatius Loyola, and Sallie McFague—found God very present within nature. I have learned through the years that *Lectio Divina*, a contemplative tradition to engage scripture, is equally applicable to listening and learning from nature.[20] Listening to nature is a sacred and different experience from ordinary listening and engaging nature, for it is unlike listening to human speech. It is a silent, untranslatable language of encounter and appreciative attentiveness to surrounding life and noises. The language of nature is entered into with silence, to experience the plants and the beauty of a nature and the community of life, and experience the network of interconnected life.

Just as I slowly and mindfully read scripture several times, I translate this practice daily, sitting outside in an amazing church garden often with my companion dog Friskie, I mindfully attend to the trees, the flowers, the succulents and desert-scape plants. I watch and listen to the birds and the insects in the garden. Within the voices of trees, flowers, and cacti and the desert succulents, there is also a deep and life-giving presence of God.[21] Such contemplative encounters have the impact of creating wonder and generating a deep love for God within nature. It is not limited to religious contemplatives but includes conservationists and naturalists who love the natural world. For instance, John Muir describes from his first exploration of the Sierra Mountains: "Oh, these vast, calm measureless mountain days, inciting at once to work and rest! Days in whose light, everything seems equally divine, opening a thousand windows to show us God."[22] Muir portrays mountains as "monuments of

20. Fischer, *Loving Creation*, 116–120.

21. See Mark Wallace for finding God in the particularities of the natural world: *Finding God in the Singing River*, 2005.

22. John Muir, "My First Summer in the Sierra," http://www.theatlantic.com/past/docs/unbound/flashbks/muir/muirfeb.htm; see also, The Nature Mysticism of John Muir, http://hummingbirdworld.com/spiritnature/Muir.htm.

love," and he intuited in his mystical engagement with nature that we are interrelated with everything else in the universe and beyond

My Ecological Location

I came to the Valley Church of North Hollywood in 2004, and I have served as Senior Pastor for more than twelve years, but as the Spirit works mischievously, when doors are shut from a homophobic tenure battle, the Spirit creates unexpected new possibilities. Briefly, I am writing this in Southern California where I live in a semi-arid environment, where the majority of water is transported from the Northern California, and we experience a severe drought. Severe water drought measures are in effect in the whole state, and tens of millions of trees have died directly from drought or the dryness of the landscape leading to destruction of large tracts of forest, wildlife, and human property through wild fires.

In 2006, we, as a congregation, watched the Al Gore's *Inconvenient Truth* documentary on global warming and climate change. We started on the road to listen to the Spirit and to listen to the Earth. And we incorporated a *tonglen* (Tibetan, "giving/receiving") meditation into our communion practice before the servers and celebrant received communion: "We offer the grace of this communion for the poor, the homeless, those suffering from war and hunger, and of the Earth so exploited, ravaged, and harmed by humanity." We remembered the Earth each week, and thenby 2007.it was natural to add the Earth to our membership roster. This compassionate communion meditation reminds us of our responsibility to suffering people and the vulnerable Earth.

Pastoral care for the Earth and other life has become a central ministry for our church. It originates from the notion that we as members of the Christ's church, including the Earth, are covenanted together. We took steps to covenant also with California Interfaith Power & Light, reducing our energy usage and offsetting our carbon footprint with a number of environmental conserving measures over several. First, I showed after service for six weeks one of the six short segments from the video *Renewal*.[23] After these 10–15 minute short clips, we discussed what might we do. The films sparked creative responses to stop buying styrofoam cups to bringing coffee cups, to recycling, to composting, to growing organic vegetables fruits from our gardens, to replacing bulbs with CFL(s)

---

23. *Renewal: Stories from America's Religious-Environmental Movement*(DVD).

and led(s) wherever possible. The congregants came up with the idea of energy-saving measure of a tankless water heater to replace a water heater that required energy all to heat the water. We were determined to model what it might look for a Christian community to live responsibly and sustainable with the Earth. Some congregants adopted these habits in their homes. We secured 90 solar panels through a lease program, saving from $500–800 per month on energy costs. We incorporated more educational programs around Earthcare, included worship and sermons about the Earth, and invited speakers to meet with us to learn more about our responsibilities to the Earth. Three years previously, we scored 75 on the UCC Green Justice Congregation scale, we now score over 140.[24] We use the scale as diagnostic tool for measuring our progress in reaching a carbon neutral footprint as a congregation. It took years to attain this because we realized that solar panels were wonderful for energy conservation, but the real work was our eco-conversion to Earthcare.

Originally, my spirituality developed from the incarnational roots of Ignatian daily practice of finding God in all things, but that spirituality picked up the bodhisattva practice of compassion and the Buddhist notion of interbeing along the way. I retrieved the spiritualities of Francis of Assisi, Hildegard of Bingen, Teihard de Chardin, and Albert Schweitzer, and I cherished new saints: Rachel Carson, John Muir, Thomas Berry, Thich Nhat Hanh, Sallie McFague, and Leonardo Boff. Each morning, I sat in our church meditation garden with my dog Friskie, listening mindful through my daily *lectio divina* practice God's presence in the garden. God revealed Godself as a Gardener.

Falling in Love with God and Earth

As we mindfully engage nature, we meet God. We intuit a connectedness with everything, and we no longer experience separateness as individuals, for at the heart of the universe, nothing exists in itself but exists interrelated to something else and through the infinite reaches of the universe. Prayer and contemplation allows us to enter the heart of the universe and experience the Spirit, the incarnated Christ and Creator interrelated within nature. This book attempts to spark "an environmental imaginary" of liberative eco-spirituality that re-contextualizes and re-envisions the

24. Green Justice Congregations: http://www.ucc.org/environmental-ministries _just-green-congregations.

sources of Christianity as interrelated with the Earth and the web of life.[25] My ecological imaginary has re-shaped my spirituality by expanding my prayer to become an eco-contemplative in compassion for the Earth. I am part of the Earth and interelated community of life.

The greening of our Christian imaginations deepens our relationship with God, the risen Christ as Gardner, and provides the foundation of Christian ecological practice. There are many Christians and churches turning to Earthcare in the form of ecojustice movements and committed to Earthcare My hope is to awaken our Christian awareness of our injuring the Earth and our failure to hear God voice, saying "These are my beloved children." The late Thomas Berry called for an "ecologically sensitive spirituality."[26] Berry devoted much of life's work, writings, and mentoring scholars, Christians, and non-Christians to promote a "life-enhancing" spiritualities with "wonder-filled intimacy with the planet."[27] Brian Swimme writes,

> The great mystery is that we are intersted in anything whatsover. Think of your friends, how you met them, how interresting they appeared to you. Why should anyone in the whole world interest us at all? Why don't we experience everyone as utter, unendurable bores? Why isn't the cosmos made that way? Why don't we suffer intolerable burdens with every person, forest, symphony, and sea-shore in exitence? The great surprise is that something or someone is interesting. Love begins there. Love begins when we discover interst. To be interested is to fall in love. To become fascinated is to step into a wild love affair on any level of life.[28]

If we fall in love with God's Earth, then we will fight to preserve what God loves and we love.

25. Peet and Watts, *Liberation Ecologies,* 263.

26. Berry, *Sacred Universe* loc. 2110.

27. Ibid., 2031 & 1759.

28. Swimme, *The Universe is a Green Dragon,* 4.

1

Snakes, Worms, and Compassion:
The Legacy of Saint Francis of Assisi

*Do people have ethical obligations toward rocks? To almost all
Americans, still saturated with ideas historically dominant in
Christianity . . . the question makes no sense at all. If the time comes
when to any considerable group of us such a question is no longer
ridiculous, we may be on the verge of a change of value structures that
will make possible measures to cope with the growing ecologic crisis.
One hopes that there is enough time left.*

—Lynn White[1]

I could say I want to imagine the world as it has never been.
—Leonardo Boff[2]

In 1968, at UCLA, a medieval European historian—Lynn White Jr. shook
the Christian churches with a published article entitled "The Historic

1. White, "Continuing the Conversation," 63.
2. Boff, *Virtues*, x.

Roots of Our Ecologic Crisis."[3] White argued that Judeo-Christianity
was at fault for the impending environmental crisis that started with
the Industrial Revolution whose cultural perspective comprehended the
Earth was there for human consumption and exploitation. White writes,
"Popular religion in antiquity was animistic. Every stream, every tree,
every mountain contained a guardian spirit who had to be carefully pro-
pitiated before one put up a mill in a stream, or cut the tree, or mined the
mountain."[4] Christianity became an urban movement and stood contrary
to the agrarian religions of the Mediterranean in the first century C.E.[5]
In its opposition to competing religions, Christianity replaced all the
ancient deities connected to nature and thus de-sacralized the natural
world. He observes:

> To a Christian a tree can be no more than a physical fact. The
> whole concept of the sacred grove is alien to Christianity and
> to the ethos of the West. For nearly two millennia, Christian
> missionaries have been chopping down sacred groves which are
> idolatrous because they assume spirit in nature.[6]

He faults readings of the Bible that justify human domination over nature and establish human privilege over and against nature. White points
out that Christianity made a distinction between humans formed in the
image and likeness of God and the rest of life and creation. Anthropocentrism is the particular worldview that non-human beings (animals)
and nature are instrumentally available for human flourishing and well-
being. In other words, it reduces the status of all creation and elevates
humanity as the purpose of creation. Humans have souls, other life does
not. In other words, nature is soul-less, and nature and other life are inferior to humanity with a spiritual soul. Humanity was made to dominate
and subdue creation. Thus, two simultaneous correlations—the strong
stress on anthropocentrism and the degradation of the material world for
the spiritual—became a strong theological combination that contributed
to Christianity's ecological harm.[7] Humanity, on the hierarchical scale of
being, remains under just God and angels (spiritual beings) and above
other life and plants and the Earth (material reality without a soul).

3. White, "The Historical Roots of Our Ecologic Crisis."

4. Ibid., 1205.

5. Stark, *Cities of God.*

6. White, "The Historical Roots," 1205.

7. Kinsley, *Ecology and Religion*, 103–14.

In the last four centuries, Christian writers and theologians believed that nature and the animal world had no value except for humanity's use and disposal. Humanity was uniquely and solely made in the image of God:

> Especially, in its Western form, Christianity is the most anthropocentric religion the world has seen . . . Man shares, in great measure, God's transcendence in nature. Christianity, in absolute contrast to ancient paganism and Asia's religions . . . not only established a dualism of man and nature but also insisted that it is God's will that man exploit nature for his proper ends.[8]

Humans have understood themselves on hierarchical scale to animals as God is to humans. Some understood that we were God's vice-regents on Earth, and Earth was to be subdued, conquered, ruled, and exploited for human purposes. This anthropocentrism has contributed to the environmental crisis and the reckless arrogance of human technology and fossil fuel industry without regard to the environmental consequences.

Lynn White firmly claimed that science and technology will not solve our environmental crisis: "More science and more technology are not going to get us out of the present ecological crisis until we find a new religion, or rethink our old one."[9] Since he faulted "Christian arrogance toward nature" as the source the contemporary ecological crisis, White logically concluded that the remedy had to be religious and had to be a spiritual antidote for such arrogance. The remedy to our crisis called for a change of human hearts and minds about nature—requiring us to abandon our contempt for nature and other life, an indifference to using the Earth for our slightest needs and whims or for profit. It required religious values to provide personal and social change from its anthropocentric perspective. White argued for humility as a virtue to provide an antidote to an arrogant Christian anthropocentricism that has precipitated and contributed to the environmental crisis. He proposed the model of St. Francis of Assisi, "the greatest spiritual revolutionary in Western history," a model of humility and fellowship with nature.[10]

8. White, "The Historical Roots," 1207.

9. Ibid., 1207.

10. Ibid.

Critique of White

But nearly five decades earlier hundreds of church leaders, biblical scholars, and theologians attacked White's argument and, of course, painted
him personally with the epithets as "godless," "secular" or a "junior anti-
christ" in the employment of Communist Russia.[11] White's seminal article,
however, had a catalytic impact upon biblical and theological scholars in
the development of ecological theology. Hargrove contends that White's
complaint was essentially correct and his arguments generated vigorous
religious debate.[12] White unfortunately laid blame on Christianity with
no viable solutions for many, and Hargrove wished the debate never
occurred.[13] A few scholars perceived that White's article was a turning
point in the Christian environmental movement, launching an explosion of scholarship refuting White or recovering ecological issues from
the biblical and theological tradition.[14] Others noted that the arguments
against White fixated on his initial article and criticism of Christianity
and the dominion-stewardship debate.[15] Few ever read White's follow-up
articles. I intuited that his answer had origins in his youth and expressed
a credible solution to the environmental crisis. White's solution resonated
with my Catholic and Buddhist theological roots, and I discovered that
my intuition was correct.

What he did, however, was to introduce "ecology" into theological discourse, an accomplishment itself. Ecology was, for the most part,
ignored in biblical and theological discourse in the late 1960s. White
goaded an active apologetic response from biblical scholars to refine their
interpretation of the Genesis texts, theologians to develop Christian traditions that surfaced and valued nature in a positive light, and ethicists to
engage and re-think environmental issues. Some Christian scholars and
ethicists understood that there was a brewing ecological crisis, and they
began to re-examine the interpretations of the Genesis text about being
created in the image and likeness of God and God investing man with
dominion over the animals and the Earth. American naturalist historian
Roderick Nash calls attention to this verse in Genesis: "Be fruitful and

11. Nash, *The Rights of Nature,* 92.

12. Hargrove, "Introduction," *Religion and Environmental Crisis.* xvi–xvii.

13. Ibid., xvii.

14. Gottlieb, "Introduction," 17–18; Nash, *The Rights of Nature,* 92–95.

15. Whitney, "Lynn White Jr.," in *Encyclopedia of Religion and Nature,* 1736; Willis
Jenkins, "After Lynn White," 285–86.

multiply, and fill the earth and subdue it, and have dominion over the
fish of the sea and over every living thing that moves over the earth" (Gen
1:28). The verbs to "subdue" (*kabash*) and "have dominion over" (*radah*)
were understood by Christian tradition as meaning "to conquer" and
"have dominion over nature"—to make nature humanity's slave. Humanity is a species separated from nature and possessed with unrestricted
right to exploit nature for human benefit. Nature is simply matter, resources awaiting human development and use. Roderick Nash says such
a Christian interpretation served as the "intellectual lubrication for the
exploitation of nature."[16] Human beings understood themselves as divine
rulers over nature. After all, the story of creation is human-centric, and
humanity was made after all creation and other creatures, for humanity alone carried the likeness and image of God. The principle of human
hierarchy was embedded in what has become an arrogant logic of human
domination of nature. Christian clergy, theologians, and leaders, for the
most part, felt that humans had the right to do whatever they want to
inferior animals or soul-less Nature. They had no rights or purpose, other
than serving the needs of humanity. This position is both arrogant and
selfish, and it breeds greed and reckless actions directed to nature.

Many biblical and theological scholars attempted to correct White
by arguing that God's command is to have dominion is similar to a king's
entrusting his administrative rule to a steward or viceroy. A steward,
Christians argued, is one who has taken God's place for earth and creatures. But this modern reading still placed humanity at the top of the
hierarchy as mini-divine rulers in God's place. It was an unsatisfactory,
half-way solution that still privileged humanity in the hierarchy but also
gave humanity the responsibility to care for nature.[17]

Christian ethicist James Nash took a modified view of White's ecological complaint by arguing that Christianity does bear some responsibility for propagating an anthropocentric perspective.[18] It is true that
Christianity bears a partial guilt for its share of the ecological crisis. He
traced it to Christianity's asceticism, its disdain for the world (*contemptus
mundi*) and its obsession for the salvation of the soul. Such dualism was
carried to an extreme that has neglected and disvalued nature, resulting
in an ecological sin of omission. James Nash noted that White's ecological

16. Nash, *The Rights of Nature*, 90.

17. Ibid., 96.

18. Nash, *Loving Nature*.

complaint against Christianity also suffers from a serious historical over-simplification and "is an exaggeration of religious influence on culture."[19] There is no single cause for how we got into this ecological crisis, citing Carolyn Merchant's detailed history, *The Death of Nature*. Merchant covers the trajectory of the emergence of science and technology from 1500 to 1700 and thus refutes White's ecological complaint.[20] Merchant challenges White's notion, pointing out that the feminine images of mothering and nurturing nature gave way to the notion of nature as wild, untamed, and threatening and the need for control and domination of nature. There is a transition from organic and feminine notions of nature to the masculine technological and scientific domination of the natural world.[21] Paul Santimire traces the problem to modern secularism, not Christianity, as the culprit for the contemporary environmental crisis.[22] All the above arguments point to the need for a more detailed account for the development of Western anthropocentrism.

Elspeth Whitney provides a balanced summary of the impact of White's original article:

> Biblical scholars and eco-theologians, among them James Barr, Carl Braaten, John Cobb and Joseph Sittler could argue that the Judeo-Christian tradition could be more accurately described as mandating a care-taking or stewardship relationship to the natural world: Christianity, therefore, was not part of the problem, but part of the solution to environmental solutions . . . .Nevertheless, White's powerful and original reading of history, which has shaped a generation of scholarship, remains the touchstone for current and future discussion.[23]

But the impact of White's complaint against Christianity opened responses beyond Christianity, for Sallie McFague aptly summarizes the widening debate,

> If Christianity was capable of doing such immense damage, then surely the restoration of nature also must lie, at least in part with Christianity. I believe that it does, but also with other world religions as well as with education, government, and science.

19. Ibid., 77.

20. Carolyn Merchant, *The Death of Nature*.

21. Nash also cites:Glacken,*Traces on the Rhodian Shore* and R. H. Tawney, *Religion and the Rise of Capitalism*.

22. Paul Santimire, *Nature Reborn*, loc. 214.

23. Elspeth Whitney, "Lynn White," 1736.

The environmental crisis we face—and which is epitomized by climate change—is a planetary agenda, involving all people, all expertise, and all religions.[24]

McFague's observations hold true fifty years after White offered his initial critique of Christian anthropocentrism. It involves not only Christians but all other communities of faith, and this becomes evident in the publications from conference at the Center for the Study of World Religion at Harvard University.[25] Many faith communities have realized that we will share the climate ravages and impacts in the twenty-first century, and we see faith based environmental groups in each of the world's religions.

White's Solution: Later Conversations

Most Christians who initially reacted to White's indictment ignored his final statement of his hope for Christianity. A few scholars took White serious in suggesting that Francis of Assisi as model for ecological responsibility and hope.

> The key to an understanding of Francis is his belief in the virtue of humility not merely for the individual but for man as a species. Francis tried to depose man from his monarchy over creation and set up a democracy of all God's creatures. With him the ant is no longer simply a homily for the lazy, flames a sign of the thrust of the soul toward union with God; now they are Brother Ant and Sister Fire, praising the Creator in their own ways as Brother Man does in his.[26]

For White, Francis of Assisi's humility and kinship model with nature and animals provides a corrective to the extravagant Christian anthropocentricism above the nature.

> However, the present increasing disruption of the global environment is the product of a dynamic technology and science which were originating in the Western medieval world against

24. Sallie McFague, *A New Climate for Theology*, 84.

25. See: The Harvard Book Series: The Religions of the World and Ecology, http://fore.research.yale.edu/religions-of-the-world-and-ecology-archive-of-conference-materials/; Yale Forum on Religion and Ecology, http://fore.research.yale.edu/publications/books/book_series/cswr/index.html.

26. White, "The Historical Roots of Our Ecologic Crisis," 1207; Kiley, "A Spiritual Democracy," 241–60; Sponsel, *Spiritual Ecology*, 43–48.

which Saint Francis was rebelling in so original a way. Their
growth cannot be understood historically apart from distinctive
attitudes toward nature which are deeply grounded in Christian
dogma.[27]

He set out an ethics based on humility, spiritual courtesy, and compassion to embrace the egalitarian vision of Francis of the biotic community.
He noted that, "The profoundly religious, but heretical sense of primitive
Franciscans for the spiritual autonomy of all parts of nature may point
the way."[28] White indicates that a renewed kind of Franciscan spirituality—focusing on humanity's kinship with all other creatures and nature
in a community of creation—would disrupt Christian anthropocentrism.
It would help humanity to co-exist with nature and other life as spiritual
equals. Many Protestant critics generally overlooked Francis of Assisi as a
solution to the environmental crisis, rejecting a Catholic sacramental and
contemplative approach to nature.

White's ethical model was, in fact, very Buddhist at its core in my
initial reading, and this was later confirmed in his later articles, but was
not generally embraced by Christian ethicists. It led me to wonder if
they ever read his later articles. By investigating more of White's later
conversations after his bombshell article, I discovered a significant event
in White's youth when he traveled to Ceylon. He noticed that Buddhist
workers building a road around earthen cones or snake nests rather than
through them. Lynn White later reflected, "They were spared not because
workmen were afraid of snakes but because of a feeling by the workers
that the snake had a right to its house so long as it wanted to stay there."[29]
Buddhists have a different view of the interrelatedness of all life from
the dominant views of other life held by most Christians. He noted that
"if the men with shovels in their hands had likewise been Presbyterians,
the snakes would have fared less well."[30] White traces his connection of
religion to ecological attitudes to this early event with Buddhists in his
life. Matthew Riley points out,

> A close reading of White's texts reveals a surprising abundance
> of creatures through the entire body of his work. His writings on

27. White, "The Historical Roots," 1207.

28. Ibid.

29. White, "Continuing the Conversation," 55. Snakes (*nagas*) were understood as
protectors of the Buddha.

30. Ibid.

religion and ecology, in particular, seem to have animals leaping
out from nearly every page.[31]

White was searching for a theological language to ground a Christian
animism that would value other life: "I am searching for ways to regain
perception of the spirituality of all creatures and to demote modern man's
absolute monarchy over nature."[32] There was no coincidence that White
gravitated to St. Francis of Assisi and Buddhist notions of compassion.
His later writings expounded a general metaphysics of compassion, and
he develops a biophilic proposal for a spiritual democracy of all creatures,
akin to Francis of Assisi but also revealing a nascent Buddhist–Christian
spirituality.

   But Lynn White was also a Christian who profoundly believed
that the Holy Spirit "is still whispering to us."[33] Though there was more
than 1500 years of reading Genesis from the perspective that nature was
created to serve humanity and that all creatures were created to serve
human need, he believed that there was a biblical basis for an ethic of
environmental care. White had also made a suggestion on how humans
might model themselves after Francis of Assisi. By imitating St. Francis,
we could imagine a "democracy of creation" or community of the Earth
whereby all creatures and the elements of nature are perceived within a
kinship model as reflected in his "Canticle of Brother Sun."[34] He valued
no hierarchies in nature, no chain of being—addressing non-human beings as brothers and sisters. Francis accorded value to non-human beings
and earth systems from a theo-centric perspective.

   White takes Francis' spiritual democracy or kinship model seriously
as he later writes, perhaps taken as an absurdity by Christian ethicists,
critics of his seminal article, and those who denigrate the material world:

> Do people have ethical obligations toward rocks? . . . To almost
> all Americans, still saturated with ideas historically dominant in
> Christianity . . . the question makes no sense at all. If the time
> comes when to any considerable group of us such a question
> is no longer ridiculous, we may be on the verge of a change of
> value structures that will make possible measures to cope with

31. Riley, "A Spiritual Democracy of All God's Creatures," 247.

32. White, "Snakes, Nests, and Icons," 61.

33. Ibid., 63.

34. Doyle, "Canticle of Brother Sun," 155–74.

the growing ecologic crisis. One hopes that there is enough time
left.[35]

White's conversation explored his desire to reform, not destroy Christianity as critics had rushed to an apologetic defense of Christianity. He
writes, "Since the roots of our trouble are religious, the remedy must
also be essentially religious."[36] He pointed to St. Francis of Assisi as the
greatest spiritual revolutionary in western history and who would challenge Christian anthropocentrism and arrogance. Francis used the term
"Mother Earth." His spiritually had no hierarchies, and he addressed
non-human beings as brother or sister. White writes, "Believing that they
(all life) all independently praised and magnified God, Francis implicitly
accorded to all creatures and natural processes a value entirely separate
from human interest. Everything had a direct relationship to God." White
called for "morality based on disinterested love of nature, which, in turn,
derived from nature's membership in God's world."[37]

Francis' notion of a spiritual democracy with the Earth and all life is
one of the most radically inclusive spiritualities that have evolved. Francis
is a model of a Christian spirituality that has potential to generate an
Earth-centered, thus a theo-centric spirituality that leads to Earth Care.
Implicit in his proposal was to move Francis' theo-centric model to an
eco-centric model of relating to a community of life, uniting the two into
a singular ethical vision of compassionate care for all life. White was so
personally transformed as a Christian to such a depth of compassion that
he defended the rights of life-forms hostile to humanity, like smallpox
(Variola).

> We humans reached the ability to exterminate smallpox . . .
> From our standpoint, the advisability of the action is beyond
> debate. What the God who created both homo sapiens and Va-
> riola thinks about this, we do not yet know.[38]

He understood the dilemma that a lethal virus created by God had value
to God. In another essay, he concluded,

> Christian compassion must be based on an ascetic and self-re-
> straining conviction of man's comradeship with other creatures

35. White, "The Future of Compassion, 109.
36. White, "The Historical Roots," 1207.
37. Nash, *The Rights of Nature*, 94.
38. White, "Compassion," 109.

. . . Today we have the creaturely companionship not only of the flowering tree that so enraptured Schweitzer, or the earthworm that he removes from the perils of the sidewalk; we can sense our comradeship with a glacier, a subatomic particle or a spiral nebula. Man must join the club of creatures. They may save us from ourselves.[39]

It is in the life of Francis of Assisi that Lynn White finds the most revolutionary Christian spirituality filled with love for and solidarity with nature, and he looks also a modern re-iteration of such a reverence for nature and animals in Albert Schweitze. For White, Francis had inspired a "spiritual democracy" as one of the most radically inclusive ethical systems.[40]

White has had a lasting significance for ecology and religion but, in particular, to my focus on Christian theology and ecology. He cared enough for the environment and hoped for a reformation of Christianity to face the ecological crisis. White's critics read his seminal article but not in light of his further conversations. Others picked up his challenges, apologetically defending Christianity by unpacking the environmental elements within scripture and theological tradition. Leslie Sponsel notes,

> White also stimulated an initial surge of interest in the relationship between religions and ecology more generally . . . White's ideas continue to be reflected in numerous works in philosophy, ethics, history, religion, and other studies relate to the environment and ecology. In short, his article was also a major catalyst in the development of spiritual ecology, especially, its intellectual component.[41]

Lynn White's consequences were far more reaching than he ever imagined. Sponsel traces a revival and strengthening of what he terms as "a spiritual ecology," an umbrella term for religion and ecology and spiritual environmentalists. In 1986, the World Wildlife Fund celebrated its twenty-fifth anniversary at the Basilica of St. Francis of Assisi. The conference looked to religious solutions for the environmental crisis, and White's dream of reforming Christianity with ecology was well on its way.

39. White, "Future of Compassion," 106–7.
40. Nash, *The Rights of Nature*, 95.
41. Sponsel, *Spiritual Ecology*, 78–79.

A Revolutionary Legacy

Francis' extreme lifestyle and spirituality bordered on heretical and extreme for its age. Francis of Assisi was canonized as a saint in recognizing his "out of bounds" spirituality, and this was a church attempt to domesticate his radical spirituality. His spirituality is deeply incarnational, focused on the crucified Christ in the poor, the vulnerable, and creation and creatures. He had compassion for the poor and for God's creatures, and these were intertwined in his spirituality. Franciscan theologian Ilia Delio links Francis' vision of compassion and biophilia together:

> Francis' compassion was grounded in his depth of vision. As he shifted from ego centrism to a relational self through the deepening of love, he released control of his life and the lives of others. The knowledge and freedom became deep and wide enough to invite others into his life. Francis grew into an ecological person because he grew into a God-centered person. His "biophilia" began with the poor, the sick, the weak and fragile, and as he grew in relationship with them, he came to know God in a new way. He accepted the leper as a brother, as one related to, and this acceptance broadened relatedness to others. The weak and fragile creatures of the earth spoke to him most clearly of the presence of Christ.[42]

Compassion is directed to the other, and there is a compassionate identification with the other through love. For Francis, it was his devotion to and relationship with Christ that his vision of cosmic interrelatedness is born. His devotion to the crucified led him to identify the poor and the vulnerable as Christ. When he witnessed the vulnerability or suffering of another creature, whether human or other, he experienced the passion of Christ. Thomas Celano, Francis' biographer, details his creation spirituality:

> Even for worms he had a warm love, since he had read this text about the Savior: "I am a worm and not a man." That is why he used to pick them up from the road and place them in a safe place so they would not be crushed by footsteps of passersby . . . Whenever he found an abundance of flowers, he used to preach to them and invite them to praise the Lord, just as if they were endowed with reason.[43]

42. Delio, *Compassion*, 85.
43. Thomas of Celano, *Life of Francis*, In FA, ED, 1, 250–251. Quoted in Delio, *A*

Francis understood that the sacredness of creation and all creatures originated from a relationship to God as Creator and the incarnate Christ and the indwelling of the Spirit. John Hart comments on the radical challenge of Francis: "He (Francis) transcended the anthropocentrism of his time when he called animate and inanimate beings "brother" and "sister." There is no rivalry among these siblings but rather a mutuality of interests in a family relationship.[44] Francis' incarnational stress on Christ enabled him to find God in creation and in all creatures. All creatures became his family, and he intuited a cosmic interconnectedness of creatures and creation with the triune God.

Francis composed his Canticle of Creation" (*Praised be, You, Laudato Si*) that expresses the goodness of creation and "cosmic interdependency."[45] Everything is interrelated. Sallie McFague suggests that Christians should love nature similarly to the spirituality of Francis of Assisi, who "epitomizes this sensibility ('to love nature in all its differences and detail, in itself, for itself') in his praise of the sun, moon, earth, and water as his brothers and sisters."[46] His sacramental vision of nature accepts nature as it is, reflecting the presence and image of God. Franciscan theologians are remaining at the forefront theologies of Creation such as Franciscan scientis, theologian, and nun Ilia Delio, who bridges creation theology and emergent evolution.[47] Her creative theology of evolution and cosmology is deeply embedded in the tradition of Francis of Assisi and Teilhard.

Leonardo Boff, former Franciscan and Brazilian liberation theologian, looks to Francis' practice of poverty in the formation of a kinship model with nature:

> Possession creates obstacles to communication between persons and with nature . . . Possession represents human "interests"—*inter-esses*—that is, what is placed between persons and nature. The more radical poverty is, the closer humans come to raw reality, and the more it enables them to have an overall experience for otherness and difference. Universal kinship results from the practice of essential poverty. We feel truly brother and sister

Franciscan View of Creation: loc. 423

44. Hart, *Sacramental Commons*, 33.

45. Delio, *Compassion*, 88.

46. McFague, *Super, Natural Christians*, 27.

47. Delio, *Christ in Evolution*; *The Emergent Christ*; *From Teilhard to Omega*; *The Unbearable Wholeness of Being: God, Evolution, and the Power of Love.*

because we can experience things with no more concern for possession, profit, and efficiency. Poverty becomes a synonym for essential humility, which is not one virtue among others but an attitude by which we stand on the ground alongside things. From this position, we can be reconciled with all things and begin a cosmic democracy.[48]

For Boff, it is Francis' poverty and humility that are critical to developing our kinship with nature: "Poverty is a way of being by which the individual lets things be what they are; one refuses to dominate them, subjugate them, and make them objects of the will to power. The more radical the poverty, the closer the individual comes to reality, and the easier it is to commune with all things, respecting and reverencing their differences and distinctions. Universal fraternity is the result of the way-of-being-poor of Saint Francis."[49] Francis' love for Christ opened himself to a profound sense of compassionate kinship with nature and other life, letting nature and creatures to be themselves. Poverty and humility opens human beings to an appreciation of the radical interdependence and interrelatedness with the web of life.[50] Sallie McFague, likewise, notes that Francis of Assisi's voluntary poverty created a "wild space," "a space where one is available for deep change from the conventional model of living to another one."[51] Often people in wild space do not fit into conventional culture. His "possessionlessness" created such a wild space but involved not only giving up some possessions but also the claims of human exceptionalism.[52] Against Christian theological anthropocentrism, the Franciscans preserved the notion of humans as a part of the biotic community. And most importantly, his legacy was his vision that the natural world sacramentally mirrored the presence of God while other life revealed a kinship community of creatures between humanity and animals.

White's proposed solution to the environmental crisis, however, was taken up by an unexpected ally. He made a nomination to the Vatican for making Francis of Assisi the patron saint for ecologists.[53] In 1979, Pope John Paul II designated Francis of Assisi as the patron saint of ecology, for

48. Boff, *Cry of the Earth*, loc. 4587–4801.

49. Boff, *Saint Francis*, 39.

50. Boff, *Cry of the Earth*, loc. 2972.

51. McFague, *Blessed Are the Consumers*, xii; ibid. 46–47.

52. Ibid., 10.

53. Riley, "A Spiritual Democracy," 146 n41; Nash, *The Rights of Nature*, 93.

he refers to Francis' marvelous gift of "fostering nature."[54] But Francis of Assisi has become an inspirational, ecological model for many Christians and non-Christian. Francis' deep love of God overflowed into love for all God's creatures in his sermons preached to animals and his insistence that all creatures are brothers and sisters under God. Eric Doyle writes his observations on Francis 'spirituality about God and creation:

> To love is to be in relation with another, creating a bond between the self and a part of the world, and so ultimately between the self and creation. If one person can love one person, one unique animal, one flower, one special place on this earth, there is no reason in principle why that love cannot stretch out to embrace every single creature to the furthest reaches of space.[55]

Through compassionate love and example of Christ, Francis attains a vision and spirituality of the interrelatedness of all life, a vision and spirituality that many Buddhists would feel at home.[56] His kinship or family model of Christ, creation, and all life places himself outside of the medieval Christian view of hierarchical chain of being with a new transfigured vision of the unity of all life through God, Christ, and the Spirit.[57]

The Feast of St. Francis (October 4) comes at the end of the newly celebrated Season of Creation with the blessing of the animals. Personally, it is one of the most enjoyable functions as clergy, blessing householders and their companion animals. I bless companion animals and the household, and then give a blessed scapular medal with St. Francis. I celebrated such blessing of animals at church and at pet shops, and no matter what spiritual tradition that the householder of the companion animal, each wants the medal for their pet.

More recently Pope Francis I took the name of the St. Francis of Assisi to re-iterate the importance of human environmental responsibility.[58] He told reporters he chose Francis after St. Francis of Assisi, "the man of poverty, the man of peace, the man who loves and protects creation," the same created world "with which we don't have such a good relationship."[59]

54. John Paul II, Apostolic Letter *Inter Sanctos*, AAS 7, 1979, 1509f. Thomas Murtagh, "St. Francis and Ecology," 143. Delio, Warner, & Wood, *Care for Creation*.

55. Doyle, "The Canticle of Brother Sun," 160.

56. See Nhat Hanh, *Love Letter to the Earth*.

57. See the remarkable volume: Delio et al., *Care for Creation*, 65–104.

58. Boff, *Francis of Rome, Francis of Assisi*.

59. Cindy Wooden, Pope Francis explains why he chose St. Francis

In fact, Francis I has named human exploitation and harm of the Earth as the "sin of our time":[60]

> This is one of the greatest challenges of our time: to convert ourselves to a type of development that knows how to respect creation" . . . When I look at America, also my own homeland, so many forests, all cut, that have become land . . . that can [no] longer give life. This is our sin, exploiting the Earth and not allowing her to give us what she has within her.[61]

In his momentous encyclical on climate change, *Laudato si, mi Signore* (*Praise be My Lord*), from the title from the Canticle of Francis of Assisi, Francis I makes clear that the saint remains the inspiration within the letter when he states that St. Francis of Assisi is "the quintessential example of comprehensive care and ecology, who showed special concern for the poor and the abandoned."[62] He further writes,

> [St. Francis's] response to the world around him was so much more than intellectual appreciation or economic calculus, for to him each and every creature was a sister united to him by bonds of affection . . . Such a conviction cannot be written off as naïve romanticism, for it affects the choices which determine our behavior.[63]

Near the end of the encyclical, Pope Francis encourages readers to follow the example of the ecological conversion embodied by the saint:[64]

> I ask all Christians to recognize and to live fully this dimension of their conversion. May the power and the light of the grace we have received also be evident in our relationship to other creatures and to the world around us. In this way, we will help

of Assisi's Name," http://www.thecatholictelegraph.com/pope-francis-explains-why-he-chose-st-francis-of-assisis-name/13243

60. Catholic theologian Sean McDonagh contributed to much of the writing of the encyclical, but there is a definite strand of Boff's theology taken into Pope Francis' theology.

61. "Pope Francis News: His Holiness Calls Environmental Exploitation a Sin," *Latin Post*, July 5, 2014, http://www.latinpost.com/articles/16542/20140705/pope-calls-environmental-exploitation-sin.htm.

62. Pope Francis I, *Laudato Si, mi Signore*, June 2015, (n. 10., n 66).

63. Pope Francis I, *Laudato Si*, 2015, No. 11.

64. Horan, "The Franciscan Character of *Laudato Si*, http://americamagazine.org/issue/franciscan-character-laudato-si. There is the "greening" spirit of the Ignatian Spiritual Exercises in the letter: James Profit, "Spiritual Exercises and Ecology.".

nurture that sublime fraternity with all creation which Saint
Francis of Assisi so radiantly embodied.[65]

Francis of Assisi provides a visionary model of ecological conversion and
inspiration for people of faith who care for the Earth and all life. Christian discipleship in the twenty-first century includes not only God and
humanity but all life in a theology of creation and justice.

Francis has been retrieved as model for ecological spirituality and
biotic quality with the web of life. He teaches that God's compassion does
not stop with human beings, for he taught us that Christ's gospel includes
animals and birds. They are our siblings, our brothers and sisters. Each
being—human, animal, and plant life—has a relationship to God as the
source of life. Every creature was a mirror of divine presence, and possibly a step leading to God, and the mystery of God was at the heart of
the created world, teeming with life. Francis had little possessions in the
world, and he would spend five or six months a year in the wilderness for
contemplation and living with God in nature. He expected his friars also
to live lightly on the Earth.

Leonardo Boff: St. Francis

Leonardo Boff is one of my favorite environmental liberation theological
heroes. What makes Boff's liberation theology attractive is his weaving
Francis of Assisi, John Duns Scotus, Teilhard de Chardin, Bonaventure,
Thomas Berry, and many others, and this theological lineage leads him
to a more inclusive liberation/ecological theology. His books on St.
Francis of Assisi united liberation theology's preferential option for the
poor with the saint's stress on poverty and universal kinship. Boff writes,
"Through his deep humanity, Francis of Assisi has become an archetype
of the human ideal: open to God, universal brother, and caretaker of nature and of Mother Earth. He belongs not only to Christianity but for all
humankind."[66] Francis of Assisi provided a paradigm for Boff's liberation
theology's care for the poor and his care for the Earth.[67] Boff's theology is
driven by "God's preferential option for the poor."[68] Liberation theology
is not neutral, "Any such claim to neutrality is really admission of support

65. Pope Francis I, *Laudato Si*, 2015, No. 221.

66. Boff, *Francis of Assisi*, loc. 78.

67. John Hart: *Sacramental Commons*; Ilia, *Compassion*.

68. Boff, *Francis of Assisi*, loc. 940–1528.

for the established order that benefits a small portion of the population and marginalizes the vast majority."[69] The God of Jesus takes sides with the poor and the oppressed and Jesus' relationship with the poor is critical to his Franciscan-based theology. He states, "If we do not take the side of the wretched of the earth, we become enemies of our very humanity. By losing the poor, we also lose God and Jesus Christ, who chose the side of the poor."[70] Preferential option for the poor, however, requires a personal conversion to stand with and empower the poor, struggle for social justice, and engage society for revolutionary change. Standing with the poor is that "wild space" that Sallie McFague used to describe Francis of Assisi's poverty.

Boff's expansion of the preferential option to include the Earth originates in his Franscican spirituality:

> The Franciscan universe is never dead, nor are things simply placed within the reach of possessive human grasp or tossed one alongside of another, without interconnections between them. Everything makes a grand symphony—and God is the conductor. All things are alive and personal; through intuition Francis discovered what we now know empirically, that all living things are brothers and sisters because they have the same genetic code. Francis experienced this consanguinity in a mystical way. Because we are brothers and sisters we love one another; violence among family members is never justified.[71]

Francis' spirituality based his universal compassion in the passion and crucifixion of Christ. This same theological orientation structures Boff's theological commitment to the poor and nature grounded in Christ.[72] He insists that the poor are "the most threatened of creation."[73] These two orientations—the preferential option for the poor and for the Earth—are intimately entwined in Boff's later theological writings. In *Ecology and Liberation*, he boldly insists, "Social injustice leads to ecological injustice and vise-versa."[74] He comprehends sin as the social rupture among human relations while ecological sin is the rupture between humanity and

69. Boff, *Liberating Grace*, 67.

70. Boff, *Ecology and Liberation*, 100.

71. Boff, *Cry of the Earth*, 4502.

72. Boff, *Christianity in a Nutshell*; Boff, *Cry of the Earth*, loc. 4473–4516.

73. Ibid., loc. 2450–2502.

74. Boff, *Ecology and Liberation*, 101–2.

nature. Ecological justice is intimately intertwined with social justice. For Boff, ecology is about relationality and relationship.

In *Cry of the Earth*, Boff returns to Francis' incarnational spirituality:

> The option for the poor, against their poverty and for their liberation, has constituted and continues to constitute the core of liberation theology. To opt for the poor entails a practice; it means assuming the place of the poor, their cause, their struggle and at the limit, often tragic fate.[75]

Boff looks to the dynamics of compassionate identification and solidarity with the poor and with the vulnerable creation in life of Francis, for he identifies the suffering poor or suffering animals with the crucified Christ.

But with Francis' spiritual; democracy of humanity, other life, and the cosmos, it is natural for Boff to look around and perceive the same social system that oppresses the poor also injures and exploits the Earth:

> The earth is also crying out under the predatory and lethal machinery of our model of society and development. To hear these two interconnected cries (the Earth and the poor) and to see the same root cause that produces them, is to carry out integral liberation.[76]

Liberation for Boff includes the poor and the Earth but liberation depends upon us, becoming actively engaged in a biotic democracy. "a democracy that is centered on life, one whose starting point is the most downtrodden human life."[77] He includes the mountains and rivers, plants, animals and the Earth "as new citizens participating in human common life and humans sharing in the common life of nature."[78]

Boff retrieves a notion that is central to Celtic Christianity that the Earth and all life is not punished because of a primal human sin and develops a Franciscan notion inherited from Duns Scotus that God's incarnation in Jesus was not due to sin, but that God intended the incarnation of Godself before creation. South American liberation theology emerged from listening to the cry of the poor, and ecological theology originates from listening to the cries of the water, the forests the animals, and the

75. Boff, *Cry of the Earth*, loc. 2381.

76. Ibid., loc. 2473.

77. Ibid., loc. 2487.

78. Ibid.

Earth. Human poverty is closely interwoven with the domination and exploitation of the Earth. In a lecture, Boff observed that liberation theology was born from listening to the cries of the poor, water, the animals and the Earth:

> We need to express these cries. The greatest poor person is planet Earth, Pachamama, (Mother Earth) which is devastated and oppressed, and should be included in liberation theology. As Sobrino has rightly said, "the earth is being crucified."[79]

He points out the cries of the Earth and the cries of the poor are intertwined. He has always fought for the poor, especially, the indigenous tribes in the Amazon, which have undergone resettlement and often times extermination as the rainforests are cut down and burned to make room for cattle-raising. Global addiction to beef has led to the destruction of vast treks of the Amazon.

Finally, Leonardo Boff honors the indigenous peoples and their ancestral wisdom of living with the Amazon lands, for he believes that the experience of God of the original peoples provide lessons for us of sacramental universe and potential bearers of theophany. For Boff, a tree is not just a tree but a living being with many arms (branches) and thousands of tongues (leaves). God is everywhere immanent in nature, and if we recover such a kinship with life and the Earth from the life experiences of the original peoples, we begin to listen to the cries of the Earth, and we live out an ethics of unlimited compassion and shared responsibility for the care of the Earth. One of the strengths of Boff's liberation theology, inclusive of the poor and the Earth, is his awareness that as the Earth is harmed, so the poor suffer even more so. He boldly claims:

> Without a spiritual revolution, it will be impossible to launch a new paradigm of connectedness. The new covenant finds its roots and site where it is verified in the depth of the human mind. That is where the lost link that reconstitutes the chain of beings and the cast cosmic community begins to be refashioned. This link in the chain is anchored in God, alpha and omega of the principal self-organization of the universe. This is where al sense of connectedness is fostered, and this is the permanent basis for the dignity of the Earth.[80]

79. Wolfart, "Liberation Theology and Ecological Concerns."
80. Boff, *Cry of the Earth*, 139.

He maintains that we can only transform the oppression of the poor and the Earth proceeds from a spiritual conversion. This includes a change of heart motivated by a realization of our interconnectedness with human, all life, and the Earth herself. It is solidarity with the nature of the perichoretic (interrelated self-emptying love) relationality of the triune God, and he envisions, "the entire universe emanates from the divine relational interplay and is made image and likeness of the Trinity."[81] At the heart of Boff's green engaged spirituality for the poor and the vulnerable Earth is what Boff reminds us, the wild space and vision of Francis:

> The West has never seen such loving kindness and tenderness, as a form of life and integration, as in Francis of Assisi. Therefore, he continues to act as a cultural reference point for everyone who tries to establish a new alliance with creation. Dante called him the "sun of Assisi" that continues to shine throughout our own times, awakening in us the power and inclination to become more aware of, allied to, and compassionate toward all beings in creation.[82]

John Hart also notes that Francis of Assisi can inspire contemporary Christians as a catalyst for ecological change and care for the well-being of the Earth and its biotic communities.[83]

81. Boff, *Ecology and Liberation*, 11.

82. Ibid., 53.

83. Hart, *Sacramental Commons*, 39.

2

No Original Sin, But Anthropocentrism

*If you start with the notion that you were born a blotch on existence,
you will never be empowered to do something about the brokenness of
life. In creation spirituality, we begin with the idea that each of us is
born with a unique expression of divinity, an image of God. Teaching
our children this is the only way to build the pride and security our
culture needs so desperately.*

—Matthew Fox[1]

Matthew Fox's notion of original blessing rather original sin has been popular both in Catholic and mainline Protestant Christianities. The doctrine
of original sin has been challenged for the almost two centuries through
evolutionary biology and socio-biology, biblical criticism, and comparative religious studies of myths around theodicy and creation narratives.
Fox has maintained that the doctrine of original sin was neither Jewish
nor Christian and that the biblical sources rather support a "creation-
centered spirituality." He traces the doctrine of original sin to Augustine
and Thomas a Kempis, objecting to the Christian over-concentration on

1. Keen, "Original Blessing, not Original Sin: Matthew Fox and Creation Spiri-
tuality," 1989. http://www.abuddhistlibrary.com/Buddhism/H%20-%20World%20
Religions%20and%20Poetry/World%20Religions/Christianity/Various%20Topics/
Original%20Blessing/Original%20blessing.rtf.

the fall–redemption dynamic—it trivializes wrong-doing and sin, placing undue guilt and shame on people. Fox correctly observes,

> Jesus never heard of 'Original Sin.'" The term wasn't even used until the 4th century, so it's "strange to run a church, a gathering, an *ekklesia*—supposedly on behalf of Jesus—when one of its main dogmatic tenets, Original Sin, never occurred to Jesus." Sadly, Western Christianity is dependent on and chronically "attached to Original Sin—but what they're really attached to is St. Augustine. The fact is that most Westerners believe more in Augustine (and his preoccupation with sex) than they do in Jesus.[2]

Likewise, theologian Patrick Cheng has argued that Western Christianities promote fall-redemption spiritualities that emerged from a crime model of sin and redemption, resulting in human abuse, or "sin management through guilt and shame."[3] He turns to the Orthodox Christian notion of grace as deification (*theosis*) or salvation through Incarnation:

> That is human nature was fundamentally transformed in the incarnation and Christ event. God emptied Godself of divinity (*kenosis*) in the incarnation so that humanity could be filled with divinity. In the words of the third century theologian, Alexnder of Alexandria, God "became human (so) that we might become divine."[4]

Incarnational theologies provide an opportunity to move away from divine rescue theologies of atonement, built upon original sin and a crime based models.

Complications

Darwinism challenged many Christian doctrines, and in particular original sin. Australian theologian Denis Edwards writes,

> There is every reason for a Christian of today to embrace both the theological teachings of Genesis and the theory of evolution. But holding together the Christian view of God and the insights of evolutionary science does demand a rethinking of our theology of the Trinitarian God as work in creation.[5]

2. Fox, *Living Questions*.

3. Cheng, *From Sin to Amazing Grace*, 35–63.

4. Ibid., 57.

5. Edwards, *The God of Evolution*, loc. 128; Johnson, *Ask the Beasts*.

The twentieth century has wrestled the literalist interpretations of original sin and the human fall from Eden. Many interpreters have moved away from literalist interpretations of original sin to cultural and social interpretations of an original condition of evolving human condition. They recognized the symbolic nature of the Genesis stories as metaphorical portrayals of the human condition. Some Christian theologians have looked to the insights of evolutionary history to try to parse the symbolics of original sin by investigating and applying the insights of evolutionary biology.

There was no literal Adam and Eve: This is obvious not widely not enough accepted. Modern evolutionary biology and biblical criticism negate the historical existence of Adam and Eve as the sole progenitors of the human race. Monogenism, the descent of all humans from a single couple, has been disproved through evolutionary biology for polygenism.[6] Neither mainstream Catholic nor Protestant Churches any longer literalize the interpretations of the Genesis narratives but view them as myths and fables. From biblical criticism and comparative studies of creation myths, Genesis 2–3 is easily understood as an etiological myth, weaving disparate sources together to explain how the human condition came to be, how human mortality, suffering and illness, pains of childbirth, and the patriarchal cleaving of women to men originated.[7] Augustine and his successors understood that human nature was sinful and fallen; thus, the Earth and nature were also fallen due to human sin. The Earth (nature) was not sinful, but as Adam and Eve consisted of material nature, the notion of human fallenness was extended to nature by Augustine and his theological successors.

There is no historical Original Sin: Original Sin, the fall of humanity, is a theological construction, created and primarily promoted by Augustine and his successors in the Western Christianities. When Jews read the Genesis 2–3 story of the Garden and the transgression of the primal couple (3:1–24), early Judaism neither focuses on the first sin nor its on-going consequences. Augustine turned the story around on its head as a story of sin and human bondage. Adam's sin not only brought the

6. Korsmeyer, *Evolution & Eden*, 61. Francisco Ayala, "The Myth of Eve," 1930–36; Doming and Hellwig, *Original Selfishness*, 71–74; Williams, *Doing without Adam and Eve*; Daly, *Creation and Redemption*.

7. Claus Westermann notes that Genesis 2 and 3 originate from differing sources and that Genesis 3 can be further divided into different traditions. Westermann, *Genesis*, 190–93.

human conditions of mortality and suffering but also tainted our moral freedom with an originating sin that corrupted human sexuality, stunted our abilities our human freedom and will, and brought death into the world. Elaine Pagels remarks, "Augustine reads back into Paul's letters his own teaching of the moral impotence of the human will, along with his sexualized interpretation of sin."[8] She detailed how many traditional Christians found Augustine's notions of original sin as peculiar and Adam's sin transmitted to his descendants through sexuality as questioning the goodness of God's creation and the freedom of human will.

Anthropocentricism

What is ecological sin? To answer that question, we need to explore what are the background roots of our ecological crisis? Lynn White has suggested anthropocentric Christianity as the root. Since early Christianity, anthropocentrism dominated Christian views about nature, the Earth, for man is the center of the universe, primary focus of God's creation. Typically, we can describe this form anthropocentrism as "androcentrism," a male centered and dominated perspective.[9] Eco-feminist theologian Rosemary Ruether asks the question, "Are Gaia, the living and sacred earth, and God, the monotheistic deity of the biblical traditions, on speaking terms with each other?"[10] Ruether wants to answer the question in the affirmative, but there are some serious caveats that throw significant obstacles to answer in the affirmative. For Ruether, patriarchal Christianity barely has any speaking relationship with Gaia. Its oppression of women parallels the oppression and domination of nature. Ruether connects her social and theological analysis of sexism and patriarchy directly to ecological sin, and she applies an ecofeminist reading of the biblical sources for developing a speaking relationship with the Earth and a feminist retrieval of Christianity.

Rosemary Ruether comprehends three elements in an ecological spirituality: transience of self, interdependency of everything, and the value of personal communion.[11] What she means by personal communion is compassion for all living things and tearing down the walls of

8. Pagels, *Adam, Eve, and the Serpent,* loc. 360.

9. Ruether, *Gaia and God.*

10. Ibid., 1.

11. Ibid., 251.

otherness. Catherine Keller comprehends that males hold a "separated" self projected upon a God who is self-sufficient and disconnected, but this contradicts a God is who is loving and compassionate.[12] Patriarchal notions of God promote male superiority and foster a Christian devaluation of the physical world for the heavenly.

Anthropocentrism, its subset androcentricism, can be traced to Judeo-Christian traditions and Greek philosophy as legitimizing authorities to its cultural construction and practice. Patriarchal religion and Greek philosophy encouraged a human arrogance toward nature. Humans treat the environment in accordance of how they have interpreted or mis(interpreted) biblical texts. By the time of the Middle Ages, humanity, meaning "males," were held up at the top of the Great Chain of Being, emanating from God to angelic beings and to male humans at the top of the hierarchy of living beings to inanimate matter. Females were a subset under male control. Anthropocentrism is the belief and the cultural practice that humans are the most important species on Earth; some folks describe it as either speciism or species chauvinism or humanism. Simply stated, humanity has more value than other life. Matthew Fox describes anthropocentrism as a form of collective sin tainting creation and the natural world to his most recent writings on sins of the spirit ego.[13] Fox takes a very Buddhist definition of anthropocentrism as a cultural form of "ego-centeredness."[14]

The anthropocentric perspective separates humanity from non-human life and from nature and promotes superior intrinsic value of humanity over other life. Conflated with the industrial and technology revolution of the last centuries this has led to the consequences of human arrogance that diminishes and separates human reciprocity with non-human life. It has practical results in the human brutal treatment of animals and the reckless exploitation of the Earth. The concept of human interrelatedness and participation in a sacred web of life are forgotten for human greed and profiteering of the Earth's resources. Similarly, Matthew Fox locates anthropocentrism in our lack of understanding cosmology and interdependence with other beings.[15]

---

12. Keller, *From a Broken Web.*
13. Fox, *Sins of the Spirit,* 185.
14. Nhat Hanh, *Love Letter.*
15. Fox, *Sins of the Spirit,* 185.

Leonardo Boff naturally holds that human beings have made themselves the center of everything. Everything must be at service of the human few:

> The term (anthropocentrism) means that everything throughout the fifteen-billion-year story exists solely for the human being, man and woman. Hence everything culminates in the human being. Nothing has intrinsic value, nothing has otherness and meaning apart from the human being. All beings are at the disposal of human beings, to serve as property and under their control, so that humans may attain their desires and projects. Human beings feel that they are above thing rather alongside and with things. They imagine themselves as an isolated single point, outside of nature and above it. They arrogantly excuse themselves from respecting other beings.[16]

Humans possess an arrogant anthropocentrism that lies at the root of both contemporary poverty and ecological degradation, for they place themselves above nature and "lesser humans." Humanity de-hallows the universe and envisions the world as separate, innert matter, and a warehouse of resources. The ultimate root of the ecological crisis is the mental disconnection and human emotional isolation from nature. This spiritual disconnection includes the story of the universe, and he is so indebted to Thomas Berry, as the Brazilian theologian expands his social and ecological liberation theology to include cosmology and evolution of the universe.[17] The story of cosmos and evolutionary life on the Earth becomes means to re-situate humanity in a liberating story and reconnect to an ecological spirituality. Boff further reflects,

> When humans organized in a way that centered upon themselves, anthropocentrism takes root. They make everything—nature, living trees, beings, plants, animals, and even other human beings—serve them. They take possession of those things and subject them to their own interests. They disrupt natural kinship with all things, for we all live off the same cosmic humus and we are all involved in the same universal adventure. Such self-centeredness does not bring the immortality that we desire but rather the disruption of all connections and connectedness.[18]

16. Boff, *Cry of the Earth,* loc. 1597–1611

17. Ibid., loc. 384–772, 876–1452. Hathaway and Boff develop the story of the universe and evolutionary thought of Thomas Berry: *The Tao of Liberation.*

18. Ibid., loc.1915.

What I like about Boff's theological hermeneutic of liberation is his claim of a joint social-environmental ethic because society and the poor are impacted by the environment, and the environment is affected by injustice in society: "Social injustice affects people directly; environmental injustice indirectly and perversely attacks human life, producing disease, malnutrition and death not only for the biosphere but also for the entire planet."[19] Ecological injustice produces sickness, contamination of the atmosphere, environmental degradation, climate change, polluted rivers, toxic waste, health challenges of all sorts, drought, severe weather events, and social oppression. Ecological sin produces evil consequences for the biosphere, the extinction of species, and environmental imbalances for the present and future generations.

In *The Body of God*, Sallie McFague defines sin as the refusal to accept our place in the world; she divides into three modes of us vs.us (other human beings), them, (other animals) and it (nature). She writes about ecological sin as human separated space: "from an ecological point of view, justice means sharing the limited resources of our common space . . . injustice is living a lie, living contrary to reality, pretending that all space or the best space belongs to some so that they can live in lavish comfort and afluence, while other are denied even the barest of necessities for physical existence."[20]

Humanity: The ecological sin is the refusal of haves to share space and land with the have- nots.[21]

Other species: "The ecological view of sin deepens when we realize that other animals, beside human ones, must have space, and that they too have a place."[22]

Nature: "We are a part of the whole . . . and we need to internalize that insight as a first step toward living truthfully, living with reality."[23]

In another place, she defines ecological sin through the notion of ecological Christology:

19. Boff, "Social Ecology: Poverty and Misery," 243.
20. McFague, *The Body of God*, 116.
21. Ibid., 117.
22. Ibid., 118.
23. Ibid., 127.

Ecological Christology defines sin as the refusal to share the necessities of life with others, both other humans and other life-forms. Sin is insatiable greed, wanting to have it all. Acting justly towards nature and other human beings demand sacrifices from Christian elites. Sustainable living involves acceptance of finite limits, such as how we drive our cars, emissions controls, and carbon taxes on industry.[24]

McFague understands sin as a form anthropocentrism—the refusal to share the necessities with the poor and other life, and she follows a similar trajectory to Leonardo Boff's preferrential options. For both theologians, an incarnational christology passes judgment on the one percent of the wealthy owning almost fifty percent of the world's wealth while the poor are without and the impact that such accumulation wealth results in carbon emissions into the atmosphere. Those enjoying an abundant life do so at the expense of the poor, other life, and the Earth.

Later, McFague shifts her exploration of anthropocentrism as the root of ecological sin, utilizing the notion of "arrogant eye."

Our narrow anthropocentric perspective—what could be called the intrinsically arrogant eye of human beings—makes it very difficult for us to achieve the disinterested point of view necessary in those who genuinely respect others. One must rise above believing that one's own needs and desires are the only needs and desires—and even that human needs and desires are the only ones, realizing that if we really are co-conspirators on one planet with many other subjects, then respect for them is our first response.[25]

She uses the notion of an "arrogant eye" to describe the anthropocentric perspective; it objectifies and distances itself from involvement with nature. McFague refers to Marilyn Frye's description of "the "arrogant eye" as acquisitive, seeing everything in relation to the self, for me or against me. It organizes everything in reference to the self—as either for me or against me."[26] She follows Frye's binary description by adding an additional qualifier: "The arrogant eye simplifies in order to control, denying complexity and mystery, since it cannot control what it does not understand."[27] McFague comprehends ecological sin as the refusal to

24. McFague, "An Ecological Christology," 41–42.
25. McFague, *Super, Natural Christians,* 151.
26. Ibid., 33.
27. Ibid.

share the necessities of life with others, both other humans and other life-forms. The refusal to share is extended to space and land. Space and land are disproportionately controlled by elite humans to the disadvantaged of other humans and other life. She contrasts sin with just action: "Acting justly towards nature and other human beings demand sacrifices from Christian elites. Sustainable living involves acceptance of finite limits, such as how we drive our cars, emissions controls, and carbon taxes on industry."[28] Humanity has developed an experiential apartheid with other life and the Earth:

> It is not just that other life forms are becoming scarce or extinct, but our experience of and with them is, too. The results are deep and disturbing. We not only learn less about these earth others, but disaffection sets in, and hence we care less for their well-being. We do not care about what we do not know.[29]

Our notions of Earth are shaped by globalized industrialization, for the material body of the Earth is understood as dead matter, stuff to be transformed into commodities. For greedy eyes, it becomes valued as capital and profit. Since we have lost direct embodied experience and knowledge of other life, we have developed a callous attitude to the ongoing extinctions of species.

In *A New Climate for Theology*, she asks the question, "Are we the only ones that matter?"[30] McFague does affirm that humans are distinctive in their self-consciousness, but that all creatures matter. She suggests that we need to move away from anthropocentrism or ecological illiteracy towards an ecological literacy.[31] She quotes the poet Wallace Stevens: "We are not our own. Nothing is itself taken alone. Things are because of interrelationships."[32] Everything is related to everything else. McFague comprehends ecology "as the most fundamental imaginable."[33] Her ecological literacy includes an interpretative move from comprehending ourselves as individuals, unique, and separate from nature. McFague turns to Buddhist teacher Thich Nhat Hanh, who describes such ecological literacy with Buddhist notions of "interbeing":

28. Ibid.
29. Ibid., 118.
30. McFague, *A New Climate for Theology*, 46.
31. Ibid., 57–59.
32. Ibid., 47.
33. Ibid., 50.

> When we look at a chair, we see the wood, but we fail to observe
> the tree, the forest, the carpenter, or our, own mind. When we
> meditate on it, we can see the entire universe in all its interwoven
> and interdependent relations in the chair. The presence of the
> wood reveals the presence of the tree. The presence of the leaf
> reveals the presence of the sun. The presence of the apple blos-
> soms reveals the presence of the apple. Meditators can see the
> one in many and the many in one . . . The chair is not separate. It
> exists only in its interdependent relations with everything in the
> universe. It *is* because all other things *are*.[34]

Mahayana Buddhist metaphysics of the interconnectedness of everything to everything else becomes the foundational practice for extending
compassion to others. In a similar vein, McFague affirms, "If we were to
accept the ecological unity as the working interpretation for our deal-
ings with each other and with our world, we would have two responses:
appreciation and care. We would see ourselves as part of the web of life,
an incredibly vast, complex, subtle, beautiful web that would both amaze
us and call forth our concern. We would feel awe about and care for our
planet."[35] This ecological perspective makes the Earth a personal but interrelated space, and she describes the Earth as our only home for which
we are likely to care for it. She offers three house rules: "1) Take only your
share, 2) Clean up after yourself, 3) Keep the house in good repair for
others."[36] Her ecological economics is derived from the fact that we are
interdependent upon one another and the Earth. She idealistically claims:
Human need is more basic than human greed: we are relational beings
from the moment of our conception to our last breath. The well-being
of the individual is inextricably connected to well-being of the whole.[37]

Excursus: The Earth's Story[38]

*The myth of original sin of a primal couple is always read from a strictly
anthropocentric context. What if we shift the reading perspective to an
Earth-centered context?*

34. Ibid., 51; quoted from Nhat Hanh, *The Sun My Heart*, 90.

35. Ibid., 53.

36. McFague, *Climate Theology*, 53.

37. Ibid., 88.

38. Reading Genesis 2–3 from an Earth perspective, see; Shirley Wurst, "Beloved,
Come back to Me," 87–97.

On the day that God made me the Earth, I was born, and no plant or herbs of the fields had yet sprung up, for God had not caused it to rain upon myself. There was no one to till my soil, but waters would rise from the ground and water the soil. Then God took some humus soil from myself and formed an earth-creature (*adamah*). God breathed into the nostrils of the earthling, and the earthling became alive. I was so happy that a part of my earth body now walked upright and imagine that this earthling could till my soil.

God planted a garden called in place named Eden. Trees and plants arouse from the womb of the Earth. And I marveled at what God was doing to my body. God is a gardener, for God planted every type of tree: figs, pomegranates, bananas, olives, almond and various nut trees, numerous fruit and berry trees, grape vines, and ornamental and flowering trees adorned the grove of Eden. Communities of trees are wonderful form of life, for they stabilize the weather and are useful for cycling water. They are intelligent and have been stable children. God loved planting trees and delighted in the garden. Then God brought streams of waters called rivers to water the garden. The sun provided energy and nourishment to the plants and trees. God placed the earthling, Adam in the garden. Each new occasion of creation God gifted myself, as God called forth new creations for the garden. We were embodied together as the soil community, all interrelated. God commissioned the walking earthling to care and serve the garden. And the walking earthlings followed God in gardening, caring and tending the community of the soil. They learned to work the abundance of life in the garden and preserved the community of trees, plants and vegetative life, and other life. One instruction was given: "You may eat freely from every tree in the garden except from the tree of knowledge of good and evil."

But the trees made from my body were not enough companionship for the earthling, so God fashioned from my body once more every animal of the field and birds of the air. They were siblings who walked over the ground and flied in the skies. They were kin to accompany the earthling, for they shared my earth body. Plants, trees, non human animals and birds, and the earthling are all my children, they were part of the soil community. The earth creature named all the nonhuman animals, but he did not find the companionship he sought. So God caused a deep sleep and took one of his ribs, and God fashioned the rib into companion mate. Thus, God created them male and female. And they were given the responsibility to care for God's garden community.

A wise serpent asks the woman, "Did God say, 'you may eat the fruit of any tree in the garden.'" The woman answered, "God say, you may not eat the fruit of the tree in the middle of the garden, nor shall you touch, or you will die." The serpent replies, "You will not die, for God knows that when you eat of it your eyes will be opened, and you will be like God." The woman saw that the tree was for eating and delightful and desired the fruit." She ate. And gave some to the man who was with her, and he ate as well. Their eyes were opened and knew they were naked. They separated themselves from the nonhuman animals and fashioned coverings from fig leaves.

At the time of the evening breeze, they listened to God's coming presence and hid themselves. God say, "Where are you?" And the man said, "I heard you in the garden, and I was afraid because I was naked, and hid myself." God said, "Who told you were naked? Did you eat of the fruit of the tree which I instructed you not to eat?" The man blamed the woman, and the woman blamed the serpent. Since they ate the fruit from the forbidden tree, they lost all community with the plants and the animals. And the Earth lamented, "Sadly, they lost all connectedness to myself and their siblings. They forgot their humus origins." God placed them outside of Eden to learn how to connect to the Earth community once more. Humans forgot a deep truth of the soil that all life shares a common ancestry from the humus or soil and are a part of the community of my body.

As I wept at the loss of my earth children, God comforted me with hope. One day there will be a new earth creature (*adamah*) born again from the soil. He will be born from a cave tomb in a garden and become a great gardener, carrying on the mission of his parent who loves gardening. He will instruct humanity on gardening once more, and they will return to the community of the soil and once again learn all life forms an interdependent community of the soil. Hope was born once more in my dreams . . .

Eden: Utopian Parable

Daryl Domning writes, "The Garden of Eden is not understood as an original state of humanity but as a vision of what God desires of us in the end."[39] Several decades earlier, Carmelite scholar Carlos Mesters

39. Domning, *Original Selfishness*, 4–5.

observed that the garden story in Genesis is "a prophecy of the future, projected into the past."[40] The Garden of Eden is an utopian parable for twenty-first humanity to equip human contemplative disciplines and engaged commitment to nature, the birth of a renewed spirituality that takes Earth seriously as a partner in life and reconnects with the community of the Earth. God has created the earthling from the soil of the Earth, and God plants a garden, and Brigitte Kahl comments on God planting the trees:

> We might expect God to lean back and watch the creature taking up the spade to start digging and planting . . . But instead we see God taking the spade and planting the trees in the garden, definitely hard and dirty manual work. Only then does God out the human being there, making sure the that the trees are beautiful to the eye and bear fruit already, so there is an abundance of food. Bread and roses both are both there, and Adam's task is simply to serve the soil, God's footmarks and fingerprints already there.[41]

Kahl notes, "This is weird. We meet a God who really gets God's hands dirty."[42] God expects Adam to work with Godself to serve and preserve the garden that is so delightful. God is a gardener at heart. Norman Wirzba speaks of God as gardener:

> God is the Essential Gardner, the one who relates to the world in modes of intimacy, protection, and delight. Moreover, given that God is cast as the First Gardener (Gen. 2:8), we are led to think that human participation in the work of gardening is also growing in our understanding of God's creative, attentive, patient and nurturing ways.[43]

God creates nonhuman animal siblings from the material of the earth for the garden. He breathes spirit into the soil to fashion the earthling and later his companion, entrusting them with care taking and tending the garden. But Carol Newsome comments, "It apparently does not occur to the storyteller (Yahwist poet) that animals have been created for their

---

40. Mesters, *Eden*, 29. See his discussion, 28–56. See also Merchant, *Reinventing Eden*.

41. Kahl, "Fratricide and Ecocide," loc. 720.

42. Ibid., loc. 713.

43. Wirzba, *From Nature to Creation*, 103.

own sakes or for God's sake."[44] Humans, nonhuman animals, and plant life are united in the Earth's community of the soil and interrelated with each other. Wendell Berry notes, "The soil is the great connector of lives, the source and destination of all. It is the healer and restorer and resurrector, by disease passes into health, age into youth, and death into life. Without proper care for it we can have no community, because without proper care for it we can have no life."[45]

God places the couple in a garden divinely designed and instructs them to care for the garden but to refrain from eating from the tree of knowledge of good and evil. They live peacefully with their siblings, animals created with humanity on the sixth day and the older siblings the trees and plants. The myth teaches that animals are peaceful, non-violent, neither wild nor domesticated. There is no use of animals for food, and. nonhuman animals, the trees, and human animals live as part of the soil community and in harmony with God.

The serpent beguiles the woman to eat of the fruit of the tree forbidden to her and Adam. She gives the fruit to Adam to eat, and they become aware of their nakedness and sew leaves to cover themselves. When they hear God coming in the evening, they hide from God in the bushes. The act of hiding is a conscious concealing of self from God's unconditional offer of grace; it is a refusal of grace, either an instinctual or conscious action. God surrounds the two with a radical proximity of grace and presence. The couple turns away or hides from God's radical nearness of love and their vocation as gardeners, but they fail to take responsibility for their actions and turn away from God in a conscious choice of hiding themselves. They disrupt the grace-filled interrelatedness with God by abandoning the destiny as gardeners and caretakers that God has bestowed upon them to tend the garden. The covering of their sexual organs with fig leaves sewn is symbolic of their severing a relationship with the naked animals. Newsome remarks, "since the eyes of the man and the woman are opened, the common ground that united human beings with other creatures are broken."[46] Environmental philosopher Baird Callicott notes that they are self-aware, separated, and this becomes the framework for their experience of shame. Callicott provides an insightful reading here:

44. Newsome, "Common Ground," 65.
45. Berry, "A Native Hill," 204.
46. Newsome, "Common Ground," 68.

> For once aware of themselves, (the man and the woman) may
> treat themselves as an axiological point of reference. Indeed,
> the text suggests by its very silence on any alternative to Yah-
> weh's banishment or any compromise, and by the finality of the
> banishment, that once aware of themselves, they will inevita-
> bly treat themselves as an intrinsically valuable hub to which
> other creatures and the creation as a whole may be referred for
> appraisal. Self-consciousness is a necessary condition for self-
> centeredness, self-interestedness.[47]

Newsome describes Callicott's description as the birth of anthropocentrism or what Sallie McFague names as the "arrogant eye."[48] This the
original condition for our committing ecological sins against the Earth
and all life.

The Antidote

There is an antidote to anthropocentrism arrived through the practice
of prayer and contemplative engagement with nature. These can be retrieved from some specific Catholic spiritualities, Orthodox and Celtic
Christianity's stress on the sacramentality of nature, some naturalist and
scientists aying attention to nature meditatively carefully. Wallace contextualizes the environmental crisis:

> The environmental crisis is a *spiritual* crisis because the contin-
> ued degradation of the earth threatens the fundamental goods
> and values that bind human beings to one another and all other
> forms of life. At a very deep level we no longer feel our common
> kinship with other beings as the basis for earth-friendly action
> and commitment. We have lost that primordial sense of belong-
> ing to a whole web of life that our kind and otherkind need for
> daily sustenance.[49]

Wallace argues that Christian teachings have distanced us from human
experience of "co-belonging with other life-forms." He describes our lifestyle of ecocide as an addiction that we can no longer stop ourselves on
a destructive path.

---

47. Baird Callicott, "Genesis and John Muir," 123–24.
48. Newsome, "Common Ground," 69; McFague, *Super, Natural Christians*, 67–90.
49. Wallace, "The Green Face of God."

> If ecocide is a disease of the soul then it requires spiritual
> medicine—the medicine of healthy, rather than toxic, Christian
> values and ideas . . . Christianity, then, is the *pharmakon* of
> looming environmental disaster: in part, it is both the cause of
> the problem and its solution. It is both the origin of the ecocidal
> "disease" from which we suffer and its "cure," insofar as it pro-
> vides resources for a new green mindset toward nature that is a
> prophylactic against antinature attitudes and habits.[50]

For Wallace, the antidote for human addiction to its destructive and toxic
path of ecocide is the recovery of the Spirit immanent in nature. The
Spirit is the healing and subversive presence in nature:

> Spirit and earth are *inseparable* and yet at the same time *dis-*
> *tinguishable*. Spirit and earth are internally indivisible because
> both modes of being are living realities with the common goal
> of sustaining other lifeforms. But Spirit and earth also possess
> their own distinctive identities insofar as the Spirit is the unseen
> power who vivifies and sustains all living things while the earth
> is the visible agent of the life that pulsates throughout creation."[51]

By engaging nature, we can encounter the presence of the Spirit, who
helps us to break our addiction to ecocide and discovers a healing and
loving connection to the Earth.

What many of the above have in common is their compassionate
engagement and identification with nature. The environmentally aware
poet William Merwin came to understand a profound insight of ecological grace: "We as a species define ourselves by our relation to the rest of
life."[52] He was sickened by the environmental devastation that he witnessed at strip mining in Pennsylvania. He writes,

> What turned me into an environmentalist, on my eleventh
> birthday, was seeing the first strip mine. To treat the Earth like
> that, to me, is like murder. Rape. I just hate it. I don't think we
> have the right to treat the living world like that. We have to do
> something about our needs in that case. My house has been so-
> lar for thirty years.[53]

50. Ibid.

51. Ibid.

52. Sponsel, *Spiritual Ecology*, 105.

53. Ibid.,101.

Such ecological engagement results in a discovery of ecologies of God's grace and presence. In Merwin's case, the ecological damage from strip mining aroused his passion to identify with the web of life and move him to compassionate action. He made it a spiritual praxis to plant a tree each day.

Thomas Berry similarly speaks of human origin and identification with the Earth:

> We come into being in and through the Earth. Simply put, we are Earthlings. The Earth is our origin, our nourishment, our educators, our healer, our fulfillment. At its core, even our spirituality is Earth derived. The human and the Earth are totally implicated, each in the other. If there is no spirituality in the Earth, then there is no spirituality in ourselves.[54]

Berry and other theologians recognize that a conversion to the Earth is to reconnect with the source of our spiritualities. It is essential for us to recognize our spiritual roots in the soil community. I would add our incarnate roots. For Berry, his engagement with cosmology and science, Buddhism, and indigenous peoples highlighted a profound truth of interrelatedness within the universe, life, and time. Our spiritual realization of our interconnectedness would lead us to a recovery of our capacity for communion with the Earth. It would breakdown our human alienation with the Earth and the web of life.

Boff offers a related solution with our discovery of our earthliness:

> Human beings must discover our place in the global community along with other species, not outside or above them. There is no justification for anthropocentrism, but it does not mean ceasing to regard human beings as unique, as that being of nature through whom nature itself achieves its own spatial curve, breaks out in reflex awareness, become capable of copiloting the evolutionary process—assuming responsibility for bringing the entire planet to happy fate.[55]

Boff comprehends humanity as beings of the earth; we are "the earth-thinking, hoping, loving, dreaming, and entering into the phase in which decision is no longer by instinct but conscious."[56] . He quotes an ecological observation of Thomas Berry: "This is the ultimate daring venture

54. Berry, *The Sacred Universe*, 69.
55. Boff, *Cry of the Earth*, loc. 2360.
56. Ibid., loc. 2350. Berry, *The Dream of the Earth*, 19.

of the Earth, this confiding its destiny to human decision, the bestowal upon the human community of the power of life and death over its basic life systems."[57] Leonardo Boff writes in a blog, "The Path as Archetype":

> Each human being is a *homo viator*, a walker through the paths of life. As Argentinean Native poet and singer Atahualpa Yupanqui says: "the human being is the Earth who walks." We do not receive our existence ready made. We must build it. And to that end, we must open the path, starting with and going beyond the paths that preceded ours, and have already been walked. Even so, our personal path is never completely given. It must be built with creativity and without fear. As the Spanish poet Antonio Machado says: "walker, there is no path; the path is made by walking."[58]

We are made from soil (Latin: *humus*) as the Genesis accounts poetically narrates. Boff in many writings never forgets his Franciscan heritage of seeing Christ in the faces of the poor and inclusifies the poor to include nonhuman animal life and the Earth herself. Boff's incorporation of Atahuakpa Yupanqui's earth-centered metaphor, "the human being is the Earth who walks," is theologically useful for uniting human embodiment with Earth embodiment, for human beings carry the Earth in their flesh and blood. Boff notes that humans are in solidarity in an earth-embodied path since the big bang billions of years ago and through ancestral descents as hominids. We have a fundamental option to choose whether or not that we will choose the right path: "we have to choose the path to build and how to follow it, knowing that 'living is dangerous' (Guimarães Rosa). But we never do it alone. Multitudes walk with us, solidarians in the same destiny, accompanied by someone named: "Emmanuel, God with us."[59]

The words "humility" and "humble" derive from the Latin *humus,* soil, Earth. Humans have disregarded the powerful myth of our origins from the soil of the Earth. The soil, the land, and the Earth are places we encounter God. In interaction with the soil, God teaches us humility or what Buddhists describe as "selflessness." Humility and selflessness both denote a spiritual path without ego-centeredness. When we engage the soil or the Earth we begin a spiritual journey of recognizing that we are

57. Ibid., loc. 2360.

58. Boff, "The Path as Archetype."

59. Ibid.

"the Earth who walks." Our roots are in the soil. We sprout growth as we interface with the Earth community and processes, for there we experience the sacramental presence of the God within:

> In terms of eco-spirituality, love leads us to identify ever more with the Earth . . . we must think ourselves as Earth, feel ourselves as Earth, love ourselves as Earth. Earth is the great living subject feeling, loving, thinking, and through us knowing that it thinks, loves, and feels. Love leads us to identify with the Earth in such a way we no longer need to become aware of these things, for they have become second nature. Then we can be the mountain, sea, air, road, tree, animal. We can be one with Christ, with the Spirit, and ultimately with God.[60]

Pope Francis echoes a similar sentiment when he says directly, "We have forgotten that we ourselves are dust of the earth (cf. Gen 2:7); our very bodies are made up of her elements, we breathe her air and we receive life and refreshment from her waters."[61]

The anthropologist Richard Nelson spent much of his life studying indigenous cultures of Alaska and writing about their relationship to nature. He realizes life, including himself as part of the Earth:

> There is nothing in me that is not of the earth, no split instant of separateness, no particle that disunites me from the surroundings. I am no less than the earth itself. The rivers run through my veins, the winds blow in and out with my breath, the soil makes my flesh, the sun's heat smolders inside me. A sickness or injury that befalls the earth runs through me. Where the earth is cleansed and nourished, its purity infuses me. My eyes are the earth gazing at itself.[62]

Nelson experiences a compassionate solidarity and identification with nature so to understand that "I am no less than the earth." Such intimate identification as part of the Earth is also found in Rachel Carson, John Muir, Aldo Leopold, ethologist Mark Bekoff, nature poets and conservationists. Their embodied connection to the Earth open themselves to fall in love with the natural world and discover ecologies of God's grace.

Dr. Chrisopher Uhl, a biologist and environmental studies professor, has noted that our anthropocentrism has resulted in our psychological,

60. Boff, *Cry of the Earth*, loc.4308.

61. Pope Francis I, *Laudato Si*, # 2.

62. Nelson, *The Island Within*, 249.

intellectual, cultural, and personal separation from the Earth. Such exclusivity has negative impact on the Earth, the web of life, and upon ourselves, and he proposes an ecocentrism to replace our anthropocentrism. We are conditioned to think and relate separately to the natural world. His focus has shifted from repairing the damage to the Earth to repairing ourselves by dissolving our separateness. It requires us to include the Earth, the natural processes, and other life into re-envisioning ourselves:

> Inclusivity is grounded in relationship whereas exclusivity stems from separation. A consciousness rooted in inclusivity generates trust, one moored in exclusivity foments fear—especially, the fear of the Other. When our goal is exclusivity, we silence those with whom we disagree; but when inclusivity becomes our goal, we create a world that works for all.[63]

There is no better way of cultivating ecocentrism than to learn to pay attention to the wild creatures that we live among.[64] He advocates a contemplative solution to our separation by advocating mindfulness of our connections with natural life.

From her perspective of "the loving eye," Sallie McFague re-connects to the Earth in an embodied and lovingly intimate fashion. She speaks of her soil origins,

> I am of the earth, a product of its ancient and awesome history, and I really and truly belong here. But I am only one among millions, no billions of other human beings, who have a place, a space, on the earth. I am also a member of one species among millions, perhaps billions, of other species that need places on earth. We, all human beings and other species, are inhabitants of the same space, planet earth, and interdependent in intricate and inexorable ways. I feel a sense of comfort, of settledness, of belonging as I consider my place in this cosmology, but also a responsibility, for I know that I am a citizen of the planet.[65]

McFague writes from an incarnational compassionate perspective about kenotic spirituality—in particular, the spiritualities of the Quaker John Woolman, Simone Weil, and Dorothy Day. All three practice forms of meditative engagement of their world that opens themselves profound interconnections with God and human life. McFague's feminist

63. Uhl, *Developing Ecological Consciousness*, loc. 4116.

64. Ibid., Loc.2234.

65. McFague, *The Body of God*, 114.

hermeneutic expands to include a planetary hermeneutic, and this trig-gered suspicions in myself because of her use of sacramental language and meditative language of careful attentiveness to nature, even use of Buddhists on compassion. I suspected that her theological praxis was rooted in meditative encounter with nature. Her theology was incar-national, inclusive, ecological, mindfully aware, and compassionate. McFague reveals her personal experience of meditation:

> I am becoming acquainted with God. This conversion has oc-curred quite deliberate: I engaged a spiritual director and have undertaken a daily pattern of meditation. I am doing what is called "practicing the presence of God," setting aside time for relating to God. To say that it has been instructive would be a gross understatement; it has been revelatory. Revelation, as I now see it, is God's loving self-disclosure, and that is what I experienced. I am meeting God and God is love.[66]

McFague has engaged meditatively the Earth, and this makes sense when she states "I am of the earth, a product of its ancient and awesome history, and I really and truly belong here. But I am only one among millions, no billions of other human beings, who have a place, a space, on the earth. I am also a member of one species among millions . . ."[67]

Incarnational Conversion

The turn to the Earth is an incarnational response to anthropocentrism and the ravages of climate change. It takes serious the core of Christian theology that God became enfleshed and embodied in the human person Jesus. Australian theologian Denis Edwards writes, "Resisting ecological conversion is, theologically, resistance to the Incarnation. To be ecologi-cally converted to Earth in a fully theological sense will involve a con-version to the Incarnation."[68] A Christian ecological spirituality actively incorporates an incarnational vision and praxis—that at the heart of the universe is God's incarnation and that an interrelatedness of fleshliness and spirit converge. Christian ecological conversion is God's incarnation in Christ, the dynamics of divine interrelatedness woven into the fabric of the universe. Such divine interrelatedness and interconnection embody

66. McFague, *Life Abundant*: 8.

67. McFague, *The Body of God*, 113.

68. Edwards, "Foreword," in Delio et al., *Care for Creation*, 3.

the compassion dynamics of identification, solidarity, and active engagement with the Earth and all life. God with us means God compassionately with us all and the whole universe.

Karl Rahner, Denis Edwards, Norman Wirzba, Jurgen Moltmann, and others turn to the notion of incarnation in the theology of Athanasius, the 4th century bishop of Alexandria, to take up and sustain an alternative orthodoxy of the grace-filled notion of *theois*, deification or becoming like God. This alternative Christian tradition of salvation precedes Anselm and his successor's atonement theologies. Contemporary theologians move away from the doctrine that Jesus was sent as part of a divine rescue mission for fallen humanity and the world. The strength of *theosis* model is that it predicates humanity nature was transformed by the incarnation, the Christ event, and through the ongoing activity of the Spirit. God emptied Godself in the incarnation, and we become divine not by nature but through the grace event of Christ's incarnation, death, and resurrection and through the Holy Spirit.[69] This model of salvation through Christ's incarnation lends itself to an ecological re-envisioning of God, Christ, and the Spirit ecologically.

How do we as Christians change our hearts to accept our vocation to be gardeners for Eden? How do we fall in love with the Earth and other life? Denis Edwards gives us a clue,

> What theology can affirm is that human beings are intimately connected with the whole universe in its evolutionary unfolding and they have a capacity to relate to each other, to other creatures and to God as creatures in whom the universe has come to self-conscious awareness.[70]

Our eco-conversion to the Earth and the community of life is to recognize our incarnational interrelatedness with Christ and the soil community of the Earth. It is also certainly a turn towards the Incarnated Christ. And it is remarkable how many conservationists, nature writers, ecocontemplatives, indigenous peoples, and folks of other faith traditions practice the dynamics of incarnational spirituality. Karl Rahner's notion of "Anonymous Chrsitianity" and Raimundo Pannikar's radical trinitarianism decades ago recognized the presence of incarnational dynamics outside of Christianity.[71] Our conversion to the Earth and recognition of

69. Keating, *Deification and Grace.*

70. Denis Edwards, *The God of Evolution*, loc. 771.

71. Rahner on Anonymous Christianity: *Foundations of Christian Faith,* 178–203.

incarnational interrelatedness points to the necessity of building inter-faith relations with those practicing what we can identify as incarnational dynamics of compassion to save the planet. The Spirit is bringing us now to a spiritual place where we are building eco-contemplative coalitions of incarnational compassion.

Pannikar: *The Unknown Christ of Hinduism; Christophany.*

3

The Ecology of Jesus:
Jesus as the "Green Face of God"

Jesus' sensitivity to nature, so vivid in his parables, is derived from living close to the natural world and from familiarity with Jewish scriptures and their metaphors of cosmic order.

—Edward P. Echlin[1]

Gospel-based compassion tolerates no outsiders. It embraces and seeks to bring in all, who are marginalized, oppressed, and excluded from empowering fellowship. It evokes a double response requiring a reawakened heart that know it cannot withhold that liberates and empowers.

—Diarmuid O'Murchu[2]

Jesus of Nazareth was a real life, historical figure in first-century CE Palestine. As a human being, he shared the physiology and psychology of a human being in a predominantly Galilean pastoral culture with several urban Hellenistic cities. He suffered the economic and political

1. Echlin, *Earth Spirituality*, 76.
2. O'Murchu, *Inclusivity*, loc. 615.

oppression under Roman domination and exclusive religious theologies. Mark Wallace calls for a "nature-based retrieval of Jesus":

> One of the best ways to rehabilitate Christianity's earth identity is through a nature-based retrieval of Jesus as the green face of God. Recovering the Gospel narratives through environmental optics opens up Jesus' ministry as a celebration of the beauty of the Earth and committed search for justice for all the denizens of the good creation. Jesus is a green prophet; he ministered to the poor and forgotten members of society and criticized extreme wealth based on a disregard of one's neighbor and the exploitation of the gifts of creation.[3]

Earlier biblical scholars noted that Jesus' parables have an origin in his ecological location of Galilee as part of first-century CE Palestine. When we look closely at Jesus' message of God's reign, we notice that his compassionate concerns for humanity and the disadvantaged, the outcast, and the sinner are intertwined with symbolic language and action that originates from daily encounter with nature and his theology grounded in the Creator God, Abba, who has a dual concern for human and non-human animals, and the plants of Earth. We will divide our discussions in Jesus and his ecological location of God's reign, his inclusive and compassionate vision of that reign, finally his actions in the Temple on behalf of the poor and non-human animals.

Jesus' Ecological Location

Any eco-Christology, or what Wallace description of "Jesus as the green face of God," finds its foundational stirrings in the historical ecological location of Jesus: the role of Galilee's geography and the surrounding area in the formation of Jesus, the agrarian and later wilderness environment reflected in his teachings on the reign of God, his religious immersion in popular Jewish creation theology, and his spiritual relationship with nature, especially, discovering the presence of God within the natural world and learning from nature. These along with Jesus' unique experience of God as Abba become personal precursors for his teaching and praxis of the reign of God.

The story of Jesus started at the margins, outside human residences in Bethlehem, and his life ends outside of Jerusalem on a cross. Wallace

3. Wallace, *Green Christianity,* 31–32.

makes the observation: "Jesus entered consciousness already intimate, then with the plight of the poor and the rhythms and flow patterns of agricultural life."[4] Jesus' birth was depicted in a cave used to shelter non-human domesticated animals as we portray in our Christmas crèches. And in Luke, shepherds, marginalized Jews, came to venerate him in a feeding trough as Savior and God's Child. His birth is draped in pastoral imagery and outside an urban setting, reflecting the disadvantaged poor and non-human animals.

Jesus lived most of his life as a child and young man in Nazareth in the region of Galilee. Nazareth was 4–5 miles outside the rebuilt city of Sepphoris, about an hour's walk, and a farming peasant community, where Jesus' family subsisted as peasant artisans or wood carpenters. John Meier observes that Jesus and his family members probably engaged in part-time farming a small plot for vegetables, herbs, and other items for family meals.[5] Wheat and barley, garden vegetables; olive, pomegranate, and fig trees; and grapes vines were the mainstay of Galilean agriculture. Greater attention has focused on the environmental and social factors of Galilee to understand the historical Jesus.[6] Jesus' life and ministry is impacted by the ecological location of Palestine: from the peasant farms of Galilee, shepherds tending their flocks, the Jordan where he was baptized by John, the wilderness where he discovered his full relationship with Abba God and his messianic ministry, sleeping under the skies in his itinerant ministry, using mountains and olive gardens to pray, sermons outside at natural sites, fishing and crossing the Sea of Galilee. Edward Echlin offers a glimpse into the ecological milieu of first-century CE Galilee:

> Jesus knew aquatic birds near the Jordan and larger scavengers in the life-filled lake. He would have seen raptors patrolling the sky above fertile land with its groves, fields, and vines. He would have observed pigeons and doves resting in the ubiquitous Palestine rocks where they lay eggs and feed vulnerable fledglings.[7]

4. Ibid., 35.

5. Meier, *A Marginal Jew,* 279.

6. Freyne, *Jesus, a Jewish Galilean*; Oakman, *Jesus and the Economic Questions of His Day.*

7. Echlin, *Earth Spirituality,* 63–64.

There were Palestine wolves, comparable to the modern day Syrian wolves prowling the hills and scrub brush, near the pasture fields.[8]

Douglas Oakman, likewise, stresses Meier's affirmation of Jesus' farming background:

> It cannot be doubted, even if it is granted that Nazareth special-ized in carpentry, that most of the residents of the village, oc-cupied themselves regularly with subsistence agriculture. Jesus came from peasant stock and without question was socialized early to the routines of farming.[9]

Galilee was a fertile land for agriculture, and large Greco-Roman planta-tions with tenant farmers grew by accumulating peasant farms because of spiraling indebtedness and displacingment. The Sea of Galilee provided a vigorous fishing economy. Herod Antipas built up two Hellenized cities, Sepphoris and Tiberius, as political and economic centers. Jesus grew up familiar with farming practices and the agriculture of Galilee. His para-bles reflect his familiarity with Galilean agriculture. C. H. Dodd points out that Jesus' parables indicate "an inward affinity between the natural order and the spiritual order."[10] There is "the sense of the divineness of the natural order is the major premise of the parables."[11] Later Dodd asks, "Was all this wealth of loving observation and imaginative rendering of nature and common life used merely to adorn moral generalities?" He proceeds to answer his own question, "This is not the impression conveyed by the Gospels as a whole."[12] More recently, Sean Freyne com-mented that Jesus' parables "are the products of a religious imagination that is deeply grounded in the world of nature and the human struggle with it, and at the same time deeply rooted in the traditions of Israel which speak of God as creator of heaven and earth and that is in them."[13] Likewise Echlin reaches the same conclusion: "Jesus' sensitivity to nature, so vivid in his parables, derived from living close to the natural world and from familiarity with Jewish scriptures and their metaphors of cosmic order."[14] Many of Jesus' parables are drawn from his ecological context

8. Ibid., 65–66.

9. Oakman, *Jesus and the Economic Questions of His Day*, 179.

10. Dodd, *The Parables of the Kingdom*, 20.

11. Ibid., 21.

12. Ibid., 25–26.

13. Freyne, *Jesus, a Jewish Galilean*, 59.

14. Echlin, *Earth Spirituality*, 76; also ibid., 37–102.

of Galilee; their images are employed from peasant agricultural experience, the plantation system of faming, and the economic upheavals from peasant displacement from their lands. There is a sense of God's agency in nature, transposed to humanity.

Jesus' experience of farming and animal husbandry are reflected in his parables as well as the oppressive agricultural system within which Jewish peasant farmers lived.[15] Douglas Oakman has noted the close connection between the Kingdom of God and the agrarian social vision of Jesus, demonstrated in his parables:

> The historical context of Jesus, therefore, reflects a social and economic situation in which exploitative urbanism, powerful redistributive central institutions like the Roman state and Jewish Temple, concentration of land holdings in the hands of the few, rising debt, and disrupted horizontal relations in society were becoming the norm.[16]

The reign of God, as Crossan tells us, is like an agricultural season. The peasant begins the growing season with sowing, then continues with the affairs of life as the seed sprouts and grows. In this mystery of growth, the earth produces of its own.[17] Jesus saw the agency of God in nature, and its sheer graciousness and growth. His ministry began as a renewal movement within Judaism, but incorporated "problems endemic to agrarian, indeed all class, societies."[18] And if we study his sayings we find a Jewish creation theology, very theocentric with notions of God's providential care for creation for plants (lilies of the field) for animal life (birds of the air).

> Where God's care for nature's birds and flowers should obviate human worries about food and clothing . . .The serenity and security passed by Jesus to his followers derives not from knowing hidden mysteries of past or present but from watching nature's rhythms of here and now.[19]

In his itinerant ministry, Jesus is mentioned found crossing the Jordan River into wilderness area and later into the region of the ten cities, Tyre in Phoenicia, or journeying to villages, town, and hamlets all around

15. Meier, *A Marginal Jew*, 279.

16. Oakman, *Jesus and the Economic Questions*, 211.

17. Waetjen, *A Reordering of Power*, 107.

18. Oakman, *Jesus and the Economic Questions*, 217.

19. Crossan, *The Historical Jesus*, 295.

Galilee. His wisdom sayings reflect a Jewish wisdom theology, predecessor to the later attributions of Jesus as the Prophet of Wisdom or even the Wisdom of God. Jesus finds God in the heart of nature as well as the marketplace and ordinary life. God is experienced in the sowing of seeds; seeds with the capacity to grow and multiply, subversive weeds, harvesting, and the husbandry of sheep. Decades ago, Amos Wilder observed, "[In the parables], it is not only human life that is observed but nature as well, or man in nature."[20] Scholars have often made the ecological elements subservient rather than inclusive in Jesus' notion of God's reign.

Jesus traveled the landscape of Galilee, and he would frequently isolate himself in prayer, listening to the stirring of God's presence and activity in the voices of nature, plants and animals. A primary observation from peasant harvests is the cooperation between peasants as well as the cooperation of God's agency in the soil and the natural elements and the sower to produce crops. He watched as the wealthy elite and the Roman plantation system disrupted the peasant connections with the soil community of life and how the large-scale production of crops harmed the land because they did not observe the Jubilee precepts to leave the land fallow for the seventh year. He communicated creatively through the poetry of his parables, the sharing of his sayings and their explanations, and symbolic praxis of God's reign. Harmonious relationship with nature was harmonious relationship with God and the soil. The reconstitution of society into a just and loving reign of God was a gradual process, germinated from a seed and nurtured by God's grace and forgiveness and flourished in their willingness to care for and share with others.

But Abba God for Jesus is also Creator God who makes the sun rise and sends the rains, for God is intimately in the processes of the cosmos. God is also the God for all creatures and connected to the Spirit. Luke claims that the Spirit was there in conception and birth of Jesus, and the Spirit was present to Jesus at his baptism, leading him into the wilderness, where God through the wilderness instructed Jesus in the wild dynamics of grace, and preparing him for God's ministry of compassionate care for the outsider. The Spirit was present with Christ in his death and raised Jesus to the resurrected Christ.

When we hear how Jesus experiences God's love for sparrows and lilies and wild flowers, he looks at them with loving eyes and sees them as loved by God and the revelation of God's providential care for nature.

20. Wilder, *Early Christian Rhetoric*, 82.

For Jesus, nature is the place of encounter with the living Spirit of Abba. When you listen to Jesus' parables, there is a sense of divineness present in the natural order. Jesus looks at nature as the gift of creation from Abba God, but it is also the place that we as human beings can encounter and meet Abba God as Spirit and the Spirit who lives in wild space and acts in a wild and unpredicted fashion.

For Jesus, mustard seeds are a subversive and wild symbol of God's spreading reign. Fig trees that produce fruit are a sign that God is near. Growth of a seed expresses God's intention that we are to thrive and flourish. And in another place in the gospel, the growth of a seed is God's grace. Jesus describes himself as a vine and us as the branches. Lost sheep expresses human alienation. And the wind becomes a metaphor for the unseen but felt experience of the Holy Spirit. For Jesus, nature instructs us continuously about God's grace.

One of my favorite parables is the mustard seed. John Dominic Crossan brilliantly unpacks the ecological context of the parable and how subversive it was. In planting the mustard seed is wildly dangerous. Jesus' audience would find the idea absurd. It is first crazy to sow mustard seeds in any field with other plants. Secondly, Jewish holiness rules prohibit planting and mixing mustard seeds with the seeds of other plants in gardens. It is first a purity issue, just like the mixing of fibers in cloth. You cannot mix things that are unlike. It offends the ancient priestly purity codes in Leviticus. So Jews would never consider planting mustard seeds in a vegetable garden. To sow mustard seeds in your garden would be unclean at best and at worst reckless. Mustard is a nuisance plant: it is a pesky weed that rapidly spreads. No farmer would ever sow such a pesky weed in their gardens, for a mustard seed grows by spreading under all of the other plants. What it does is it spreads so far unseen until it covers the undergrowth of the garden. This is why Jewish gardeners hated it, it just took over, no matter what you did, it went where it wanted to go. It works in small steps with small seeds to slowly but surely take over the entire garden, unnoticed, from underneath. Each flower on the plant can produce thousands of seeds. The potential of each flower to pollinate and seed multiplies inexponentially, it is almost unstoppable.

For Jesus, God's reign is a subversive movement like the mustard seed. The mustard plant takes over where it is not wanted. God's reign is a movement of people empowered. It is an out of control weed; it attracts birds which spread the mustard seeds to other locations where it is not particularly desired. The power of God's inclusive love is subversive and dangerous like the mustard seed; the power of God's love is stronger than the power of violence. But the mustard plant is not entirely useless; it has medicinal properties for healing. The Roman naturalist and author Pliny wrote:

> Mustard . . . with its pungent taste and fiery effect is extremely beneficial for the health. It grows entirely wild, though it is improved by being transplanted. But on the other hand when it is sown, it is scarcely possible to get the place free of it, as the seed when it falls germinates at once.[21]

Thus, Jesus points out the main character of God's reign as an empowered movement. It has dangerous "take over properties" with medicinal capabilities of healing.

Jesus' Empowered Companionship

Jesus proclaimed the reign of God. John Dominic Crossan has translated the usual patriarchal translation "kingdom of God" as the "companionship of empowerment."[22] Diarmuid O'Murchu translates it into the English idiom, "empowerment," but qualifies it even further with "empowerment through mutuality."[23] "Empowerment through mutuality" or "companionship of empowerment" open up new images of God not as a patriarchal ruler, king, or judge but co-creator in our midst—Emmanuel, God with us. O'Murchu writes,

> The Companionship of Empowerment make a double shift; from power over to power with, and from domination to communal collaboration . . . it marks a seismic shift from exclusivity to radical inclusivity . . . nobody is out, and therefore, everybody is considered to be included.[24]

Another translation I like to use for translating kingdom is "kin-dom." It is appropriate for apprehending the ecological dimensions of Jesus' message and praxis. Canadian author and clergy Bruce Sanguin observes about his usage of kin-dom:

21. Pliny, *Natural History*, 19, 170–71. Quoted in Crossan, *The Historical Jesus*, 278.

22. Crossan *The Birth of Christianity*, 337. Crossan notes, "Disciples (or students) can all be equal and still subordinate to a teacher.

23. O'Murchu, *Christianity's Dangerous*, 30–32; O'Murchu, *Inclusivity*, loc. 741–53.

24. O'Murchu, *Inclusivity*, 741–63.

The metaphor of kin-dom is a family metaphor. In an evolutionary universe, I'm interested in kin as a metaphor that includes
"*all of us*," not just "us." From this perspective, kin is not just
about our tribe, our nation, our family, our relation or even our
species. Kin suggests the radical belonging of all our relations,
human and other-than-human.[25]

Kinship denotes a relationship with a larger group, and in this case, Jesus' kin-dom message inclusively incorporates humanity and the web of
interdependent life.

Jesus lived out his parables' inclusivity and compassionately in his
healings and open commensality. Crossan amazingly communicates the
egalitarian depth of God's companionship of empowerment:

> The Kingdom of God was not, for Jesus, a divine monopoly
> exclusively bound to his own person. It began on the level of
> the body and appeared as shared community of healing and eat-
> ing—that is to say, of spiritual and physical resources available
> to each and all without distinctions, discriminations, or hier-
> archies. One entered the Kingdom as a way of life, and anyone
> who could live it could bring it to others. It was not just words
> alone, or deeds alone, but together as life-style.[26]

It was an inclusive life-style, a praxis of radical inclusion, a spirituality
openness to all, and radical egalitarianism. Jesus' lifestyle incarnates the
companionship of empowerment—wild grace with God in our midst.
His companionship of empowerment resulted in social and political
pushback with charges: "Behold a glutton and a drunkard, a friend of
tax collectors, and sinners. (Luke 7:34) In his healings, he is charged of
healing and exorcizing in the name of Beelzebul (Luke 11:14–15; Mark
3:23). All attempts in churches to sanitize or spiritualize Jesus; ministry
removes the "dangerous memories" of Jesus, the radically subversive and
politically and religious challenging message and the symbolic praxis of
the companionship of empowerment through discipleships, healings and
exorcisms, his practice of compassion, practice of open commensality,
and the symbolic challenges of his last week in Jerusalem to the Temple
leadership and Romans.

O'Murchu claims that radical inclusivity is at the heart of Jesus message and praxis of empowered companionship. This builds upon Crossan's

---

25. Sanguin, *Darwin, Divinity, and the Dance of the Cosmos*, 171.

26. Crossan, *Jesus: A Revolutionary Biography*, 113–14.

insight that Jesus promoted an inclusive and brokerless egalitarian kin-dom of nobodies and the poor.[27] He inspired a wildly compassionate inclusiveness and excited the dangerous depths of human longing and imagination of alternative world. Wendell Berry, American novelist and ecological activist, recognized three principles of the "kingdom of God":

> The first principle of the Kingdom of God is that it includes ev-erything in it, the fall of every sparrow is a significant event. We are in it whether we know it or not and whether we wish to be or not. Another principle, both ecological and traditional, is that everything in the Kingdom of God is joined both to it and to everything else that is in it, that is to say, the Kingdom is orderly. A third principle is that humans do not and can never know either all the creatures that the Kingdom of God contains or the whole pattern or order by which it contains them.[28]

Berry envisions two economies: the "Great Economy" and human econ-omy. The Great Economy is based on part of the Sermon of Mount in Matt 6:24–34:

> Therefore, I tell you, do not worry about your life, what you will eat or drink; or about your body, what you will wear. Is not life more than food, and the body more than clothes? Look at the birds of the air; they do not sow or reap or store away in barns, and yet your heavenly Father feeds them. Are you not much more valuable than they? Can any one of you by worrying add a single hour to your life? (Matt 6:25–26)

For Wendell Berry, the Great Economy is what Jesus includes in his notion of the companionship of empowerment, for Jesus expressed the economy that God designed in creation. It is a considerate economy found in nature, and all human economies need to fit harmoniously with the companionship economy. It is an extension of the Great Economy of companionship of empowerment into the natural world.[29] Berry per-ceives an ecological and economic sustainability with the above words of Jesus.

For Jesus, companionship denotes community, mutuality, co-creat-ing together through the mobilization of diverse gifts. It involves forgive-ness, unconditional love, non-violence, compassion, sharing goods, care

27. Crossan, *The Historical Jesus*, 292.

28. Berry, *Jayber Crow*, 220.

29. Berry, "Two Economies."

for the vulnerable, and God's wild grace, inclusive of human animals and nonhuman animals. My exploration of Jesus' vision of empowered companionship is divided in the following subsections: Discipleship, Compassion, and Open Commensality. Then I will include the discussion of Jesus' inclusion of nonhuman animals.

Discipleship

Jesus recruited men and women from rural communities and towns, many of which were social outcasts or considered social misfits. He invited men and women disciples to an itinerant lifestyle, leaving family for a greater family where all were beloved children of God. He taught them in a Jewish pedagogy of listening to his instruction and imitating his example, apprenticing and practicing God's companionship of empowerment. It is a learning that is practiced intentionally and mindfully focused on God now in our midst. Some of the salient elements of discipleship will become significant in our discussion of a kenotic spiritually of compassionate action in the world, inclusive of humanity and nonhuman life.

Jesus' commandment of love of God and love of neighbor: In Matthew sermon on the Mount (5:43–44), Jesus pushes the commandment of love beyond its traditional tribal boundaries: "You have learned how it was said: you must love your neighbor and hate your enemy. But I say this to you: love your enemies." It extends love of neighbor, (Lv. 19:18) inclusive of Gentiles and even the Romans. When asked who is my neighbor in Luke. Jesus gives an example in the Parable of the Good Samaritan, shattering Jewish cultural and religious prejudices against Samaritans (Luke 10:29–37). Both answers would have a shock impact on his audience, stretching them to understand enemies, the Samaritans, as neighbors. He elucidates the particulars of the requirement to love: (Luke 10: 27–28, 32).

His principle of love extends to nonviolent responses to enemies. In Matt 5:40–32, he gives example of anyone who wants your shirt to give your cloak as well. Or if Romans conscript you to carry their packs for a mile, go for another mile. South African theologian Albert Nolan writes, "Jesus is appealing for an experience of solidarity with humankind, an experience that is not exclusive, an experience that is not dependent upon reciprocity because it includes, even those who hate you, persecute you, or treat you badly."[30] Nonviolence towards enemies includes non-retaliation against them, Mark Kurlansky, in his book, *Nonviolence*, notes that the Romans had to kill Jesus cruelly:

> Jesus was seen as dangerous because he rejected not only warfare and killing but any kind of force. Those in authority saw this as a challenge. How could there be authority without force? This was trouble for the rabbinate, and was even more trouble for the military occupiers, the Romans. Jesus built a following that was attracted to his uncompromising point of view—the kind of people who are called troublemakers. He was tortured to death by the Romans in a manner so grisly and violent, it was surely designed to repel his followers.[31]

Christians followed the example of Jesus' enemy love and nonviolence in their pacifism and antimilitarism until Constantine's co-opting of Christianity into an empire religion.

John Dominic Crossan maintains that the heart of Jesus' ministry was a "shared egalitarianism of spiritual and material resources," an un-brokered reign of God.[32] The discipleship of equals became a form of egalitarian relating between men and women.[33] This included giving up wealth and sharing it with the poor. Jesus instructed the rich young man to sell his wealth and give it to the poor (Mark 10:17–31). Jesus remarks about the young man's turning away from discipleship: "It is easier for a camel to go through the eye of a needle than for someone who is rich to enter the kingdom of God" (Mark 10:25). Jesus envisioned a sharing of goods with the poor and the vulnerable, building a community of empowered care; he enacted such sharings in his meal and, in particular, the feeding of the multitudes.

Jesus instructs his disciples on loving service of the rest. He takes on the notion of slave who serves. He points out,

> The kings of the Gentiles exercise lordship over them; and those in authority over them are benefactors. But not so with you; rather let the greatest among you become as the youngest, and the leader as one who serves. For which is the greater, one who

---

30. Nolan, *Jesus Before Christianity*, 76.

31. Kurlansky, *Nonviolence, loc.* 328. Kurlanksy traces how nonviolence of Jesus and others create a trajectory of nonviolence in history.

32. Crossan, *The Historical Jesus*, 341–46.

33. Schüssler Fiorenza, *In Memory of Her*, 140–50.

> sits at table, or one who serves? Is it not the one who sits at table?
> But I am among you as one who serves. (Luke 22:24)

In his own words, Jesus modeled God's reign as one who serves at table and who washes the feet of his disciples. Foot washing was restricted to inferior status folks: women, slaves, and children. He asked his disciples to imitate these actions of women, slaves, and children as model of God's empowered companionship. His practices of etiquette at table also criticized domination politics—the hierarchical politics of Jewish aristocracy and Temple leadership, Herod Antipas, Pilate, and the Roman imperial system. For disciple service, he maintained: "there are those who are last who will be first, and first who will be last" (Luke 13:30; Mark 10:31; Matt 19:30). This was style of service leadership of the upside-down companionship of empowerment. His instructions of service as the least or the last highlights a critical alternative to the domination politics, based on status and power of the clerical aristocracy and the Roman Empire. God turns social and political hierarchies inside out, upside down. We hear this charge in priestly aristocrats turning Jesus over to Pilate, "He perverted the nation" (Luke 23:2).

The selfish person loves no one but him/herself. Such self-centeredness lacks compassion; it promotes an individual view of power, independence, and greed. Jesus, on the contrary, endorsed and exemplified humility for his disciples. He taught an egolessness, an ethic of interdependence, mutuality, and interrelationality. Jesus had a spirituality of interconnectedness to humanity and nature. There are a number of sayings where Jesus calls his disciples to take up their cross and to follow him or deny yourself.

> If anyone wishes to come after me, he must deny himself, and take up his cross and follow me, for whoever wishes to save his life will lose it; but whoever loses his life for my sake will find it. (Matt 16:24–25)

> If anyone wishes to come after me, he must deny himself, and take up his cross daily and follow me. (Luke 9:23)

Jesus imagines that as we lose our self-centeredness, we surrender to a network of companions of God, who let go of their self-centeredness. Once we identify with those who are suffering, hungry, weeping, thirst for justice, meek, lovers of peace, we realize the need for restraint of ourselves for compassionate care and engagement with the world. We deny self-interest for the values of the Beatitudes of God's companionship of empowerment.

Compassion

Jesus was a prophet of compassion in his ministry of living out empowered companionship in the stories of healings, his discipleship of equals, and his practice of open commensality. Compassion in Hebrew and Aramaic comes from plural word "womb."[34] Borg points out that Jesus' saying in Luke 6:36, "Be compassionate as your compassionate" stands as apart the various holiness groups who practiced a priestly code in Leviticus 19:2, "Be holy as God is holy." The priestly holiness code shaped various holiness groups in Second Temple Judaism, in particular, the Qumran community, the Pharisees, the Sabbath fundamentalists, and the Temple priesthood.

There was conflict between the dominant social paradigm of holiness and Jesus' compassion paradigm of the companionship of empowerment. Marcus Borg writes, "For Jesus, compassion was more than a quality of God and an individual virtue: it was a social paradigm, the core value for the community. To put it boldly, compassion for Jesus was political. He directly repeatedly challenged the dominant sociopolitical paradigm of his social world and advocated what might be called a politics of compassion."[35] Various holiness codes in the first-century CE Palestine were at odds with Jesus' open commensality. Sufficient to point out that the purity codes were based on the creation of various social maps of purity around animals, people, and location with the Temple's holy of holies as the center of the geographical purity map. It was a priestly vision implemented by the Jewish biblical tradition, the priests and, in turn, with the Pharisees who attempted to duplicate the purity of the Temple priests by their commitment to the purity codes and the commitment to

---

34. Marcus Borg explains, "In the Hebrew Bible, compassion is both a feeling and a way of being that flows out of feeling . . . it is very specifically linked to the association of womb; a woman feels compassion for the child of her womb; a man feels compassion for his brother, who comes from the same womb. As a feeling, compassion is located in a certain part of the body—namely, in the loins. In women, as one would expect, this means the womb; ion men, in the bowels. Thus, we have the somewhat odd biblical expression, 'his bowels were moved with compassion.'" Borg, *Meeting Jesus*, 47.

35. Ibid., 49.

tithing.[36] Marcus Borg argues that Jesus' practice of compassion served as an antidote to ritual purity/holiness codes. The holiness code was embedded in first century CE Judaism as a whole, in particular holiness groups but also on a popular level. It shaped the lives of those adhered to the purity code but those outside, whose lives were equally shaped the purity system.

In her study of compassion, Maureen O'Connell makes four points which are relevant to Jesus' practice of compassion:

> 1. Compassion is not comfortable and private but rather dangerous and political . . .[37]

> 2. Compassion unleashes the interruptive and liberating power of contrast experiences and hones our ability to feel, to imagine, and to enact alternatives to what is.[38]

> 3. Compassionate love is counter-cultural. It creates upheavals in the ways we understand ourselves, others, and the world.[39]

> 4. Compassion does not just alleviate suffering, but rather it transforms it.[40]

Jesus practiced God's companionship of empowerment, and it expressed a politics of compassion that was dangerous and political—Jesus' dramatic entry into Jerusalem, his controversies with Pharisees and Sadducees, and the Temple protest.

Compassion "unleashes the interruptive and liberating power of contrast experiences" (in particular, the Prodigal Son, the Good Samaritan, and the Dinner Party). Bernard Scranton Scott has a wonderful book, exploring the re-imagined world of Jesus' parables.[41] For example, Scott explores the parable of the woman who stealthily places the leaven in the three measures of flour until it is all leaven. Here Scott proposes, Jesus' radical message is "God becomes unclean."[42] Jesus imagines an

36. Neyrey, "Reader's Guide to Clean/Unclean, Pure/Polluted, and Holy/Profane: The Idea and System of Purity," https://www3.nd.edu/~jneyrey1/purity.html; "A Symbolic Approach to Mark 7," https://www3.nd.edu/~jneyrey1/symbolic.html.

37. O'Connell, *Compassion*, 3.

38. Ibid., 51.

39. Ibid., 70.

40. Ibid., 2.

41. Scott, *Re-Imagine the World*.

42. Ibid., 121.

alternative world of empowered companionship without the barriers of clean/impure, turning religious and social norms inside/out.

The Parable of the Good Samaritan is an incisive critique of the daily life shaped by the politics of holiness or purity codes. The man robbed, "half-dead," gives the ambiguity that the Levite and the priest perceive the man left on the side of the road as dead. Dead bodies are considered unclean, highly contagious. The priest and Levite pass by the body without investigating whether he was dead or not. They represent the heart of the purity system. It is the compassionate Samaritan, an unclean outsider and cultural enemy, that stops to care for the beaten man, placing him on his mount, and bringing him to an inn and paying for his convalesce. The outsider breaks purity boundaries out of compassion. Jesus' parable interrupts the purity system. Again the insight of Scott is incarnated here: God is unclean, breaking human categories.

Likewise, Diarmuid O'Murchu stretches the limits of Jesus' message, healings, and parables into poetry with alternative visions for then and now.[43] Jesus' politics of compassion shattered social barriers and religious boundaries that included the elite and excluded others. In *Christianity's Dangerous Memory*, O'Murchu describes Jesus' parables, healings, and ministry. He calls the parables "queer stories," for he claims, "Jesus is into queering on a big scale. And we remember that he is doing so at the service of a new vision, the Companionship of Empowerment."[44] When we take "queer" as a verb, it means to "interfere with or spoil." It disrupts and transgresses the oppressions of the ritual purity system, excluding folks for a variety of unclean reasons. Jesus' queer parables defy the purity scheme and stretch the creative imagination of his hearers to a creative to engage his politics of compassion and live an alternative dream of God's companionship. O'Connell points out that compassion is political and countercultural, but it also has the capacity to unleash "interruptive and liberative power," a power to change society.

O'Murchu notes that compassion cogently transforms the person who stands in solidarity with the outcast and marginalized:

> Gospel based compassion tolerates no outsiders. It is embraces and seeks to bring in all who are marginalized, oppressed, and excluded from empowering fellowship. It evokes a double response requiring a reawakened heart that knows . . . it cannot

43. For example, O'Murchu, *Jesus in the Power of Poetry*.

44. O'Murchu, *Christianity's Dangerous Memories*, 61.

withhold the just action that liberates and empowers. The transformation of the heart which might also be described as the
contemplative gaze, asks us to go where it hurts, to enter into
the places of pain, to share in brokenness, fear, confusion, and
anguish. Compassion challenges us to cry out with those in
misery, to mourn with those who are lonely, to weep with those
in tears. Compassion requires us to be weak with the weak, vulnerable with the vulnerable, and powerless with the powerless.[45]

Compassion is an important element of gospel inclusivity, but compassion is not for the faint of heart. It is a committed vision of justice to
relieve the suffering of the poor or the outcast or the ill. Compassion
recognizes an interrelatedness of the person suffering that can transform
the person experiencing the wombness of God in his or her life and with
the suffering party. Both are transformed in their forged bonds and empowered to mutual action for justice. Jesus used the imagery of taking up
the cross and denying yourself to indicate the seriousness of compassionate discipleship.

Jesus made an inclusive table practice as a central symbol of his
compassionate ministry. Just as God opens the feast without social and
religious purity boundaries, so Jesus encouraged his disciples to open
their feasts of God's empowered companionship to those in need and
unable to repay the favor. Jesus challenged exclusive religious boundaries by practicing what Borg calls a "boundary-subverting inclusiveness",
Dunn refers to his practice as "an absence of boundaries," and Crossan
describes it as "open commensality."[46] All these descriptions indicate an
untamed or wild hospitality practiced by Jesus as signs of God in our
midst.

Jesus' Open Commensality

John Dominic Crossan underscores that Jesus' open table fellowship as
a core component of the reign of God and symbol of his ministry. Jesus'
practice of "open commensality (rules of tabling and eating) is the symbol and embodiment of radical egalitarianism, of an absolute equality
of people that denies the validity of any discrimination between them

45. O'Murchu, *Inclusivity*, loc. 618.

46. Borg, *Meeting Jesus*, 142; Dunn, *Jesus Remembered*, 599; Crossan, *The Historical Jesus*, 261–64.

and negates the necessity of any hierarchy among them."[47] Crossan understands the Parable of the Feast (GThom 64:1–2; Luke 14:15–24; Matt 22:1–13) as an expression of open commensality:

> It is the random and open commensality of the parable's meal that is the most startling element. One could, in such a situation, have classes, sexes, ranks, and grades all mixed up together. The social challenge of such egalitarian commensality is the radical threat of the parable's vision . . . And the almost predictable counteraccusation to such open commensality is immediate: Jesus is a glutton, a drunkard, and a friend of tax collectors and sinners. He makes, in other words, no appropriate distinctions and discriminations.[48]

The banquet vision of the parable affirms that God's empowered companionship is not about power over but about a non-reciprocal gifting of lesser status people with abundant welcome of acceptance and forgiveness. Jesus' open commensality expressed a notion of "unbrokered egalitarianism," an open access to God through one another without the brokerage of priests or Temple. Borg also stresses the focal point of Jesus open and inclusive table, "The inclusive vision incarnated in Jesus' table fellowship is reflected in the shape of the Jesus movement itself."[49] Jesus invited sinners, tax collectors, prostitutes, and deviants with a mixture of poor and artisans into a fellowship meal that celebrated God's forgiveness and unconditional love.

Jesus broke the existing pattern of exclusive eating practices of his time as he redefines meal boundaries from exclusions to inclusions. Elisabeth Schüssler—Fiorenza describes this as the "praxis of inclusive wholeness."[50] When you invite someone for dinner, he said, "do not think of the rich, not even your family and friends, not the socially respectable, but the poor, who cannot reciprocate the invitation." The general scholarly consensus finds that Jesus' open commensality and his eating habits critique the asymmetrical religious patronage exchanges, both asymmetrical and even symmetrical giving and receiving favors, and he disrupts them. His etiquette of open hospitality, service at table, unbrokered egalitarianism, and celebration of God's forgiveness of sins, around

---

47. Crossan, *Jesus: A Revolutionary Biography*, 79.
48. Crossan, *The Historical Jesus*, 262.
49. Borg, *Meeting Jesus*, 56.
50. Schüssler Fiorenza, *In Memory of Her*, 119–30.

meals criticizes cultural, social, and religious hierarchies and inequalities. Jesus replaces hierarchies for egalitarianism—proposing a transgressive religious vision of role reversals, upturning of hierarchies, and radical equality and inclusive hospitality. Jesus indiscriminately welcomes men and women of all classes and purity/impurity statuses and fosters a community. He symbolizes in his table practices what Donald Kraybill calls the "upside-down kingdom" or companionship.[51] Stephen Patterson indicates such an open table is a table "far less manageable and far more threatening."[52]

Jesus triggers a terror of open commensality to his religious critics and political opponents, whose group centered personalities cannot comprehend eating together without discriminations and hierarchies, but it stills triggers a terror of unbrokered egalitarianism. Crossan insightfully remarks, "Generous almsgiving may be conscience's last refuge against the terror of open commensality."[53] There were no hierarchies at table, no one in charge and in power. There were only those who voluntarily served others, gladly washed the feet of their companions, who assisted folks at table to heal from the years of religious abuse and oppression. Jesus encouraged them to dream a future with hope, with God with shared resources and the abundance of food created by the companions of the bread and the cup. Mark Bredin views Jesus open table of sharing as "a way of challenging a world where the abundance of God's creation is mistreated and manipulated for the use of the elite."[54]. These meals were ritually loaded with empowering intent:

> Jesus shared food with a wide range of people at the table of radical inclusiveness, marking not merely a revolutionary concept with far-reaching implications . . . but also carrying cosmic potentialities that have gone largely unobserved . . . for Jesus the open table is an icon of both local and cosmic empowerment. It represents a dispensation of communal sharing in which nobody ever need be hungry. By the same token, it denotes the cosmic creation that nourishes all God's people abubdantly, and . . . all forms of charitable almsgiving subvert the the cosmic abudance that God intends for every earthly creature.[55]

51. Kraybill, *The Upside-Down Kingdom*.
52. Patterson, *The God of Jesus*, 86.
53. Crossan, *The Historical Jesus*, 105.
54. Bredin, *The Ecology of the New Testament*, 111.
55. O'Murchu, *Dangerous Memories*, 103.

God intends flourishing for all creatures, and Jesus' commensality embraces a cosmic inclusivity of God's abundance for planetary well-being. Open commensality embeds a symbolic intuition of God's open and extravagant grace for all life.

Matthew narrates how the disciples are plucking grain on the Sabbath and how the Pharisees criticize them for violation of the Sabbath law (Matt 12:1–2). For Jesus, denying food to anyone hungry is wrong. He gives the example of David and his companions broke into the house of God and ate the bread of presence or how priests violate the Sabbath, remaining guiltless. Jesus responds, "I desire mercy and not sacrifice (Matt 12:7)." In the several accounts of feeding the crowds, Jesus uses the later Eucharist formula of taking bread, blessing, and giving the loaves to the disciples (Matt 14:13–21 and parallels). Bredin remarks, "His actions embody an alternative system marked by generosity and shared resources as he also taught in the beatitudes."[56] These narratives contrast the practices of the urban rulers that deprive food to the hungry.

Borg interweaves Jesus' practice of compassion and open commensality:

> There is something boundary shattering about the *imitatio dei* that stood at the center of Jesus' message and activity: "Be compassionate as God is compassionate." Whereas purity divides and excludes, compassion unites and includes. For Jesus, compassion had a radical sociopolitical meaning. In his teaching and table fellowship, and the shape of his movement, the purity system was subverted by an alternative social vision affirmed. The politics of purity was replaced by a politics of compassion.[57]

The companionship of empowerment was a movement of nobodies, who practiced a radical inclusivity, a radical egalitarianism (discipleship of equals), open commensality, and care for the poor. Bread and wine were central to Jesus' meals; they symbolize both the growth of grain and grapevines, human farming, harvesting, milling grain or pressing the grapes into wine, and sharing these resources. Mark Bredin stresses the ecological symbolism of sharing bread and wine: "In sharing food and drink with those considered unholy, he (Jesus) show his acceptance and love for them, He shares with the very essence of creation that God intended for humans to enjoy and share regardless of culture or economic

56. Bredin, *The Ecology of the New* Testament, 113.
57. Borg, *Meeting Jesus*, 58.

class or, for that matter, species."[58] When we recall the principles of the Great Economy of Wendell Berry, we live in harmony with God's intention of shared abundance. It is likely that Jesus gave thanks and blessed the bread in the feeding of the crowds, each meal he would offer thanks to the Creator of life and the abundance shared. Jesus' gratitude recognizes how God provides all good gifts in the companionship of empowerment.

Finally, I contextualize the Last Supper in the line of meals of open commensality during Jesus' ministry. The synoptic and Pauline accounts (Matt 26:17–30; Luke 22:7–23; Mark 14:12–26; 1 Cor 11:23–26) of the Last Supper mention that the disciples were in attendance, and I follow Elisabeth Schüssler Fiorenza's understanding a discipleship of equals, inclusive of male and female disciples.[59] Therefore the later construal of the twelve only in John's final discourse becomes the ideological justification for male clericalism even though there is little historical involvement in Jesus' ministry and the post-Easter Jesus movement.[60] O'Murchu addresses the issue of participation in Jesus' final meal:

> If all the other meals were inclusive, and this seems to have been a nonnegotiable for Jesus, then the Last Supper consisted of more than the twelve apostles. Moreover, we know that most, if not all, of the twelve had fled in fear by the time of Jesus' death; if the meal happened sometime close to his imminent death, then some of those sacred apostles would have already fled. To suggest that all of them were present at the Last Supper seems to be defying common sense itself.[61]

First, such an inclusive contextual reading of the Last Supper seems to be consistent with Jesus' practice, and secondly with practice of a discipleship of equals.

Author Nick Page reiterates the egalitarianism in Jesus' communal meals and implicitly realizes the interrelatedness in Jesus' final meal:

> Proper messiahs would have had a victory banquet. Jesus had bread and wine the universal foods of the Greco-Roman world. The sound of the mill stone and the smell of baking bread filled the streets of every city, town, and village. Equally, vineyards were everywhere on the hillside and in the villages; even in the

58. Bredin, *The Ecology of the New* Testament, 111.

59. Schüssler Fiorenza, *In Memory of Her*, 135.

60. Torjessen, *When Women Were Priests.*

61. O'Murchu, *Christianity's Dangerous Memories*, 99.

city we may assume that vines were grown, effectively forming roofs along some of the narrower streets. There was nothing exotic about this feast: Just a cup, bread, and wine. A simple prophesy of what to come, and a celebration which would spread around the world.[62]

The outcast and socially marginalized had the right to sit at meals with Jesus, and there were no distinctions between sinners and righteous. Jesus takes bread and wine to indicate the ordinariness of the symbolic elements, the participation of God and nature in the growth of the wheat and grapes, the working of planting and harvesting the crops, the making of bread and the pressing and fermentation of grapes into wine. These symbolize a life in mutual companionship with the poor and marginalized but also with God's world of nature. He indicated that his death was compassionate sacrifice; he died for his "praxis of inclusive wholeness."[63] Denis Edwards claims, "Eating and drinking with outcasts and sinners is an authentic witness to the God of Jesus. These meals are acts of fidelity to the God of boundless compassion and familial inclusivity. For Jesus, the practice of inclusive table companionship is fundamentally and immediately linked to the issue of what kind of God God is."[64] Jesus died for the compassionate inclusiveness and unconditional love of God for humanity and all life. Here he symbolic partitions his bodiliness in anticipation of death and the composting his dead body for continued life. The compassionate God of life will birth justice and life through his sacrificial martyrdom. It becomes his last act of compassionate living for God. God is at the heart of everyday life, the giver of food and sustenance. His body and blood become food and drink for inclusive compassion.

Crossan points to the ancient notions of sacrifice to contextualize the death of Jesus. He explores the etymology of sacrifice (*sacrum facere*, "make holy"). Jesus' death can be construed as a sacrifice or martyrdom for God's empowered companionship. People sacrifice their lives to rescue another such as mother for child or dying for a cause, Jesus died for the non-violent vision of the companionship of empowerment. The ritual of the bread and cup of wine indicates that he understood his impending execution as sacrificial. He shares the bread and the cup of compassionate care for all present, all those connected together in God's companionship

62. Page, *The Wrong Messiah*, loc. 4338.

63. Schüssler Fiorenza , *In Memory of Her*, 119–21.

64. Edwards, *Jesus the Wisdom of God*, 47.

and its vision of non-violent love and forgiveness. It is a martyr's compassionate sacrifice for all life, ending the shedding of blood in the name of God and Empire, the ending of animal blood sacrifices.

Jesus and Nonhuman Animals

There are three stories I explore about Jesus' relationship to nonhuman animals: Jesus' journey into the wilderness (Mark 1:13), a floating Coptic gospel story about Jesus and the mule, and finally Jesus' protest in the Temple. There is a single phrase in Mark 1:13 that Jesus went to the wilderness and he "was with the wild animals." The messianic child of God begins in the wilderness his mission of empowered companionship, He first establishes a relationship nonhuman animals (*theria*), wild animals or predators. Bredin presents a context for understanding this verse: "Jesus being 'with the wild beasts' provides a countercultural witness to cultures that perceive animals and the rest of creation as existing only to satisfy human needs."[65] He begins his public ministry with the least of the least, nonhuman animals. Similarly, Richard Bauckham notes that this reflects the Jewish prevailing attitude of conflict between human animals and their domesticated nonhuman animals with the wild nonhuman animals.[66] It alludes to the messianic vision in Isaiah 11:6–9 that portrays peace between the human animal and their domesticated nonhuman animals (lamb, kid, calf, bullock, cow) with the wild nonhuman animal world (wolf, bear, leopard, lion, poisonous snakes). It is an end to enmity with a vegetarian paradise restored. Bauckham writes, "Jesus is portrayed at peace with the wild animals as the paradisal state of humans and animals was supposed to be in Jewish thought. By means of this motif Mark represents Jesus as the eschatological Adam, who, having resisted Satan, instead of succumbing to temptation as Adam did, then restores paradise: he is at peace with animals and the angels serve him."[67] Jesus with the wild animals is a Christological warrant and messianic symbol, and the retrieval of such a perspective occasionally glimpsed in Christian history as in the life of Francis of Assisi is necessary for Christians: "This is the possibility of living fraternally (I use the word because Francis' sense of all creatures as brothers and sisters.) with wild creatures, and experi-

65. Bredin, *The Ecology of the New Testament*, 44–45.
66. Bauckham, *Living with Other Creatures*, loc 2845–3027.
67. Ibid., loc. 2783.

encing thereby the grace of otherness which God gives us the diversity of animal creation and which is missed when animals are reduced merely to usefulness or threat."[68]

This story of Jesus in the wilderness indicates a peaceable companionship, and the temptation of domination is absent from this scene in Mark's gospel. Mark Bredin quotes Thomas Berry in regard to Jesus in the wilderness: "We misconceive our role if we consider that our historical mission is to 'civilize' or 'domesticate' the planet as though wilderness is something destructive rather than the ultimate creative modality of any form of earthly being. We are not here to control. We are her to become integral with the larger Earth community."[69] A number of authors suggest that Jesus learned and accepted his messianic ministry in the wilderness; some of have suggested that he learned his lifestyle there.[70] Rene Dubois also speaks of the impact of wilderness upon human experience: "The experience of the quality of wilderness in the wilderness helps us to recapture some of our own wildness and authenticity. Experiencing wildness in nature contributes to our self-discovery and to the expression of our dormant potentialities."[71] Thus, the wilderness presented Jesus with natural opportunities to learn about the "wild grace" of God, his dependence upon God, and perhaps an itinerant, carefree lifestyle dependent on the providence of God and human beings. Wendell Berry understands "wilderness as a place "where we must go to be reborn—to receive the awareness, at once humbling and exhilarating, grievous and joyful, that we part of creation, one with all that we live from and all that, in turn, lives from us."[72] Berry's notion of rebirth is consistent with the baptism narrative; new directions were stirring in Jesus.

Bauckham lists two more instances in Mark's Gospel of the peaceableness of the messianic reign: Jesus stilling of the storm (Mark 4:35–31) and Jesus' symbolic entry into Jerusalem on a donkey (Mark 11:1–10, parallels). Zechariah's prophecy in 9:9–10 serves as the interpretative lens of Jesus staged entrance into Jerusalem at Passover time. The stress is

68. Ibid., 3050.

69. Bredin, *The Ecology of the New Testament*, 41.

70. See ibid., 28–30; Loader, "Good News—for the Earth?," 28–43; McDonagh, *Greening the Christian Millennium*, 17.

71. Dubois, *The Wooing of the Earth*, 17.

72. Berry, *The Art of the Commonplace*, 99–100. The wilderness is a metaphor for God or God's Spirit. Erickson suggests a zoological *imago dei* of wilderness. Erickson, "The Apophatic Animal," 97–99.

on Jesus' stress on the peaceable reign among humanity, but this staged event is assisted by a donkey. In all likelihood this entry differed than the Roman procession of Pilate days before on a war horse and Roman troops carrying the standards of Rome into Jerusalem. Bauckham unpacks this episode, "In ancient Near Eastern cultures, horses were associated with war, but a king in peacetime might be expected to ride a mule, not a donkey (cf. 1 Kgs. 1:33). Jesus rides the animal that was every peasant's beast of burden."[73] Jesus dramatizes a counter-empire demonstration of peace over Roman violent conquest or in the cricus arenas where human and fierce beasts are sacrificed in combat. He subverts the symbols and gestures of empire and violence with a counter symbolic demonstration, laying the foundations for his disciples of God's "upside-down" kin-dom.[74]

Jesus and the Mule

There is a Coptic version of this floating gospel story, and it is impossible at this point to know whether it derived from an early gospel tradition.[75]

> It happened that the Lord left the city and walked with his disciples over the mountains. And they came to a mountain, and the road which led up it was steep. There they found a man with a pack mule. But the animal had fallen, because the man had loaded it too heavily, and now he beat it, so that the mule was bleeding.
>
> And Jesus came to him and said, "Man, why do you beat your animal? Do you not see that it is too weak for its burden, and do you know it suffers pains?" But the man answered and said, "What is that to you? I may beat it as much as I please, since it is my property, and I bought it for a good sum of money. Ask those who are with you, for they know me and they knew about this." And some the disciples said, "Yes, Lord, it is as he says. We have seen how he bought it." But the Lord said, "Do you then not see how it bleeds and do you not hear how it groans and cries out?" But they answered and said, "No, Lord, that it groans and cries out, we do not hear." But Jesus was sad and exclaimed, "Woe to you that you do not hear how it complains to the Creator in heaven and cries out and complains in its pain." And he came up and touched the animal. And it stood up and its

73. Bauckham *Living with Creatures*, loc. 1951.

74. Kraybill, *The Upside-Down Kingdom*.

75. Bauckham, *Living with Other Creatures*, loc. 2147.

> wounds were healed. But Jesus said to the man, "Now carry on
> and from now on do not beat it anymore, so that you too may
> find mercy."[76]

The story was translated from ancient Coptic into English in 1957. It is a loose narrative fragment floating around in the early Christian world. There were other such stories that floated around for awhile.[77] The precise age of this fragment is difficult to determine. Roderic Dunskerly, who translated it into English in 1957, felt that it is entirely keeping with the spirit of the gospels. He goes on to say, "since kindness to animals was not an aspect of Christian charity which the Early Church largely ignored", and this resulted in "such an incident falling out of notice."[78] Likewise, Bauckham explains this story: "So the story might go back to a Jewish Christian source in which the Jesus' teaching that love is the overriding principle in interpreting the law was extended, as it is not explicitly in the canonical Gospels to concern for animals as well as people."[79] The extra-canonical story expresses the spirit of Jesus in the canonical gospels. Kindness to animals was ignored by Greek speaking Christians, and this early story may conceivably go back to the historical Jesus.

Jesus left a city and was walking with his disciples over a steep mountain when he notices a mule has fallen from the heavy load the mule was carrying. Of course, the solution is not to relieve the mule of the heavy over load but to beat the mule. Jesus says, "Friend, why do you beat your animal? Do you not see that it is too weak for its burden, and do you know it suffers pains?" He responds back to Jesus, "What is that to you? I may beat it as much as I please, since it is my property, and I bought it for a good sum of money. Ask those who are with you, for they know me and they knew about this." He claims that the mule is his property, and he can do as he wishes. Jesus' disciples agree with him.

But Jesus asks his disciples: "Do you then not see how it bleeds and do you not hear how it groans and cries out?" But they answered and said, "No, Lord, that it groans and cries out, we do not hear." His disciples are blind to pain inflicted upon the mule and don't hear the cries of the animal. It is the failure of human beings to respond compassionately to the cries of the innocent creature, and the disciples too have made the

76. Ibid., loc. 2136.

77. For example, John 8:1–12; see Brown, *The Gospel of John*, 1:336–37.

78. Dunskerly, *Beyond the Gospels*, 143–44.

79. Ibid., loc.2147.

mule's cries inaudible. This invites a rebuke from Jesus for the lack of mercy and care. Even his own disciples have failed to hear the cries of the mule. Those who should hear do not. Kate Rigby comments on this story and the deafness of the disciples to the cries of the mule: "What this suggests is the ability to respond to the ethical call of other- than-human suffering is contingent on the recognition of a shared creatureliness."[80] She reads this story intertextually with the Good Samaritan parable in Luke 10:25–37. In both cases, Jesus highlights compassion for the other as the driving motive for an ethical response to the other. I add Brian Patrick's voice: "Who is our neighbor? The Samaritan? The outcast? The enemy? Yes, yes, of course. But it is also the whale, the dolphin, and the rain forest. Our neighbor is the entire community of life, the entire universe. We must love it all as our self."[81] The nonhuman animal cries out to its creator for mercy, suggesting that the animal also has its own relationship to God who hears its cries. The Hebrew scriptures declare God's instructions, "You shall not see your neighbor's donkey or ox fallen on the road and ignore it, you shall help to lift it up" (Deut 22:4). The Hebrew scriptures are filled with rules on the compassionate care for domesticated animals. The fourth commandment concerning the Sabbath requires rest for one's livestock as well as humanity (Exod 20:10; Deut 5:14). There is also the law forbidding the yoking of animals of unequal strength because such a yoking would cause pain to the weaker animal. The basic principle in the Hebrew Bible governing human animal relationships is considering "the pain of living creatures" (*tza'ar ba'alei chayim*).

It is easy to imagine Jesus reciting the line from the Psalms: "You save humans and animals alike, O God" (Ps 36:6) Jesus often spoke about God's providence in caring for the sparrows of the sky. The nonhuman animal cries out to its Creator for mercy, suggesting that Jesus believed that the animal has its own relationship to God who hears the cries of the mule. But Jesus rebuked, "Woe to you that you do not hear how it complains to the Creator in heaven and cries out and complains in its pain." He chides both the disciples and the mule owner: "Now carry on and from now on, do not beat it anymore, so that you too may find mercy." Some early followers of Jesus saw his teachings as extended to suffering animals in preserving this story. Jesus exemplifies the principle of saying: "the measure you give will be the measure you receive" (Matt 7:2; Luke

80. Rigby, "Animal Calls," 122.

81. Patrick, *Earthspirit*, 40.

6:38). Or "Blessed are the merciful, for they will receive mercy" (Matt 5:7). If people do not show mercy to their nonhuman animals, for they cannot expect mercy from God. That is the reality of Jesus' final saying and teaching.

We should certainly expect that Jesus treated animals with care and compassion. When I hear the parable of the Good Shepherd (John 10:11–18; Luke 15:4), I wonder what experience of Jesus stands behind these analogies. It is imaginable that Jesus filled in for a neighbor and searched for the one lost sheep on his watch. In the Sabbath controversies over healing (Luke 13:14–16; 14:5; Matt 12:10–14), Jesus points that acts of compassion for domesticated animals is permitted by the Torah as an exemption from the prohibition of work on the Sabbath. Jesus is well aware of the arguments that actions on the Sabbath to relieve suffering of nonhuman animals are compassionate and permissible under the law. If domesticated nonhuman animals serve humanity, humanity also has reciprocal responsibilities to care.

In a saying, Jesus asks, "Are not two sparrows sold for two pennies? Yet not one of them is forgotten in God's sight" (Luke 12:6–7; Matt 12:29–31). He presents sparrows, creatures of very limited value in the marketplace, to his audience, but these birds never escape God's providential care. God cares for the very least of nonhuman animals. Bauckham speaks of a hierarchy of value with the community of created life, but it is not the Greek hierarchy of Aristotle and Greek philosophy that predicates human superiority and nonhuman animal inferiority.[82] Jesus often comes to the defense of his actions on the Sabbath with Jewish scriptural traditions of human responsibilities to domesticated nonhuman animals (Luke 23:25; Matt 12:11). Bauckham makes a strong point that Jesus never uses the Greek argument of the hierarchy of human animals' superiority over nonhuman animals of later Christian theologies influenced by Greek philosophy. Jesus presumes a mutuality of fellow creatures. Elizabeth Johnson writes, "Jesus' vision of the reign of God includes wholeness and shalom for all creatures, even the least important in the hierarchy of values, the nonhuman, God's peace links all creatures in a community of life and stands against exploitation even of the least powerful. In the new heaven and the new earth, every created thing will have its own integrity in relationships of mutuality and interdependence."[83]

82. Bauckham, *Living with Other Creatures*, loc. 2319.

83. Johnson, *Consider Jesus*, 140.

Jesus' general practice of love and compassion is of course of great importance for our treatment of animals. This text of the mule invites us to understand that Jesus was compassionate to nonhuman animals, and this is not a far-fetched idea as healer of their suffering. Jesus' general practice of love and compassion is of course of great importance for ethical treatment of nonhuman animals. This reflects the Jesus' inclusive ministry of compassion and his "being with the wild animals" in the wilderness. There is no life, be it human animal or nonhuman animal apart from God's care and concern.

Stop the Temple Action

When I first wrote Jesus' Stop the Temple action twenty years or so ago, many scholars still explained Jesus action as a spiritual cleansing or were just beginning to speak of it as a prophetic demonstration of the Temple's destruction. Catholic social and political critic Garry Wills correctly writes, "The most striking, resented, and dangerous of Jesus' activities was his opposition to religion as that was understood in his time. This is what has led to his death. Religion killed him."[84] "Jesus did not come to replace the Temple with other buildings, whether huts or rich cathedrals, but to instill a religion of the heart."[85] Generally, Wills' assessment is correct but needs some fine-tuning with what Jesus was resisting in his "stop the Temple" demonstration. Jesus in some of the controversy stories in the gospel, quotes Hosea 5:1 and 6:6: "I desire mercy, not sacrifice" (Matt 9:13). It is a response to the Pharisees' question to Jesus' disciples, "Why does your teacher eat with tax collectors and sinners?" (Matt 9:11). The Pharisees attempt to duplicate the purity of the Temple priests through strict adherence to the purity codes and tithing as their holiness agenda of their fellowship meals. Pharisees required for their table fellowship observing comparable holiness and purity as the Temple priests.

Jesus challenged the purity/holiness codes of not only the Pharisees but also the Temple code through his practice of open commensality and forgiveness. N. T. Wright notes that the seeds of conflict with the Temple existed during Jesus' ministry: "His (Jesus) offer of forgiveness, with no prior conditions of Temple-worship or sacrifice, was the equivalent of someone in our world offering as a private individual to issue someone a

84. Wills, *What Jesus Meant*, 59.
85. Ibid., 75–76.

passport of a driver's license. He was undercutting the official system and claiming by implication to be establishing a new one in its place."[86] The Temple was also the national banker, lending monies to Jewish peasants to pay for seed, pay their taxes to Romans, and tithes. The Temple also foreclosed after several years on peasant families, selling family members into slavery as well as the peasant farmland. Spiraling indebtedness was a problem leading to social displacement of farmers. If we look at Jesus' parable of the Good Samaritan, we find a scathing criticism of the priest and Levite failing in compassionate care to the man robbed, beaten, and left for the dead.

Jesus criticized the Temple leadership and priesthood, and this is confirmed in all four canonical gospels in his staged protest.[87] Richard Horsley indicates that Jesus' staged protest was directed at the heart of the Temple, its integral business of money exchange and selling of animals for sacrifice, and these businesses were administered by the aristocratic priestly families. Horsley concludes, the protest was a "prophetic act symbolizing God's imminent judgmental destruction, not just of the building, but of the Temple system."[88] Marcus Borg similarly asserts that Jesus challenged the purity system in his ministry and he staged a protest in the heart of the purity system in the Temple and the vested economic interests of the Temple elite.[89] The evangelist Mark has Jesus in an ever escalating conflict with the Sadducees and scribes during his last week in Jerusalem. Over twenty years ago, I wrote: "His (Jesus) action was premeditated and carefully orchestrated and staged. There are three components to Jesus' symbolic action or messianic theater: the overturning of the money changers' tables, the driving out of those selling sacrificial animals, and the stopping of those working on the rebuilding of the Temple."[90] He stopped the selling of sacrificial animals. Jewish pilgrims would not be able to bring pigeons on their journey to the Temple so they procured them for sacrifice. Mark 12:15 and Matthew 21:12 indicated that he stopped the selling of pigeons, while John 2:14–15 added sheep and oxen to pigeons. I earlier interpreted the messianic theater protest

86. Wright, *The Challenge of Jesus*, 65.

87. McLennan, "Resisting Religion, Spreading Love," 62–69; Chilton, *Rabbi Jesus*, 222–29; Wright, *The Challenge of Jesus*, 65–68, 77–78; Borg, *Jesus: A New Vision*, 174–76.

88. Horsley, *Jesus and The Spiral of Violence*, 300.

89. Borg, *Meeting Jesus*, 55.

90. Goss, *Jesus ACTED UP*, 145–47.

as an attack on the sacrificial system, the priesthood, and the economic exploitation of the poor.

The selling of sacrificial animals was a lucrative business, and with the numbers required during festivals point to the development of proto-factory farming that supplied sacrificial animals needed for the year. It is reasonable to expect that the Temple had ownership of a number of agrarian and animal husbandry plantations or had a financial stake in the proto-factory farming operations. In John 2:16, Jesus says, "Stop making my Father's house a marketplace." In Mark 11:17, he levels the charge that the vendors have made the Temple a "den of thieves." All fees were certainly tithed, for the Temple took its share of all revenues. Jesus' criticism was leveled against the priesthood and the Temple itself as a religious institution.

In the ancient world, temples were the slaughterhouses and the butchers selling the meat of the sacrificed animal. Stephen Webb images the scenario of the Temple:

> The stench of the blood and roasting flesh can hardly be drowned by the smoke of incense, nor can the cries of the traders, or uplifted voices of priests and pilgrims at prayer, have drowned the screeching of the beasts as they had their throats cut.[91] The Temple economy was based on the selling, buying, and killing animals. Whatever Jesus was doing, it had to be directly related to the animals that dominated the temple activities.[92]

Webb concludes, "Jesus came to liberate the animals so that worship would not depend on the spilling of innocent blood." He arrives at the conclusion from Hammerton-Kelly's argument that Jesus cursed the fig tree and that this represented the sacrificial system of the Temple.[93] Therefore, he curses the tree: "May no one ever eat from fruit from you again" (Mark 11:14). Webb understands the allegorical interpretation of the fig tree for Temple sacrifice, for he claims, "Jesus is saying that nobody needs to benefit from animal sacrifices anymore. And since Jews in Jerusalem limited their meat consumption to animals that were properly killed in the temple, Jesus could be interpreted as advocating a vegetarian

91. Wilson, *Jesus: A Life*, 174.
92. Webb, *Good Eating*, 95.
93. Hammerton-Kelly, *The Gospel and the Sacred*, 19.

diet."[94] Later Webb asserts that Jesus was not a strict vegetarian; he ate fish and a general peasant diet of grains, vegetables, and fruits.

If Jesus is performing messianic theater as he similarly staged with his dramatic entry into Jerusalem, then nonhuman animals are included in three of the messianic actions: the wilderness, the entry into Jerusalem, and now the Temple. When I read again the four accounts of the Temple actions, the incident is reminiscent of where Jesus recited the words from Isaiah in the synagogue of Nazareth in Luke 4:18–19, Jesus proclaims "release of the captives" and "a year of favor" or jubilee. Do we have another messianic action that symbolizes the "peaceable kin-dom" with the abolition of animal sacrifice? Webb gives some direction to my claim of messianic action including the peaceable reign and the liberation of nonhuman animals: "To say that Jesus came to save the world means not only that Jesus came to save us, but also that Jesus came to save the animals, Jesus quite literally took the place of the animals so that they would not take place of us."[95] In John's Gospel, John the Baptist proclaims Jesus "the Lamb of God (John 1:29). Later, the evangelist brings out the fact that Jesus is crucified as the paschal lambs are slaughtered in the temple. The cries of the lambs, whose throats are cut in the Temple, parallel the cries of agony of Jesus on the cross. They bleed and die as Jesus on the cross bleeds and dies.[96] The post-Easter community of Jesus was naturally divided at first about meat eating of sacrificial animals as evidenced by Paul's arguments about eating meat sacrificed to deities. But more importantly, Christian abstention from sacrifice and from meat eating often resulted from the undersanding of the death of Jesus as a sacrifice (1 Cor 8:4–13). Steve Patterson notes, "So the unclean and unsettling death of Jesus became the sacrifice to end all sacrifice."[97]

Seemingly, Jesus' mission to bring God's companionship of empowerment fails on the cross. He dies as a marginal outcast, one crucified as a slave criminal for his rebellion to Rome and to the Temple; he dies in solidarity with the poor and the disadvantaged. Cardinal John Henry Newman, part of the 19th century Oxford movement of Anglicanism and later a convert to the Catholic Church, preached at St. Mary's Church in Oxford on Good Friday.

94. Webb, *Good Eating*, 97.

95. Ibid., 100.

96. Wallace *Finding God in the Singing River* (no page numbers for the plates).

97. Patterson, *Beyond the Passion*, 101. See Patterson's discussion of sacrifice and Christian abstention in ibid., 86–101.

> Since the scripture compares (Christ) to this inoffensive and
> unprotected animal, we may without presumption or irrever-
> ence take this image (of the lamb) as a means of conveying to
> our minds the feelings which our Lord's suffering should excite
> within us. I mean consider how very horrible to read accounts
> which sometimes meet us of cruelty inflicted upon brute ani-
> mals . . . For what was this but the very cruelty inflicted upon
> the Lord.[98]

Cardinal Newman finishes: "Think then, my brethren, of your feelings at
cruelty practiced on brute animals, and you will gain one sort of feeling
which the history of Christ's cross and passion ought to excite you."[99]
Cardinal Newman correlates the cruelty inflicted upon animals with the
affliction of suffering lambs.

Green Christians understand that if God cares about every sparrow,
every insect, every creature in the seas, in the air, or on land, and the wild
beasts. Jesus' death invites his disciples to love fellow creatures as God
loves them. We are called into a kinship with God's creatures and the
earth, not the domination of nature. Jesus taught that all life, disadvantaged and poor, have a God-given value. Mark Wallace claims,

> In the Christian story, the cross is green. It is green because Jesus'
> witness on the cross is to a planet where all of God's children are
> bearers of life giving Spirit. It is green because of the goodness of
> creation is God's here-and-now dwelling place where everyday
> life is charged with sacred presence and power. The kingdom of
> God is not some far-off possibility never to be realized on Earth
> rather, it is the always-here reality of God's enfleshed presence
> now being realized through caring for one's neighbor and seek-
> ing justice for the oppressed. By modeling our lives after Jesus'
> life, we realize the truth of the prophetic teaching.[100]

Jesus cries out on the cross for the poor and suffering. It is a cry a pain of
humiliation and suffering for those people who are suffering and dying
without voice. But it is also the cry for the terrified cries of nonhuman
animals, slaughtered at the Temple through a religious factory farming
system. Humanity continues a system of domination, not the ancient Roman Empire and coopted Temple aristocracy, but by the new promoters
of global and corporate empire, desecrating and exploiting the Earth and

98. Quoted in Linzey, *Animal Gospel*, 65.

99. Ibid., 65.

100. Wallace, *Green Christianity*, 38.

careless disregard for human flourishing or the flourishing of other life. Wallace continues,

> Jesus' suffering on behalf of all of us who cry out for restoration and compassion, human and nonhuman alike, enables us, in turn, to reach out to a dangerously warming planet and heal it as well. It is this sense that his suffering makes us whole—his life of service empowers us to commit ourselves to social justice and planetary well-being . . . The kingdom of God is in our midst. In the power of the green cross, our task is to realize the gospel truth that the sacred earth is God's kingdom where the vital needs of all God's children are to be met with compassion and integrity.[101]

There is no question that Jesus' life story, from birth through death, represents a parable of God's compassion or the "green face of God."

---

101. Ibid., 38–39.

4

Christ the Gardener

For I saw the Lord sitting like a man. I watched, wondering what kind of labor it could be that the servant was to do. And then I understood that he was to do the greatest labor and the hardest work there is. He was to be a gardener, digging and ditching and sweating and turning the soil over and over, and to dig deep down, and to water the plants at the proper time. And he was to persevere in his work and make sweet streams to run, and fine and plenteous fruit to grow which he was to bring before the Lord and serve him to his liking.

—Julian of Norwich[1]

Gardening is an active participation in the deepest mysteries of the universe.

—Thomas Berry[2]

The first epigraph is from the *Showing*, written by Julian of Norwich, fourteenth–fifteenth-century English anchoress and mystic. Julian narrates

1. Julian of Norwich, *Showings*, 1978, 273–74.
2. Thomas Berry, quoted on http://blog.gaiam.com/quotes/authors/thomas-berry/35118.

the parable of "The Lord and the Servant," God and a servant identified with Adam and the second with Jesus. Adam is placed in Eden to garden, to sweat and dig and water, but Adam and Eve give into temptation to eat from the Tree of Knowledge of Good and Evil. They eat the fruit and are banished from the garden, Adam fails in his task of gardening. Like the first gardener, Jesus comes to Earth to replace the failed gardener. His labor is metaphorical, for Julian, his garden is the human soul, and through his labor he restores us to the original garden. Julian reflects Anselm's satisfaction/atonement theology, which I find violent and reject. But Julian's parable has the metaphorical surplus of meaning to reflect on the work of Jesus as gardener.

The symbolic of risen Christ the Gardener has wonderful ecological possibilities. Gerard Loughlin observes how during the Renaissance the images of Christ with hoe in hand or watering can adorned devotional altar cloths and book covers, "reminded people that gardening was a godly activity."[3] The garden is no longer the individual human soul, but it includes, on microcosmic level, human animals, nonhuman life, the web of life and the planet Earth and on macrocosmic level it includes all created reality—the entire universe. The garden is a place of encounter for Mary Magdalene with the risen Christ and becomes a place for all future encounter with the risen Christ.

Orthodox Christianity portrays the icons of Jesus' crucifixion with Adam's scull at the foot of the cross. Orthodox Christianity takes Golgotha, "the place of the skull" (Mark 15:22, Matt 27:33) as the location of the Garden of Eden. In a medieval sermon, Jesus tells Adam that he was crucified in a garden: "For the sake of you who left a garden, I was betrayed to the Jews in a garden, and I was crucified in a garden."[4] This leads back to Julian's visionary parable. Jesus sweats blood in the Garden of Gethsemane, beginning the greening of the soil. For Julian, Jesus wears the crown of thorns from Adam's crop of thorns, and Julian sees that Christ now wears the sweat-stained gardener shirt of Adam while his passion on the cross dries up the sweat of Adam and all humanity.

> Christ the gardener irrigates the desert with water flowing from his pierced side, making "sweet streams to run fine and plenteous fruit to grow." Christ the gardener harrows hell, raising up

3. Loughlin, *Alien Sex*, 270–271 and 288, n. 76.

4. Cited in International Commission on English in the Liturgy, *The Liturgy of the Hours*, Vol. II, New York, Catholic Book Publishing Co., 1976, 497.

the great root out of the deep depth, which rightly was joined to him in heaven."[5]

Adam, representing all humanity, now enjoys Christ the flourishing Tree of Life.

The ecological Christ expands aspects of Incarnation intuited in the early formulations of a Wisdom Christology. In their experience of Jesus' resurrection, the disciples began to develop a metaphorical language about the risen Christ. There are evolutionary dimensions, cosmological dimensions, and the emergence of the notion of "deep incarnation." Our focus now is on the metaphor of Jesus as the Gardener.

The Truth of Gardens

I love our church garden, for it remains a surprising gift in an urban setting with a desert landscape and indigenous California plants. Each day, I sit in the garden for prayer, often joined by my companion dog Friskie. He loves the garden fragrances and enjoys chasing the birds eating the bird seed. Sometimes he just sits with me in meditation, and I wonder if he is meditating with me. He pays attention to the garden. The garden teaches me about abundant life, for it teaches me the language of God grace.

The Garden of Eden is a mythic projection of God's graced space for a future ecotopia, for we alienated ourselves from the garden of the Earth over the last centuries. This is perhaps more truth in the myth for contemporary humanity as we have further disconnected ourselves from nature and gardens. For myself and many of the congregants, our church garden is God's graced space; it was dedicated as the "Resurrection Garden." It evolved from my sermon one Easter on Mary Magdalene's mistaken recognition of Jesus as Gardener.

Our garden is truly a gift, literally because every plant has been donated by members, non-member stakeholders, even by strangers. Gardens are gifts of natural beauty, with an abundant network of life. Gardens are works of art, cultivated and intended to be enjoyed.[6] We co-live with them and participate in them whether as gardeners or visitors. We have a relationship with a garden whether we cultivate and care for the plants or are a visitor meditating and enjoying the garden. One of my

5. Healy, "Christ the Gardener," 78; from Julian, *Showings*, 277.
6. Garcia-Rivera, *The Garden of God*.

Sunday pleasures is to witness congregants exploring the latest blooms, sitting peacefully in the garden to talk after service.

Our gardener is a living parable of Christ's gardening as have watched him for many years, tenderly caring for each plant and lovingly watering, pruning, planting or transplanting, fertilizing, mulching, or enjoying and mourning the death of plants. The garden has become his spiritual practice, and he is attentive and listens to each plant. His relationship to the garden exhibits a profound mutuality or a reciprocal relation. Each benefits from a relation of shared needs. Our gardener is a deacon, taking seriously that he has a pastoral responsibility to care for the Earth since we made the Earth a member of our congregation. As gardener, he finds himself mindfully attentive to what plants need and provides for their need. But the garden plants reciprocate by instructing him on the need to slow down from the hectic pace of contemporary life and be mindful of the moment as well as eco-location of being part of the garden. Bruce Sanguin writes about the relationship between garden and gardener:

> A relationship is established in which the garden silently communicates its needs and desires. Any good gardener knows that there is a genius particular to each piece of land, which will determine what will flourish . . . Our best gardeners operate not as masters over the garden, but as one intelligent source of creativity among other centers of creative intelligence, the plants.[7]

One day I commented to the church gardener how much his listening skills and compassionate care for congregants have matured. He attributed his growth in pastoral skills to his daily practice of listening and being attentive to life in the garden. The garden has provided him with pedagogy of listening and care, transferable also to congregants. He is truly an "eco-chaplain" to the church garden flock. Furthermore, the garden has been a life-preserving spiritual practice in his struggle with a chronic illness, and it continues to keep him alive with a purpose in life by its requirement of care, but it often instructs him about his own life. One morning, we sat in the garden and shared about life challenges that we both faced. He shared: "I have learned a lot from gardening. I have experienced plants dying, and just when I think they are completely dead, they surprise me with coming back to life. The garden teaches me continuously about myself and how God surprises us with life here and

---

7. Sanguin, *Darwin, Divinity, and the Dance of the Cosmos*, 38.

beyond." Theologian Norman Wirzba writes: "At the root of agrarian life, we find the experience of waiting and watching, of letting go and trusting the grace of life to accomplish what we cannot perform."[8]

Gardens can be planned or be eclectic; they can be professionally landscaped and designed such as botanical gardens, the landscapes for parks or buildings, or small enclaves of home and church gardens. Eleanor Perenyi writes, "A garden is a world, and its parts are not separable."[9] Even the smallest eclectic gardens connect us with the larger natural world. By connecting to our garden, we ground ourselves in a community of birds, insects, pollinators, soil, water, and sun. It requires personal engagement with the Earth and a community of life.

The second truth about gardens is that they become a "second nature, nature interpreted, landscaped, cultivated, built upon, and transformed in innumerable ways."[10] Sallie McFague repeats Pollan's insight that the "second nature" of gardens is an improvement or transformation of nature.[11] This understanding makes the garden as second nature, an ideal metaphor for resurrection and the resurrected transformed universe. Gardens are transformed natural spaces, and they become transformational space, often creating a holy or sacramental places where the sacred and nature come together. There is no question that God loves gardens and creates gardens. Numerous gardeners testify to the spiritual connections that their gardens provide. Dorothy Francis Gurney writes, "One is nearer God's heart in a garden/ Than anywhere else on earth."[12] Then the Irish playwright George Bernard Shaw also observes, "The best place to seek God is in a garden."[13] Many of us similarly find God in our own gardens, church garden prayer time in our garden, often spent with companion dog, the plant life, and the birds and butterflies. Norman Wirzba astutely remarks that gardens integrate us with biological processes that are part of the web of life:

> The garden is the most practical prism through which we can observe the diverse strands of plant and animal and human life, coming to together in terms of bewildering array of biological,

8. Wirzba, *The Paradise of God*, 73–74.

9. Perenyi, *Green Thoughts*, 175; quoted in *The Paradise of God*, 113.

10. MaFague, *Super, Natural Christian*, 159; Polland, *Second Nature*, 233–34.

11. Ibid., 160.

12. Dorothy Francis Gurney, "God's Garden," lines 13–16.

13. George Bernard Shaw, *The Adventures of the Black Girl*, 51.

chemical, and physical processes. It is, we might say, the site through which wildness comes home.[14]

Gardeners place themselves in service of their gardens and their biological, chemical, and physical processes. They plant, water, prune, talk to and care for their plants, fertilize, and enjoy the plants of their gardens. They talk about individual plants intimately and proudly as if they were family or close intimate friend. They are sad when a plant is stressed and dies. Gardeners are intimately involved with their gardens. As they nurture their gardens, their gardens nourish themselves with beauty and feed their spirits. Wirzba speaks of the ecological value of gardens: "As we garden, that is, as we weed out the non-nourishing elements within us and train our habits to be more life promoting, we participate in the divine life, and learn to see and feel the creation as God sees and feels it."[15] Gardens train gardeners to be attentive to the fragility and vitality of life and to appreciate the surprises and miracles of life sprouting before them. Most gardeners, I know, have a meditative focus on their gardens.

The final truth is that God's hands are dirty from garden care, fashioning and creating from the soil. In the poetry of Genesis 2–3, God the Gardener takes clay, breathes into clay, and fashions the first earthling— *adamah*. Dr. Daniel Hillel, a soil physicist, observes that the feminine Hebrew noun *adamah* indicates humanity's origin and humanity's destiny. In other words, we are tethered to the Earth from beginning of our lives to the end of our days.[16] This is a profound truth of earthly embodiment and foreshadowing our destiny to return to the Earth until we are resurrected from the tomb as plants arises from the soil. In Genesis 2, God creates human beings and places them in a garden, and it is paradise because it is the place where humans can walk, talk, and intimately meet God in a graced space, and are part of a community of the soil. Daniel Hillel writes,

> The ancient Hebrew association of man with soil is echoed in the Latin name for man, *homo*, derived from *humus*, the stuff of life in the soil. This powerful metaphor suggests an early realization of a profound truth that humanity has since disregarded to its own detriment. Since the words "humility" and "humble" also derive from *humus*, it is rather ironic that we should have

14. Wirzba, *The Paradise of God*, 114.

15. Ibid., 118.

16. Hillel, *Out of the Earth*, 14.

assigned our species so arrogant a name as *Homo sapiens sapiens* ("wise wise man"). It occurs to me, as I ponder our past and future relation to the earth, that we might consider changing our name to a more modest *Homo sapiens curans*, with the word *curans* denoting caring or caretaking, as in "curator." ("Teach us to care" was T.S. Eliot's poetic plea.) Of course, we must work to deserve the new name, even as we have not deserved the old one.[17]

Gardens provide not only a Sabbath delight for God, but also they delight ourselves because they are space for intimate encounters with life that have been made fragrant to the smell and pleasurable to our senses. We can develop two primary relationships to a garden—actually as a caretaker or as a visitor enjoying the garden. God loves and takes delight in gardens whether it is the immense garden that we name as universe or the smaller Earth garden. Our church garden is sacred like our sanctuary used to celebrate eucharist and looking out of large window at grape vines, purplish red bougainvillea, red and yellow roses trees. Our sanctuary is integrated with the garden, but our garden is a cathedral of grace that embeds our sanctuary.

Czech writer and gardener Karel Čapek writes the following in his lovely book *The Gardener's Year*. He describes a gardener, but imagine that he is speaking about God:

> I will now tell you how to recognize a real gardener. "You must come to see me," she says; "I will show you my garden." Then, when you go just to please her, you find her with her rump sticking up somewhere among the perennials. "I will come in a moment," she shouts to you over her shoulder. "Just wait till I have planted this rose." "Please don't worry," you say kindly to her. After a while she must have planted it; for she gets up, makes her hand dirty, and beaming with hospitality she says: "Come and have a look; it's a small garden, but—Wait a moment," and she bends over a bed to weed some tiny grass. "Come along. I will show you *Dianthus musalae*; it will open your eyes. Great Scott, I forgot to loosen it here!" she says, and begins to poke in the soil. A quarter of an hour later she straightens up again. "Ah," she says, "I wanted to show you that bell flower, *Campanula Wilsonae*. That is the best campanula which—Wait a moment, I must tie up this delphinium . . ."[18]

17. Ibid.
18. Čapek, *The Gardener's Year*, Feb. 19, 2002.

In the above description, I find the delightful image of God as a female Gardener with a wonderful hat—tilling, fussing, watering, and tenderly caring over her garden. The picture of God as a female gardener fussing over her garden hearkens back to Ignatius of Loyola who proposes that we contemplate God as laboring for us in creation. The image of God as an older female gardener refreshingly breaks with male patriarchal images of God.

Gardens are pure gift and occasions of sheer joy. We receive them as networks of abundant life—places of life-giving beauty—splashes of color, designs that still our soul, and intoxicating scents that incite enjoyment. They signify the abundant life of God. They still the storms of raging emotions and center us on beauty of life and the Gardner who made this possible for enjoyment. Norman Wirzba insightfully writes, "Gardens are places where people learn that death is not simply an end to life, but a vital ingredient and partner in furthering life."[19] Christian farmers have understood this for centuries in their close relationship to the soil. For myself, our garden teaches me about God's ecological grace, for it speaks of Christ' resurrected life.

Jesus and Magdalene in the Garden

Early Christians grasped the depth of meaning of the garden exchange between the risen Christ and Magdalene. They understood that God is a gardener, for God began the gardening process of creation, and God the Gardener is lost in a kind of revelry or enjoyment on the Sabbath in Genesis. Since the garden is so lovely and so interesting, there is no other place that God wants to be, for God wants to attend to the garden and the gardeners. If we take this Hebrew perspective of God's Sabbath delight in the garden, this enriches the Johannine text (John 20:1–16).

On Easter morning, the eschatological first day indicates a new cosmos and Sabbath. Magdalene stood weeping outside the empty tomb in the garden where Jesus' body was entrusted, but she discovers the stone of the tomb rolled away, the burial garment strewn around the tomb, and empty. She informs Peter and the Beloved Disciple, who run to the tomb to find it empty with face napkin neatly folded and the burial clothes scattered around. The Beloved Disciple has faith from the sign of the neatly folded up face napkin. She felt anguish that Jesus' body was stolen or

19. Wirzba, *From Nature to Creation*, 99.

desecrated. She spoke her emotional anguish and grief to one she thought was as a gardener. Jesus appears to her in the garden, symbolic of Eden resurrected and the cosmos yet to be restored to a new fullness. She recognizes the gardener as her Teacher only when he calls her by name, "Mary."

John's Gospel symbolizes the new Adam and Eve in the garden of the resurrection. What John's garden narrative proclaims is the good news that, out of destruction and death, Jesus rises from the earthen tomb as the new Adam or resurrected *adamah* from the soil. God the Gardener, who planted a Garden in Eden, then raised Jesus to new life in a garden, is still at work creating life and beauty in our world.[20] The identity of Jesus with the God (John 10:30) transfers the function of God the Gardener to Christ the Gardener. No wonder at the empty tomb in the garden did the risen Christ appear to Mary Magdalene as the gardener. Her mistaken identification of the risen Jesus as the gardener bears much prophetic truth about his risen glory. Echlin interprets this gospel scene,

> Mary's initially mistaking Jesus for the gardener is profound irony with many connotations. Jesus in fact is the Gardener, the New Adam, as the open side of the cross intimates, Master of garden Earth, the One in whom, with whom, and under whom all human gardeners garden.[21]

Likewise, Mary Coloe confirms Echlin's earlier observation:

> Mary's perception that Jesus is the gardener is accurate. The Risen One has passed through death into the glory that was originally his, with God in the beginning. He returns to Mary as the divine Gardener walking in the garden of creation (John 1:2).[22]

Jesus is the Gardener who transforms our lives now and becomes at the same time the ultimate Garden where we meet the God of life anew and profoundly. Thus, there is a biblical affirmation that the resurrection garden is the dwelling place of God, replacing the Jewish association of the Temple with Eden. The risen Jesus, as the Tree of Life, replaces the presence of God in the Temple. And this hearkens to the story of the Jesus incident in the Temple (John 2:13–22), where Jesus says, "Destroy this

20. God as Gardener: See Gen 2:8, 13:10; Num 24:6; and Ezek 31:18. See Risik, "Discovering the Secrets of God's Garden," 84.

21. Echlin, *The Cosmic Circle*, 125–26.

22. Coloe, "Creation in the Gospel of John, loc. 1767.

Temple, and in three days I will raise it (v. 19)." The editor inserts in v. 21: "he actually was talking about his body." The disciples would make this connection after Jesus' resurrection.

Magdalene reaches out to cling to Jesus, but Jesus tells her that she cannot continue to hold on this way as his resurrection transformation is incomplete. First, Coloe understands that this is a reference to the Genesis tree of life as a replacement of the cross, She notes in Genesis that the woman explains God's prohibition to the serpent: "you must not touch it" (Tree of Life) Gen.3:3. Mary Coloe concludes, "Whereas the first woman's disobedience in touching the tree brought death, Mary Magdalene's obedience brings the Easter proclamation of life as children of God."[23] An ecological interpretation might interpret "not to touch" until his body becomes transformed from one plane of existence into the entire ecosystem. The deep incarnation is taken root into the flesh of all life and into the Earth and cosmos.

Hildegard of Bingen writes: "The Spirit of God is life that bestows life on root of the world-tree and wind in its branches. She is glistening life, alluring all praise, all awakening, all resurrecting."[24] Christ, the Tree of Life has expanded into every tree and all green life through the resurrection, and these trees take in carbon dioxide and breathe out oxygen for life on the planet. The resurrection of Jesus is not only the radical transformation of the crucified Christ but the "green" transformation of all things in God. This clear from theological assertion of the enfleshment of Christ for the world: "God so loved the world that God sent God's only beloved child" (John 3:16). Or as Ambrose of Milan stated: "In Christ's resurrection, the earth itself rose."[25] All things become divinely interconnected through the risen Christ as he imagined himself to his disciples at the Last Supper as the vine connected to the branches and Abba God is the vine-grower or the gardener (John 15:1ff.). This strengthens the irony of Magdalene's mistaken identity of Jesus as the gardener and makes a theological statement on the divine identification of Jesus with God as Gardener. Ultimately, what gardens and Christ's resurrection have in common is the gift of abundant life and the transfigured presence of God. The sense of gift is the heart of the Easter experience—bringing surprise, abundant life, hope, and emotional peace and tranquility. And gardens

23. Ibid., loc. 1782.

24. *Hildegard of Bingen: Smyphonia*, 140–41.

25. Ambrose of Milan, *Prologia Latina*: 16, 1354. Quoted in Johnson, "Jesus and the Cosmos," 148.

may have the same gracious surprise, abundant life, and a calming impact. An early tradition in Irenaeus of Lyons (second century) compared Christians grafted onto Jesus, the olive tree.[26] Cyril of Jerusalem, living on the outskirts of Jerusalem, also compared Christians grafted onto the true olive tree, the risen Jesus.: "You have been separated from the wild olive tree and grafted on the cultivated tree and given a share in the richness of the true olive."[27]

Mary Magdalene and the other disciples were called to follow in the steps of the Christ the Gardener. They were invited to participate in the mission of co-creating and co-participating, co-living with the Spirit in giving life to the garden. As gardeners, Christians co-create gardens to help others find and meet God, for they extend their cultivation skills to the world God so loved. The model of gardener, rather than the quasi-biblical notion of steward, is far more productive and generative paradigm for compassionate and effective, eco- action.

Stewardship Model: The Priestly Tradition

Christian apologists advanced the stewardship model to counter Lynn White's complaint that a dominion model emerged from reading early Genesis chapters. The dominion model has re-gained prominence with eco-feminist critiques and some biblical scholars of the Earth Bible Project that read the priestly account in Genesis 1. The Genesis texts have been interpreted as justifying exploitation of nature. In Genesis, when God reflects upon the possibility of creating humans, God says, "Let us make humankind in our image, according to our likeness; and let them have dominion over the fish of the sea, and over the birds of the air, and over the cattle, and over all the wild animals of the earth, and over every creeping thing that creeps upon the earth" (Gen 1:26). But the domination and mastery perspective is grounded in Gen 1:28 "Be fruitful and multiply, and fill the earth and subdue it and have dominion . . ." Theodore Hiebert provides an analysis of the two verbs—*rada* and *kabas*:

> When used of kings, *rada* is used primarily for the rule over Israel's enemies (Ps. 110:2) and it occurs in descriptions of military conquest, where it is paired with such verb as "destroy." (Num. 24:19) and "strike down" (Is. 14:6).

26. Echlin, *Earth Spirituality*, 49.
27. Ibid.

> ... *kabas* "subdue" (v. 28) means to rule, to exercise power and
> authority ... The verb *kabas*, "subdue" (Gen. 1:28) is even more
> forceful than *rada*, describing the actual subjugation, of forcing
> another into a subordinate position.[28]

Hiebert notes that the domination theme is reinforced and even amplified
by the priestly narrative's view that humanity is created in God's image
and likeness (Gen 1:26–27).[29] The priestly tradition has construed humanity in the image of God, creating a hierarchical control and mastery.
In Psalm 8, humanity is made a little lower than God with domination
over the earth and the animals. Hiebert notes that made in God's image
"grants humanity, not a unique essence, but a unique function within the
created order: to exercise authority as God's representative in creation."[30]
The priestly tradition remains thoroughly anthropocentric, comprehending humans with greater intrinsic value over other species even though
humans and animals are both created on the sixth day. Non-human life
becomes a resource for human use and exploitation. The position is typi-
fied by the androcentric perspective: The Earth was made for man, not
man for the Earth.

The stewardship model originates from the domination and subjugation command of the priestly tradition. Nowhere are "stewards"
mentioned in scripture, it is derived from the priestly function of rep-
resentation of God on Earth. The representative function of God comes
from the king, delegated power and authority to the steward of his household. The most articulate proponent of the stewardship model is the Canadian theologian Douglas John Hall. His position takes the exegesis of
the priestly tradition and Psalm 8 for notion of stewardship, and Hall
softens the priestly hierarchic function a bit from the harshness of the
Genesis 1 account with a creation and covenant theology, in which the
steward represents God in the sphere of creation. The steward imitates
God's rule and character. He turns to the Christian Testament and to Jesus as Lord (*Dominus*), the theology of stewardship defines its function
Christologically and Jesus' lordship as servanthood. Jesus' servanthood
brings the upside down notion of the companionship of empowerment,
where the first are last, and the last first. Hall succinctly states his premise: "My thesis, stated in the most rudimentary manner, is the that the

28. Hiebert. "The Human Vocation," 137.

29. Ibid.

30. Ibid., 138.

vocation of the human being within creation is to image God, and that imaging of God (Dominus) described in the tradition of Jerusalem would mean exercising the dominion of stewardship."[31] But Hall recognizes the divine image as relatedness to God, relatedness to human to human and human to nature relatedness. For Hall, this relatedness is exercised in humans acting as stewards. He brings Christological reflection of service to nature in his definition of stewardship, and I find a lot that of his argument commendable in relational theological responsibility to nature, but stewardship has little scriptural warrants for Earthcare, except for a few parables of Jesus.[32] Hall recognizes "The fact is, the symbol (of stewardship) has played almost no role at all in the history of European Christianity."[33]

Criticism has been level against the constructed metaphor of an environmental steward. For example, Clare Palmer critiques the applicability and suitability of the metaphor, and locates the popularity with Protestant annual congregational financial campaigns in the 1950s on.[34] My own participation in stewardship campaigns more often functions as raising funds for the institutional church than church mission. It is wedded to some capitalist economic premises and notions of resource management that contribute to environmental degradation.[35] Likewise, Norman Wirzba comments on the paucity of prior historical use of the symbol of stewardship in Christian history:

> A primary reason is that the symbol of steward, at least in the popular imagination, maintains the notion that human beings are in control, and stewardship stands in contrast to other environmental approaches that stress a more egalitarian view. Stewardship recognizes that unique powers and responsibilities that equip them for the role of management of the earth. In affirming species superiority of humans it can thus make it easier for us to live with a history of exploitation, since all we need to acknowledge is that our domination has at times gone astray. Though some of the means of our mastery may have been improper, the

31. Hall, *Imaging God*, 60; Hall, "Stewardship as Vocation."
32. For example, Luke 12:35–48; 16:1–13.
33. Hall, *The Steward*, 65.
34. Palmer, "Stewardship," 67–86.
35. Sallie McFague explores the economics that contribute to climate change: *Climate Change* and *Blessed Are the Consumers*. Both of these start to tackle the economic foundations for global climate chage.

overall trajectory of mastery escapes sustained examination of
critique.[36]

Ecologists have frequently offered similar critiques of the Christian stewardship model, for it inflates the importance of humanity over nature and
other species. Like the priestly tradition, theological stewardship model
incorporates a strong anthropocentrism by privileging humanity over the
natural world with the claim of the divine image and rule. Stewardship
model, that proposes someone having power to the running a household
or palace, is entrusted with responsibility. It acknowledges God as owner
of creation and humanity as God's representative. Hall modifies Hebrew
creation theology with the Lordship and servant hood of Jesus, and this
remains problematic in its androcentricism and anthropocentricism.

Douglas John Hall and others define stewardship as loving service
to creation, while others use stewardship as a means for management
of natural resources or even exploitation for human benefit. Ecofeminist
theologians such as Rosemary Ruether remain highly critical of the androcentric features of this model, she describes this model as "the toxic
waste of sacralized domination":[37] "Domination of women has provided
a key link, both socially and symbolically, to the domination of the Earth,
hence the tendency in patriarchal cultures to link women with the earth,
matter, and nature, while identifying males with sky, intellect, and transcendent spirit."[38] While the Christian Orthodox position develops the
human role as priestly ,it is both androcentric and clerical.[39] John Zizioulas argues that humanity has a liturgical mediating link between God
and creation and that in the Eucharist, the priest can sanctify and bring
nature into communion with God. One salient difficulty is the abiding
clericalism and gender discrimination of male ordination in a number
of churches.

Christian discussion of human responsibility towards creation
must move beyond stewardship for the sake of an ecological theology
that places humans as part of creation, not above creation. A Franciscan
critique of the stewardship points a danger of some forms of Christian
creation theology:

36. Wirzba, *From Nature to Creation*, 129–30.

37. Ruether, *Gaia & God*, 3, 250.

38. Ibid.

39. Zizioulas, "Preserving God's Creation," 1–5; 12:2, 1989, 41–45, 13:1, 1990, 1–5.
See also Barker, *Creation*.

When the image of stewardship dominates our imagination, God can be removed from the scene as human beings are given oversight of the earth and move to the center stage in the drama of creation. Too easily the duty of caring for God's world becomes a task of shaping our world. Just as stewards are not anxious for the master's presence lurking over their shoulder, so humanity is content to keep God in a distant heaven.[40]

Conservationist John Muir also questions the stewardship model as well, "Why should man value himself more than a small part of the one great unit of creation?"[41] He further counters it with the Yahwist author in Genesis 2: "From the dust of the earth, from the common elementary fund, the Creator made *Homo sapiens*. From the same material, He has made every other creature, however, noxious and insignificant to us. They are earth-born companions and our fellow mortals . . . How narrow we selfish, conceited creatures are in our sympathies! How blind to the rights of all the rest of creation!"[42] Muir places humanity back into creation as minor part of creation, for humanity is an integral part of the soil community of life as all other creatures. Humanity is affiliated with other life, not in a managerial position over the land and the web of life. Also Aldo Leopold asserts, "Human beings are intended to be 'plain members and citizens of nature . . . neither its tyrannical masters, nor benign, managerial stewards."[43] This critique of human management of creation reflects the land ethic and conservation philosophies of John Muir, Aldo Leopold, Wendell Barry, and J. Baird Callicott.

The Gardener: The Yahwist Tradition

Hiebert names this second model based on Genesis 2–3 as "human as farmer."[44] While the Earth creature, like nonhuman animals, are fashioned from the soil (Gen. 2:9, 2:19), the nonhuman animals are made helpers in the garden. Hiebert writes,

> Animals, too, share the agricultural identity of humans, as they are legitimate "helpers" on the farm even if they are not sexually

40. Hines and Hines, "Sacrament of Creation."

41. Muir, *A Thousand Mile Walk to the Gulf*, 137.

42. Ibid., 98–99, 139.

43. Leopold, *County Almanac*, 216.

44. Hiebert, "The Human Vocation," 138.

compatible partners (2:18–20). Receiving the breath of life (2:7) does not grant the first human being a soul or spiritual character different from the animals, since the breath is the physical breadth of all animate life (cf. Gen, 7:22). The human being and animals are called "living beings" (*nephesh hayya*, 2:7, 2:19), an identity English translators have been unable to accept.[45]

God places the earth creature and assigns him/her (at this point this Earth creature is androgynous) to till or cultivate the garden's soil. The Yahwist author employs a different verb *abad*, "serve."

> In the Hebrew scriptures, *abad* is the customary term to express servitude, of slave to master (Gen, 12:6), of one people to another (Ex. 5:9) and of Israel's service to God in its life and worship (Ex. 4:23) . . . Yet its use for cultivation must stem from a sense if the vital power of the land over its creatures and of human submission to this power of the land over its creatures and of human submission to the power in the act of farming. This way of speaking of agriculture views the human as the servant, not the master of the land. It emphasizes human dependence and the service, rather than domination over the earth.[46]

There is a significant contrast to the domination and subjugation principle of hierarchy of the priestly writer with the Yahwist stress on service and submission. The relationality of the Earth creatures with nonhuman animals in the garden and service to the soil community of the garden remain distinctive. Hiebert stresses the Yahwist narrative as similar to the land ethic of the American pioneers—John Muir and company—who found subservience and humble service to the soil community as a central feature of the agrarian perspective of relating with the Earth. If a person wants to live with the land, that person cannot exploit or abuse the soil community, for that person needs to listen and learn from the soil community to live sustainably and healthily with the soil community. Such a gardening perspective leads to human flourishing and the flourishing of the soil community.

The Franciscan companionship model evokes a different attitude toward creation than with the priestly model of stewardship:

> But the Franciscan theological tradition presents an additional model. I believe that Francis left us a familial model of relating

45. Ibid., 139.
46. Ibid., 140.

to Creation. In the stewardship model, humans care for the earth because we want to take care of ourselves and future generations. God "put us in charge" of the beauty and bounty of the Earth. We are to care "on behalf of." The familial model values relationship with beauty and diversity of Creation, celebrating the interaction between ourselves and Earth's many creatures. We are called to care for, as a member of God's family of creatures. We exist by God's grace, together, side by side. We can marvel at the miracle of life's diversity, and humbly acknowledge our simple membership, and at the same time recognize that there are certain responsibilities that we have as a species.[47]

The Franciscan model of kinship moves beyond the stewardship limitations and opens cooperative interrelationality as the primary value for living with nature and nonhuman life. The prerequisite for Francis' kinship with nature was his commitment to poverty, an egolessness, living interrelatedly and humbly. Wirzba includes ecological and spiritual humility like Francis in his own gardening aesthetic. Wirzba quotes Eloi Leclerc on Francis of Assisi:

> To be brother to all creatures, as Francis was, in the last analysis to choose a vision of the world in which reconciliation is more important than division. It is to overcome separation and solitude and to open oneself to a universal sharing in which 'the mystery of the earth (comes) into contact with the mystery of the stars' in a vast movement of pardon and reconciliation.[48]

The service to the soil and interrelatedness with nonhuman animals of the Yahwist is compatible with the Franciscan kinship model or the biotic democracy.

Resurrection: Earthly Gardeners

The resurrection of Jesus as Gardener and the Tree of Life proposes not only Christological implications of the divinity and the development of trajectories of deep incarnation and the cosmic Christ, but also commissions Mary Magdalene and the disciples. Going back to Julian Norwich's parable of the tree of life, Denise Nowakowski Baker writes, "Like Adam, Jesus came to earth to be a gardener, however his task is metaphoric, not

47. Warner, "Get Him out the Birdbath," 369.

48. Leclerc, *The Canticle of the Creatures*; quoted in Wirzba, *From Nature to Creation*, 121.

literal, for the ground he cultivates the human heart."[49] Here resurrection of Jesus the Gardener inaugurates a metaphorically green, albeit gardening mission, for his disciples. One of the memorable lines of Edward Echlin is "Ecology is inherent to be a disciple of Jesus."[50] Theologies of the resurrection promote a mission of gardening that takes serious gardening activity. Norman Wirzba asserts,

> To garden is to enter into our most authentic vocation. On the other hand, this needs to be taken quite literally—we need the experience of taking care of plants, of learning the patience and discernment that comes with such activity in the physical and practical act of gardening we will come to feel from the inside the pace and measure of life, that is attuned to God's delight and rest.[51]

We garden, we engage plants and the garden, and we learn to live with the garden carefully and caringly. We learn the habit of living interconnectedness, living instinctively and consciously as responsible interrelatedness to lfe. The subordination to agrarian life is in no way a demeaning subordination, because we subordinate ourselves to ecological grace. Humility before the land serves rather, as introduction to the grace of life, an unfathomable network of which we are a part, and so begins our education.

Our service to creation is patterned on Jesus' open commensality and his inclusive hospitality. Jesus' inclusive ministry focused on the poor, the vulnerable, the lame, and those who could not repay the invitation. This needs to take another step inclusivity to include other life that is vulnerable and without voice. Norman Wirzba proposes that the extension of Jesus hospitality of the companionship of empowerment exceed the limit of the human community to include the whole Earth community. It means the inclusive love that God has for creation and all life. Our relatedness to others includes the Earth and other life. Theologically articulate, Wirzba writes,

> As created in the image of God, the bearing of desire and our activity is to be informed by the divine pattern of generosity that makes room for the lives of others, that provides for the well-being of others. Insofar as our desire remains focused on

49. Baker, *Julian of Norwich's Showings*, 103.
50. Echlin, *Earth Spirituality*, 32.
51. Wirzba, *From Nature to Creation*, 119.

ourselves, we deny our authentic vocation. How practically speaking might this theological insight be combined in the lives of countless organisms? Are we for instance to sacrifice ourselves for the preservation of inanimate natural elements and the well-being of nonsentient, nonrational beings?[52]

For Wirzba, the gardening perspective includes the foundation of the Christological image of the self-emptying Christ in Philippians 2:7–8. Jesus "emptied himself, taking the form of a slave, he humbled himself and became obedient to the point of death—even death on a cross." Christ' service is expressed in the imagery of a slave (*doulos*). "The model of servanthood developed here, however, assumes a context of creation in which interdependence and the grace of mutuality, rather than patriarchal oppression, are the guiding norms. Authentic servanthood, in other words, can be realized only in its creation context."[53] The kenotic or self-emptying spirituality of Christ serves as model for our service as gardeners to disadvantaged humanity and to disadvantaged Earth and the community of life. We will explore the dimensions of living a kenotic spirituality for social justice and environmental justice.[54] God's risen Christ, incarnationated as Gardener and the Tree of Life, desires human social well-being and flourishing as well as the flourishing of the Earth. Wirzba beautifully expresses our gardening interrelatedness: "In serving others, we participate in God's self othering life."[55] Christ's resurrection makes foundational for our mission that we are like everything on Earthand that we do not exist for ourselves, but exist and live co-interrelatedly. This is the primary insight from the resurrection. Interrelatedness leads to solidarity with suffering life, whether human or nonhuman.

Wirzba sees the vocation to gardening as the "artful living, of life attuned to the integrity and rhythms of creation."[56] It will include a Sabbath economy of restraint and finding the only wealth as life itself. The gardener delights in the just distribution of God's grace, the vision of Jesus' empowered companionship and the equitable distribution of grace to the Earth's community. Norman Wirzba indicates, "The first step in our becoming servant of creation will therefore require that we make

---

52. Ibid., 145.

53. Ibid.,136.

54. In the meantime, consult McFague, *Blessed Are the Consumers*.

55. Wirzba, *From Nature to Creation*, 137.

56. Ibid., 155. "Artful" and "attuned" denote the contemplative tradition.

ourselves the patient and earnest students of creation."[57] He encourages an attention to place and a sustained commitment to make our practices attuned to the Earth processes and life. To my ears, it sounds very much like the Benedictine vow of stability and commitment to the land. Benedict of Nursia, the founder of Western Christian monasticism, required monks to perform manual work such as domestic work, gardening, tilling, planting, and caring. The Benedictine monastics became part of the soil community, learned how not to deplete soil vitality but to enhances fertility. Other contemplative Earth-caring spiritualities provide us with garden models for responsibly and compassionately relating with the environment.[58] One of the primary benefits the spiritual and earthly vocation of gardening is that it focus our attention to what plants need and so to adjust our lives accordingly. Another feature of gardening care for the Earth and the land is humbly recognizing that we are a part of creation. Wirzba points out "Being a creature within the larger creation requires that we learn to attune our desires of God (this is what the life of faith is finally about) and so come to see the whole of creation—every bit of it and not just the scenic parts—as God sees it. It will mean letting go of our contentious grasp on the world so that we can engage all of creation through God."[59] In the Ignatian *Spiritual Exercises*, the recognition of your "creatureliness" is the first step in a journey towards a vision of finding God transparent in all things and among all creatures.[60] Our creatureliness removes our deep ego-centeredness and recognizes our interrelatedness with everything. Wirzba insightfully comments, "There can be no substitute for the activity of gardening because it is the richest, most multifaceted entry into the expertise of being a creature."[61] It helps us to see life as God sees life.

The Christian vocation of gardening has the contemplative benefit of slowing us down in the modern world, become aware of our ecological location and life surrounding us, and taking appropriate action for ecojustice. Some form of contemplative practice of gardening transforms our perspective from an egoistic agenda to Earth-centered, Christ-centered encounter. Eco-Christians understand gardening as Christian

57. Ibid., 145.

58. Taylor, *Green Sisters*.

59. Wirzba, *From Nature to Creation*, 193.

60. Wirzba wants to restore to humanity a sense of "creatureliness"; ibid., 96–129.

61. Ibid., 194.

resurrection practice, empowering community building activity in inter-faith, and cross ecological communities and movements. Discipleship re-covers the dangerous memories of Jesus' empowered companionship and his ecological vision of feeding the poor, standing with the vulnerable, and caring for the Earth. The interrelatedness of the risen Christ is God's compassion in action, and it is thoroughly inclusive and green. Ambrose of Milan preached, "In Christ's resurrection the earth itself arose."[62] But God's garden, the Earth, is dying, and human beings are responsible for killing the garden through our impact on climate change. Today the most urgent need is the eco-transformation of humanity to reconnect intimately with our garden the Earth. We can counter this Earth damage by fostering a gardening spirituality that not only connects us with our foundational experience of Easter but overcomes our arrogant separation from nature by learning to reconnect reverently to interrelated life. The key to natural immersion is to re-discover the wonder and beauty of God immanent in the natural world. Thomas Berry points out how we need to listen to the language of the Earth. Natural phenomena have their own language, and the natural world resonates with the voice of Christ the Gardener. Just as the gardener in my church learned to listen to the voices of each plant and the birds in our church garden. I sit attentively and lis-ten to the voices of the Earth in the garden as the risen Gardener teaches me what Berry describes as "wonder-filled intimacy." McFague notes,

> Global concern—care for the earth—often arise from local en-counter—such as care for garden. It is hard to care for the earth if one never cared for a piece of it. The particular is the basis for the universal. Teaching a child to care for goldfish—learning about its needs, respecting its otherness, delighting in shimmer-ing colors and swimming skills—is a better education in caring than a lecture on global warming.[63]

All human resources are required to heal, nurture, cultivate, and restore health to God's garden. Gardening reminds Christians of the mission to feed the hungry, care for the poor, and manage God's ecological house-hold with compassion and justice:

> When God created the earth, God "made room" for us all and in so doing showed us the heart of divine life, indeed all life, is the generous and gracious gesture. As we garden, that is, as we weed

62. Ambrose of Milan, PL, 16:1354.Quoted in Johnson, *Ask the Beasts*, 208.

63. McFague, *Super, Natural Christians*, 155.

out the non-nurturing elements within us and train our habits
to be more life promoting, we participate in the divine life and
learn to see and feel the creation as God sees and feels it.[64]

Gardening is a restoration, predominantly a justice term that incorporates redress of injustice with resurrection. It includes human flourishing,
letting go self-centeredness, and a self as interrelated to all human life
and the community of life. Stephen Evans notes, "the Incarnation seems
to shout at us that God is intimately involved with the temporal world.[65]

---

64. Wirzba, *The Paradise of God*, 164.
65. Evans, "Kenotic Theology and the Nature of God," 197.

5

"God Gave God"[1]:
Ecological Interrelatedness

*There was no place in the universe that was separate from the
originating power of the universe. Each thing of the universe had its
very roots in this realm . . .*

—Brian Swimme and Thomas Berry[2]

*The universe is a communion of subjects rather than a
collection of objects . . .*

—Thomas Berry[3]

When teaching creation in Genesis 1:1—2:4a, I draw a map of the world
on the board for students as the priestly writer understood. It is a flat
world with pillars anchored into the primordial waters with a vault of
heaven, circled by the primordial waters. Obviously, it was how the
ancient Hebrews envisioned the world. Of course, we know from our

---

1. The title is taken from Rowan Williams; the full quote is "God gave God,
nothing else to give," in McIntosh, *Mystical Theology*, 166.

2. Swimme and Berry, *The Universe Story*, 17.

3. Ibid., 242.

experience that the Earth is round from spectacular pictures from the moon. Like all maps, they need revision as our knowledge increases. Certainly, the mainline Christian denominations no longer hold to a literal map of the Earth envisioned in the opening verses of Genesis 1 but hold to the metaphorical truth expressing the goodness of creation and God's participation in that creation.

In an interview with the *New York Times*, Tim Maudlin, the author of *The Philosophy of Physics, Time and Space*, notes:[4]

> Modern cosmological knowledge has refuted such an account. We are living in the golden age of cosmology: More has been discovered about the large-scale structure and history of the visible cosmos in the last 20 years than in the whole of prior human history. We now have precise knowledge of the distribution of galaxies and know that ours is nowhere near the center of the universe, just as we know that our planetary system has no privileged place among the billions of such systems in our galaxy and that Earth is not even at the center of our planetary system. We also know that the Big Bang, the beginning of our universe, occurred about 13.7 billion years ago, whereas Earth didn't even exist until about 10 billion years later.
>
> No one looking at the vast extent of the universe and the completely random location of *homo sapiens* within it (in both space and time) could seriously maintain that the whole thing was intentionally created for us.[5]

Maudlin expresses the scientific perspective in the current golden age of cosmology discoveries, pushing human knowledge back to less than one second following the Big Bang.

Thomas Berry argued that the story of the universe, story of the Earth and human evolution, need to spark theological imaginations to re-envision God's participation in this unfolding of the universe and evolutionary life on planet Earth. New theologies of evolutionary origins starting from the Jesuit paleontologist Teilhard de Chardin, the contemporary dialogue between theology and science, and the cultural writings of Thomas Berry. For Berry, the re-telling of the universe story from the big bang to now was pivotal to his overall project of restoring a sense of sacred and wonder to the natural world through a nw cosmological story. Berry wrote, "We have moved from cosmos to cosmogenesis, from the

4. Maudlin, *The Philosophy of Physics.*

5. Gutting, "Modern Cosmology versus God's Creation."

mandala journey toward the center of an abiding world to the irreversible journey of the universe itself, as the primary sacred journey. This journey of the universe is the journey of each individual being on the universe. So this story of the great journey is an exciting story that gives us our macrophase identity with the larger dimensions of meaning we need."[6] Thomas Berry saw the possibility of telling the universe story, embedding the Earth story within a comprehensive narrative. New creation stories, based on cosmological models and evolutionary processes starting with Darwin and emergent evolutionary thought have provided a creative interplay with theological reflection on God in cosmic processes and within microcosmic processes.

Thomas Berry and Brian Swimme wrote and produced the documentary the *Journey of the Universe*. Both the documentary film and book evoke a sense of wonder and awe within me and others.[7] It is the grand cosmic narrative within which the stories of the Earth, the evolution of life, and the emergence of humanity. Swimme and Tucker speak of wonder:

> Wonder is not just another emotion; it is rather an opening into the heart of the universe. Wonder is the pathway into what it means to be human, to taste the lusciousness of sun-ripened fruit, to endure the bleak agonies of heartbreak, to exult over the majesty of existence. The universe's energies penetrate us and awaken us. Through each moment of wonder, no matter how small, we participate in the entrance of primal energies into our lives.
>
> However, insignificant we may feel with respect to the age and size of the universe, we are, even so, beings in whom the universe shivers in wonder at itself. By following this wonder we have discovered the ongoing story of the universe, a story that we tell, but a story that is also telling us.[8]

Wonder produces religious affection that binds us to the vastness of the universe and its cosmology but intimately connects to the story of the evolution and the emergence of humanity as two pages of the vast narrative. Sallie McFague explains, "One of the most profound lessons we can learn from the common creation story is appreciation for life, not just for our own, but that of all creatures in the family of life. We are the only ones

6. Berry, *The Great Work*, 163.

7. Swimme and Tucker, *Journey of the Universe* DVD.

8. Swimme and Tucker, *Journey of the Universe*, p. 113.

on our planet, who know the story of life and the only ones who know that we know: the only ones capable of being filled with wonder, surprise, curiosity, and fascination by it."[9] Both McFague and Berry judge that human engagement with the common story of the universe could re-ignite a sense of ecological sensibility and our interconnectedness to nature and the universe.

A common mistake is to view cosmology and creation as opposed to one another. As a theologian, I accept cosmology with its scientific discoveries and its stories, but I also realize the word "creation" is a theologically constructed notion with a particular metaphorical story of God's unfolding in creation, in the incarnation of Christ, and the sustaining presence of the Spirit. It is from the cosmological story that people of faith develop a sense of wonder and connection to the universe, and there is also need to describe the story of God in metaphorical language as theological story. When we look at the expansive processes of the universe from the Big Bang to the formation of galaxies and stars with planets or to the evolutionary processes of life on Earth, we cannot deny the integrity of these scientific descriptions. There are naturally gaps in our knowledge yet to be filled in the future.

We need to truly search to understand how God really acts in the universe, our world and evolutionary processes, and in our individual lives.[10] God does not act in the ways we were conditioned by outdated philosophical and theological notions of divine causality. God is closer to us than our jugular vein and is present in the cosmological processes of the universe and the emergence evolutionary processes of life. The cosmological and evolutionary stories of emergence of the universe and of life point to unanswered questions within these stories and echoes of these stories enfleshed in nature and in our lives. Thomas Berry writes,

> The universe story is the quintessence of reality. We perceive the story. We put it in our language, the birds put it in theirs, and the trees put it in theirs. We can read the story of the Universe in the trees. Everything tells the story of the Universe. The winds tell the story, literally, not just imaginatively. The story has its imprint everywhere, and that is why it is so important to know

9. McFague, *The Body of God*, 123.

10. Edwards, *Breath of Life*; Edwards, *How God Acts*; Johnson, *Ask the Beasts*; Boff, *Cry of the Earth*; Boff and Hathaway, *Tao of Liberation*.

the story. If you do not know the story, in a sense you do not know yourself; you do not know anything.[11]

The universe's story does not answer the specific questions of our hearts how God acts within the cosmological and evolutionary processes. It is at the secondary level of scripture and theology that requires dialogue with the foundational scientific hypotheses and answers. We find some directional trajectories along with the cosmos that lead to the foundation of life and that the creativity of life emerges with innumerable movements of trial and error and the memory genetically successful life developments. When we move away from the media sensational accounts of conflict with Christian creationists, we discover that science and theology have been in dialogue for awhile in an effort to understand that the universe is incomplete, evolving at all levels.[12] My goal here is to propose ecological directions for our personal and communal theologies and spiritualities and how to live in the world as contemplatives in action, seeking justice and reverence for all life. My focus is to pick up a small bit of this paradigm shift and reframe our metaphorical understandings of God and creation, incarnation and salvation. Scientific explanations address our minds, but metaphorical stories touch our hearts of faith and motivate our ways of living in the world.

What Was God Doing before the Big Bang?

What was God doing before the Big Bang? I start with this Zen like koan or question precisely knowing that many physicists find themselves at a loss to explain what had preceded the Big Bang or the explosion of the infinitely dense singularity. It seems cosmological investigation is at loss to really explain what was before the Big Bang since the laws of physics were begun with space and time in the Big Bang For myself, I answer "God." I want to cover three points about God and creation: 1) the perichoretic nature of God, 2) the inclusive interrelationality of the Trinity, 3) the primacy of God's intention for Incarnation prior to creation. These three theological notions are foundational for an ecological model.

11. Berry, quoted in Loy, *The World Is Made Up of Stories*, 71.

12. For example, Polkinghorne, *Science and Religion*; Russell, *Time in Eternity*; Johnson, *Ask the Beasts*; Delio, *The Unbearable Wholeness of Being*; Edwards, *Ecology at the Heart of Faith*; and Edwards, *How God Acts*.

The Jesuit theologian Karl Rahner maintained the theological axiom that "the economic Trinity is the immanent Trinity and vice versa."[13] Let me explain Rahner's axiom. First, he is denying that there is any notion of a God behind the God that is revealed in history, scripture, and experience. It means that we can speculate about God through God's economic relations with humanity in history. Rahner provides us with a window to extrapolate some limited knowledge to plumb the mysterious depth of God as a triune community of love. Rahner's Trinitarian axiom first stresses the undeserved and gratuitous God's self-communication to humanity as the basis of creation. He chooses the theological notion of the Franciscan theologian/philosopher John Duns Scotus (1266–1308 CE), who affirms that God chose to incarnate God's self prior to the act of creation.[14] God intended to incarnate the Word and pour out the Spirit; it is God's self-bestowal in creation, incarnation, and the final transformation of creation. Rahner takes a more radical notion of God's self-expression of Incarnation as the core of creation and the Spirit poured out to creation, involved in the Word become flesh, and the final fulfillment. For him, the unique insight of Christian view of God is that God is distinct from the world, yet God is giver and both gift simultaneously. God's incarnated Word becomes integral to the evolution of the Earth and the entire universe.[15]

Let me start with a rich metaphor of Orthodox Christianity that understands God as three and one as universal spiral dance (*perichoresis*) of a community of love. God is three: Parent begetting Child, God Child begotten, and the Holy Spirit generated from their love as procession. It is the divine community of radical inclusive love, but this radical inclusion of three loving partners is metaphorically image as a spiraling, ecstatic dance (*perichoresis*) that breaks down all barriers of other by its dynamic and loving movement of interpenetrating communion.[16] Mark Wallace writes about the perichoretic life of God:

> The life of God is an eternal dance. As *perichoresis*, God's inner life is a cotillion of joy and companionship, with the Spirit's performing the role of ensuring the reciprocal love among all three members. The Spirit is God's celebratory act of interpersonal

13. Rahner, "The Economic Trinity is the Immanent Trinity and vice versa," 79,

14. Edwards, *How God Acts*, 40.

15. Rahner, "The Specific Character of the Christian Concept of God," 191.

16. Cheng, *Radical Love*, 56.

unity, the bond of harmony and affections that consummates the
friendship and love that define the inner relations of Godself.[17]

Wallace's notion of a cotillion, a popular eighteenth-century dance in
Europe and America and the precursor to the American square dance,
is a wonderful metaphor of the spiraling dynamism of dance partners.
Leonardo Boff describes this dynamic of communion:

> *Perichoresis* means one person's action permeates the other and
> allows itself to be permeated by that person. The interpenetra-
> tion expresses the love and life that constitutes the divine nature.
> It is the very nature of love to be self-communicating; life natu-
> rally expands and seeks to multiply itself. Thus, the divine Three
> from all eternity find themselves in an infinite explosion of love
> and life from one to the other.[18]

Both an explosion of love and life and the spiraling dynamism of the
dance metaphor appeal to my pluralistic inclinations that resist mono-
theist conformity. The Triune nature of God is a divine communion of
radical inclusive love expressed in the creative image of line dancing. The
partners in God are dancing, circling each other, changing positions in
love, and the whole floor is whirling around. The partners inter-permeate
or interpenetrate each other in an eternal and egalitarian dance. Each
person spirally empties self and mutually surrenders to the other two,
giving life, love, wisdom, goodness. The dancing of the three within God,
circling in mutual love is dynamic and playful mystery of love, conta-
giously spiraling open and inclusively and lovingly pulling us into that
dance of love. If God is dancing, God invites us to join in a community of dance. Mark Wallace wonderfully reflects: "As trinity, God bodies
forth divine compassion for all life-forms in the rhythms of the natural
order."[19]

Creation, at this point, can be described as "bodying forth" dynamic
energy of love to create materially the universe and to share in radical
inclusive divine love. There is unity and diversity within God. To say that
God is one is to affirm the unity of God. To say that God is three is to
affirm dynamic diversity and a community of love. There is an inclusive
community love that is within the nature of God and provides a radical
inclusivity and openness in creation and within ourselves. Denis Edwards

17. Wallace, *Finding God in the Singing River,* 41.

18. Boff, *Holy Trinity,* loc. 360.

19. Wallace, "The Wounded Spiri," 57.

affirms, "The universe can be understood as unfolding 'within' the Trinitarian relations of mutual love."[20] God's mutual perichoretic dance of radical inclusive love does not immediately overflow into creation. Rather, within the infinite space of the divine *perichoresis* of mutual love, God makes inclusive room for creation within God's own space. God is in creation and present to every atom, every star, and each and every creature. The Trinitarian God is both anterior to creation and involved in continuous creation. Edwards like many recent theologians understands this model as panentheism (all things in God) and yet God exceeds creation itself. Edwards here references Jurgen Moltmann's notion that the triune divine community of mutual love is so infinitely expansive that provides room in God's space to permit the universe. Moltmann uses Isaac Luria's kabbalistic notion of *tzimtzum* ("contraction, constriction") or God's withdrawal to make space for creation:[21] Luria tries to image spatially the presence or indwelling of the infinite God in the world (*shekinah*) and world outside of God's infinite space (*ein-sof*).[22] God's infinite space withdraws God's space and power to make room for creation. Thus, God can step into the world, "a God evacuated space," to manifest God's presence.[23]

Moltmann, likewise, writes, "The very first act of the infinite Being was therefore not a step 'outwards' but a step 'inwards,' a 'self-withdrawal of God from himself into himself . . .'"[24] In *God in Creation*, Moltmann connects God's self-withdrawal to make space for creation with the self-emptying or kenotic nature of the Incarnation in the hymn in Philippians 2:5–11. Therefore, God makes space for the explosion of the infinitely dense singularity into the infinitely emerging universe by self-limiting God's space and power. Jurgen Moltmann further develops,

> In a more profound sense he (God) creates by letting be, by making room, and by withdrawing himself. The creative making is expressed in masculine metaphors. But the creative letting-be is better brought out through motherly categories.[25]

20. Edwards, *The God of Evolution*, loc. 304.

21. Moltmann, *The Trinity and the Kingdom of God*, 108–11; Moltmann, *God in Creation*, 88.

22. Drob, *Kabbalah and Postmodernism*, 67; Moltmann, *God in Creation*, 87–88.

23. Lee, *Celebrating God's Cosmic Perichoresis*, 41.

24. Moltmann, *The Trinity*, 109.

25. Moltmann, *God in Creation*, 88.

Denis Edwards picks up this suggestion of creation unfolding inside of God's space with the insight of Elizabeth Johnson, who speaks of Moltmann's notion of self-contraction to move from male imagery to the metaphor of a "mother:[26]

> Such exclusive use of male metaphors is a blatant anomaly because to be so structured that you have room inside yourself for another to dwell is quintessentially a female experience. To have another actually living and moving and having being in yourself is likewise the province of women . . . (every human) has lived and moved and had their being inside a woman for a better part of the year it took for them to be knit together. This reality is the paradigm without equal for pantheistic notion of the coinherence of God and the world.[27]

Johnson points out that God's kenotic or self-emptying nature is not a divine stinginess, but God's self-emptying nature indicates that at the heart of the universe is a divine generosity.[28] Sallie McFague's panentheistic or sacramental theology fits well with her model of God as Mother and the world as God's body. She observes,

> And it is clearly the parent as mother that is the stronger candidate for an understanding of creation as bodied forth from divine being, for it is imagery of gestation, giving birth, and lactation that creates an imaginative picture of creation as profoundly dependent on and cared for by divine life. There simply is no other imagery available to us that has power for expressing the interdependence and interrelatedness of all life with its ground. All of us, female and male, have the womb as our first home, all of us born from the bodies of our mothers, all of us are fed by our mothers.[29]

Bryan Lee comments on Moltmann's image of maternal womb making room or space for life; this is pertinent to the maternal images of McFague and Johnson as well:

> The mother makes in herself room for the baby, wherein the baby could exist apart from the mother. The room is made possible by the mother who lets the baby exist; however, the space

---

26. Edwards, *The God of Evolution*, loc. 322.

27. Johnson, *She Who Is*, 234; McFague, *Models of God*, 101–23.

28. Johnson, *She Who Is*, 234.

29. McFague, *Models of God*, 106.

is still in her. Then, she enters into the space within her—a space
she neither completely controls nor controls—for the benefit of
the baby and reaches out with the umbilical cord through the
space-within to the baby to give life.[30]

Lee describes the Holy Spirit as the umbilical cord for Moltmann, for the
Spirit provides both the creative divine energy of God and vitality that
links and sustains all life.[31] This offers a metaphorical model for theological and ecological speaking of divine transcendence and immanence
simultaneously.

God as Being Interrelationality

At the heart of the divine community of love, is the interpenetrability
of each member of the Trinity. Creator, Christ, and Spirit are distinct
but not self-contained but move out in love into the other. *Perichoresis* is interpersonal interrelatedness that expands to bestow the gift of
life. Franciscan scientist and theologian Ilia Delio describes the dance
between God and the universe: "God is eternal, self-sufficient divinity;
yet the universe contributes something that is vitally necessary to God.
Creation is integral to God. It contributes to God what God lacks in his [/
her] own divinity, namely, materiality. Evolution is not only the universe
coming to be, but it is *God who is coming to be*."[32] As we explored in the
previous section, the *perichoresis* of the divine community of love flows
outwards in the action of making space for creation. Divine intimacy as
self-emptying love is shared with creation and creatures alike. The movement of love between these three persons flows outwards into the created
universe. Or perhaps we can say the intra-relational community of love
expresses God's love through interrelationality—that is with others distinct and yet connected to the divine community of love.

Denis Edwards picks up Karl Rahner's notion of God's self-bestowal
to the universe:

> God creates a universe of creatures in order to give God's self to
> them in love. Self-bestowal is the meaning of the universe. We
> human beings have experienced this self-bestowal in the Christ

30. Lee, *Celebrating God's Cosmic Perichoresis*, 41.

31. Ibid.

32. Delio, unpublished Conspire 2014 conference, quoted by Richard Rohr, Science Week 1 "We Are One," Daily e-mail meditation, November 3, 2015.

even and in the experience of the Spirit given in grace. In the
Word made flesh and the Spirit given in grace, God is revealed
as a God of self-bestowing love. Creation is the addressee of divine bestowal. This self-bestowal is already at work in our world
in God's creative presence to all things. It will reach its culmination only when the whole of created reality is transfigured in the
power of the resurrection and taken up into God.[33]

Edwards summarizes Rahner's theology of grace as originating within the
inner life of God and spilling out into creation and creatures. Creation is
united in its origin from God and is continually linked by God's bestowal
of divine love and grace in Christ and through the Spirit. Irenaeus of
Lyons designating Christ, God's Logos, and the Spirit as the two hands
of God operative in the world of the deification (*theosis*) of the universe.

There is a community of mutual love between the Creator, Christ,
and the Spirit, and this perichoretic interrelatedness is extended into the
universe through the incarnate Christ and the Spirit as divine bestowal
in creation, incarnation, and salvation. One of the major contributions
of Rahner to 20th century theology is his breakdown of the partition of
divine bestowal into the triadic creation, incarnation, and salvation (final
deification of the universe).[34] For Rahner, creation and incarnation are
part of the single flow of divine self-bestowal that looks to consummation
at the end of time.

God's perichoretic life—reciprocal relations of intimate and interrelated communion—becomes a part of the divine bestowal. The Greek
Orthodox bishop John Zizioulas affirms. "It is communion that makes
things 'be'; nothing exists without it, not even God . . ."[35] Creation is a
stunningly amazing act of God's grace and interrelating communion,
and within creation and here on the Earth, we perceive that cosmological
processes are interconnected and all biological life on Earth is interdependent upon the processes of the Earth and interrelated to life. The cosmos is a dynamic web of interrelated processes. Biological life does not
allow us to comprehend itself outside of evolutionary interconnectedness
as well as planetary interconnected as well as galactic interconnected
and ultimately cosmological interconnectedness. The image of the Celtic
trinity knot or *triquetra* symbolizing the inifinite unity, continuous interweaving knotted rope, was appropriated by Celtic Christians to indicate

33. Edwards, *Ecology at the Heart of Faith*, 61.
34. Rahner,*Foundations*, 197.
35. Zizioulas, *Being as Communion*, 17.

the interconnectedness of triune life to nature and all interrelated life. A number of Christian theologians turn to Buddhism's notion of inter-relatedness as the spiritual practice for solidarity with other life and the Earth community and foundation for compassion. The Buddhist notion of compassion is comparable to the Christian notion of grace (uncondi-tional love). For Christians, God as community of kenotic or self-empty-ing love tries to communicate how the living God is a dynamic mystery of interrelated love, pouring out that love and extending salvation to us and all the universe.

The Primacy of the Incarnation

The thirteenth-century Scottish theologian and Franciscan priest John Duns Scotus (1266–1308) affirmed theologically that Christ was first idea or thought in the mind of God and that thought originated from love. God has never stopped thinking and loving the eternal Christ or Logos Incarnated. Christ was the masterpiece of love, *the summum opus Dei* (God's masterpiece).[36] Delia Ilio further writes about Scotus:

> The idea of all of creation is made for Christ means that for Christ to come about there had to be a creation, and, in this creation, there had to be beings capable of understanding and freely responding to divine initiative. Creation was only a pre-lude to a much fuller manifestation of divine goodness, namely, the Incarnation.[37]

Christ's Incarnation is primary because God desires to be loved perfectly as God does. The first intention of God is love for Christ, and thus cre-ation is an absolute gift of love.

Delio argues that Scotus' notion included Christ as the blueprint of creation, for he is the purpose of the universe and the model for what the universe will become through its transformation into God through the incarnation of Christ. Scotus uses the medieval theological notion of the final cause for the determining factor of the God the Artist's work:

> When Jesus comes as the Incarnation of God, there is a "perfect fit" because everything has been made to resemble Jesus Christ. This means that this sun, moon, trees, animals, stories, all have

36. Delio, *A Franciscan View of Creation*, loc. 779; Delio, *Christ in Evolution*, loc. 1079ff.

37. Delio, *A Franciscan View of Creation*, loc. 782.

life in Christ, through Christ and with Christ, for Christ the
Word through whom all things are made (cf. John 1:1).[38]

All creation is "christoform." This notion proceeds from two principles.
First, Scotus' philosophical principle of univocity of being affirms that
God's being and created being are related. Creation and each creature is
endowed with the light of the Creator; in fact, each being reflects the light
of God. His second principle is *haecceitas* ("thisness") or the individua-
tion of everything. It points to the singularity of each thing that is set off
from everything else. Each thing does itself, and "This do-being is doing
Christ."[39] Delio points out how the Jesuit poet Gerard Manley Hopkins,
whose notion of "inscape" of nature is an expression of Christ . . ."[40]

John Duns Scotus also moves away from the divine rescue mission
redemptive theology of Anselm and others who maintain the purpose
of the Incarnation was to come to save humanity when humanity goes
astray with original sin. For Scotus, this notion of atonement is to reduce
God's love to a lesser good. The primacy of Christ—Christ is the first
priority in God's intention to love—is an innovative element to medieval
Christian theology. Scotus writes,

> Therefore, I argue as follows; in the first place, God loves him-
> self. Secondly, he loves himself in others and this is most pure
> and holy love. Thirdly, God wills to be loved by another who can
> love him perfectly and here I am referring to the love of some-
> one outside of God. Therefore, fourthly, God foresees the union
> between the Word and creature Christ who owes him supreme
> love, even had there never been a Fall.[41]

Creation is not an independent act of divine love that was followed by
the divine self-revelation in the covenant. Rather, the divine desire to
become incarnate was always the plan and intention of God. God wills to
be loved by another who can love God perfectly in return, and that other
is Incarnate Christ. The Incarnate Christ would be God's masterpiece and
greatest creation in flesh. Sallie McFague's quotation of Arthur Michael
Ramsey is theologically insightful here: "God is Christlike."[42]

38. Ibid., loc. 789–790.

39. Ibid., loc. 846.

40. Ibid., loc. 858.

41. Scotus, *Reportata Parisiensia*, III, d. 7. Q 4, n. 5. Quoted in Osborne, "Incarnation, Individuality, and Diversity," 209.

42. Quoted in McFague, *Collected Readings*, 197, from Arthur Michael Ramsey as

There is a tradition in Christian history of Christ's incarnation not dependent upon the fall of the primal couple, but that the incarnation was always the plan of God from the beginning. Edwards associates this tradition to include Irenaeus, Duns Scotus, Teilhard de Chardin, and Karl Rahner.[43] The motive for incarnation emerges from God's free loving communication to humanity. These theologians have envisioned that the Word's incarnation was always intended by God.

The theological innovation of Scotus is to place the Incarnation within the context of creation and not within human sin. It was always in God's mind before the physical creation of the universe and before humanity's sin. What Scotus does is to shift from the sin-centered model of comprehending Incarnation to love-centered focus. If humanity never sinned, God still willed Christ's Incarnation as supreme manifestation and communication of God's love to creation. God loves us first through the Incarnation and then saves us. It places salvation in the divine matrix of unconditional love and gift. This blends well with the Orthodox Christianity's notion of divinization. Secondly, Duns Scotus, in the Franciscan tradition, highlights that God is in us and in everything created. Franciscan author Richard Rohr writes about the incarnation of Christ as overcoming the gap between God and the created world: "Because of incarnation, we can say, "God is with us!" In fact, God is in us, and in everything else that God created. We all have the divine DNA; everything bears the divine fingerprint, if the mystery of embodiment is true."[44]

Duns Scotus reflects the Franciscan spirituality of the Incarnation is centered on love and not sin. Christ expresses God's love and God's intention of communion with creation. All creation will be transformed into a communion with God. Each creature radiates inwardly with the light of God. Thus, each creature speaks to us something about God. Duns Scotus thus reflects the spirituality in the Franciscan tradition of Bonaventure that perceived an intimate connection between creation and Christ, for both grounded in God's infinite love. Scotus is optimistic about the goodness of creation—all reality is good and beautiful. Sallie McFague reflects a Franciscan view of the presence of God through the Incarnation:

---

quoted in McGrath, *Christian Theology*, 323.

43. Edwards, *Jesus the Wisdom of God*, 71–72.

44. Rohr, "Incarnation: God Is Not Out There."

The radical intimacy of God's presence in the ecological model means we can perceive god's presence anywhere and everywhere. There is no place that God is not . . . God is always present in mediated forms, through something or someone else. We do not meet God "face to face", but we do meet God in the world. As the body of God, the world is a sacrament, the sacrament, the incarnation of God, so that while each thing is itself in all its marvelous particularity and uniqueness, it is the same time and in and through its specialness, the presence of God.[45]

Some modern theologians such as Karl Rahner and Jurgen Moltmann have grounded the Incarnation as a primary expression of God's self-communication and unconditional love. More importantly, they connect intimately creation and Incarnation not as separate events but as the perichoretic love of God's self-emptying love poured into the heart of creation. Rahner, for example, incorporates the theological notion of the primacy of Christ to interpret the purpose of creation. God always intended Christ's incarnation for creation, for the incarnation was not linked to an originating sin, but the incarnation of Christ revealed God's grace and forgiveness for us. The incarnation was primarily intended for God's self-giving to creation.

Jesus as God's Wisdom

There are several decades of history of scholarship from feminist theologians and other scholars recognizing that Paul and the gospel traditions comprehended Jesus' ministry, death, and resurrection with the Hebrew wisdom traditions. Feminist theologians began to develop this vector of interpretation that Jesus as the wisdom of God to avoid androcentric theological constructions.[46] There were numbers of biblical studies on Jesus as the wisdom of God as well.[47]

The earliest Christian communities, for example the Q community source, identified Jesus as Wisdom's envoy (Luke 7:35, Matt 11:19) and

45. McFague, *Collected Readings*, 223–24. McFague comes very close, if not reflective, to Duns Scotus' philosophical notion of *haeccitas*. See Mulhodland, "Christ: The Haeccitas of God," 305–12.

46. For example: Johnson, "Jesus, the Wisdom of God." 261–94; Johnson, *She Who Is*, 150–69; Elisabeth Schüssler Fiorenza, *Jesus, Miriam's Child*.

47. Gary, "Wisdom Christology," 448–59; Brown, *The Gospel of John*, 1:cxxii–cxxviii; Edwards, *Jesus and the Cosmos*; Edwards, *Jesus the Wisdom of God*.

the prophet of Wisdom (Matt 23:24, Luke 23, 34). Q understands John the Baptist and Jesus as successive prophets of Wisdom executed (Luke 11:49). The earliest Christians understood Jesus as the child of Sophia God, "The reign of God suffers violence from the days of John the Baptist until now and is hindered by men of violence" (Matt 11:12).

Edwards affirms: First the liturgical hymns and confessional writings of the early church perceived Jesus as incarnate Wisdom as in 1 Cor. 1:14, "Jesus is the Wisdom of God." Edwards' second affirmation is critical to our discussion in this chapter:

> Historically this ancient Wisdom Christology is the essential structural link in the development of the doctrine of incarnation in the early church. It is in and through the identification of Jesus with pre-existent divine Wisdom that we find in the early Christian hymns the beginning of a theology of incarnation, a theology which reaches a clear and unambiguous articulation in John's gospel. Here is Jesus the eternal Word made flesh.[48]

Christian communities used the Jewish Wisdom, with its creation theology and its notion of personified Wisdom, to interpret Jesus as the envoy/prophet of Wisdom and to the theological developments of pre-existent Logos and the incarnate notions of Wisdom/ Logos. The theological language of Wisdom provided them a Jewish theological matrix to understand the human Jesus and his ministry, his death, and to make sense of Jesus' resurrection. His humanity was unified by and united to divine Wisdom.

Three Wisdom Hymns

There are three hymns to Christ from first-century CE liturgical celebrations, offering insights on Jesus as God's Wisdom and the Incarnate Word: The hymns are Philippians 2:6–11; John 1:1–8; and Colossians 1:15–20. Each of these hymns provides insights into our later discussion of "Deep Incarnation" and manifest three dimensions of incarnation as *kenosis* (emptying), the fleshliness of incarnation, and the cosmic Christ. These liturgical affirmations of the risen Christ expand the process of Christian theological reflection on God and evolve into the Trinitarian notions of "God with us." For early Christians, God's incarnation in Christ opens the exploration of their faith experience that God is with us, God is in

48. Edwards, *Jesus the Wisdom of God*, 51.

our fleshliness, and God is in everything that has been created and in the fulfilling process of creation. Richard Rohr use the wonderful phrase: "We all have divine DNA, everything bears the divine fingerprint, if the mystery of embodiment is true."[49] The revolutionary insight of "God is near and within" has deep ecological implications for a Christian eco-theology and eco-spirituality.

In the hymn of Christ (Phil. 2:6–11), scholarly discussion focuses on Christ's *kenosis* (emptying), self-emptying of divinity of the God, "taking the form of a slave, becoming obedient to death, even death on a cross." It has included the incarnation of Christ, Trinitarian life, divine action and cosmology, and the vulnerability of Christ on the cross and suffering.[50] The kenotic dynamic of God is self-emptying divine love vulnerable in the life of the universe in creation and its freedom, through the vulnerability of the incarnated Christ on the cross, and the ensouling dynamic of the Spirit in suffering and death in life. God becomes Christ-like, and God empties God's self into each other and into creation, incarnation, and fulfillment of creation. George Ellis forms an inclusive definition of human life congruent with notions of a kenotic Creator God, and self-sacrificing incarnate Christ and the Spirit in emergent evolution:

> *Kenosis*: a joyful, kind, and loving attitude that willing to give up selfish desires and to make sacrifices on behalf of others for the common good and the glory of God, doing this in a generous and creative way, avoiding the pitfall of pride, guided and inspired by the love of God and the gift of grace.[51]

Sallie McFague offers a complementary explanation:

> A kenotic theology . . . a theology that begins with need, both God's need and ours; a need that runs all the way from the most elemental biological processes of the energy of transformation to understand the Trinity (the being of God) as one of continuous and total exchange of love. Kenosis is the process that begins and continues life all the way from the splitting of cells to the sacrifice (and Death) of some human beings for the nourishment of others and, and of God's quintessential act of self-emptying both with the divine being and for the creation and salvation of the world.[52]

49. Rohr, "Incarnation: God Is Not Out There"; Butler Bass, *Grounded*.

50. Polkinghorne, ed., *The Work of Love*.

51. Ellis, "Kenosis as Unifying Theme for Cosmology," 107.

52. McFague, *Blessed Are the Consumers*, 172.

Both descriptions express a deep spirituality of kenotic living at the level of Christ enfleshed as God's compassionate action in the universe. The example and words of God's Christ inspires imitation: "Be compassionate as God is compassionate (Luke 6:36)." God's love is expressed in the fleshy parable of Jesus' life of compassion and sacrificial love. It expresses our potential at graced companions living through the Spirit but also reveals the abandonment of God's omnipotent power for the vulnerability of compassionate suffering love and care. Ellis quotes William Temple: "What we find is power in complete subordination to love."[53] Ellis continues, "for the exercise of creative power of the Creator is voluntarily restricted to that which enables a universe where a free and loving response by humankind is possible, despite the costs and sacrifice entailed, specifically ordaining things so that humans with free will can act as they will."[54] Wherever the Spirit of Christ inspires folks to live, serve, and love kenotically, God kenotically extends love into the world.

For McFague, a kenotic theology perceives the "world as God's beloved" for "God is always incarnate, always bound to the world as its lover, as close as we are to our own bodies, and connected before all else to see that the body, God's world, flourishes."[55] This enables McFague to unpack the kenotic dimensions of the spiritual lives of John Woolman, Simone Weil, and Dorothy Day. She comprehends their examples of saints, whose kenotic living of Christ inspires us to shape our lives and act as a channel for such love. The self-surrender of St. Francis, "make me an instrument of your peace" or the *Suscipe* ("Receive") prayer of Ignatius of Loyola.[56] The self-surrender in compassionate loving service to others is a central wisdom revelation of God in Christ. In the Wisdom theology, Jesus becomes the radical praxis of God's compassion: "the prophet of compassion" of Marcus Borg, "the compassion of God" of Monika Hellwig and "the inclusive praxis of wholeness" of Elisabeth Schüssler-Fiorenza.[57] Jesus becomes the incarnation of compassion in the world

53. Ibid., 117.

54. Ibid.

55. Ibid., 172.

56. Ibid., 118. *Suscipe* Prayer: "Take, Lord, and receive all my liberty, my memory, my understanding, and my entire will, all I have and call my own. You have given all to me. To you, Lord, I return it. Everything is yours; do with it what you will. Give me only your love and your grace that is enough for me."

57. Borg, *Meeting Jesus Again*, 46–68; Hellwig, *Jesus*; Schüssler Fiorenza, *In Memory of Her*, 119–30.

or embodies the interrelated compassion of the triune God. McFague pushes this direction for an ecological Christology:

> An ecological Christology means that God is with us—we are dealing with the power of love of the universe; it means that God is with us—all of us, all people and all other life-forms, but especially for those who do not have justice, health, or fulfillment.[58]

God empties Godself to be with us, and this revolutionary theological model has only just been realized in its incarnational potential in popular writings on current Christian spiritualities.[59] The ecological incarnation widens the breadth and depth of the incarnation not only in the cosmos but within the web of life.

The second hymn is the prologue of John 1:1–18. Gerald O' Collins underscores the wisdom matrix for the prologue:

> For the source of "the word became flesh," we should turn rather to Baruch: "Wisdom appeared on earth and lived among human beings" (Bar. 2:17, see also Sir. 24:8). To sum up, John's prologue may speak explicitly of the Logos, but in doing so it consistently transposes into the key of "word" what has been said of wisdom. It uses "logos" as an equivalent for the "Sophia" found in Jewish Wisdom Literature.[60]

Christians sang this hymn in worship as many Christians now recite this Prologue every Christmas Eve service or Christmas day. The Word (*logos*) begins before creation and became flesh (*sarx*) in Jesus. The Prologue interweaves two important insights for the notion of God's Logos connected to the event of creation and its embodiment in the human fleshliness of Jesus. Jesus' enfleshment is also part of an interrelated web of life and interconnected with all fleshliness. Elizabeth Johnson writes,

> In the incarnation of Jesus, the self-expressing Wisdom of God, conjoined the material conditions of biological life forms (grasses and trees), and experienced the pain common to sensitive creatures (sparrows and seals). The flesh assumed in Jesus Christ connects with all humanity, all biological life, all soil, the whole matrix of the material universe down to its very roots.[61]

58. McFague, "An Ecological Christology," 34.

59. See Butler Bass, *Grounded*; Bourgeault, *The Wisdom Jesus*.

60. O'Collins, "Word, Spirit, and Wisdom in the Universe," 77.

61. Johnson, *Ask the Beasts*, 195–96.

As a direct result of this incarnated event, Jesus remains interconnected with all physical matter and spiritual realities. The "I am" verses throughout point to these physical/ spiritual interconnections. Bread of life, the light, the good shepherd, truth and the way, resurrection and the life, and vine, and the tree of life. Jesus is Incarnate Wisdom interconnected to all—the tree of life (Prov 3:18).

The Colossians hymn to Christ (1:15–20) expands Christ's death and resurrection to what the pioneer Lutheran eco-theologian Joseph Sitter describes as a "vast cosmic vision."[62] This hymn originates from a Pauline community that acknowledges the role of Christ in creation (1:15–18a) while in the second strophe (1:18b–20) lists a series of cosmic attributes of Christ: He is the firstborn the dead, "that he is in everything so he might be pre-eminent," "in him the fullness of God was pleased to dwell," "through him to reconcile all things, whether on earth on in heaven," and "making peace on the cross." Christ, "the fullness (*pleroma*) of God is linked to creation as well as to the fulfillment and end of that creation."[63] The community, from which the Colossian hymn originated, recognizes that through Christ's death and resurrection, the transformation of creation has begun. Edwards quotes Rahner on the crucified and risen Jesus' radical new relationship with the universe from this hymn. Rahner writes, "When the vessel of his body was shattered in his death, Christ was poured over the cosmos, he became actually, in his very humanity, what he had always been in his dignity, the very center of creation."[64] In the resurrection, Jesus becomes the agency of transformation to a new fulfilled and transfigured creation; he is interconnected with all life and the Earth.

Easter affects everything alive and dead, the Earth and the complex web of interrelated processes and life, and the cosmological processes of the universe, past and present, into the future. The shift to the cosmic Christ in Colossians through the early patristic period finds its flowering in the Franciscan theological and Orthodox Christian traditions.[65] The cosmic Christ has developed into two directions: 1) Evolutionary Christogenesis has moved to explore the cosmic implications of the incarnation in the recent theological explorations of the notion and expansion of deep

---

62. Joseph Sittler, "Called to Unity," 179.

63. Schillebeeckx, *Christ*, 189–91; Edwards, *Jesus the Wisdom of God*, 77–88.

64. Rahner, *On the Theology of Death*, 66.

65. See Bauckham, *The Bible and Ecology*, 141–78; Bourma-Prediger, *For the Beauty of the Earth*, 105–10.

incarnation. 2) Popular spirituality/meditative movements spearheaded by Franciscan Richard Rohr and Matthew Fox have popularized the cosmic Christ and have influenced the formation of Christian clergy and laity and non-Christian contemplative seekers. Both spirituality teachers have suffered from charges of Gnosticism, monism, pantheism (not panentheism) by conservative Catholics. But their impact on the growing and popular contemplative in action spirituality and the Earthcare movement outweighs the ecological apathy of their critics. Their contemplative practices include ecological dimensions and shift the model of a distant God, God with us and within the cosmos.

Richard Rohr promotes a perennial Catholic contemplative spirituality with the cosmic Christ immanent in the natural world, other contemplative traditions, and within us. He is featured among numerous prominent interfaith ecological contemplatives and religious practitioners in *Spiritual Ecology: The Cry of the Earth*.[66] He explores the contemplative and ecological aspects of the cosmic Christ on a YouTube talk[67] Matthew Fox similarly has developed an impressive body of writings on the cosmic Christ and creation spirituality for three decades.[68] He has created the University of Creation Spirituality that morphed into the interatih University of Wisdom.[69] His training of thousands of folks in engaging the cosmic Christ, the wisdom traditions of the world, creativity and spirituality, ecological spirituality, introduction of the cosmic mass, and his poly-evangelical attempts to re-awaken the practice of the mystical, contemplative practices, commitment to social justice and protection of the Earth earns him the status of global bodhisattva. Matthew Fox has had the most sustained and praxis-oriented theological trajectory of the cosmic Christ outside Orthodox Christian theologies. The Wisdom traditions are connected to co-living with nature, and it was an easy way of translating the ecology of Jesus and his message of the companionship of empowerment. Theologian Denis Edwards connects the theology of Jesus as divine Wisdom incarnated and the cosmic Christ to ecology: "a Wisdom Christology can begin to show the interrelation between the expanding, interconnected and self-organizing universe

66. Rohr, "Creation as the Body of God," Ibid., 239–48.
67. Rohr, "Cosmic Christ," https://www.youtube.com/watch?v=4LYQQO5uFtA.
68. See Fox, http://matthewfox.org/; Fox, *The Coming of the Cosmic Christ*.
69. University of Wisdom, http://www.wisdomuniversity.org/aboutus.htm.

and all its creatures, and the saving work of Jesus Christ."[70] Edwards and other contemporary theologians have moved from atonement models of redemption to the Scotist notion of the incarnation as the flow of divine community of love and grace and the Orthodox tradition of divinization of the universe. They move closer to the theologies of Eastern Orthodox Christianity's notion of incarnational salvation as *theoisis* (divinization). This inclusion of Trinitarian *perichoresis* and the Scotist notion of the primacy of Christ's incarnation originating from love lends itself creatively to emergent evolutionary and cosmological theologies, pertinent to an eco-spirituality.

Deep Incarnation

Theologians such as Dunscan Reid, Dennis Edwards, Niels Gregersen, Elizabeth Johnson, and others have creatively embedded eco-Christology in a deep incarnational model.[71] "Deep incarnation" opens some new horizons of meaning on the deep death and resurrection of God's Christ, Jesus of Nazareth. The Danish theologian Niels Gregersen speaks of God's co-living with all creatures that face suffering and death: "The incarnation of God in Christ can be understood as a radical or deep incarnation, that is, an incarnation into the very tissue of biological existence, and system of nature. Understood this way, the death of Christ became an icon of God's redemptive co-suffering with all sentient life as well as with the victims of social competition. God bears the cost of evolution, the price involved in the hardship of natural selection."[72] Gregersen widens the incarnational scope to include biological existence (grass and lilies) and nonhuman evolutionary life (sparrows and wolves). In his introduction to the book *Incarnation*, he asks: "What does the incarnation in Christ have to do with the world of star formations, animal suffering and the restless productivity in nature, as we have come to know cosmic and biological evolution from the sciences?"[73] Through incarnation, God enters creation, evolutionary emergence and biological life in a radically new mode. This means the incarnation started with the big bang and within the gaseous expansion. Edwards claims that the body of Jesus, like

70. Edwards, *Jesus the Wisdom of God*, 69.

71. Gregersen, ed., *Incarnation*.

72. *Gregersen, "The Cross of Christ in an Evolutionary World,"* 205.

73. Gregersen, "Introduction," in *Incarnation*, 3.

our own bodies, was produced from the atoms in the starry furnace of the sun as well billions of microbes that resided in his body. The body of Jesus of Nazareth existed in interdependence and interrelated with all other biological life.[74] God's incarnation in Jesus was interrelated with the divine community of love, and Jesus becomes "a scorned-human being and a human animal body, at once vibrant and vital and yet vulnerable to disease and decay."[75] God's incarnation in Christ identifies with all those who have died namelessly from violence, died from natural catastrophse, and with animal suffering and extinctions. And Gregersen continues, "the incarnate Logos, sent by the Father, is present for and with all creatures, including in their suffering."[76]

The resurrection of Christ signifies that salvation is neither solely human nor merely spiritual—it must be for the entire creation of fleshly life and even all the material universe, all biological and emergent evolution and cosmological processes. Elizabeth Johnson expresses the fact that the "deep" interpretation of John 1:14 where God's Word is a "densely expression of God's love" that has entered into solidarity with biophysical life, and this act of solidarity with fleshly life confers dignity on life on the Earth and the cosmological processes upon which our planet depends.[77] She claims: "Deep incarnation in the event of the cross extends the presence of the Word/Wisdom made flesh all the way into the groan of suffering and the silence of death. Conjoined with flesh, the living God bears 'the cost of new life' . . . being in solidarity with all creatures living and dying through endless millennia of evolution from the extinction of species to every sparrow that falls to ground."[78] Johnson pushes the notion beyond anthropocentricism with biocentric and cosmocentric inclusion. In the risen Jesus, some aspect of biological life and the Earth community is incorporated into and interrelated with God, and the risen incarnated Christ is a proleptic sign of the future deification of the whole universe.

Johnson retells the story ing of John Muir coming across the dead body of a bear in Yosemite Valley, where Muir complains that there is no room in heaven for the bear: "Not content with the taking of all the earth, they also claim the celestial country as the ones who possess the kinds of

74. Edwards, *Partaking of God*, loc. 1072.

75. Gregersen, "The Cross of Christ," 193; see also Gregersen "The Extended Body of Christ," in *Incarnation*, 225–51.

76. Gregersen, "The Extended Body of Christ, 240.

77. Johnson, "Jesus and the Cosmos," 140.

78. Ibid.,146.

souls for which that imponderable empire was planned." Johnson says: "To the contrary, he figured, God's charity is broad enough for bears."[79] Evolutionary theologian John Haught similarly affirms,

> An evolutionary theology, I would suggest may picture God's descent as entering into the deepest layers of the evolutionary process, embracing and suffering along with the entire cosmic story, not just the recent human chapters. Through the liberating power of the Spirit, God's compassion extends across the totality of time and space, enfolding and finally healing not only human suffering, but also all the epochs of evolutionary travail that preceded, were indispensable to our own experience.[80]

Cosmic history—the story of the universe and evolutionary life—are embraced by God's redeeming love so that the whole of creation will participate in the resurrection of Jesus, God's Christ.[81] God taking flesh in Christ has salvific significance beyond humanity to include the whole world of interrelated organisms. God's Incarnation includes not only Jesus but also the web of interconnected life starting from the first moment of biological life on Earth. God has embraced the whole universe of interconnected life and material existence through Christ and the agency of the Holy Spirit. In fact, God's Incarnation brings incarnational transformational change to all flesh, all biological life. Neil Darragh comments on consequences of "the Word becoming flesh" to the biosphere: "To say that God became flesh is not only to say that God became human but to say also that God became an Earth creature, that God became a sentient being, that God became a living being, that God became a complex Earth unit of minerals and fluids, and that God became an item in the carbon and nitrogen cycles."[82] The incarnated Christ became a part of the Earth's eco-system. God's incarnation became a deep incarnation into the fleshy tissue of biological life on the Earth, to include human bodies but all the bodies of other creatures and plants themselves, and is now evolving within creation in a radically new way towards divinization. God becomes incarnated from microscopic level to the macro-biosphere of

79. Ibid., 149.
80. Haught, *Christianity and Science*, 92.
81. Edwards, *Ecology at the Heart of Faith*, 58.
82. Darragh, *At Home in the Earth*, 124.

the Earth, and God communicates divine life to all flesh: "God became human so humanity can become divine."[83]

Mark Wallace adds Spirit Christology by drawing a parallel between God's self-communication of green grace through the incarnated Christ and the carnal Holy Spirit.

> God incarnated Godself both in Jesus and in the Spirit—both as human and non-human animal life-forms. The full implications of this realization can be only imagined as Christianity broadens the circle of God's identity and compassion to include not only the human sphere but also the wider expanse of non-human living beings. In becoming all things—human and nonhuman—the biblical witness testifies to us that God eagerly desires the health and vitality of the whole created order, not just the human sphere.[84]

Jesus and the Spirit are interconnected as two "carnal expressions of God":

> As once God became earthly at the dawn of creation and as once God became human in the body of Jesus, so now God continually enfleshes Godself through the Spirit in the embodied reality of life on earth. In this sense, God is carnal. God is earthen, God is flesh, The Spirit has always and continues to indwell the earth as its inmost source of life and breath, and the earth has always arrayed and continues to array, the Spirit in garments of the cardinal elements.[85]

The Word is the fleshly form that God takes on, and the Earth is the body of the Spirit.[86] Moreover, Jesus and the Spirit are interconnected in suffering and death: "The crucified Jesus and the cruciform Spirit are bound together in common affliction."[87] They both take on together the pain and bruises of suffering life, whereas Jesus suffered on the cross for the sins of the world, the Spirit suffers in the cruciform of the suffering Earth for the sins for human complicity in the degradation of the Earth.

83. Irenaeus, *Adversus haereses*, book 5, preface.

84. Wallace, *Green Christianity*, 44.

85. Wallace, *Finding God in the Singing River*, 23.

86. Marya Riversa develops a theological poetics of flesh (*sarx*) for multiplicities and incarnational living. It is the basis of loving our neighbors and the Earth (Rivera, *Poetics of the Flesh*).

87. Wallace, *Green Christianity*, 45.

Wallace's dual carnal expressions of God in the world, the redemptive work of Christ and the Holy Spirit are both integrally interconnected as the one movement of God's communication of green or life-sustaining grace and co-suffering love. God incarnates Godself in Christ while the Holy Spirit ensouls herself carnally or greens herself in humanity and creation. The connection of Christ's incarnation and the Spirit's ensoulment respect the trinitarian nature of God. Wherever and whenever, one "person" of the triune community acts, the other two participates in creation. This requires a re-envisioning of the Christ event as an action of the Spirit. Irenaeus explained the intertwining of the Logos and the Spirit active in creation as the "two hands of God."[88]

For Wallace, the Spirit manifests herself carnally in the four elements—earth, air, fire, and water.[89] The elemental metaphors of the Spirit abound in the scriptures. As earth element, Wallace points to the symbolization of the Spirit as earthen avian form, who hovers over the waters of chaos in Genesis 1:1, appears at the baptism of Jesus in the Jordan. As air, the Spirit is the breath (*ruach*) of God; she blows where she wills (John 3:8) or is revealed in a gentle breeze to Elijah (1 Kgs 19:12) or speaks to Phillip (Acts 8:29). The Holy Spirit is like air, it is the vitality for and within life.

The Spirit ensouls herself with divine grace and sustaining life and creative love in human and nonhuman life, material reality of the universe. As water, the Spirit brings life and healing. Water as the vitality, the waters of the Earth forms the blood of the Earth. She is involved with life-giving faith (John 1–15), baptisms (Acts 8:26–40; 11:1–18). She is the Spirit in the water flowing from the pierced Jesus' body on the cross. As fire, there is the story of tongues of fire descending on the disciples in the upper room on Pentecost (Acts 2:1–4). The Spirit sparks the inclusive and multicultural mission of the Jesus movement to the nations. For Wallace, God's Spirit has been infusing the universe and the Earth, in particular, since their inception. It is in its Earth-centered mode; the Spirit is cruciform—that is, She suffers the pain and torment of the Earth and its life: "God as Spirit lives among us in great sorrow and deep anguish. From the viewpoint of green spirituality, as the God who knows death through the cross of Jesus is the crucified God, as also is the Spirit who enfleshes

88. Irenaeus, *Adversus haereses*, book 5, Preface.
89. Wallace, *Green Christianity*, 39–43.

divine presence in nature the wounded Spirit."[90] Through Christ crucified and the wounded Spirit, God refuses to be aloof from suffering and
sin of humanity experiences and is in solidarity with suffering and death
in nature, and compassionately remains present to the Earth and inclusively all life. Wallace's notion of on the carnal Spirit wounded, taking
up ecological damage and exploitation of the whole Earth system and
life, complements the deep incarnation exploration of Gregersen and his
colleagues with an equally deep Spirit.

God's Divine Image

With our exploration of deep incarnation and deep pneumatology, we
can address the image (*tselem*) and likeness (*demuth*) of God. Just as we
widen and deepen the incarnational scope of Christology and widen
pneumatology with the carnal Spirit, the theological affirmation of the
image of God needs to be re-envisioned beyond its anthropocentric
constraints. A parallel interpretation trajectory to own my interpretation
of the carriers of God image is Rabbi David Seidenberg's *Kabbalah and
Ecology*, who provides a genealogical history of the widening the notions
of God's image reflected in humanity in later rabbinic Midrashim and
Jewish Kabbalah writings.[91] He establishes in detail how Jewish extra-
biblical reflections envision creation and nonhuman creatures participating in the divine image. He demonstrates that Jewish rabbinic texts
do not ground human value through the notion of God's image. In fact,
the rabbis extended the divine image beyond humanity also to include
angels and the heavens. With the Kabbalah, Seidenberg elucidates that
the notion of God's image is expanded to non-human creatures and the
dimension of the earthly or lower realm.

Christians have theologically conceived the divine image historically into two fashions: substantially and relationally. The substantial position incorporates the perspective that human nature or capacities such
an infinite soul or rationality which separate us from nonhuman animals
while the relational approach assumes human responsiveness or relation
to God endows us with the divine image above the non-responsiveness
of nonhuman animals to God. In both cases, the image of God (*imago
dei*) has been used to justify human separation and domination over

90. Wallace, *Finding God*, 131.
91. Seidenberg, *Kabbalah and Ecology*.

nonhuman animals. Larry Rasmussen summarizes the distinctiveness and exclusive of the divine image restricted to humanity: "*Imago dei* set us apart from the rest of nature as free agents who act upon it in responsibility before God . . . But it was stewardship in the mode of mastery, control, and good management, all determined by an anthropocentrism of interests."[92] The divine image was restricted anthropocentrically, justifying Earth domination.

Hebrew biblical scholars Claus Westermann and Walter Brueggemann both stress that "image of God" indicates how God engages human creatures relationally and intimately through speaking and human capacity in freedom to respond.[93] Karl Barth proposes a relational "I–thou" response as bearing the divine image.[94] And Karl Rahner understands that humans have become creation self-conscious with the ability to respond freely to God's invitation to unconditional love.[95] And it is contemporary eco-theologians who have widened the divine image beyond anthropocentrism.

Australian Denis Edwards provides a superb description of divine image:

> Being created as the *imago Deo* means that God creates human beings as persons in order to embrace in interpersonal love . . . Precisely because human beings are made in the image of God, they are called like God to care for every sparrow that falls to the ground. They are called to love their fellow creatures as God loves them . . . in a way that respects the distinctiveness and otherness of a kangaroo, an eagle, or a whale.[96]

Edwards develops an ecological perspective of Rahner's notion of God's inclusive grace surrounding us and in our midst; he notes "To be called into relationship with the living God is to be invited into a world of grace, a world in which God is present to each person (and all life, my emphasis) in self-offering love."[97] He finds that God's image in nature: a mountain range, a wild flower, soaring redwood tree, all life and the Earth. He

92. Rasmussen, *Earth Community,* 189.

93. Westermann, *Creation,* 58; Brueggemann, *Genesis,* 31.

94. Miller, *Animal Ethics and Theology,* 35–36; Barth, *Church Dogmatics* III/1, 184–85.

95. Rahner, *Foundations,* 189.

96. Edwards, *Ecology at the Heart of Faith,* 16.

97. Ibid.

notes, "They are expressions of God, sacraments of divine presence in the world. They image God in specificity."[98] Edwards places the image of God in God relating to the Earth and all other life. There are two refinements: incarnation of Christ and the Spirit carnal ensouling herself in the Earth and nonhuman life. This is to make more explicit what I believe is implicit in Edwards' theology: Trinitarian notion of *perichoresis* and interrelationality is the divine image that links not human animals but nonhuman animals, other life, and the universe.

Interrelational communion within the divine community of life is beyond full comprehension, and we can hardly understand the intimacy of the risen, cosmic Christ and the Spirit in their interrelatedness. Interrelated love, open and generous, self-emptying, and extravagantly inclusive is the operation mode of the divine community love in the universe. Interrelatedness is the air humanity breathes, but it is also the operational matrix for the biotic community of life, individually and macro-biotic. There is nothing on this planet that is isolated and without connections to something else. Interconnection and interrelatedness include a web of interconditional causality of everything that is interdependent in cosmological, earthly, and biological interprocesses. The *imago Dei* is reflected in the universe's macro interrelatedness and smaller planetary interrelatedness', and all life, whether human or nonhuman life are interrelated. The universe reflects the image of Trinitarian interrelatedness. Everything participates in this cosmic web of interbeing. Dennis Edwards writes,

> When such a God creates a universe, it is not surprising that it turns out to be a radically relational and interdependent one. When life unfolds through the process of evolution, it emerges in "patterns of interconnectedness and interdependence that 'fits' with the way God is."[99]

The universe unfolds within the life of God, and God, in turn, is reflected in the unfolding of the interrelating patterns of the universe. Trinitarian interrelating is located within cosmological, evolutionary, and ecological interconnectedness through the incarnation of Christ and the ensoulment of the Holy Spirit; these fleshy interconnection express the divine intimacy and perichoretic "entanglements" within the universe, evolving open-endedly.[100]

98. Ibid., 17.
99. Edwards, *The God of Evolution*, 28.
100. Simmons, *The Entangled Trinity*, 150–63.

The incarnated Christ introduces biological life and physically into the triune God. Thomas Torrance notes how the incarnation interrelates temporally:

> The incarnation was not just a transient episode in the interaction of God with the world, but has taken place once-for-all in a way that reaches backward through time and forward through time, from the end to the beginning and from the beginning to the end.[101]

Through the incarnation, God is interrelated and biologically, physically, and materially entangled with the universe. God's re-creation or deification is not just a restrictive promise in the risen Christ to humanity only but to the universe in its entirety. Incarnation becomes interbeing of Christ as the risen one "inter-is" in every particle of matter and life. God the Creator is acting with the process of creation, inclusive of incarnation as causality of deification or re-creating the universe in the image of the cosmic Christ as well as the Spirit ensouling herself with life and life processes. For Niels Gregersen, God's grace is interrelated or engaged in the particulars of ongoing creation and emergent evolution: "For if God is not in the particulars, God is not in the whole of reality either."[102] Gregersen notes that God kenotically is present in all the particulars of continuing creative and self-organizing processes, "giving room—from moment to moment, from event to event—to the explorative capacities of God's creatures."[103] God's spaciousness, God's kenotic capacities for self-limitation or making room for creation and other life, continues within the process of the incarnation and the interweaving ensoulment of the Spirit continues the panentheist creation. God, by making space for creation, does not remove the presence of the divine community, for Trinitarian interrelatedness has a "transcendent proximity."

Now the extension of the divine image beyond humanity has been entertained by some theologians. David Cunningham argues that the differences between creatures is a "matter of degree rather than a simple opposition of inclusion and exclusion from the attribution 'created in the image of God'"[104] For Cunningham, all creation carries the marks of the Creator. It does not provide a meaningful description for all created

101. Torrance, *The Christian Doctrine of God,* 216.

102. Gregersen, "Laws of Physics," 98.

103. Ibid.

104. Cunningham, "The Way of All Flesh," 100.

order for human claims for dominion and the domination of nonhuman animals. Cunningham takes up the notion of "flesh," and he contends that flesh is the element of creation shared by Jesus primarily with creatures and secondarily with humanity. God's incarnation is not defined by accidental properties of human, male, or Jewish but by fleshliness. Nonhuman animal activist and ethicist Andrew Linzey observes, "By becoming flesh, the Logos identifies, according to the paradigm, not only with humanity but with all creatures of flesh and blood."[105] This is critical for an ecological inclusivity, the dynamics of incarnation for deification of the universe.

Cunningham's critique of *imago dei* as inclusive of all flesh in creation expands theological traditions that maintain a restrictive anthropocentrism to privilege humanity. Rabbi David Seidenberg notes that the rabbis' inclusion beyond anthropocentrism to include creation provided a mode for perceiving creation and its diversity bearing elements of God's image. No creature, human or otherwise, can bear the full divine image: "we . . . reveal the image of God in other creatures and things through a right relation with them."[106] He wonderfully describes that "the divine image is not inherent within the Other, nor within oneself, but rather comes into being through relationship with the Other. The *telos*, the goal, is a relationship that reflects the image of God, and the means for achieving this is relation itself."[107] When we as humans realize the contemplative insight of imagining God's image in all Being and in all beings, then we live in a spirituality of compassionate action for life and all creation. He concludes. "But on the most direct level, we are called upon to open ourselves to simply encountering and listening to the creatures and orders of being that inter-penetrate our lives."[108] We thus hear prayer in our actions with the lives of other creatures.

As God's self emptying love in the incarnation of or becoming fully human in Christ, the combination of the kenotic impulse toward creation and incarnation become a redemptive movement of grace. Ilia Delio wonderfully affirms: "Redemption, therefore, is not being 'saved from' but rather being 'made whole' for the healing and wholeness of God's

105. Linzey, "Introduction: Is Christianity Irredeemably Speciessist?," xvi.

106. Seidebberg, *Kabbalah and Ecology*, 342.

107. Ibid., 347.

108. Ibid., 362.

creation, and this wholeness is ultimately the transformation of created reality through the unitive power of God's love."[109]

109. Delio, "Revisiting the Franciscan Doctrine of Christ," 18.

6

Greening Biblical Hermeneutics

I am self-conscious about my earth-centered hermeneutic and believe that such a hermeneutic allows the Bible to speak from the center of its love and passion for the good creation God has made. God is not distant from our planet, unmoved by earthly concerns, dispassionate and unaffected by the environmental degradation that despoils the beauty and the bounty of the created order.

—Mark L. Wallace[1]

Earth justice obligates us, as members of the Earth community, to be advocates for Earth and to interrogate our biblical heritage to ascertain whether Earth is silenced, oppressed, or liberated in the Bible.

—Norman C. Habel[2]

Christian contentiousness has surrounded the Bible and its interpretation for centuries, but in the modern/post-modern era, this contentiousness has escalated as various contextual and constructionist theologies have engaged, critically read, resisted, subverted, inclusified, queered and read

1. Wallace, *Finding God in the Singing River*, 11.
2. Habel, *Readings from the Perspective of Earth*, 27.

anew the scriptures. Readers of the scriptures come from diverse contexts, genders and gender variance, sexual orientations, ethnicities, races, economic status, and diverse Christianities. The Bible has been politically misread as a meta-narrative, read allegorically, literally, exclusively and imperiously, androcentrically, racist, heteronormative, while others have read the text metaphorically, liturgically, contemplatively, critically, subversively, liberative and personally transformational. The Bible has been blamed for legitimizing anthropocentricism, a dominion perspective that the Earth, all life and all its resources are there for human benefit. Lynn White has leveled the complaint of human and spiritual apartheid from nature, resulting in our developing ecological crisis. The Bible has been become a source of interpretative contention for environmentalists, climate change deniers, people of faith from commitments for or against the Earth.

In this chapter, we explore a variety of reading strategies of the Bible addressing our environmental crisis: Retreival strategies for discovering God's intention for stewardship, liberation theological strategies that expand preferential option for the poor to include the Earth, and the Earth Bible project and its hermeneutical ecojustice strategies to surface the voice of the Earth, read from beyond anthropocentricism and committed to eco-justice.[3] Eco-location is critical for reading and engaging the scriptures because it provides the contextual experience of nature, the passion to practice Earthcare. Eco-reading strategies starts with these specific features of eco-location just as a variety of contextual theologies provide the hermeneutical lens for reading and engaging the biblical traditions.

Retrieval Strategies

Before the emergence of mainline Protestant and evangelical Protestant churches became invested in the environmental movement and tried to recover God's call to a stewardship in the Bible, there was the Lutheran theologian Joseph Sittler.[4] He brings a hermeneutical complexity to reading the biblical text, incorporating the works of Paul Ricoeur and Hans Georg Gadamer. Sittler discards any literalist framework of interpreting the text but uses an overall theology of grace, grounded in the

3. Horrel et al., *Greening Paul*, 11–48.
4. Bourma-Prediger, *The Greening of Theology*, 61–102, 175–216.

cosmic Christ in doxological hymn in Colossians 1:15–20. His stress in reading the scriptures was less on the original meaning but placing stress on Paul Ricouer's notion of the surplus of meaning and engaging the text as the living reality of God in the present moment.

When you read the Lutheran theologian, he cites poets—Keats, Whitman, Shakespeare, and Hopkins as well the writings of Rachel Carson and John Muir. He stressed the natural world as place for encountering God's grace. His love for the natural world intersects his theological writings and sermons as he attempts to develop God's grace within creation. Joseph Sittler was determined to bring the natural world and a theology of grace together in a theology of creation. This fusion of the natural world and the theology of grace form his ecological location for reading the scriptures and preaching a message of the cosmic Christ. From his studies of ecology and the natural world, he comprehended the "fundamental postulate of ecology that anything is related to everything."[5] He perceived the environment as a living organism, and he echoes Muir: "nature is like a fine piece of cloth, you pull a thread here, and it vibrates throughout the whole fabric."[6] Sittler understood the interrelated web of life and its interconnections, and he connected this to grace, designating nature as "a theater of grace." The theologian did not develop a stewardship retrieval reading of the scripture, for he saw the stewardship perspective as too narrow, and he aspired to theology of creation, infused by the gracious life of the triune God whose interrelated life interrelated with all creation and life. All creation is interrelated web of God's grace, and his environmental commitments arose from this foundational theological insight. He wrote at a time in 1950s and 1960s when his theological ideas were perceived as unorthodox, and his originality was to thoroughly make ecology into a theological issue and part of his overall theology of creation. Sittler is an authentic pioneer in ecotheology and an eco-hermeneutical reading of scripture.

It was the pivotal article of Lynn White in *Science* that spurred the development of counter-apologetics to White's complaint against Christianity. Many biblical scholars and theologians attempted to refute his conclusion that Christianity interpreted the opening texts of Genesis as anthropocentric. They challenged White's interpretation of anthropocentric Christianity's notion of dominion over nature and human

5. Sittler, *Essays on Nature and Grace*, 113; Sittler, *Gravity and Grace*, 22.
6. Muir *My First Summer in the Sierra*, 110.

exceptionalism. American evangelicals and mainline Protestant biblical scholars, ethicists, theologians, and leaders countered White analysis with the stewardship notion of creation care. In 1971, the National Association of Evangelicals issued two resolutions calling for responding to environmental problems:

1. Today those who thoughtlessly destroy a God-ordained balance of nature are guilty of sin against God's creation.

2. We pledge our cooperation to any responsible effort to solve critical environmental problems and our willingness to support all proven solutions developed by competent authorities. We call upon our constituency to do the same, even at the cost of personal discomfort and inconvenience.[7]

In 1979, Calvin DeWitt founded the Au Sable Institute to blend ecology and with biblical principles of stewardship to assist Christians to develop a stewardship practice.[8] With the 1980s, a number of evangelical associations developed, and they culminated in theologian Ron Sider's founding an environmental activist group, Evangelical Environmental Network.[9] The Network released "An Evangelical Declaration on the Care of Creation", which raised the issues of caring for the poor and those suffering from climate change.[10] There has subsequently been a proliferation of evangelical and Protestant organizations responding to creation care and the environmental crisis.

The stewardship reading of scripture attempted to recover the texts that manifested God's intention for humanity to responsibility for creation care. One of the significant ecumenical projects was the publication of *The Green Bible*, which promoted a retrieval hermeneutic in reading and interpreting the scriptures from Genesis to Revelations. The Preface states its retrieval strategy of God's word on creation:

> Is God green? Did Jesus have anything to say about the environment? What is my role as a Christian in caring for the earth? With over a thousand references to the earth and caring for creation in the Bible, the message is clear: all in God's

7. Wilkinson, *Between God & Green*, 16.

8. Ibid., 17. See: http://ausable.org/.

9. Wilkinson, *Between God & Green*, 19. See: http://creationcare.org/.

10. Ibid.; see also: http://creationcare.org/creation-care-resources/evangelical -declaration-on-the-care-of-creation/.

> creation—nature, animals, humanity—are inextricably linked
> to one another. As God cares for all of creation, so too, we can-
> not love one dimension without caring for the others. We are
> called to care for all God has made.[11]

It places in green all those verses and passages that speak about God's vision for creation and its care *The Green Bible* advertises itself as text for Christians who want to live the scriptural values of stewardship, love of neighbors, and care for the underprivileged. In addition, there are twelve essays from a variety of evangelical Protestant and Catholic authors concerned for Earthcare. Calvin DeWitt derives from the stewardship perspective biblical principles for creation care: Earthkeeping, fruitful-ness, Sabbath, discipleship, kingdom priority, contentment, and praxis.[12] The introduction from Christian leaders, theologians, and faith activists each take up the retrieval interpretative strategy with the assumption that there are "environmental truths" within the scriptures that promote envi-ronmental responsibility.

One of the downsides of this interpretative strategy is that few evan-gelicals challenge the pre-dispensational Christian interpretative strate-gies in prioritizing the eschatological texts over creation theology texts.[13] Evangelical biblical scholar N. T. Wright has consistently presented in-novative interpretations of and corrections to the Christian eschatologi-cal texts and the Second Coming of Christ.[14] His response to Christians denying climate change or expecting the rapture is: "Jesus is coming, so plant a tree."[15] There has been an ever-increasing growth of Evangelical and Protestant presence in Christian environmental networks, joining together on education on Earthcare, learning to make their church cam-pus more sustainable, political advocacy and alignment to fight climate change.

Preferential Option for the Poor/Earth

The phrase "preferential option for the poor" was first used in 1968 by the Superior General of the Jesuits, Father Pedro Arrupe, in a letter to the

11. Ibid.; *NRSV The Green Bible*, I-15.

12. Ibid., I-28-I-34.

13. Liederback and Bible, *Tru-North*, loc. 2385–3473.

14. Wright. *Surprised by Hope*.

15. *NRSV The Green Bible*, I-72–83.

Jesuit order in Latin America. It deeply informed the formation of Jesuits through their identification with the poor and, in particular, my own spirituality. The notion of the preferential option was included in Jesuit apostolates and formation programs working in poor urban neighborhoods, First Nation reservations, and overseas. The preferential option for the poor was first developed by liberation theologian Gustavo Gutierrez as a principle grounded in the Hebrew and Christian scriptures.[16] He understands the preferential option for the poor as the central element of Jesus' ministry. The term was later developed by the Catholic bishops of Latin America at the conferences at Medellin and Puebla. In its early usage, particularly, the option for the poor highlighted biblical texts, where God has a demonstrable preference given to powerless individuals who live on the margins of society. The liberation theology movement fully embraced this concept, particularly when they closely associated the poor and vulnerable with Jesus, "Whatever you did for the least of my family, you did for me" (Matt 25:40).

Leonardo Boff used both Jesus and Francis of Assisi's identification with the poor for his theological explorations of the preferential option for the poor.[17] For Boff, the care of the poor goes back to Jesus and in apostolic times to the church prior to Constantine, when the church was merged with the Roman imperium. He asserts,

> The poor are considered *vicarious Christi:* the individual makes real the presence of Christ as judge, demanding the practice of charity and justice with the naked, the hungry, the jailed, etc. Furthermore, the poor individual is "judge and porter of heaven," acting as intercessor before the Eternal Judge. Finally, the poor prolong the incarnation of Jesus, suffering servant within history. Service to the poor implies a service to Christ himself.[18]

Boff traces this option for the poor to lived spiritual practices of the Franciscans, Servites, Dominnicans (and Jesuits) to the modern development of the preferential option for the poor within liberation theology and mainstreamed recently by Pope Francis I. Boff claims that personal solidarity with the poor remains at the hermeneutics of liberation theology. In a later work, Boff affirms that the God of Life "takes the part of

16. Gutierrez, *A Theology of Liberation.* See also Gutierrez and Muller, *On the Side of the Poor.*

17. Boff, *St. Francis,* loc. 940–1540.

18. Ibid., loc. 1074.

the poor and the oppressed, whose lives are threatened."[19] He claims that "the rights spoken in the Bible belong to the orphan, the widow, the pauper, the immigrant, and the alien. There is no sidestepping that fact that biblical rights, especially, in the Prophets, the Wisdom Literature, and the New Testament, are the rights of the oppressed."[20]

The scriptures exhibit God's concern for the poor (*anawim*), for God has always been partial to the poor, the vulnerable, and the oppressed. To practice care for the poor means that we identify with the poor, listen to their struggles to survive and the tragedies that they experience. Boff extends God's option for the poor to include the vulnerable Earth and all life that inhabits the Earth. In *Cry of the Earth*, Boff explicitly expands the preferential option for the poor to include the cries of the Earth: "The option for the poor, against their poverty, and for liberation, has continued and continues to constitute the core of liberation theology. To opt for the poor entails a practice; it means assuming the place of the poor, their cause, their struggle, and the limit, their often tragic fate."[21] Boff claims an epistemological priority of the poor in theology: "that is, the poor constitutes the point from which one attempts to conceive of God, Christ, grace, history, the mission of the church."[22] The poor has to be accorded a central location within liberation praxis and theology as it is accorded in scripture. They are, in fact, the most threatened in creation. He contends a need for a more inclusive notion of liberation: "It is not only the poor and oppressed who must be liberated but all human beings, rich and poor, because all are oppressed by a paradigm—abuse of the Earth, consumerism, denial of otherness, and of the inherent value of each being that enslaves us all."[23] Boff notes the greatest challenge is to broaden understanding of liberation to include a paradigm that "will enable Gaia to love and all beings in creation, especially, human beings, to exist in solidarity."[24] He writes, "The earth is also crying out under the predatory and lethal machinery of our model of society and development. To hear these two interconnected cries and to see the same root causes that produce them

19. Boff, *When Theology Listens to the Poor*, 61.

20. Ibid., 59.

21. Boff, *Cry of the Earth*, loc. 2380.

22. Ibid.

23. Ibid., Loc 2487.

24. Ibid., 2495.

is to carry out integral liberation."[25] The incarnational identification with the poor and the vulnerable becomes extended to what humanity considers the least—vulnerable other life. For the Brazilian theologian, his theological notion of incarnation in the Franciscan tradition opens us to a new ecological paradigm and epistemological priority of the interconnectedness of all with all.

The recent papal encyclical *Laudato Si* on climate by Francis I utilizes the preferential option for the poor and intertwines this hermeneutical principle with environmental degradation: "The human environment and the natural environment deteriorate together; we cannot adequately combat environmental degradation unless we attend to the causes related to human and social degradation. In fact, the deterioration of the environment and of society affects the most vulnerable people on the planet."[26] The encyclical speaks of the depletion of fishing reserves and how this harms fishing communities; lack of water and water pollution affects the poor in developing nations, and potential sea level rises that displace coastal populations. He points out how the impact of climate change and environmental degradation impacts the poor more disproportionately than the affluent in industrialized nations. He argues that the church in its identification with and empowering the poor needs to advocate for environmental policy to change the reckless course of action toward the Earth. A policy position paper of the Catholic German Bishops' Conference on Climate Change (2007) applied the preferential option for the poor also to the victims of climate change.[27]

Pope Francis concludes, "Today, however, we have to realize that a true ecological approach always becomes a social approach; it must integrate questions of justice in debates on environment so as to hear the cry of the earth and the cry of the poor."[28] Francis echoes a number of themes found in the writings of Boff: The Earth as "common home", the "cry of the Earth and the cry of the poor", the "care" of the "interdependence of all beings", of the "poor and vulnerable". In other parts of the encyclical, he integrates a retrieval hermeneutic of scripture to support

25. Ibid., loc. 2478.

26. Laudato Si, no. 48. See Bishops Confereence, "Pastoral Letter on the Environment and Human Development in Bolivia El universo, don de Dios para la vida," (23 March 2012), 17.

27. Commission for Society and Social Affairs/Commission for International Church Affairs: *Climate Change*.

28. Ibid., no. 49.

a stewardship ethic for care of the Earth and the community. Here like Boff, Francis I retrieves an ecological context from Francis of Assisi and the biotic community.

The biblical theology of God's preferential option for the poor provides a hermeneutical Catholic inclusion of the Earth. This theological construct of the preferential option is well grounded in various texts of the Judeo-Christian biblical heritage and plays a prominent position within Latin American liberation theologies. Commenting on Boff's liberation theology of the poor and nature but applicable to the official recension in the papal encyclical, Ernst Conradie provides his evaluation, "One may develop this into a fairly comprehensive notion that would address the tensions between God's good creation, the suffering of the vulnerable in creation due to human oppression, prophetic critiques of such oppression and hope for the liberation of creation . . . The strength of this construct is its ability to confront socio-economic forces that lies at the roots of the current environmental crisis."[29] The preferential option for the poor and the Earth offers the most possibility for social and economic analysis against the ravages of a climate change and a rise of temperature to 4 to 4.5 Celsius by the end of this century and that afflicted on the poor and poor nations. This liberative praxis and orientation are critical to any ecological hermeneutical strategies. In addition, Leonardo Boff connects other hermeneutical keys for interpreting the biblical texts. He includes the Franciscan notion of love and interconnection with the Earth and other life as well as a developed cosmogenesis and evolutionary perspective to speak that at the heart of these processes is an interrelatedness of processes and life and humanity is embedded in these interdependencies and interconnections. This leads him to make integral connections between social ecology and ecology, and it provides him with the crucial theological link between liberation and ecological theology:

> The dominant ethics of present day society is utilitarian and anthropocentric. Humankind believes that everything culminates in the human being. Human beings believe that they are lords and masters of a nature that simply exists to satisfy their needs and to realize their desires . . . this conviction leads to violence and to domination of others and nature. It denies the subjectivity of other peoples, justice, classes, and intrinsic value of certain other living creatures in nature. It does not understand that rights do not belong only to humankind and nations, but also to

29. Conradie, "What on Earth Is Ecological Hermeneutics?" loc. 4863.

other beings in creation. There is a human and social right, but there is also an ecological and cosmic right.[30]

Boff does not derive an ecojustice theology merely from the biblical text, but he employs a Latin American connection of social ecology with environmental ecology within his liberation theology. He looks to inspiration from Jesus, Christ's Incarnation, and Francis of Assisi, the poor and indigenous people of the Amazon basin as models for integral praxis of social justice and ecojustice.

Boff has been one of the pioneers of Catholic ecojustice theology, and he weaves together the evolutionary insights of Teilhard de Chardin and Thomas Berry, Franciscan theologians, and Catholic creation theology.[31] He perceives humanity as daughters and sons of the Earth; humanity is Earth becomes conscious. In an Advent sermon, he describes human beings as "Earth walking." In *Cry of the Earth*, he asks his readers to "feel, love, and think as the Earth."[32] Empathic identification with the suffering Earth is absolutely critical for an ecological sustainable spirituality, an incarnational inclusion of the Earth and interrelated life. This hermeneutical approach points to a Catholic theological model reflected in the encyclical *Laudato Si* of developing a strong ecological and social ecology with theology that integrates the poor around the world and the Earth.[33] The encyclical reflects an integration of the "preferential option for the poor" as a core hermeneutical praxis in defense of the poor from harm due to climate change and expanded to a preferential option for the vulnerable Earth, called "our common home." There is strong evidence that the poor are harmed disproportionately through climate changes caused by humanity. Secondly, the letter reflects the rich heritage of evolutionary and creation theology in the Catholic Church developed from the twentieth century into the present. Similar to evangelical and Protestant recovery reading strategies, there is a strong theme of Earthcare and Catholic creation theology, but it invites a liberation praxis for the poor and the Earth.

30. Boff, *Ecology and Liberation*, 29–30.

31. In fact, every one of the six principles of ecojustice of the Earth Bible Project is found in Boff, *Cry of the Earth*, which was published prior to the ecojustice principles.

32. Boff, *Cry of the Earth*, loc. 4008–4318.

33. McDonagh, *Passion for the Earth*.

Ecological Hermeneutics: The Earth Bible

Norman Habel and the scholarly team involved in the Earth Bible Project have developed a complex ecological hermeneutics in reading the biblical text. Their strategy is dependent upon earlier feminist biblical scholars and their retrieval of female voice within the scriptures. Gene McAfee suggests that an interpreter needs to understand as much as possible the physical environment of particular biblical authors or what Daniel Spencer describes ecological location. He asks potential readers to discern whether that the ideas of a biblical author transcend that particular physical environment. McAfee wonders if theological readings of our anthropocentric biblical texts can really assist us to live responsibly ("justly") on the Earth on her terms. He asks, "What kind of anthropocentricism will we embrace? Will we embrace anthropocentricism, in which human beings will be the locus of meaning and authority, or the theocentric monism in which the meaning and authority derive from the perspective of reality as a seamless whole with God and God's creation (including humans) at its center?"[34] McAfee re-envisions a post-anthropocentricism that places humanity in the midst of creation and interdependent on creation and other life. These early precursors to an ecojustice hermeneutics raise legitimate questions of textual suspicion of anthropocentrism and patriarchy, asking for a new hermeneutical engagement of the scriptures within a context that re-contextualizes humanity as part of God's creation.

Norman Habel and other team scholars of the Earth Bible Project have built upon feminist and various contextual approaches to the Bible with a hermeneutics of suspicion, identification, and liberative engagement or retrieval of the biblical text, and they owe a major debt to the pioneering work of feminist theological and liberation theological hermeneutics.[35] Habel is quick to point out that an ecological hermeneutic is not just trying to focus on what a given scriptural text is saying about creation or on ecology and theology. He highlights, "An ecological hermeneutic requires a radical change of posture in relation to the Earth as subject in the text. (Here the term "Earth" refers to the total ecosystem, that is the web of life—the domain of nature which we are familiar, of which we are an integral part, and which we face the future."[36] Habel's description of the radical change of posture of the Earth within the text

34. McAfee, "Ecology and Biblical Studies," 43.

35. Eaton, "Ecofeminist Contributions to Ecological Hermeneutics," 54–71.

36. Habel, "Introducing Ecological Hermeneutics," 3.

includes two elements: the first is what Daniel Spencer describes as eco-location in the introduction of this book and secondly, a conversion experience that now comprehends that eco-location as part of a regional ecological location, the community of interdependent life and Earth process, and the Earth herself. This radical re-orientation to the text presupposes an eco-conversion as well as intellectual and metholodological conversion to the Earth. Approaching the text with suspicion already signifies a reading strategy that understands the interpretative history is surrounded with particular social interests, in particular, anthropocentricism. Ecological location presupposes anthropocentric suspicion, and the goal is to retrieve a non-anthropocentric or alternative tradition, the marginalized voice of the Earth.[37]

Norman Habel articulates six ecojustice principles, developed over the years in dialogue with ecologist Charles Birch:[38]

1. The universe, the Earth and all its components have intrinsic worth. All creation is loved by God.

2. The Earth is a community of interconnected living things that are mutually dependent on each other for life and survival.

3. The Earth is a subject capable of raising its voice in celebration and against injustice.

4. The universe, Earth and its components are a part of dynamic cosmic design within which each piece has a place to play in the overall goal of that design.

5. Earth is a balanced and divine domain where responsible custodians can function as partners with, rather than rulers over Earth, to sustain its balance and a diverse Earth community.

6. Earth and its components not only suffer from human injustice but actively resist them in the struggle for justice.[39]

These ecojustice principles are developed to clarify the criteria for the perspective of the Earth, and they not exhaustive but suggestive as principles, to be revised, and others may be added to as we dialogue with

37. Habel, "Introducing the Earth Bible," 35.

38. Birch, *Confronting the Future*.

39. Habel, "Introducing Ecological hermeneutics," 2; The Earth Bible Team, "Guiding Ecojustice Principles," 38–53.

ecologists. These principles provide *a priori* principles to engage text and read it from an ecological location. Thus, Habel writes,

> When reading the text, an interpreter participating in the Earth Bible project, taking into account one or more of the above principles, asks critical questions to ascertain whether there is justice for the Earth in the orientation, ideology or focus of the text or its interpreters. Typical questions are: Is the Earth viewed merely as a resource for humans or as a subject with intrinsic worth? Is the Earth treated as a subject with a "voice" or as an object to be exploited?[40]

We read as creatures, part of the interdependent relationships and interconnected processes of the Earth. The Earth Bible Team intends to re-contextualize or re-locate the human in the ecological web of relations, the Earth community and the kinship of all creatures. Similarly, Leonardo Boff notes that eco-spirituality involves "feeling, loving, and thinking as Earth."[41] He takes up an Earth centered metaphor for humanity: "the human being is the Earth who walks."[42] And this is hemeneutical sympathetic to the Earth Bible project.

The first stage of reading involves suspicion. We must be weary of our own anthropocentric prejudices and the anthropocentricism within a given text, privileging ourselves and humanity over all other perspectives. It is the view of human exceptionalism that rejects a kinship context of our interrelatedness. Both the ecojustice principles of interconnectedness (number 2) and of purpose that the Earth and all its components are part of whole cosmic design (number 4) raise the question of suspecting our own prejudices and textual prejudices (number 5). Anthropocentricism asserts itself in the text when humanity is totally different, exceptional, and hierarchically above other life. By shifting our perspective to a kinship model of interrelatedness to other life, inanimate nature, or the Earth herself, we can understand and expose the anthropocentricism within the text, for instance, acknowledging Genesis 1:28 as anthropocentric. How do we shift from an anthropocentric acting towards the Earth to identify with the Earth community as siblings and seek the voices of the Earth community who are our sibling relatives? Thus, there is an experiential priority of an eco-conversion from a strong individualist

40. Ibid., 2.
41. Boff, *Cry of the Earth*, loc. 4007-4315.
42. Boff, "The Path as Arcehtype."

perspective to perceive ourselves as partners in the world to members of an interrelated community. Initial care for the environment motivates us to shift our perspective to kinship model of the Earth and its community of life espoused by Francis of Assisi. We no longer understand ourselves as the apex of creation but as siblings within a biotic community. There are conflicting anthropocentric perspectives and theo-centric perspectives when we read the priestly creation account with Genesis 2. In Genesis 2:15, the Yahwist (J tradition) poet does not have the elevated position of the priestly claim in Genesis 1:28. In the second creation narrative in Genesis 2, the J tradition affirms that humanity, the animals, and plants are made from the same dirt and share the same breath that gives life. Humanity as a member of the creaturely community of the Earth is placed in the garden by God to cultivate and serve the garden. We raise the anthropocentrism of Genesis 1:28 and its troubled interpretation in human domination and exploitation of the Earth, but we can raise the intertextual alternative perspective of humanity among the interrelated web of life.

The second stage of ecological interpretation involves identification. In Catholic liberation theology, it is the personal solidarity with the Earth and the poor. Solidarity is a particular term or process in liberation theology that takes on the perspective of hermeneutical compassion, in this case, identification with the Earth or the Earth community. Sallie McFague understands the power of being empathetic, "being able to feel into another's mental and emotional needs" as key process of personal and social transformation.[43] She observes, "Great compassion is the kind of love for others that not only wishes their suffering to be diminished but involves the willingness to make it so oneself." McFague quotes the Dalai Lama, "Great compassion is, in fact, an even deeper type of compassion, an undifferentiated type of compassion towards all beings. But it is not only undifferentiated. There is a strong sense that 'I wish to protect.' It's engaged, it's taking on responsibility, taking on the burden."[44] Solidarity with the suffering or hermeneutical identification with the other is what McFague describes as "empathy for others that includes the responsibility to act."[45]

43. McFague, *Blessed Are the Consumers*, 125.
44. Ibid.
45. Ibid.

From a hermeneutical perspective of socially engaged Buddhism, there are three stages in the development of social praxis for transformational change: 1) mindful awareness, 2) deep or compassionate identification of the self and the world, and 3) engagement or contemplative action to respond to the world.[46] This threefold process of awareness or contemplative attentiveness, compassionate identification with suffering, and contemplative action to alleviate suffering, provides a personal, emotional, and spiritual context for environmental praxis. This process allows one to become attentive to the suffering of the Earth, empathetically enter into the suffering of the Earth or the specific life endangered by humanity; finally, I do something to assist or change the suffering. Jewish Zen teacher Bernie Glassman comprehends the need for decisive compassionate action: "If this is me, and it's bleeding, I take care of it. I don't mean join a discussion group or wait for the right equipment or wait until I am enlightened or go off to get trained. I immediately get some rags to stop the bleeding because it's me bleeding."[47] For engaged Buddhists, this threefold process provides the motivation for committing themselves to mindful social action for transformational change of society. They utilize the religious principles of non-violent action or the Buddhist principle not to harm, a state of equanimity to engage friend or foe with compassion, and stress on collective grassroots action. We find these principles in the writings of Buddhists committed to personal and social transformation. Similar principles are found in Boff and the Catholic stress on spiritual and personal solidarity in identification with the poor and the Earth. "Contemplative in action" has the same threefold dynamics as Engaged Buddhism. We take up the cause of the injured Earth or harmed creatures for compassionate action. An example for myself is Hosea 4:1-3 as the cries and mourning of the Earth and the prophet Hosea hears those cries.

> Hear the words of the Lord, O people of Israel, for the Lord has a case against the inhabitants of the land. There is no faithfulness and loyalty, and no knowledge of God in the land. Swearing, lying, murder and stealing and adultery break out; bloodshed follows bloodshed. Therefore, the land mourns, and who live in it languish, together with the wild animals and the birds of the air, even the fish of the sea.

46. Queen, "Introduction," 6–7.
47. Quoted in ibid., 7.

The text points to our need to carefully hear the cries of the Earth community today and empathetically give them voice to those unable to listen to the Earth. The ecojustice principles, in particular, the interconnected of Earth and all life and listening to the voice of the Earth, shifts our reading from an anthropocentric context or a history of anthropocentric biblical interpretation to counter-praxis of interpretation, or what Michel Foucault has termed the "insurrection of subjugated knowledges."[48] The voice of the Earth and the cries of the Earth community have been silenced by anthropocentric authors and interpretation. Our "green" conversion to an Earth perspective, realizing that we are members of the Earth community, generates an anthropocentric suspicion that motivates us to creative attentiveness searching for counter-intuitive readings of resistance to anthropocentrism and the development of alternative views. Hosea observes, that the land mourns over those who live in it languished. The prophet and the Earth indict "the inhabitants of the land with the charge there is no faith in the land no knowledge of God in the land." The Earth mourns the subversion of God's created order depicted poetically in the creation account of subduing and having dominion in Genesis 1:28. This time creation in the Hosea passage is reversed, from humanity to wild animals, the birds of the air, and the fish of the sea.

For 2015 Season of Creation, the last Sunday celebrated mountains. Prior to the scripture reading of Psalm 48 (Mt. Zion, God's holy mountain) and sermon, we included a centering prayer meditation; we showed the segment "Crimes Against Nature" from the video series, *Renewal*, we witness how mountain tops are wastefully harvested through explosions, toxic chemicals polluting the water table and streams harming humans and other life.[49] The testimony of the mother who bathes her child in water laced with arsenic and other toxins is poignant. We hear the cries of the land as the coal companies explode the mountain tops and the cries of animal and human life as they are displaced and poisoned by toxic chemical in the pollution of the streams and the water table. Here the poor are the cries of the Earth community and all life, human and non-human. They are the poor and vulnerable, and they are the ones to most suffer the climate changes from our over-addiction to fossil fuels. The poor always suffer while the wealthy have means to escape the ravages. What is significant is that we unpack the voice of the mountains in seeing

48. See, Goss, *Jesus ACTED UP*, 182–84.

49. *Renewal: Stories from America's Religion Environmental Movement* (DVD). http://www.interfaithpowerandlight.org/resources/films/.

the visual human devastation of mountain top removal and the sermon that spoke about the ravages of the mountain and its impact upon human and other life in the bioregion.

The third feature of ecological hermeneutics is retrieval. I want to distinguish the retrieval strategies of ecojustice readings from the evangelical and mainline Christian retrieval of God's word for environmental care. For Habel, retrieval is an engaged reading or liberative process related to the previous two processes. Retrieval involves exposing the anthropocentric dimension of a given text, the prejudice of past interpretations, or the anthropocentric bias of the reader. Liberative or ecojustice retrieval surfaces anthropocentric harm of the text, subsequent Christian interpretations, theologies, and practices. Such retrieval raises to awareness the anthropocentric culture of Earth violence and oppression, but the identification with marginalized or silenced Earth or Earth community produces counter-readings of resistance and hope. It can re-envision the Earth as subject rather than as secondary and unimportant background object.

The second aspect of identification within the retrieval process is discerning the voice of the earth or members of the Earth community. Habel asserts,

> Discerning Earth and members of the earth community as subject is a key part of the retrieval process. In some contexts, their voices are evident but have been traditionally ignored by exegetes. In other contexts, the voice of the Earth and Earth community is not explicit, but nevertheless present and powerful. These subjects play roles in the text that are more than mere scenery or secondary images. Their voices need to be heard. It is a voice that needs not correspond to the languages of words we community associate with human voice.[50]

The ecojustice interpreter can bring imaginative vision to the retrieval of the voice submerged in the text. Habel gives an example of listening to the voice of the Earth in Genesis 1, placing humanity as one many species in the chapter, and re-imaging the creation narrative told from the perspective of the Earth and with the Earth's voice.[51]

> I am Earth, I was first revealed when God summoned the primal waters to part. I came forth from the waters as a living domain

50. Habel, "Introducing Ecological Hermeneutics." 5.

51. Ibid., 5–8.

with the potential to give birth. I count this a great honor and grounds for celebration. I am a valuable part of the cosmos.

At the request of God, I brought forth, like a mother, all the flora that covers the land. I gave birth to vegetation that has the capacity to reproduce. After the flora that comes from within me is interconnected with me and is nurtured through me.

At the request of God, I also brought forth, like a mother, the fauna that live on the Earth. They are my offspring and depend upon me for subsistence. All fauna depends on the vegetation I produce for their survival and enjoyment of life. I am Earth, the source of daily life for the flora and fauna that I have generated from within me.

Sad to say, there is another story that has invaded my world, the story of the so-called god-image creatures called humans. Instead of recognizing that these god-image creatures are beings interdependent with Earth and other Earth creatures, this story claims that the god-image creatures belong to the superior riling class or species, thereby demeaning their nonhuman kin an diminishing their value. Instead of respecting me as their home and life source, the god-image creatures claim a mandate to crush me like an enemy or slave.

My voice needs to be heard, and the intrusive story about the humans in Gen. 1:26–28 named for what it is from my perspective: the creature of a group of power hungry humans.[52]

Habel re-envisions the Genesis creation account by discerning the voice of the Earth and imagines her perspective in retelling the story. The Earth unmasks the anthropocentrism of the Genesis verses to "subdue" and "have dominion" over her and the community of life. From the ecojustice interpretative lens, a counter-narrative is created to reveal a distorted human relationship to the Earth and is intended to motivate folks to cultivate an alternative relationship of interconnectedness with life and the Earth processes.

Green Hermeneutical Praxis

For years, I have been an exegetical activist for social justice causes and now for the Earth. I have engaged the biblical text for contemplation, pastoral practice, preaching and teaching, and theological writings; I am textually formed from my previous contemplative and interpretative

---

52. Ibid 8.

encounters of the biblical text as well as my personal commitments and social context. Hans Gadamer comments, "Understanding always involves something applying the text to be understood to the interpreter's present situation."[53] The so-called hermeneutical circle of encounter with the text unfolds in a "to and fro movement" between the interpreters who brings his/her interpretative context, skills, and imagination to the encounter. I bring my own theological interests—environmental knowledge and contemplative imagination, and my passion to the interpretative process. Together these strategies recognize the interrelated priorities of the poor and the Earth. It is the poor on the coastline, extreme deforestation in the Amazon for Northern Hemisphere's addiction to beef, or climate changes deepening drought, and the continued degradation of the Earth and continued toxic pollution of the environment. This is not readily apparent in the ecojustice context of the Earth Bible strategies. Theologian Paul Santmire writes.

> We Christians will be a voice for the voiceless for the sake of the creatures of nature who have no voice in human affairs. We will listen to the plaintiff cries of the great whales and hear the groaning of the forest, and we will be their advocates in the village square and in the courts of power, by the grace of God. All the more so, we will hear the bitter wailing of the little children who live on the trash mountains and who wear clothes that have been washed in streams overflowing with heinous poisons and who sometimes drink these waters.[54]

Norman Habel argues that the ecojustice hermeneutics needs the liberation strategies of Leonardo Boff: "We also need to hear the Scripture the voice of suffering nature itself. Leonardo Boff argues that we need to listen to 'the cry of the poor' and to 'the cry of the Earth.' This is critical reorientation in worship, namely, that we attune our ears to hear in Scriptures the voice of Earth. If God knows the fall of every sparrow, then 'who will speak for the sparrow?' Scripture does."[55] I have noticed that using the Season of Creation promoted by Norman Habel from the Earth Bible Team, clergy do not normally leave behind the anthropocentric features of Scripture when they preach about sky, mountains, forests, rivers, oceans, animals, and so on. Unless they understand with greater zeal that

53. Gadamer, *Truth and Method*, 306–7.

54. Santmire, *Nature Reborn*, 121.

55. Habel et al., eds., *The Season of Creation*, 34.

socio-economic dimensions of poverty and economic addiction to fossil fuels and unbridled myths of endless economic expansion, it is difficult to really pick up the voice of the underrepresented voice of the Earth or Earth element. It requires a thorough re-working of human understanding and individual self-understanding to an ecologically interrelated self as part of the earth community. My green spirituality impacts my textual encounter as it provides the textual formation of an ecological church. A praxis interpretation from an Earth-centered conversion is about radical re-orienting our reading perspective but also empowering change.

7

Greening the Heart of Faith

The Church is ecological.

—Sallie McFague[1]

Ecological conversion means falling in love with the Earth as inherently valuable, living community in which we participate, and bending every effort to be creatively faithful to its well-being, in tune with the living God who brought it into being and cherishes it with unconditional love.

—Elizabeth Johnson[2]

Ritual is a generalized category in comparative religion, inclusive of meditation and prayer, communal rituals and rites of passages, religious festivals, pilgrimage, various rites of passage, and sacraments. Ritual originates in mythic narratives that explain origins, destinies, and the meanings of life. It includes all forms of individual and communal religious practices from praying the rosary, yogic practices, prayer, Tai Chi, and sitting and walking meditation practices. Greening rituals can be an effective means of eco-conversion, individually and communally. Many

1. McFague, "The Church Is Ecological," 124.
2. Johnson, *Ask the Beasts*, 259.

of the ritual practices discussed here are ones that I used in the "greening" transformation of myself and the church that I served for twelve years. They become effective when used with climate change and environmental videos, outside speakers from an environmental organization, and educational programs. We need rituals to transform our hearts and change or "green" lifestyles, for "greening" indicates a change of heart born from God's grace embedded in a love for gift of the natural world and reverence for all life. Effective rituals can be used to facilitate the "ecological conversion" of individuals and communities from anthropocentricism to be embraced by the heart of the interrelated universe, encountering self-emptying divine love.

Christianity, like most religions, is well acquainted with conversion experience; we can jump to Saul of Tarsus on the road to Damascus and his dramatic conversion experience. We can include many in a lineage of conversions: St. Paul, Augustine, Francis of Assisi, Ignatius of Loyola, Martin Luther, Simone Weil, and Dorothy Day to name a few. My own conversion experience to Christianity was deepened through the thirty-day retreat in silence, mentored through Ignatius Loyola's *The Spiritual Exercises*. Ignatius begins his *Exercises* with a meditative consideration, "The Principle and Foundation."[3] This meditation allows one to realize creatureliness, generating a spiritual indifference, much like Buddhist equanimity that generates, "strong feelings of compassion for one's fellow creatures . . . (A)s one progressively acknowledges with gratitude and love, one's own creaturehood before God, one simultaneously experience one's interdependence with other creatues . . . Knowledge of one's true place in the world allows one to make room for others, to give others likewise a fair chance for existence and well-being."[4] This foundational practice finds its culmination in the contemplation for attaining love (*contemplation ad amorem*), where the heart of the universe, expressive and incarnated with self-emptying divine love, embraced my own heart and I discovered God's presence transparent in all things and all life. This was the spiritual roots of my own ecological conversion to nature. Contemplative practices deepened my awareness and connection to the natural world. It became a space of spiritual encounter and taught me to fall in love God's Earth and web of life.

3. Sears and Bracken, *Self-Emptying Love*, 24–33.
4. Ibid., 32–33.

Ecological Conversion

Larry Rasmussen sums up the need of our spiritual revolution:

> The long term task . . . is the conversion of Christianity to the Earth . . . It means experiencing the presence and power of none other or less than the God incarnate in the more than human universe that surrounds and surpasses the burning mysteries of our own fragile and precious lives, wherever they are lived. It means the embrace of Earth as the providing ground that is bone of our bone and flesh of our flesh and the only habitat for living the lives we can and desire to have . . . It means a practical everyday mysticism, an aesthetic, and an ethic that knows the gut and hearts as head that redemption of each creature is required for the redemption of all and the borders of all life, indeed of inorganic being and the galaxies themselves, all leak into the presence of God and bespeak the power of the same.[5]

His notion of conversion to the Earth is a break out experience from Christianity's alienation to the natural world. Catholic theologian Elizabeth Johnson offers her own description of ecological conversion: "Ecological conversion means falling in love with the Earth as inherently valuable, living community in which we participate, and bending every effort to be creative faithful to its well-being, in tune with the living God who brought it into being and cherishes it with unconditional love."[6] Hugh O'Donnell understands ecological conversion as "a call to contemplation."[7] This ecological conversion requires meditative awareness of nature as an interrelated web of life, discovering the Earth as God's handiwork and falling in love.

Norman Wirzba turns to the Orthodox Christian notion of ascetism as a practiced discipline of iconic perception: "By iconic I mean a perceptive approach to things in which others are not reduced to the scope of utilitarian and instrumental aims. In this mode of perception, people are called to open themselves to the integrity and sanctity of the world."[8] The iconic perception, described by Wirzba, is the disciplined contemplation of nature, which is transformed into a perception of nature as creation. It is to engage the natural world and see God's creation, but it is also to

5. Rasmussen, "The Church's Mission to Society," 526–27.

6. Johnson, *Ask the Beasts*, 272; Delio et al., *Care for Creation*, 182.

7. O'Donnell, *Eucharist and the Living Earth*, loc. 946.

8. Wirzba, *From Nature to Creation*, 70.

see the natural world as God sees it. Wirzba rightly describes what I call contemplation in action or Buddhist or mindfulness in compassionate action: "Put simply, we cannot learn to perceive the world as God's creation if we do not at the same time also learn to live in ways that make that kind of perception possible."[9]

Sallie McFague quotes the poet, Wallace Stevens: "Nothing is itself taken alone. Things are because of interrelations and interconnections."[10] American Christians almost always think of themselves as individuals, even when as members of a church community and even less so a part of the Earth. McFague calls for a new ecological literacy that moves us from our maps of individual ego-centeredness to a kinship model of interrelationality.[11] She encourages us to view immersed in the web of life, realizing how complex and wonderfully amazing this network of life invites us to claim our participation.

Catholic theologian Denis Edwards cites several descriptions of ecological conversions.[12] He cites Elizabeth Johnson's notion as the transformation from anthropocentricism: "Woven into our lives is the very fire from the stars and the genes from the sea creatures, and everyone, utterly everyone, is kin the radiant tapestry of being."[13] Edwards entitles the subtitle of his book: "The Change of Heart That Leads to a New Way of Living on the Earth." For Edwards, eco-conversion is a heart to heart relation with God and learning to love the Earth as God loves:

> Adopting the kinship model demands a form of conversion. It involves a new way of seeing and acting. It involves extending the law of neighbor to embrace creatures of other species. It involves extending the love of enemy to involve creatures that confront us as other and inspire fear in us. It involves loving and valuing others as God loves and values them. Ultimately, it is a God-centered (theocentric) view of an interconnected community of creatures that have their own intrinsic value.[14]

Edwards' notion of ecological conversion adopts a kinship model with humanity and other life, and McFague's kenotic spirituality specifies the

9. Ibid., 72.

10. McFague, *A New Climate for Theology*, 47.

11. Ibid., 48–56.

12. Edwards, *Ecology at the Heart of Faith*, 24–25.

13. Johnson, *Women, Earth and Creator Spirit*, 39.

14. Edwards, *Ecology at the Heart of Faith*, 24–25.

way of living out that conversion of falling in love with the Earth.[15] An Earth-centered conversion requires not only contemplative attention to the natural world but also involves the discipline of continual study of nature, learning about climate change, on-going ritual living to connect ourselves to the web of life, communal nurturing our change of heart, and practice responsible caring for the Earth as a sibling member. For full life-style transformation to an Earth-cenered spirituality, we need some discipline of contemplative practice to detach ourselves from ego-centeredness and involvement in action for Earthcare. For many of us, the transformation starts with ourselves and expands to our faith communities.

Communal Eco-Conversion

Sallie McFague makes the bold assertion: "If ecological catholicity is a mark of the church, it is central to the mission of the church, to preach the good news to all creation."[16] For McFague, "The (natural) world cannot be left out. The church must become ecological through and through." She claims that there is needed an additional mark to include in the traditional marks of the church—one, holy, catholic, and apostolic.[17] "Ecological" needs to become an additional mark by which a Christian church understands her mission. "Ecological literacy" is a means to a more profound self and communal transformation that Sallie McFague describes as *kenosis,* a self-emptying of self in humble and loving service. "Ecological conversion" or greening seems to me a better description of the process of individual transformation as well as the process of the grassroots transformation of the local church and hopefully beyond.

How do we make our faith communities lives less anthropocentric, more ecological? Individual eco-conversion is intertwined with ecclesial eco-conversion. How do we as individuals and members of a church and the Earth community transform ourselves to co-live with God's Earth? Frequently, it is one or couple of people motivated to commit themselves to Earthcare or environmental justice. It is easy for church eco-justice team to focus on specific issues to transform the church campus on a jour-ney of reducing a carbon footprint, environmental advocacy, planning an

15. McFague, *Blessed Are the Consumers,* 147–70.

16. McFague, "The Church Is Ecological," 126.

17. Ibid., 124–27.

Earth Day event, public seminars on water conservation, green coalition building with denominational environmental justice networks or Interfaith Power & Light.

Communal eco-conversion is similar to personal transformation, for the inner work includes contemplative engagement with the natural world. There is no universal or fixed guide for communal transformation. There are many ways to experience ecological grace, for it is inclusively available to everyone but each person's journey is distinct from others. It is an open way like spiritual mentoring that requires a creative pedagogy of ritual and discipline study and praxis to generate the conditions for ecological conversion. Matthew Fox understands the spiritual dimensions of contemplative creativity require various rituals to connect us to the divine presence:

> Creativity is intimate because it is most truly, spontaneously, and totally. It is also intimate because it is the Spirit through us in so profound a way that Eckhart says God "becomes the space where" we want to act . . . it is a place, a space, a gathering, a union, a where—wherein the Divine powers of creativity and the human power of imagination join forces. Where the two come together is where beauty and grace happen and, indeed, explode. Creativity constitutes the ultimate in intimacy, for it is the place where the Divine and the human are most destined to interact.[18]

Fox links creativity, imagination, art and ritual, play and meditation all intertwine as a space where God and us can ineract. Christian rituals can create incarnate space where Christ and the Spirit inhabit and where we may find in incarnate in ritual space within nature. Christian rituals have suffered Christian disconnection with nature. Fox turns to suggestions of Thomas Berry that "the universe . . . is 'the primary artist,' and it brings into being all our knowledge and our artistic and cultural achievements."[19] He quotes Berry, "In every phase of our imaginative, aesthetic, and emotional lives, we are profoundly dependent on this larger context of the surrounding world. There is no inner life without outer experience."[20]

For Fox and Berry, the human apartheid from the natural world is a tragic loss of soul; humanity has restricted their imaginations, emotions,

18. Fox, *Creativity*, 4.
19. Ibid., 43.
20. Ibid.

their contemplative lives, intellect, and creativity. Fox insightfully remarks, "The communion between creativity of the universe and our own
creativity is profound and continuous. We need to be constantly prod-
ded and provoked by the beauty and the aesthetics of the world around
us."[21] Our rituals return us to the natural world to engage God's creativity
and grace, creating an ecological space where God "becomes the space
where" we want to act." And that space is found in the natural world as
we ritually connect to interrelated grace. An Earth centered conversion
requires not only contemplative attention to the natural world but also
involves the adoption of a kinship model with the Earth community, continual appreciation, learning about climate change, communal nurturing
ge of heart, and a kenotic spirituality that embodies the way of living our
ecoconversion.[22]

Lectio Divina

We schedule a monthly walking an Earth-centered labyrinth, designed
after the pattern of the Chartres Cathedral but designed by my two Druid
friends, who painted an Earth-centered design on a large canvas, with
stepping stones, green vines and occasional flowers. My instructions in a
hand out for walking the labyrinth are very specific: "Our labyrinth dif-
fers from the geometric pattern labyrinths. As a Green Church committed to Right Relations with the Earth and with much of our electric usage
generated by solar panels, we had an earth-centered labyrinth designed
with stepping stones, the four directions, and green vegetation. Each
time you walk our labyrinth, we ask you to also walk for healing human
relations with the Earth and for world peace." Labyrinth meditation is
similar to Zen mindful walking but with the formality of the labyrinth
structure. Originally, the labyrinth practice in Christian practice is traced
back to the inability of Medieval Christians to undertake pilgrimage to
the Holy Land because of the Crusades. The labyrinth practice was a
meditative journey or symbolic pilgrimage, and it was encapsulated into
three meditation stages: purgation, illumination, and union. Walking to
the center is a purgative, shedding ego-centeredness. At the center, one
rests receptively in a place of illuminated wordless exchange with God,

21. Ibid., 43–44.

22. McFague includes her earlier notion of ecological literacy with a kenotic spirituality. McFague, *Blessed Are the Consumers*, 147–70.

and in retracing steps meditatively, one brings back that intimate union with God into ordinary space and time.

I and the church gardener have graduated from the monthly practice to daily mindful walking or sitting in church garden. Labyrinth meditation practice became a training ground for listening for God's presence within nature for several of us. The garden has become the labyrinth where we practice *lectio divina* of the plants and trees.

Lectio divina was a Christian contemplative practice arising in proto-monastic communities of the Desert Fathers and Mothers, where meditative reading the scriptural text aloud and slowly for several times and let the words or even a single word or an individual image may catch your attention and speak to you.[23] It led to the Desert Mothers and Fathers mindfully attending the flow of emotions and thoughts in their lives or applying the same contemplative awareness to their desert environment. The meditative dynamics in *lectio divina* of a scriptural text can be transferred to the natural world or landscapes in specific locales. Often times focusing on one specific aspect of the natural setting is helpful in becoming attentive to what God is saying in nature. I walk the garden as I do the labyrinth, and I am amazed as the discovery of the bloom of roses or an exotic cactus blossom or the beautiful display of orange or purple colors of the bougainvillea plants. There I encounter God as Gardener, and I find myself in the midst of democracy of living plants and ecological grace. *Lectio divina* has been transferred to walking in forests or botanical gardens, or the dog park as I bring my companion Friskie to play and socialize with other dogs. The range of meditative practices can expand from simple paying attention to our natural surroundings and finding God there.

Lectio Divina: Nature and Bible

Preaching engages the scriptural text with green hermeneutical strategies, chapter, exegetical work to reconstruct the various levels of the text (original content, context, author and/or editor), engagement from one's own personal context and ecolocation, reconfiguring the text to be applied to the congregation. In *lectio divina*, I add the additional meditative

23. *Lectio Divina* includes four stages of the flow of meditation practice: *lectio* (Reading and Listening), *meditatio* (Meditation), *oratio* (Prayed), and *contemplatio* (Contemplation). This trains an individual for Christian centering prayer.

dynamic of encountering the text with an openness to be transformed. Slow repetitious reading allows the reader to pay attention to the flow of words or a particular word of image. It leads to reflective thought connecting emotions, imagination, and creativity to listen and learn from the encounter with particular text. The Protestant reformer Martin Luther remarked, "God writes the Gospel, not in the Bible alone, but also on trees, and flowers, and clouds and stars."[24] My normal *lectio divina* practice is included for "green" sermons. It led me to pay attention to the ecological location of Jesus, comprehend the green cross and the risen Christ as Gardener, and the practicing contemplation with nature.

Ecologically based spiritual immersion is elaborately described by Douglas Christie as "contemplative ecology":

> The term *contemplative ecology* suggests . . . that there is a way of thinking about spiritual practice that has an ecological character, or a way of thinking about ecology that includes reflection on the moral or spiritual dimensions of experience . . . The aim of contemplative living, in its wider application, is to address the fragmentation and alienation that haunts existence at the deepest possible level and, through sustained practice, come to realise a different, more integrated way of being in the world.[25]

Christie understands Christian contemplation going back to the desert ascetics and developed in the monastic tradition as a particular way of seeing and whose goal is the vision of God. It starts in the ancient contemplative tradition with its profound commitment to the simple practice of *prosoche* or attentiveness or listening. And often this meditative attentiveness was directed to the natural world:

> To orient oneself toward the non-human, to give one's conscious attention fully and deeply to a place, an animal, a tree, or a river is already to open oneself to relationship and intimacy with another. It is to see and feel the presence of the Other not as object, but as a living subject. To experience this Other as part of 'a larger whole,' part of the vibrant and complex ecology, and to seek to immerse oneself in that larger whole, is to open oneself to the larger whole completely without reservation.[26]

24. Quoted in Abbate, *Gardening Eden*, 114.
25. Christie, *The Blue Sapphire of the Mind*, 17, 36.
26. Ibid., 7; Habel, *Rainbow of Mysteries*.

This attentiveness has been found not only Christian contemplatives of the natural world, but Christie takes pains to document how poets such as Wordsworth, evolutionary attentiveness of Charles Darwin, or naturalists such John Muir practice or Rachel Carson practice ecological contemplation.[27]

The naturalist John Muir understood the natural world as scripture. He wrote, "Here were miles and miles of scripture along the sky, a bible that will one day be read. The beauty of its letters and sentenced burned me like fire, through all these Sierra seasons."[28] Muir saw Jesus' beatitudes "channeled "by winds, falling water; thunderheads, and whispered by a thousand, thousand small still voices of birds and plants."[29] Stephen Hatch remarks about the contemplative approach of Muir to nature: "Taking a contemplative perspective, we read Muir as a monk would read the sacred scriptures ruminating on each phrase until it reeals its meaning for our lives. In common with contemplatives the world over, we can experience this meaning in terms of union with the divine."[30] Muir encountered the Sierra Mountains as scripture, and though he was raised as a Scottish Calvinist Christian, he developed naturally a *lectio divina* or contemplative encounter in experiencing God within the natural world.

When I combine *lectio divina* of the natural world with that of the scripture text, we find a conflation of the ecological location in the scriptural text with the ecological context for preaching. When I preach on ecological theme, I often bring the two together. I can imagine and visualize, for example, Jesus in the wilderness for forty days. I heard many sermons about Jesus in the wilderness from the temptation scenes in Q but none on Jesus' experience of the wilderness. Sean McDonagh observes, "It was during this sojourn in the desert that Jesus came to accept and appreciate his messianic ministry he was about to embrace. In order to be fully open and receptive to his call, Jesus forsook the company of people and spent time with the wild animals in the wilderness."[31] Jesus may have separated himself from human contact, but he immersed himself in the wilderness or what Sean McDonagh poetically describes as

27. Abram, *The Spell of the Sensuous.*

28. Worster, *A Passion for Nature,* 329.

29. Hatch, *The Contemplative John Muir,* loc. 1007.

30. Ibid., loc. 196. See "The Natural World Is a Scripture," in ibid., 959–1036.

31. Ibid., 29; McDonagh, *Greening the Christian Millennium,* 17.

"the cathedral of nature."[32] I envision Jesus entering the wilderness, and I ask, "What did Jesus hear from the wilderness?" He learned much about God's wild grace. There in the wilderness community, Jesus forged his vision of God's empowered companionship. Ecological contemplation brings a familiarity of God's presence in the natural world; it becomes the locus of grace and learning. Thus, Richard Bauckham cites the work of C. H. Dodd, Claus Westermann, and Sean Freyne, who comprehend Jesus' parables as drawn from nature and note his close experience of God's presence in creation.[33] Sean Freyne states, "The parables are products of the religious imagination that is deeply grounded in the world of nature and the human struggle with it, and at the same time deeply rooted in the traditions of Israel which speak of God as creator of heaven and earth and all that is between them."[34] Jesus prepared his message about God's reign from his meditative experience of nature.

For my sermon preparation, Jesus in the wilderness and in a place of solitude at night becomes a model for bringing the natural world into sermons. I live and pray the text for at least a week. I pray to the Spirit to assist my ministry of encountering the word. Beyond normal exegetical practices, I add contemplative techniques: *lectio divina*, imaginative placement into the narrative, and the use of the scripture for contemplation. All three stages of prayerful engagement often take place in the church garden. And the natural setting become sacred space to find God and listen to God's word.[35] Listening to nature and the scriptural text in wilderness (natural parks) and in gardens, I experienced God's grace ecologically. The garden has taught me that God continues life in surprising ways even when plants seem to die. There is surprising resilience to life

Let me conclude this section with formative experience of attentiveness of geologian Thomas Berry describes a pivotal moment of grace that became foundational for his commitment to Earthcare:

> At the time I was eleven years old. My family was moving from
> a more settled part of a small southern town out to the edge
> of town where the new house was being built. The house, not
> yet finished, was situated on a slight incline. Down below was
> a small creek and there across the creek was a meadow. It was

32. McDonagh, *Greening the Christian Millennium*, 17.

33. Bauckham, *Living with Other Creatures*, loc. 1784–1901.

34. Ibid., loc. 1733; Freyne, *Jesus, a Jewish Galilean*, 59; Eichlin, *Earth Spirituality*, 76.

35. Campolo and Darling, *The God of Intimacy and Action.*

an early afternoon in late May when I first wandered down the incline, crossed the creek, and looked out over the scene. The field was covered with white lilies rising above the thick grass. A magic moment, this experience gave to my life something that seems to explain my thinking at a more profound level than almost any other experience I can remember. It was not only the lilies. It was the singing of crickets and the woodlands in the distance and the clouds in a clear sky.[36]

Here described is the moment of grace that began the ecological conversion of Thomas Berry, who felt a deep sense of belonging to the universe and the goodness of the Earth, this event shaped his destiny as a priest, geotheologian, and lover of Earth and all life. In any retreat or instruction on connecting with nature, it is good to canvas what similar grace moments of nature have had. This past Lent I invited my church to choose a plant in the garden, to listen and experience a relationship, to apply the tools of *lectio divina* or meditative awareness to the plant. What I discovered is that many folks have found their favorite rose, cactus, or native plant that they now regularly visit each Sunday.

Following Jesus into wilderness experiences, the wilderness, even in the tame experiences of botanical gardens or in a church garden, can instruct us about God's grace and word. Some church folks for the season of creation joined myself in a meditative walk in Descanso Botanical Garden in Los Angeles. Promoting such meditative connections open us to an on-going incarnational conversion, finding the cosmic Christ in the heart of nature and discovering the green word in scripture.

Greening the Pulpit and the Liturgical Seasons

Both the word and sacraments are interwoven church rituals in the life of the church, and if a church is to become ecological, its word and sacramental life must also retrieve its ecological origins. Susan Bond observes, "Preaching is a sacramental activity that makes Christ present to the community . . . Preaching is nothing more and nothing less than the invocation of the dangerous memory, the subversive presence, and the transformed future of the God we know in Jesus Christ."[37] Preaching

36. Berry, *The Great Work*, 12. See also the Center for Education, Imagination, and the Natural World, https://www.beholdnature.org/beingbeholdingbelonging.php.

37. Bond, *Trouble with Jesus*, 150.

is sacramental through the ritual efficacy of proclaiming the word and unpacking the word for today and invoking the dangerous memories of Jesus. Spirit and Logos are the two modes of God operative the world, and they make present the subversive presence of the risen Christ through remembering proclaimed word in the Spirit. Likewise, the sacramental word—the symbolic action of the memorial narrative of Jesus from the Last Supper includes a proclamation and symbolic re-enactment of the dangerous memories of Jesus as subversive grace. Christ becomes present in the word and in the symbolic sacrament "through a remembering of faith with power of the Spirit."

Preaching at least seven to ten times during the liturgical year on climate change as well as our responsibilities to care for the Earth is necessary for ecological conversion and formation of the congregation.[38] If we are not doing this on a regular basis, clergy will soon find themselves in the predicament of preaching on climate change every couple weeks in the near future as the severe weather events and their frequency impact us and disaster relief assistance fatigue sets in our churches. Paul Santmire's issues a cautionary warning about the frequency that congregations need to hear stories of creation and care of the Earth:

> Unless the preachers of the church persistently and imaginatively and forcefully tell the cosmic story of faith in their sermons and in their teaching, the whole case of liturgy that is ecologically and socially formative, according to the cosmic Word of God, could easily be lost. The faithful need to hear the whole biblical story told and retold in this manner so that they can see with new eyes the ministration of the cosmic Word of God in their own midst, especially in the sacraments of baptism and Eucharist, and know, too, that it is Christ himself who addresses them as the proclaimed Word.[39]

One Sunday early in the year is the National Preach-In against Global Warming, aligned with Evolutionary Science, during February. We join interfaith communities to sponsor a preach-in or a community event on climate change.[40] I have often use the occasion to invite guest preachers. Druid friends, an outside clergy, or advocate from a green organization adds a different voice for Earthcare. Additional outside

38. Schade, *Creation-Crisis Preaching*.

39. Santmire, *Revitalizing Nature*, 143.

40. Interfaith Power and Light provides resources for the preach-in. http://www.preachin.org/.

green voices and testimonies reinforce the church's commitment to environmental spirituality and Christian Earthcare.

This past Lent we promoted a day long series of community workshops for the greater community on water conservation, converting from grass lawns to semi-arid plants, and individual household water conservation. The severity of the drought in Calfornia has forced water conservation measures on citizens. The water conservation day full of workshop was well attended and sponsored by community conservation groups such as the Tree People, the Theodore Payne Society, and other groups on water conservation. I preached on water justice and the drought as well introducing the congregation to water conservation as spiritual Lenten practice for forty days, and it continued as a congregational and individual spiritual practice beyond the season of Lent.

Easter or Paschal Triduum (Maundy Thursday, Good Friday, and Easter Sunday) are the core of Christian Faith. We invite a neighborhood Disciples of Christ church for our Maundy Thursday Green Seder for the oppressed Earth, and on the next night to celebrate a joint Tenebrae service that remembers Christ's passion in suffering poor and Earth. It is easy to create for the Seder a new set of ten plagues afflicting the Earth community and look to healing the Earth.[41] For the Tenebrae, we modify the traditional stations of the cross for the passion and crucifixion of the Earth and the vulnerable with slides to visual considerations for each station and a response in song and prayer from the community.[42] For myself, Easter Sunday with the story of Mary Magdalene visit to the empty tomb and her mistaken Jesus for the Gardener lends itself to stressing , God and Christ as Gardeners, our vocation as gardeners of the Earth, and the cosmic ministry of Christ's Resurrection.[43] Easter is the ecological celebration that empowers our vocation to care compassionately for the garden of the Earth. Mary Magdalene becomes not only the apostle of the

41. A basic format is provided by The Shalom Center: https://theshalomcenter. org/haggadah-for-the-earth.

42. Fox and Andrus, *The Visionary Stations of the Cosmic Christ*; Cuthbertson, "An Earth Tenebrae: A Liturgy for the Vernal Equinox," http://www.earthspirituality. org/rituals/An%20Earth%20Tenebrae.pdf; the Columban Fathers have an environmental and ecological stations of the cross: http://columban.org/11414/columban-center-for-advocacy-and-outreach/economic-and-ecological-way-of-the-cross/. The Green Sisters or Sisters of the Earth have included labyrinth walks and Earth Stations into their forms of embodied prayer in nature: See Taylor, *Green Sisters*, 231–59.

43. Shore-Goss, "Easter is the Source of Our Green Faith."

resurrection and commissioned to garden but also the second century community that produced the Gospel of Mary stands alone in its emphasis on healing and reconciliation. It reminds us that our prime mission to heal ourselves and repair the damage to the Earth.

The Season of Creation is an optional season, ecumenically practiced, that starts with Creation Day, September 1st, the four Sundays of September and ends with the commemoration of St. Francis Assisi's feast day and his blessing of the animals on the first Sunday of October. The Season of Creation turns our liturgical attention in preaching and ritual to God's relationship with all creation and with our relationship with creation.[44] For our experience in the Valley church, it is a wonderful season to appreciate and become mindful of our connection with God in creation. You take elements of the Earth as the context for preaching: water, mountains, the Earth, and so on, and it is an opportunity to introduce Earth-centered rituals into the Sunday liturgy.

Sacraments

Sacraments and the numbers have varied from churches. Roman Catholic Church identified seven at the Council of Trent while the Reformation Churches maintained two. The Orthodox Churches use the Greek term "mysteries" for the Roman Catholic "sacraments." They overlap with many of the sacraments in the Latin Church. For my theological schema, I understood two families of sacraments: baptism and Eucharist. The rest might be folded in as ritual extensions of these two sacraments.

Sacraments were defined in early Catholic education as visible signs of invisible God's grace. Through the millennia, sacraments have been removed from their natural elements, with theological Midrash. The natural elements include water, oil, bread and wine, the human body, the cycles of life (birth, marriage, ordination, sickness and death). Theologian John Hart offers a definition of natural sacrament: "A natural sacrament is a place, event, or creature in nature that as a sign of Spirit's immanence and presence, draws people toward the Spirit and simultaneously invites them to relate not only to the Spirit but to all living and nonliving creation."[45] His definition of natural elements includes food (human

---

44. A helpful resource is Habel et al., eds., *The Season of Creation*.

45. Hart, *Sacramental Commons*, xiv.

made from harvesting and human effort), for the sacramental elements need to be embedded in the material reality of the natural world that we inhabit and celebrate. Dutch Dominican scholar Edward Schillebeeckx called Jesus "the sacrament of the encounter with God."[46]

As we integrate sacraments with nature and the cosmos, we develop a spirituality that is intertwined with notions of a sacramental universe and sacramental commons. Again let me tap Hart's definitions:

> *Sacramental universe* and *sacramental commons* express complementary perceptions of divine immanence in, and engagement with humanity through, the created universe. A *sacramental universe* is the totality of creation infused with the visionary, loving, creative and active power of the Spirit's transcendent-immanent and creating presence. A *sacramental commons* is creation as a moment and locus of human participation in the interactive presence and caring compassion of the Spirit who is immanent and participates in a complex cosmic dance of energies, elements, entities, and events. It is a place in which people in historical time integrate meaning of the *sacramental* with the social meaning of *commons* and, and consequently is characterized by a community consciousness that stimulates involvement in concrete efforts to restore and conserve ecosystems.[47]

What John Hart describes as the levels of sacramental moments, events, and locations is oriented to a ritual and meditative connection with the Earth, all life, and the cosmos. It is the subject on what we discuss previously and now with discussion on baptism and Eucharist. My intentions are to restore Christian sacraments to their natural elements to comprehend profound connections to the incarnate Christ and the presence/activity of the Spirit. For if we are connected to the transforming opportunities of such sacramental celebrations, two consequences may result: 1) It becomes a sacramental pattern for viewing Christ with the natural elements of the world, 2) We can celebrate sacraments connected to physical world, re-centering us into an incarnational spirituality rather the discarnational spiritualities that disvalue the body and the world for the spiritual.

46. Schillebeeckx, *Christ*.

47. Hart, *Sacramental Commons*, xvviii (italics original). Hart uses sacramental to reconnect Christian ethic actions to live and experience and act justly toward the Earth and the community of life. He derives much of his spirituality from Francis of Assisi, Leonardo Boff, and indigenous peoples (ibid., 23–57).

Baptism

Jesus traveled to John the Baptist from Nazareth in Galilee because he heard of John's ministry. Jesus entered the waters at the edge of the wilderness where the wild baptizer immersed him in the flowing currents of the Jordan River. He entered the wildness of the river. His baptism is not just a ritual cleansing for sin; it is a unique conversion moment whereby Jesus connected with the Earth Spirit and experienced the revelation as a beloved child of Abba.[48] The sensible world of natural elements placed him in touch with the transfigured mystery of God's Spirit ensouled in the waters. And it did this for Jesus as he entered unclothed into the waters of the Jordan. The life-giving waters and the ensouled Spirit bathe the body of Jesus in the radiance of God's abundant life, and water surrounding his body form an Earth covenant.

Water is an important natural symbol in all of the world religions because every living creature depends upon water to live. Our bodies contain 60–70% water. Hydration of our bodies is essential to life. Water is a richly complex substance without which there would be no life on Earth as we know it. Water is the Earth's blood, its vitality, and water then becomes literally part of our blood flowing through our bodies and most of other life. There is an intimate symbolic connection with water and life. Without water, there is no life, yet water has the power to destroy as well as to create.

Water becomes a Christian symbol through Jesus' baptism in the Jordan River. In a baptismal sermon, Tertullian shares, "Christ is never without water."[49] The Jordan becomes a cosmic incarnational symbol. Edward Echlin writes, "When Jesus enters the Jordan, the waters and the creatures, dependent upon water, are sanctified by the presence of God's Word. All waters are connected—water is like the blood of the earth. All waters are cosmic Jordan. All waters are Jordanised, sanctified, recreated by the Spirit again moves over the waters at the baptism of Jesus."[50] Christ's grace—like living water—reaches every pore of our bodies, the bodies of creatures and plant-life, into the soils of the earth, with the rains from heaven falling on to the soil, in the wells and oasis streams, in bub-

48. Brown, *Tradition and Inspiration*, 282.

49. Echlin, *The Cosmic Circle*, 79.

50. Ibid., 78. See Echlin's whole chapter on the cosmic Jordan, 77–88. See also McDonnell, *The Baptism of Jesus in the Jordan*; and Robinson "Sanctified Waters."

bling springs and rivers, lakes, and the oceans that comprised much of our planet. Jesus becomes interrelated with the waters of the Earth. He becomes a microcosm of the Earth alive. Every particle of water in our bodies and other creatures, in the streams, rivers, lakes, oceans, aquifers, and rains is sanctified and consecrated with the incarnational presence of Christ in the earthly waters. The orthodox Syrian bishop Jacob of Serugh claims, "The entire nature of the waters perceived that you had visited them—seas, deeps, rivers, springs and pools all thronged together to receive the blessing from your footsteps."[51] Many Christian writers have comprehended the baptism of Jesus as the beginning of the new creation and new birth for us, but baptism recognizes that we are the blood of the Earth and the incarnated Christ in our flesh. We are creatures of the Earth, and we carry the Spirit in our fleslhy lives.

In *A Watered Garden*, Benjamin Stewart details four eco-theological characteristics of water for baptism: waters of life as an oasis, living water as pouring and flowing, pooled waters as mysterious depths, and a place that welcomes what we might call the untamed or wild nature of water.[52] Jesus reminds us of the mystery of living water and its connection to Earth Spirit in conversation with the Samaritan woman. Jesus speaks in John's Gospel of the living water from God's abundance that is able to renew and sanctify all of creation. "Everyone who drinks this water will become thirsty again. Anyone, who drinks the water, I give will never become thirsty again. The water I give him will become a spring of water, springing up to eternal life" (John 4:14). Jesus uses the image of water as indispensable to life, then he points to himself as the 'living water' which he offers eternal life. Water is vital to human and all life, and in dry or desert climates, water becomes an oasis of life. Baptismal waters give life to us, and Jesus becomes an oasis of water. We need to have plants and stones in areas when we baptize anyone, and this means our garden oasis becomes a more appropriate place for baptism—with its water and plant features.

The second ecological feature is the symbol of living waters as flowing. That day as Jesus entered the flowing waters of the Jordan, he understood the action that John performed as entering into the waters of God's life. Stewart observes, "When new Christians are made in flowing baptismal, all of those associations—the overflowing blessings of God, the

51. Jacob of Sarugh. Quoted in Echlin, *Cosmic Circle*, 70.
52. Stewart, *A Watered Garden*, 27.

nourishing water over landscape, the always new quality of flowing water, and the life-giving power that flows to us from beyond our control—wash over the newly baptized and deepen our significance of baptism."[53] The baptism of Jesus and our own baptism into Christ communicates vividly the ecological goodness and connectedness of God's creation. The third ecological characteristic is the mysterious depths of pooled waters, great lakes, and oceans. Deeply pooled waters hold mysteries, and we cannot fathom the full depth of the dangers and the euphoric experience of connecting with life infinitely greater than ourselves but intimately weaves all life together in a grace-filled ecology on interrelatedness. Such deep and great pools remind us that the Holy Spirit hovered over the primal oceans of the earth billions of years to create a spark of cellular life. Above the waters of the Jordan, God appeared to Jesus in the form of a dove, the Holy Spirit, the Earth Spirit. Earth Spirit ensouls Herself in us and Earthly elements.

Many early Christian writers understood Jesus' baptism had ecological significance of water as the bearer of the Spirit. Maybe we should recapture this notion that as Jesus was immersed in the Jordan waters and surfaced that he was linked to the Spirit as the beloved child of God and child of the earth. The Spirit led him into the wilderness where Jesus grew closer to the Earth Spirit. In the baptismal waters and wilderness experience, God transformed the Jesus into the beloved child and the prophet of compassion, leading back to begin the ministry to preach the good news to the poor, the sick, and the oppressed.

Stewart understands the fourth characteristic as the welcoming the untamed waters. When Jesus was immersed into the Jordan River, his hair was messed up and his body dripping wet. Stewart writes, "Baptism into Christ is a radical thing; it profoundly rearranges your life. The water, poured out, disrupted the careful grooming and neatness of the baptismal party as if something of the wilderness baptism of John had flowed."[54] The waters of the river Jordan represented death of an old self and new birth from the waters of the Spirit. It was a moment of revelatory disruption and personal transformation. When we welcome the living waters of the Earth, the wildness or untamed Spirit that led Christ to the Jordan and into the wilderness, this practice also infuses us with the Spirit's wildness, who works outside orthodoxies as Jesus became a

53. Ibid., 29.
54. Ibid., 31.

religious rule breaker with his upside/down kin-dom. This feature may unleash some out of the box and compassionate action for ecojustice. Christian baptism links to the commitment to water justice.[55]

Whenever possible we perform baptismal rites in the garden or in the sanctuary with redwood burl altar with the sanctuary opens to spectacular burst of colors from the garden. In my baptismal rite, I ask the godparents: "Do you promise to reverence the Earth that God created and teach (child's name) how much God loves the Earth and all life? And teach (the child) to love to the Earth and all life?" I baptize the child into the Earth Spirit and the incarnate Christ. Our baptism into the waters of Christ is baptism into the experience that Jesus had the Jordan River, stressing his ministerial and incarnational responsibility towards God's creation. We are linked by baptism to the body of Christ and that body of Christ is linked to the elements of the Earth, water, clean air. Our baptism stresses that we are entrusted with mission to protect and co-live with the Earth, the waters of the Earth, the air we breathe. The Earth Spirit who appeared at the baptism of Jesus continues to baptize us into the waters and call us explicitly to work for water justice and water rights. I have found that Christian parents, who love and care for the Earth, want their child baptized in a green church and outside. Restoring an ecological dimension to baptism holds promise for celebrating new life on God's beloved Earth, but it celebrates hope for sustained life and makes sustainability a virtue for which parents, family members, and community can commit themselves to the restoration of the natural world.

Eucharist: The Ecological Imagination

I became acquainted with the writings of the Jesuit paleontologist and mystic Pierre Teilhard de Chardin at a young age. I used sections of Teilhard's *Divine Milieu* and *Hymn of the Universe* for my daily spiritual reading and meditation. It was decades ago that a few Jesuits and myself read the Teilhard's Mass of the World on the rocks of Gloucester (MA) on the Atlantic Ocean. While in the Ordos Desert in Mongolia on the Feast of the Transfiguration in 1923, Teilhard de Chardin neither had the elements of bread and wine nor the altar vessels for the celebration of the Eucharist. He contemplatively celebrated the Eucharist by envisioning

55. The United Nations on the Human Right for Water: http://www.un.org/waterforlifedecade/human_right_to_water.shtml.

the Earth as his altar and the toil and work of the day as the Eucharist elements of bread and wine.

Teilhard's Eucharistic imagination is primarily incarnational and simultaneously ecological. The incarnation of Christ is deeply embedded with the Earth and physical matter. He is driven by spirituality influenced the Ignatian Exercises, and in particular, the contemplation for divine love (*contemplatio ad amorem*), which stresses that God's love shines down on us like the rays of the sun, permeating everything. It is the pinnacle of Jesuit spirituality finding God in everything and becoming a contemplative in action. Denis Edwards writes,

> He (Teilhard) sees the power of God at work in Christ and present in the Eucharist as transforming the Earth from within. Because the Word is made flesh, no part of the physical universe is untouched. All matter is the place of God. All is being divinized. All is being transformed in Christ: "Through your own incarnation, my God, all matter is henceforth incarnate." Because of this, Earth, the solar system and the whole universe become the place for encounter with the risen Christ: "Now, Lord, through the consecration of the world, the luminosity and fragrance which suffuse the universe take on for me the lineaments of a body and a face—in you."[56]

In his communion prayer of the Mass, he stretches his hand to touch the fire of Christ within the heart of the world as fiery bread and then to taste it in communion:

> To take it is, I know, to surrender myself to the forces which will tear me away painfully from myself in order to drive me into danger, into an austere detachment where my affections are concerned. To eat it is to acquire a taste and affinity for that which is everything is above everything—a taste and affinity which will henceforward make impossible for me all the joys by which life has been warmed. Lord Jesus, I am willing to be possessed by you, to be bound to your body and led by its inexpressible power towards solitary heights which by myself never dare to climb.[57]

Here Teilhard's communion prayer unites his incarnational vision of Christ deeply ingrained in the Earth with an ecological vision of the contemplation or divine love, finding Christ interrelated and interconnected.

56. Edwards, *Ecology at the Heart of Faith*, 104. Internal note; Teilhard, "Mass," 24.

57. Teilhard, "Mass," 30.

He loses his center, "tear me away painfully from myself," to "affinity for that which is everything and above everything." It is a joyful communion or transfiguration of the self into a wider ecological and spiritual communion with everything and simultaneously with Christ, the fire of all matter. Teilhard de Chardin's Eucharistic imagination extends to nature—with his self, decentered into a cosmic web of evolutionary life.

His comment in the Mass, "I firmly believe that everything around me is the body and blood of the Word," was formative of incarnational theology and stretched my Eucharistic imagination to include nature.[58] The eucharist becomes an incarnational, ecological sacrament for myself.

Matthew Fox has developed a Cosmic Mass, a post-modern celebration and Eucharist event.[59] Hew writes about his experience of the Cosmic Mass experience:

> There was beauty going on wherever I looked. It was like being in a forest, where every direction displayed beauty and something interesting to behold. This included not only the singers, dancers and rappers, but also the projections on large video screens, on television sets, on a huge globe suspended over the beautiful altars (one a sun altar, the second a crescent-moon altar). On the screens were hummingbirds hovering, galaxies spinning, flowers opening, human beings marching, protesting, embracing, and polluting (sin was present and indeed renamed for us at the mass). Life was there in all its panoply of forces, good and not so good, human and more than human.[60]

I participated in Fox's Cosmic Mass in an abbreviated form at the 2015 Parliament of World Religions. It is a blend of the four stages of Christian spirituality outlined in his book *Original Blessing*: *via positiva*, *via negativa*, *via creativa*, and *via transformativa*.[61] It blends spirituality with youth raves, techno-music, and dancing. The Cosmic Mass also includes a DJ plus multi-media visuals on screens, physical (yogic postures) and ends off with fifteen minutes of dancing to drumming rhythmic beats within the music for dance and carrying Earth figures of animals and the Planet. It was a shamanic-style dance with a commitment to become

58. Ibid., 27.

59. Fox, *Original Blessing*; Fox, "Finding the Divine Everywhere"; Fox, *Creativity*, 224–27.

60. The quotation is an excerpt from *Confessions*: http://thecosmicmass.com/the-history/.

61. Fox, The Vision of the Cosmic Mass, http://thecosmicmass.com/the-vision/

"warriors" protecting the Earth. I envisioned myself as deer in a forest. This style of Eucharist liturgy has the potential to pull millennials and spiritually non-affiliated folks into non-traditional worship that appeal to their sense of community, club dancing, and incarnational Earthcare.

Other ecumenical theologians and even interfaith authors have connected ecology to the Eucharist.[62] The celebration of the Eucharist provides a contemplative arena for ecological imagining and reflection. Tony Kelly expresses one such notion:

> The Eucharistic imagination thus animates its own ecological perspectives. Everything has its part in God's creation; everything has been owned by the divine Word in the Incarnation; everything is involved in the great transformation already begun in the resurrection. We are bound together in a giving universe, at the heart of which is the self-giving love of God: "Unless a grain of wheat falls into the earth and dies, it remains just a single grain, but if it dies, it bears much fruit" (John 12:24). We are living and dying into an even larger selfhood to be realized in a network of relationships pervading the whole of the universe and reaching even into the Trinitarian relationships that constitute the very being of God.[63]

The death and resurrection is embedded in the intersections of incarnational theology sacramental memory of the church in John 12:24. It expresses interrelatedness and interconnections of the conditions and causality in the process of life, which Thich Nhat Hanh describes with his term "interbeing." The Eucharist gifts at the altar interrelate with past, present, and future. The gifts of bread and wine originate from the gift of nature and the gift of human toil. Thich Nhat Hanh comprehends the Eucharist as an example of mindfulness in which Jesus attempts to awaken his disciples to life and its connectedness:

> When a priest performs the Eucharistic rite, his role is to bring life to the community. The miracle happens not because he says the word correctly, but because we eat and drink mindfulness. Holy Communion is a strong bell of mindfulness. We drink and

62. Edwards, *Ecology at the Heart of Ecology*, 99–118; Kelly, *Bread of God:* loc. 1686–2000. Theokritoff, *Living in God's Creation:* 155–210; Theokritoff, "The Cosmology of the Eucharist," 131–35; Patriarch Batholomew, *Cosmic Grace*, 156–57, 162–63, 200–201, 288–89. From a Buddhist-Christian perspective, see Bruteau, "Eucharistic Ecology and Ecological Spirituality," http://www.crosscurrents.org/eucharist.htm.

63. Kelly, *Bread of God*, loc 1919–1928.

eat all the time, but we usually ingest only our ideas, projects, worries, and anxiety. We do not really eat our bread or drink our beverage. If we allow ourselves to touch our bread deeply, we become reborn, because our bread is life itself. Eating deeply, we touch the sun, the earth, and everything in the cosmos. We touch life, as we touch the kingdom of God.[64]

Thich Nhat Hanh observes further, "The practice of Eucharist is a practice of awareness."[65] He notes that "if his (Jesus) disciples would eat one piece of bread in mindfulness, they would have real life."[66] With a similar context of interbeing, I have celebrated the prayer over the elements, noting how the grain is grown in a field, seed sown by the farmer, the field watered through irrigation or rain, the sun shines upon the land, and the soil and the mixtures of conditions conspire to make the seeds to sprout and grow. Humans harvest the grain, mill it into flour, and the flour is used to bake bread, Likewise, the grape vines are planted on a hillside; sun and water nurture the vines until sprout grapes. The grapes are harvested, crushed, and made into wine. The wine is here on the table. This litany brings home the interdependent causes and conditions of the bread and wine and how they are interrelated to the Earth and God's incarnated Christ's mission.

But I apply the Buddhist notion of interbeing, probing the interrelatedness and interconnections of life before, now present, and joined in a cosmic transformation of life. Conservationist Wendell Berry speaks of authentic spilling over the Eucharist style liturgy (literally, the service of the people) into their daily lives: "To live, we must daily break bread with the body and shed the blood of creation. When we do this knowingly, lovingly, skillfully, reverently, it is a sacrament. When we do it ignorantly, greedily, clumsily, and destructively, it is desecration. In such a desecration, we condemn ourselves to spiritual, moral loneliness, and others to want."[67] The ritual practice of the Eucharist stimulates our contemplative and ecological imagination to ritualize our daily living as liturgy. Hugh O'Donnell argues, "To live a Eucharistic spirituality is to live in awareness

64. Nhat Hanh, *Living Buddha, Living Christ*, 30–31.
65. Nhat Hanh, *Peace in Every Step*, 22.
66. Ibid., 23.
67. Berry, *The Gift of the Good Land*, 281.

that all is one: that God is in all—from the dandelion to the teeming life in a spoonful of earth."[68]

The Eucharist celebration originated in the radical inclusive ministry of Jesus and his indiscriminate invitation to table, culminating in the symbolic ritual of his sharing bread and a cup of wine indicating his life "given for all." Then his life giving death and resurrection become an act of compassionate, self-emtying love for all life or what I have termed green or incarnational inclusivity. Anglican bishop and biblical scholar Tom Wright sums up the early Christian view of transformation of Jesus in the event of the resurrection: "They believed that God was going to do for the whole cosmos what God had done for Jesus at Easter."[69] In other words, Christ is the pledge and beginning of the perfect fulfillment of the world—Jesus risen from the dead is the representative of the cosmos yet to be perfected—the beginning of the transformation of all things in God. This is the inclusive green grace celebrated in Eucharist. Ecotheologian Sallie McFague understands that an ecological Christology has two features, embodiment and inclusion:

> By bringing God into the realm of the body, of matter, nature is included within the divine reach. This inclusion is possible only if incarnation is understood in a broad, not narrow fashion: that is, if Jesus as the incarnate Logos, Wisdom, or Spirit of God is paradigmatic of what is evident everywhere else as well . . . Incarnational Christology means that salvation is neither solely human nor spiritual. It must be for the entire creation . . . Incarnational Christology says that God wants all of nature, human beings and all other entities, to enjoy well-being in body and spirit. Incarnational Christology, then, expands the ministry and death of Jesus, the model for Christians of "God with us" to envelop the entire universe.[70]

What McFague argues for is an "incarnational inclusivity," that starts with the Big Bang and explodes the incarnated limits of God to include all matter, humanity and all beings, to the limits of the universe. Incarnation is the flowering and evolving grace of creation, made present in a specific time and place, but expanded exponentially by the death and the resurrection of Christ and through the outpouring of the Spirit. McFague

68. O'Donnell, *Eucharist and the Living Earth*, loc. 964.

69. Wright, *Surprised by Hope*, 104.

70. McFague, An Ecological Christology," 37–38.

192 GOD IS GREEN

continues: "An ecological Christology means that God is with us—we are dealing with the power and love of the universe; it means that God is with us—on our side, desiring justice and health and fulfillment for you, all people and all other life forms, but especially those who do not have justice, health, and fulfillment."[71]

Catholic ecotheologian Sean McDonagh highlights the ritual capacity of the eucharist, especially, an imaginative liturgy, to transform participants in how they relate to the Earth and to humanity:[72] "While everyone accepts that good ritual is first and foremost an act of worship of God, nevertheless sensitive liturgies can also help the process of reconciliation with nature, especially, for people living in an urban environment who no longer have an intimate dependant relationship with nature."[73] He understands the eucharist in Hebrew covenant theology and the covenant Jesus establishes with his disciples in his last meal. McDonagh contends that the eucharist, Jesus' new covenant, calls us to be aware how humans have harmed and exploited the environment. By understanding the eucharist as the renewal of the covenant, McDonagh creates an ecological Decalogue to review our human destructiveness to the Earth.[74] Eating was holy for Jesus, it intersected with and envisioned God's empowered companionship. Creation, gratitude, justice, and interconnectedness are prevalent in Jesus' meal. Wendell Berry observes, "To live, we must daily break the body and shed the blood of Creation. When we do this knowingly, lovingly, skillfully, revereverently, it is a sacrament."[75] The eucharist roots to the soil community are deep, for we eat bread from the Earth and drink the fruit of the grape. The Earth becomes part of our bodies, for we are flesh of the Earth. Marya Rivera writes, "Air, water, and soil nourish my flesh and constitute it accordingly, imperceptively, without my knowledge or conset. What is flesh but earth, in so many forms?"[76] The eucharist forms us as companionship of bread and grape juice, welcomes others in hospitality, and reminds us of our intimacy with the Earth and

71. Ibid., 34.

72. McDonagh had the opportunity to study with Thomas Berry for 4–5 months. McDonagh was a major writer for Pope Francis' encyclical *Laudato Si*. He has a similar commitment to the poor and the Earth as Leonardo Boff.

73. McDonagh, *Greening the Christian Millennium*, 192.

74. Ibid., 200–201.

75. Berry, *The Gift of the Good Land*, 281.

76. Rivera, *Poetics of the Flesh*, loc. 3187.

all life. We shared the malleable incarnational flesh of Christ rooted deep into the Earth. We do this in memory of the Incarnate Christ. The eucharist becomes what Jesus envisioned as empowered companionship with God and the Earth community.

Once a year on Earth day Sunday, the Sunday nearest to Earth Day, April 22nd., we renew our covenant with the Earth" Several years ago, the church made the Earth a member of our congregation. The Earth needs a great deal of (eco) pastoral care because She has been traumatized, exploited, suffered rape, experienced profound losses of life and degradation. We usually invite folks from outside the congregation committed to Earthcare to preach, and it is not limited to Christian clergy. Immediately, after the sermon on issue of Earth and before the eucharist covenant, the community renews its covenant to the Earth:

> We, the (Church Name), proclaim our love for God's Creation and profess our belief that the Earth, ourselves, and all life are an interconnected as part of the sacred Web of Life. We acknowledge that the Web of Life is the Body of risen Christ. We covenant together to commit ourselves as a church and individuals in the great work of healing, preservation and justice as we strive to reduce our individual and collective negative impact on the environment and to repair the damage that has been done to God's Earth. In worship and church life we will express our appreciation and give praise for the Earth and display a reverence for the Earth community of life. We commit ourselves to principles of taking only what we need, clean up our damage to Earth we do, and keep the Earth in repair for the future.[77] We make this covenant in the hope and faith that through our Earth care we will be able to help improve and sustain the health of the land, air and water for the benefit of all current and future inhabitants of this Planet. Amen!

It would be negligent for me not to point out that Celtic Christianity, the Franciscan tradition, and the Orthodox Churches' sacramental transfiguration of natural elements are Earth-centered. Only our sacramental and meditative imaginations can expand incorporate many more elements of the natural world into our worship. We can bring the elements of the Earth into our meditative rituals and worship just as Teilhard celebrated the Mass of the Earth or Matthew Fox's Cosmic Mass. The altar in the sanctuary is a red wood burl table slab and on the central wall a cross

77. McFague, *A New Climate for Theology*, 53.

made from six woods from around the world with two twenty foot windows looking out to our garden. We have brought the natural landscape into the sanctuary or rather brought the church into the cathedral of our garden.

8

"Who Is My Neighbor?"

A God who suffers only with humans is too small. Our task is to
recognize that there are countless crosses in the world, non-human as
well as human, to which countless victims are involuntarily nailed,
often by powers that have nothing to do with human agency.

—Jay McDaniel[1]

Coverage of nonhuman animal theology is unusual in environmental theology with several recent exceptions. There is frequently a disjuncture between nonhuman animal ethics and environmental theological reflection that I want to bridge because it makes no eco-theological sense to me.[2] Compassion toward the Earth and other life is intimately interwoven of humanity's relationship to nonhuman animals.

Anyone person that knows me for a period of time or follows me on Facebook knows how deeply I love my companion nonhuman animal Friskie and other dogs and nonhuman animals. One of my favorite days is the feast of St. Francis of Assisi and the blessing of companion nonhuman animals. I bless the whole household and their interspecies bonding and give out a blessed Catholic medals for their companion animals with

1. McDaniel, *Of God and Pelicans*, 29.

2. Linzey, "Explorations in Animal Theology," 29; and Linzey, "The Conflict between Ecotheology and Animal Theology," in Linzey, ed., *Creatures of the Same God*, 49–71.

St. Francis of Assisi on side and St. Anthony of Padua, patron saint of the lost. We are dog inclusive church! On many Sunday services, there are a number of congregants, who bring their dogs to service. Stephen Webb notes that in seventeenth century England, churches invented the office of "dog-whipper" to keep dogs out of church. "Before that, dogs were common in many English churches, and the practice did not desist completely until the nineteenth century."[3] We have restored that practice before I discovered this tradition of dog inclusion in English churches.

Most of my life I have lived with companion dogs. Several years ago I lost my companion dog, a bichon friese. He was a faithful and loving friend, and I grieved at his loss after years of companionship and care for him through back-surgery and his rehabilitation. Two weeks later, a congregant had rescued a little white dog, a Chihuahua-Spaniel mix with some light brown markings on ears and his back, into church. I still grieved the loss of my companion dog, and I intentionally kept my distance from the white little dog with brown markings. When I sat down to talk to another person after church, the dog ran up to me and jumped into my lap, starting to kiss my face. How could I resist?

Back in our distant preliterate human history, it has been common assumption that human hunter gatherers tamed wolves. However, Dr. Brian Hare and Vanessa Woods of the Canine Cognition Center at Duke University maintain it was the reverse.[4] It evolved from wolves scavenging at the edges of human encampment for food. Bold and aggressive wolves were killed, but wolves, bold and friendly, were the ones that tamed human beings. They initiated a history of human inter-species friendliness. Inter-species friendliness from wolves led to the domestication of humans. Over time and with generations of breeding, we now have thousands of canine species with wagging tails, different sizes and coats, some with floppy ears and others with pointed ears. But these former wolves developed a different psychology from their ancestors. Stephen Budiansky advances the notion that certain "domesticated animals chose us as we chose them."[5] Daniel Miller writes, "Dogs have even adapted

3. Webb, *On God and Dog*, loc. 2736.

4. Brian Hare and Vanessa Woods, "We Didn't Domesticate Dogs"; Clutton-Brock, "Origins of the Dog."

5. Budiansky, *The Covenant of the Wild*, 24; Hobgood-Oster, *A Dog's History of the World*.

behaviorally and psychologically in order to communicate better with their human companions."[6]

In his wonderful animal theology book, *On God and Dogs*, Stephen Webb writes about his spiritual experience with dogs, disturbing the speciesist assumptions of many:

> Being a pet involves listening without speaking, talking through touching, finding joy in ceremonial greetings and submissive behavior, as allowing oneself to be touched. It consists of certain kind of giving as well as receiving, an economy of generosity that transgresses the usual and expected. It also provides an opportunity for feelings of devotion that border on the sacred. "A loving worship of God should be fulfilling for people who want to have comfort from submissive, obedient love. Perhaps a dog is fulfilling a religious vacuum." In the dog not only do we experience the obedience that we ourselves can know before God on occasion, but also we give to dogs as we want God to give to us. We enter a relationship that is unbounded, intense, and all encompassing. It is also a relationship that changes us, and we can imagine moving outward into other relationships with the same dynamic of giving and taking.[7]

He comments that the notion of animal theology must be a "little absurd," especially when he starts an animal theology from the perspective of human-dog relationships. Webb compares the divine- human relationship to the human-companion dog relationship:[8]

> The interconnections among God, humans, and dogs are rich. Both God and dogs love unconditionally, both God and humans are masters in their own realms, and both dogs and humans are creatures and servants. Humans are in between both masters and servants, loved by God and dogs alike. God's venture across a great divide to identify with humanity is not unlike the human project of domesticating and adopting canine species. Moreover, dogs, like God, are both infinitely close to us and mysteriously far away, everyday and unfathomable, immanent and transcendent.[9]

6. Miller, *Animal Ethics and Theology*, 104.

7. Webb, *On God and Dog*, loc., 1276–1283.

8. Ibid., loc. 1884.

9. Ibid., loc. 1907.

There is a love relationship between a human companion and a dog, and there is a joy of caring that God and a human companion share. Webb notes, "To pet a dog is not such a bad way to practice theology."[10]

This chapter originates from my relationship to FrisKie. It involves playing together, knowing each others' patterns, routines, and body and voice signals for communicating. We are engaged in interspecies learning. Friskie communicates his desire for me to take him to work and sitting next to me (though he prefers my lap) while I work but then nagging me with smiles, kisses, and grabbing my fingers with his mouth to drag me to tell me that it is time to go to the small dog park across the street, or to nap together placing his head on my heart or jumping across from lap into Joe's lap to play. There are times he sits on my lap and gazes into my eyes with what I describe as a "contemplative gaze of affection and connectedness" and my reciprocal gaze. Dog-lovers will be the first to tell you that dogs are family members, perhaps even spoiled.

The love between a dog and human companion is reciprocal, mutual, and playful, but it is certainly asymmetrical in power and intelligence. Certainly, I would add that there is an asymmetry between God and humanity, a gulf lessened by Christ's incarnation and the Spirit enfleshing her presence in bodies, and life.[11] I readily confess that God has tamed me a long time ago, and I have no difficulty viewing the above comparison as anything but complementary, pious, and analogous to our relationships with God. I don't mind if I am God's pet. If God is like me in any fashion, then I expect to be spoiled as a pet.

Companion Nonhuman Animals

There are three explorations from which my theological praxis for companion nonhuman animals starts: 1) the emotional context for theological action and reflection; 2) how companion nonhuman animals surprise and gift us; and 3) extension of incarnational theologies.

In *Loving Animals*, ethicist Kathy Rudy starts her study of human-animal relations, similar to Webb's approach but dissimilar to the hermeneutical approaches of animal rights and animal theology writers.[12] "Put differently, this approach to advocacy is not only about humans loving

10. Ibid., loc 1886.

11. Wallace, *Finding God in the Singing River*, 32–33.

12. Rudy, *Loving Animals*.

animals but also animals loving us back. It recognizes that animals have choices, and one of the choices many of them make is to become loving, to be loving animals. They transcend the boundaries of their bodies and their species by trusting, caring for, and communing with us. Thus, "loving" is both a verb and an adjective, something both of us also are."[13] Her approach to animal advocacy develops from a contextual perspective that sees nonhuman animals as "subjects, agents, and actors in their own right."[14] Rudy adopts a hermeneutics of emotion and "love" as the starting point of the complex and multi-dimensional question of human animal/ nonhuman animal relations. Rudy's includes "emotions—and in the way that connections can change culture—in theory and practice of animal advocacy."[15] Her purpose to tap readers' intense emotional bonds with specific nonhuman animals to speak up and work to change people's hearts in nonhuman animal advocacy movement. For Rudy, this affective movement to nonhuman animal advocacy has spiritual and sacred dimensions; it does not reside only with indigenous peoples but also with folks who are connected intensely with their nonhuman animals. Rudy's passion and eloquence, almost Buddhist, tries to bridge the species divide:

> I firmly believe that given the right opportunity most humans can connect with animals, can look in their faces and see the spirit of a fellow being, and can make the changes necessary to improve their lot in life . . . Few people really want to see another being suffer. The problem is always either that see the suffering (in factory farms or labs, for example) or they don't understand that an animal's life is made of the same "stuff" as yours or mine.[16]

Rudy's hermeneutic develops a compassionate solidarity by exposing our deep emotional connections to animals; and her intention is to change hearts and transform human relationships nonhuman with animals by their similarity to humans. For myself, this is a spiritual and passionately personal exploration, and it remains a critical for humanity's recovery of a humane and ethical relationship with animals but with our compassionate selves.

13. Ibid., loc. 49-loc. 55.
14. Ibid., loc. 50.
15. Ibid., loc. 55.
16. Rudy, *Loving Animals*, loc. 181.

My second author is Ken Stone, a Hebrew Bible scholar and fellow lover of his Beagle Mack. Stone narrates the following story about Emmanuel Levinas, the Jewish French philosopher, drafted into the French Army to fight in World War II and captured by the Germans, and he was confined to the Jewish barracks in a military prison camp. Levinas relates a story in the prison camp about a dog named "Bobby." "One day he came to meet this rabble as we returned under guard from work . . . We called him Bobby, an exotic name, as one does with a cherished dog. He would appear at morning assembly and was waiting for us as we returned, jumping up and down and barking in delight. For him there was no doubt that we were men."[17] The philosopher clearly distinguishes between Bobby the dog and the Nazi guards in the camp: The Nazi guards dehumanized their Jewish prisoners, treating them as animals. Levinas observes, "We were subhuman, a gang of apes." Bobby recognized the prisoners as human, part of the pack, and greeted them with joy and unconditional love as dogs are wont to do when you leave and return. Again Levinas points out, "For him (Bobby) there was no doubt that we were men."[18] He reminisces, "He (Bobby) was a descendant of the dogs of Egypt. And his friendly growling, his animal faith, was born of his forefathers on the banks of the Nile."[19] Levinas compares Bobby to the dogs of Egypt in Exodus 11, where Moses speaks about the last plague, the death of the first born, yet that the dogs do not bark. They silently recognized the humanity of the Hebrew slaves in Exodus. Stone observes, "By holding their tongues, the dogs mark the liberation of Israelite slaves. And here, Levinas observes we see what it means to say that the dogs are friends of humanity, for 'with neither ethics nor *logos*, the dog will attest to the dignity of its person.'"[20] Levinas speaks of "animal faith" and "friendly growling" of Bobby that recognize the humanity of the prisoners. Levinas associates dogs in the scriptures with human freedom from slavery in Egypt and the dog Bobby with humanity. The dog is given a human name for his humaneness to the Jewish prisoners while the Nazi guards "stripped us of our human skin. We were subhuman, a gang of apes."[21] Through the history of anti-Semitism, Christians often construed the

17. Stone, "The Dogs of Exodus," 40.

18. Ibid., 40.

19. Ibid.

20. Ibid., 39.

21. Gross, "The Question of the Creature," 126.

otherness of Jews as "animals." Levinas narrates a wonderful story of how dogs humanize us, and implicit behind this story is that no nonhuman animals ever committed the atrocities and barbarisms of human animals. Aaron Gross comments, "they (nonhuman animals) are the root others who help us imagine ourselves and who call us to, and constitute our being."[22] Levinas' story of Bobby lifts the dog out from the typical human category of a thing, an "it" into a dialogical subject, who imparts dignity and freedom. Ann Benvenuti speaks about what her dog Molly Brown taught her: "Perhaps the grandest thing I learned from Molly Brown slowly over the years is that we cannot be human without the guidance and support of the non-human world, not merely as crass commodity for consumption, as we are taught to see 'it,' but as companion, as friend, as teacher, as parent."[23] Molly Brown became her gateway to gain confidence to engage other nonhuman creatures by imitating their behaviors, make sounds, and to wait for their returned responses. These canine engagements were stepping stones to learning real empathy, listening attentively to the communication of other creatures, and ultimately learning so much from each engagement. She comprehends rightly, "The whole world is here, waiting to be heard, but I am too busy producing words and thoughts to listen to it . . . In silence, we learn love. You do not need information about bats to know a dry tongue and a hand reaching for a parched throat, but you are unlikely to see that reaching hand unless you are still inside."[24] Benvenuti has taken a quantum leap in interspecies communication and empathetic understanding, and this is what Levinas experienced and I and many others have learned from our nonhuman animal companions.

Companion animals may help us to learn about ourselves and teach us about the interrelationality of the web of life. These interspecies engagements are playful, mutually committed interactions, and entirely a spiritual practice. And the conversation of spiritual practice opens to Stephen Webb's claims:

> Like forgiveness, animals are a gift; they come to us with their own beauty and dignity, and they plead for patience and understanding. In turn, they give us more than we could otherwise have known about ourselves by allowing us to venture into a

22. Ibid., 136.

23. Benvenuti, *Spirit Unleashed*, loc. 3393.

24. Ibid., loc. 3442–3453.

relationship that goes further, due to its very awkwardness and limitations, than the boundaries of human language normally permit, "The fact that animals are so generous in answering us is what makes it okay to train them but a human duty one way we enact our gratitude to the universe that animals exist."[25]

Companion animals bring joy but expect a return, care, attention, and love. They show us love and will extend that love to others. One day I was in the church social hall talking to a couple, one whose face was seriously disfigured from cancer, and he had a hard time speaking words from his impairment. Friskie intuited his difficulty, pain, and immediately jumped into his lap—starting to lick his face and giving him unconditional love and attention. I could have hugged my companion for his care and love; for it was unconsciously what I wanted to extend such comfort to him. Later I had a flashback to Levinas' story about Bobby and how a canine can humanize and instruct about care.

Loving a companion animal provides an alternative expression to human relationships and expansions of relationships. It disturbs the speciesist assumptions that only humans are worth loving.[26] I think of how therapy dogs have been introduced into nursing homes for the chronically ill or LA Childrens' Hospital for the hospitalized children, the introduction of dogs has produced remarkable successes in alleviating loneliness and helped healing.[27] Dogs are remarkable companions if we take the time to listen and learn from our dogs, and they will communicate with us in many different ways if we take the time to patiently engage them and learn how they communicate.

Stephen Webb makes an analogical comparison between God and human animals and nonhuman animals: "The interconnections among God, humans, and dogs are rich. Both God and dogs love unconditionally, both God and humans are masters in their own realms, and both dogs and humans are creatures and servants. Humans are in between, both masters and servants, loved by God and dogs alike."[28] Both relationships—God to us and dogs to us—are places where we experience unconditional love. When we return to either our companion dog or God, there

25. Webb, *On God and Dogs*, loc. 1418–1426.

26. Ibid., loc. 1238–1246.

27. On the Pet Facilitated Therapy movement, see ibid., 1268–1298. Pet facilitated therapy has been employed for autistic children, veterans with post-traumatic stress, the elderly, and even in hospice. A google search will generate a great many of articles.

28. Webb, *On God and Dogs*, loc. 1905.

is a joyful hospitality of welcoming and excitement from either or both I have often imagined Christ not as the Good Shepherd but the "Good Companion," for it is a metaphor for identifying myself with the faithful and loving companion dog as the companion to Christ and imitating Christ as the good companion to Friskie.

The third context is the significance of Christ's incarnation to other creatures. Stephen Webb comprehends that Christology gives the original covenant of God even more relevance to nonhuman animals: "The incarnation is not just a yes to human beings, but an affirmation of all sentient longing and redemption of all suffering and pain. God's embodiment in the world means God's compassion for all materiality, regardless of intellectual development or communicative skills. God does not waste anything; on the contrary, God values and saves even that which has no discernible purpose or function, that which seems superfluous and redundant."[29] The Christian affirmation of God's becoming enfleshed in creaturely *sarx* is the central symbol of Christology. Given the interconnectedness of the web of life and the material world, Christ is united with all fleshliness, not just with human animals but also with nonhuman animals and all life, the whole of creation. The incarnation is densely interconnected with all creatures. Elizabeth Johnson rightly perceives, "This deep incarnation of God within the biotic community of life forges a new union, one with different emphasis from the empowering communion created by the indwelling Creator Spirit. This is a union in the flesh."[30] Denis Edwards, likewise, argues that Jesus' incarnation in flesh indicates an interconnection beyond humanity to nonhuman animals within the theological context of developing Anthansius' theological principle that God became human might be taken up into God and deified: "The meaning of incarnation, of becoming flesh, is not restricted to humanity. The flesh is embraced by God is not limited to humanity. It includes the whole interconnected world of fleshly life and, in some way, the whole universe to which flesh is related and upon which it depends."[31] Edwards maintains that because of Christ's incarnation and resurrection, nonhuman animals participate in salvation. He reflects on Athanasius, bishop of Alexandria: "All things, including every wallaby, dog, and dolphin are created through the eternal Wisdom of God, and redeemed and recon-

29. Ibid., loc. 640.
30. Johnson, *Ask the Beasts*, 198.
31. Edwards, *Ecology at the Heart of Faith*, 58.

ciled through the Wisdom made flesh in Christ."[32] Athanasius' theology extended salvation through Christ's incarnational identification with all flesh, including animals. God's grace not only is extended to humanity, it is far more inclusive than many humans realize to embrace other life and the universe. This raises the question on nonhuman animal suffering and our responsibility. David Clough claims, "The doctrine of the incarnation does not therefore establish a theological boundary between humans and other animals; instead, it is best understood that as God stepping over the boundary between Creator and creation and taking on creatureliness."[33]

Nonhuman Animal Neighbors

Daniel Miller provocatively uses Karl Barth to expound an ethic of non-human animal neighbors and friends. Miller provides an innovative theological perspective on John 1:14: "The word was made flesh, and dwelt among us . . ." "In doing so, I will argue, Christ became neighbor to all living creatures of flesh—including animals. Consequently, by drawing near to animal life in this way, Christ's incarnation and resurrection provide the basis for our own drawing near to animals as neighbors."[34] Miller builds a narrative ethics from Jesus' Parable of the Good Samaritan, for he understands the intent of the parable is to upturn the lawyer's notion "who is my neighbor?" He wants to extend the category of neighbor to nonhuman animals: "The Parable of the Good Samaritan embraces nonhuman animals as neighbors because it focuses on the action rather than the recipient of neighborly love."[35] Prior to his exploration, Miller asserts that he agrees with Andrew Linzey, all aspects of creation possess value because it is derived from the value of the Creator as good. But he also disagrees with Albert Schweitzer's response of general reverence or respect for life because he wants to make a point that greater respect should be accorded "because of the commonalities between human and animal natures, animals demand an additional, uniquely relational kind of moral response. They, like, humans are the kinds of creatures that deserve to be treated as neighbors."[36] For Miller, it is the act of loving

32. Edwards, "The Redemption of Animals," 92 -99.

33. Clough, *On Animals*, loc. 2844.

34. Miller, *Animal Ethics and Theology*, 96.

35. Ibid., 14.

36. Ibid.

rather the esteem that we regard an individual human animal or non-human animal as emotionally near or as neighbor. He disrupts human religious and prejudicial categories as Jesus intended in the parable and commitment to the peaceable kin-dom: "Thus, for Jesus the question of neighborly love "is not a cry for limitation but for an opportunity." Caring for animals presents an opportunity to demonstrate the unlimited bounds of neighborly love. Love in this sense is not a limited resource that be cautiously reserved for a narrowly defined group."[37] Neighborly love does not need to stop at the boundary of humanity but to include nonhuman animals. Miller cites Jesus' words to the synagogue leader for the healing of a woman from an illness on the Sabbath: "Does not each of you on the Sabbath untie his ox or his donkey from the manger, and lead it away to give it water" (Matt 13:15). For Mille, this line of compassionate argument for animals provides a scriptural warrant for extending the category of neighbor to nonhuman animals.

Miller clearly wrestles with Linzey's observation about Christian theological dismissal of nonhuman animals: "What is so problematic is the way in which God's "yes" to humankind in the incarnation becomes a "no" to creation as a whole."[38] Scholars in religion in the west have started to reshape the field by dissolving categorical disavowals or breaks between human animals with nonhuman animals.[39] Many still keep nonhuman animals marginal, for there has been a theological disavowal of nonhuman animals as soulless creatures, linguistically deficient, non-rational, incapable of inner emotions, and devoid of the divine image.[40] Daniel Miller's exposes the theological failure of Barth to comprehend Christ's incarnation in flesh and its cosmic scope and impact through the resurrection.

> By taking humanity's earthly human nature, Christ becomes neighbor not only to humans, but also to creatures of the earth . . . Because Christ has become our neighbor, we can then be neighbors to others . . . Because Christ drew near as neighbor to all earthly creatures, we are able to do the same.[41]

37. Ibid., 15.

38. Ibid., 96. Barth, *Church Dogmatics*, III/1,18. Linzey, *Animal Theology*, 9.

39. Gross, *The Question of Animal and Religion*, 60–95.

40. Linzey, *Why Animals Suffering Matters*, 9–42.

41. Ibid., 98.

Miller uses the "taxonomy of nearness" to define our neighbor, for it enables us to understand "general guidelines for discerning our various responsibilities to the different kinds of animals we encounter."[42] Process theologian John Cobb, for instance, raises a number of human animal–nonhuman animal relationships that disturb our conscience:

> Domestication has also been degradation. We have reduced living, sentient beings to economic commodities considered as they contribute to monetary gain. We routinely torture millions, for inessential human purposes. To think of all things, and especially of all living things, as embodying Christ must give us pause. A creature in whom we see Christ cannot be only a commodity to be treated for our gain or causal pleasure. An animal that incarnates Christ cannot be only a specimen for our cruel experiments or an object forced to do unnatural things for our amusement.[43]

Incarnational theology, when it becomes less restrictive and more inclusive of nonhuman animals, exposes the ideological divide from nonhuman animals, commodified for food production, experimented upon, cruelly mistreated, or hunted. Restrictive incarnational theologies have elided Christians ever seeing Christ in creatures, thus making them invisible for Christian compassion.

Certainly, there is a taxonomy of nonhuman animals through their evolutionary nearness of domesticated animals. And further more distant taxonomies of nonhuman animals as wild with more limited engagement with human animals, though that is rapidly receding globally. For Elizabeth Johnson, the metaphor of the Tree of Life functions as an evolutionary diagram that links the development of humanity to other nonhuman animal species.[44] But many of us ignore the evolutionary nearness of nonhuman animals to us. Sallie McFague highlights human callousness to nonhuman animals such as hunting, eating meat, traditional zoos and circuses, vivisection, and cosmetic nonhuman animal testing. She notes that we blind ourselves to the evolutionary proximity to nonhuman animals: "In fact it is by suppressing any thought that they might have needs, wishes, or feelings, in other words, that they are anything like us (or we are like them—the more valid the exclusionary comparison) that we can

42. Ibid.
43. Cobb, "All Things in Christ?" 177.
44. Johnson, Ask the Beasts, 64–65.

continue such practices with good, or at least, numbed consciences."[45] There is an evolutionary proximity of the higher mammals to ourselves, and this raises a host of ethical concerns about treatment of nonhuman animals.

The Taxonomy of Nearness

Over the decades, the work of numerous other animal researchers—Jane Goodall, Marc Bekoff, Frans de Waal, Constantine Slobodchikoff and others—have broken down the evolutionary divide between human animals and nonhuman animals. Many nonhuman animals, especially, mammals, form emotional bonds for social living. Mammals also share a brain system that supports cognitive functions of intelligence and a range of emotions comparable to human animals. Because of these similarities, nonhuman animal researchers began to ask questions, ignored by general culture and other researchers: Do nonhuman animals have minds, hearts, families and friends, languages? Do they have emotional lives? Do they have spiritual experience?

Nonhuman animal cooperation, even empathy and compassion within animals, has been documented by animal researchers, opening the study of nonhuman animals and the rich ranges of their emotional lives and their various linguistic forms of communication. Ethologist Marc Bekoff writes, "It is clear that morality and virtues didn't suddenly appear at the evolutionary epic beginning with humans. The origins of virtue, egalitarianism, and morality are more ancient than our own species. While fair play in animals may be a rudimentary form of social morality, it still could be a forerunner of more complex and more sophisticated human moral systems."[46] There is enough research pointing to the inner lives of animals, their capabilities for emotions such as love and grief, joy, ritual, dance, love and maternal love, friendship and compassion, laughter, play, and depression. Human animals shared a common evolutionary kinship of inner lives, from the very rudimentary to more advanced sentience of mammals. As nonhuman animals make noises of barking, howling, laughter, whimpering grunts, squeals, body signals, and sounds inaudible to human ear or eye to eye gazing, these are some methods that they communicate. He notes that many species

45. McFague, *Collected Readings*, 184.
46. Bekoff, *The Emotional Lives of Animals*, 109.

live in different sensory worlds from us. Scientists have previously had wrong assumptions about animals speaking because they did not listen. The Cornell Bioacoustic Research Program has undertaken research in this area, using digital technology to record the sounds of wildlife and decode the linguistic signals. One of the program researchers, Christopher Clark notes, "By listening in on the world's creatures, we make it possible for their voices to be heard on critical conservation issues."[47] Another example of decoding nonhuman language is Professor Con Slobodchikoff of Northern Arizona University, who has spent decades studying the language of prairie dogs. He describes "Prairiedogese" warning system of alarms that describe particular predators: hawks, coyotes, dogs, snakes, and humans. They can describe the speed of a predator, individual differences of size, shape, and color.[48]

My own experience of my companion dog indicates his capacity to smile, be happy and excited by going to work with myself, or experiences pleasure in greeting people or happily jumping, dancing in circles and barking when we are off to the dog park. Moreover, Bekoff has noted that elephants, whales, chimpanzees, and dolphins demonstrate that they are self-aware. Nonhuman animals are sentient beings, facing the challenges and joys of daily life. We human animals have more in common with our nonhuman animal kin. Marc Bekoff tells a story that he had to kill a cat for his doctoral research project. He picked up the cat, whom he considered to be intelligent. He faced the cat's "piercing, unbreakable stare," which he comprehended to mean, "Why me?" He noted the cat's eyes "told the whole story of the interminable pain and indignity he had endured."[49] He broke down in tears and resolved not to conduct the research project that would cause harm, inflict pain, and result in the death of another being. Bekoff muses about the eyes as form of emotional communication: "Eyes are magnificently complex organs that provide a window into an individual's emotional world. As in humans, in many species eyes are the feelings, whether wide open in glee or sunk in despair. Eyes are mysterious, evocative and immediately communicative . . . Personal interpretation or intuition plays a role, and yet there is no more direct animal to animal

47. The Cornell Biacoustic Program, http://www.birds.cornell.edu/page.aspx?pid=2713.

48. Slobodchikoff, *Chasing Doctor Dolittle*, 51–62; also Prairie Dog Chatter, https://www.youtube.com/watch?v=y1kXCh496Uo.

49. Ibid., 50.

communication than staring deeply into another's eyes."[50] Jane Goodall, likewise narrates that a most profound experiences in interspecies communication begin with eye to eye with a dominant male chimpanzee she named David Greybeard. "(His) eyes seemed to express his entire personality . . . His eyes seemed almost like windows through which, if only I had the skill, I could look into his mind."[51] When my companion dog Friskie lays on me with his head on my chest, he stares deeply into my eyes as long as I stare back.

Bekoff relates how elephants show concern for dead elephants. He cites Cynthia Moss, an elephant expert, who describes how elephants mourn and stay with the carcass of a dead elephant, then bury the body with sand and branches.[52] Elephant grief has been documented in the story of Lawrence Anthony, an elephant conservationist, who worked to save two herds of South African elephants. He worked with traumatized elephants, and he exemplified interspecies care and compassion. He listened and studied the ways that elephants communicated to each other. Anthony writes, "To save their lives, I would stay with them, feed them, and talk to them. But, most importantly, be with them day and night."[53] With Anthony's death, two elephants made a trek to Anthony's compound and ritualized their grief of his passing.[54]

Another example is Jane Goodall's study of chimpanzee' dancing in a waterfall ecstatically for nearly fifteen minutes. There is no apparent discernible reason except they enjoy it. They throw themselves into the dance with total abandonment. Bekoff asks about the Goodall observation of the dance in the waterfall: "Could it be they are a joyous response to being alive, or even an expression of the chimp's awe of nature? Where, after, all might human spiritual impulses originate?"[55] Goodall asks this, "If the chimpanzee could share his feelings and questions with others, might these wild elemental displays become ritualized into some form of animalistic religion? Would they worship the falls, the deluge from the sky, the thunder and lightning—the gods of the elements? So all-powerful,

50. Ibid., 49.

51. Goodall, *Reason for Hope*, 79.

52. Ibid., 66. Moss, *Elephant Memories*.

53. "Elephant Whisperer: Lawrence Anthony's Remarkable Impact," http://epicvictories.com/the-elephant-whisperer-lawrence-anthony-s-remarkable-impact/.

54. Bekoff, *The Emotional Lives of Animals*, 109.

55. Ibid., 61.

so incomprehensible?"[56] Primatologist Frans de Waal has witnessed the same behaviors of male chimpanzees dance during a thunderstorm and seemingly enter a trance-like state.[57] De Waal seems to trace the origin of religious impulses and superstitions (spirituality: my word) back to our primate inheritance. In an interview, religion scholar Aaron Gross criticizes the notion that religion is exclusive to human animals: "So the first thing I would say is that to utterly exclude animals from the phenomenon of religion is to pretend we know what it is more than we do. That's bad scholarship. It's also bad theology."[58] Gross explores cultural transmission by various mammals and asks, "What is symbolic language, and can we really deny it to all animals?"[59]

Recently de Waal argues that morality has its biological roots with primates: "Mammals have what I call an "altruistic impulse "in that they respond to signs of distress in others and feel an urge to improve their situation. To recognize the need of others, and react appropriately, is really not the same as a preprogrammed tendency to sacrifice oneself for the genetic good."[60] He traces altruism to the prototype of maternal care in mammals. In his chapter, "The Parable of the Good Simian," de Waal documents in-group bias among both human animals as well as among nonhuman animals.[61] Referring to Jesus' parable, he comments about apes: "Clearly they are not as selfish as has been assumed, and might actually beat the average priest or Levite when it comes to humane behavior."[62] Frans de Waal makes the compelling point: "I refuse to use differently terminology for these reactions of humans and apes as urged by the opponents of anthropomorphism. Those who exclaim that "animals are not people" tend to forget that while true, it is equally true that people are animals."[63] Marc Bekoff also makes a strong case for the affinities of justice and fairness among the social play of nonhuman animals.[64]

56. Goodall, "Primate Spirituality," 1304–5.

57. Waal, *The Bonpo and the Atheist*, 198–99.

58. Aaron Gross reviews the evidence of the possibility of nonhuman animal rituals and symbolic organization of behaviors: Aghapour, "What if Animals Believei n God?"

59. Ibid.

60. Ibid., 33.

61. Ibid., 113–46.

62. Ibid., 146.

63. Waal, Ibid., 145.

64. Bekoff, *The Emotional Lives*, 89–104.

Nonhuman animals exhibit fairness during their play with each other, but they react negatively to unfair play behaviors. Fair play in nonhuman animals is rudimentary prototype for human animal social morality. In his book, *Wild Justice*, Bekoff and his co-author Pierce conclude, "We argue that animals feel empathy for each other, treat one another fairly, cooperate towards common goals, and help each other out of trouble. We argue, in short, that animals have morality."[65] Bekoff suggests from his animal studies that "if we try to learn about forgiveness, fairness, trust, and cooperation in animals, maybe we'll also learn to live more compassionately and cooperatively with one another."[66]

Both Marc Bekoff and Anne Benvenuti weave a spirituality that brings the nearness of nonhuman animals to themselves. Bekoff develops a Buddhist approach to nonhuman animals with his ethics for compassionate care. He espouses "rewilding," "Rewilding our hearts is about becoming reenchanted with nature. It is about nurturing our sense of wonder. Rewilding is about being nice, kind, compassionate, empathetic and harnessing our inborn goodness and optimism. In the most basic sense, 'rewilding' means 'to make wilder' or 'to make wild once again.'"[67] He speaks of paying attention that includes a Buddhist style of mindfulness that finds respect for nonhuman animals trying to identify with them and trying to figuring out what they are feeling. "'Minding animals' refers to caring for nonhuman animals, respecting them for who they are, appreciating their own world views, and wondering what and how they are feeling and why. We mind animals when try as hard to as we can to imagine their point of view."[68] This mindfulness leads to the practice of "deep ethology" but also compassion and wisdom, a signal of attributes of the bodhisattva path. I comprehend Bekoff as an ecosattva whose contemplative practice leads to compassionate action in the world on the behalf of nonhuman animals. Buddhist notions of compassion, in particular, carry an incarnational dynamic of compassion based on the Trinitarian aspect of perichoretic interrelatedness. This allows for the development of a spirituality of compassion and putting compassion into action. Bekoff writes,

65. Bekoff and Pierce, *Wild Justice*, 1.
66. Bekoff, *The Emotional Lives*, 109.
67. Bekoff, *Rewilding Our Hearts.* 5.
68. Ibid.

> I try to make kind choices; I try to increase compassion and
> reduce cruelty . . . In practice, this means walking through the
> world treating every living being like an equal—not the same
> but as being with an equal right to life. The Golden Rule applies
> to human animals, other animals, tree, plants, and even earth
> itself . . . Kindness and compassion must always be the first and
> foremost in our interactions with animals and every other being
> in this world.[69]

Any Buddhist would hear the words of a bodhisattva or ecosattva, an enlightened being dedicated to compassionate practice, in Bekoff's words.

Anne Benevenuti, an Episcopal priest and professor of philosophy/
psychology, traces her lineage of "natural spirituality" to Buddhism and
Christian practice via Franciscan spirituality expressed by Father Richard
Rohr's notion of "alternative orthodoxy."[70] Like Bekoff, Benevenuti turns
a contemplative gaze towards nonhuman animals, assuming the kenotic
life of Jesus for living the Trinitarian relationship and incarnational interrelatedness of Christ's body, "and in this vehicle by which we can come
home to the truth that all life is family."[71] The Animal Welfare Movement has achieved some successes with New Zealand and Quebec with
legislation declaring that the animals are "sentient"—banning hunting,
experiementation, and tighter controls in approving animal usage for
testing and research.[72]

Nonhuman Animals Suffering and Death

A number of ecotheologians, the animal researchers, and nature conservationists understand nonhuman animal predation as part of evolutionary biological life. But humanity kills nonhuman animals in scope
incomparable to nonhuman animal predation. This section is suggestive
for the issue of suffering and death within the realm of nonhuman animals. Theological work began on how God comprehends the suffering,
tragedies, and death of nonhuman animals. The question of nonhuman
animal theodicy—suffering and death—has been taken up by a few authors. Stephen Webb develops this issue in his chapter: "Will All Good

69. Bekoff, *The Emotional Lives,* loc. 164.

70. Benevenuti, *Spirit Unleashed,* loc. 4010.

71. Ibid., loc. 4042.

72. Buchanan, "New Zealand: Animal Welfare Recognizes Animals as Sentient
Beings."

Dogs Go to Heaven?"[73] It is an emotional question for human animals who are bonded in companionship with their dogs. The question raises the wider question of nonhuman animals in evolutionary history. Webb argues that nonhuman animals are morally innocent, and thus they are closer to God. God finds worth in all that God creates.[74] John Wesley in the 18th century preached a sermon, affirming that nonhuman animals will exceed their former state in Paradise because of their suffering.[75] C. S. Lewis, an advocate for nonhuman animals, opposed animal experimentation and even fox hunting.[76] He used his fictional writings on Narnia and his science fiction books to advocate for nonhuman animals.In his Narnia stories, his nonhuman animals have equal rights to human animals, but they also are endowed with personhood and rationality And the last volume of the *Chronicles of Narna*, both human and nonhuman animals are saved. In *The Problem of Pain*—Lewis argues that nonhuman animals live in their own right before God, but he places the possibility of the redemption of sentient nonhuman animals based on their relationship to humanity. Nonhuman animals will be saved because they have a part in our lives and matter to us, thus they must be included in the resurrection community. Jürgen Moltmann widens the argument that the suffering of innocent creatures requires just divine compensation: "There is therefore no meaningful hope for the future of creation unless the tears are wiped away from every eye. But they can only be wiped away when the dead are raised, and when the victims of evolution experience the justice of the resurrection of nature."[77] Moltmann argues that resurrection includes the resurrection of all flesh, and all refers to nonhuman animals.[78] He later qualifies his meaning that every creature, who has lived, will exist without their individual particularity.[79]

Jay McDaniel notes that predator-prey relations existed long before the appearance of early hominids; for McDaniel claims that the notion of animal predator-prey relationship existed before human sin or the myth

73. Webb, *Good Eating*, 160–78; Webb, *On God and Dogs*, loc. 2748–2856. For a Franciscan view, see Wintz, *Will I See My Dog in Heaven?*

74. Webb, *Good Eating*, 160–78.

75. See the discussion of Wesley: Clough, *On Animals: Systematic Theology*, loc. 3813–3879.

76. See Root, *C.S. Lewis.*

77. Moltmann, *The Way of Jesus Christ*, 142.

78. Moltmann, *The Coming of God*, 69–70.

79. Ibid., 306–8.

of the fall. He re-narrates an event of a grey whale being killed, attacked and eaten by a pack of orcas from the Buddhist poet Gary Synder. Mc-Daniels asks a theological question of the tragedy, at least for the grey whale. If God is Christ-like, whose side is God on in this situation? Mc-Daniel answers, "The answer is that God is 'on the side of' both creatures, to the exclusion of neither."[80] He quotes process theologian, Schubert Ogden: "Because of God's love itself is subject to no bounds and excludes nothing from its embrace, there is no creature's interest that is not also God's interest, and therefore intended in the redeeming love of God."[81] Here is an example of nondualistic theology of a compassionate God who is for the predators and with the prey's suffering and death.

Christopher Southgate presents a comprehensive exploration of extinction theodicies of nonhuman animal life by exploring the divine kenosis and divine co-suffering of God with nonhuman animals in evolution and through evolutionary extinction and redemption of nonhuman animals.[82] He claims a kenotic ethics for dealing with the extinction of nonhuman animals. Southgate boldly proposes that "a sign of our (human) liberty as children of God starting to set free whole of creation would be that human beings, through a blend of prudential wisdom and scientific ingenuity, cut the rate of natural (and "human-made") extinction."[83]

Stephen Webb offers a provocative thought about treating nonhuman animals as "disposable nonentities":

> We can only treat them (nonhuman animals) if we think that their transient lives have no ultimate standing in the universe. How would we treat them if we thought that they shared our destiny? How would we treat them if we thought what we do to them, the least among us, could rebound on us in the afterlife? How would we treat them if we knew that they would be our eternal partners in the new world that God will create to redeem the suffering in this one?[84]

Webb holds that our imagination of an embodied and incarnational afterlife can motivate human animals to change their views and behaviors

---

80 McDaniel, "Can Animal Suffering be Reconciled with Belief?' 162–63.

81. Ibid., 163.

82. Southgate, *The Groaning of Creation*.

83. Ibid., 125.

84. Webb, *Good Eating*, 178.

on how we think and relate to nonhuman animals. Webb is consistent with the logic of the dynamic of kenotic compassion of God and God's justice. The more real and inclusive resurrected life is real to us; the more motivation of future life will affect us in the present moment.

Nonhuman Animal Abuse and Killing

Humanity abuses and kills more nonhuman animals on unimaginable scale. We hunt nonhuman animals for sport and often keep parts of them for trophies; we kill 100,000 baby seals a year for their fur, we shoot deer with automatic weapons and use those guns on children and innocent folks, pharmaceutical companies experiment on beagles, dogs known for the docility and love for humans.[85] The Valley Church gave our annual Justice Love Award based on the principles articulated in Micah 6:8 to the Beagle Freedom Project.[86] A dog-loving congregant recommended the organization for their work in rescuing Beagles from corporations doing medical, pharmaceutical, and research on them. Beagles are a very mild and affable breed. On a NBC sports show "Under Wild Skies" on big game hunting, the host and his guide stalk and shoot a bull elephant, who trumpets and writhes in pain, even charging the two killers. The host then shoots the elephant again between the eyes. The elephant falls, and the two huntsmen stand next to the dead elephant to gloat over triumph kill. Hunting for sport is a human perversion; for me it is murder. The earlier question, "who is my neighbor?" is answered with the incarnation principle (Matt 25:26), "whatever you do to the least of my family, you do it to me." "The least of my family" covers nonhuman animals, who are neighbors.

Many human animal activists oppose confinement of nonhuman animals to cages in zoos or orca whales and dolphins at Sea World. It is difficult to see nonhuman animals in cages, and some zoos have widened the habitat spaces for particular in safari parks. Benvenenuti addresses our human practices of confining nonhuman animals: "I pray for caged animals, not because prayer will magically help those in cages but because it gives us the courage to be honest, and not to look away. It places us with them together in the context of the whole of Life, and call on the one to whom we pray to witness, placing us all in the context of the

85. Scully, *Dominion: The Power of Man*.
86. Beagle Freedom Project: http://www.beaglefreedomproject.org/.

whole. At the same time that I acknowledge our wrongs, I recognize that it is they, the animals, who are positioned to help us."[87] Wholeheartedy, I concur with Benvenuti's sentiments, and especially, with private collectors of wildlife large cats such as lions and tigers. Conservation strategies, while worthwhile when they are working, are optimal for creating wild life zones, but human impact globally and change threaten biodiversity of nonhuman animal species.[88] Some progressive zoos and safari parks assert that their facilities promote awareness and compassion. To a certain extent that is true. But for myself, zoos and safari parks may become the only places for preserving species that are rapidly moving toward extinction. They may function as medieval monasteries in preserving written knowledge.

Globally 70 billion nonhuman animals are slaughtered for food each year.[89] The majority of Christian history nonhuman animals have either been degraded, devalued as brutish, soulless, non-rational, and incapable of suffering. The most recent Catholic Catechism (2003) states "it is legitimate to use animals for food and clothing."[90] Philosophically, theologically, and culturally nonhuman animals have been commodified and reduced as living being to "meat." In his dominion theology, Karl Barth deals with borderline or extreme issues such as the killing of nonhuman animals for food, "and the nearness of the animal to man irrevocably means that when man kills a beast he does something which is at least very similar to homicide."[91] Barth allows for human killing of nonhuman animals by using the notion of animal sacrifice in the Hebrew Scriptures as substitutionary sacrifice. The nonhuman animal represents human guilt and human need for forgiveness. Miller observes, "For Barth, meat, as a sacrificial meal, also points towards the substitutionary death

87. Benvenuti, *Spirit Unleashed*, loc. 3839.

88. See Rudy, *Loving Animals*, loc. 1692–2265.

89. FAOSTAT, 2015. Database of the Food and Agriculture Organization of the United Nations. Animal equality uses fifty-six billion farm animals. http://www.animalequality.net/food. The Animal Killing Counter places the number above one hundred fifty billion animals per year. The counter ticking per second is haunting. http://www.adaptt.org/killcounter.html.

90. Catholic Catechism, #2417: "God entrusted animals to the stewardship of (humankind) . . . hence it is legitimate to use animals for food and clothing." It also demands a respect, compassion, and temperance in human dominion over nonhuman animals.

91. Barth, *Church Dogmatics* III/4, 362; quoted in Miller, *Animal Ethics*, 152.

of Christ that reconciles humans and all creatures to God."[92] Barth concludes, "The killing of animals, when performed with the permission of God and by His command, is a priestly act of eschatological character."[93] He offers a solution, but there is another eschatological possibility. Barth's position of sacrifice seems to be theological gymnastics, and it is does not cogently express a meaningful scriptural warrant for killing nonhuman animals on genocidal scale.

The cultural movement in the last century moved from family husbandry farming that often included animals as part of the farm community, and they treated the nonhuman animals humanely and cared for them, and used them for food on semi-regular basis. The emergence of corporate feedlots and slaughterhouses, termed "factory farming," further reduced or instrumentalized nonhuman animals into things, machines, and commodities.[94] It has led to wholesale slaughter of nonhuman animals efficiently, converting their carcasses into meat cuts. Many folks have no association of the hamburger that they are eating, was once a live and breathing cow. It is now "meat."

Factory farms prioritize efficient production often humane treatment and killing of nonhuman animals, even kosher slaughterhouse have been caught killing nonhuman animals inhumanely.[95] Nonhuman animal theologians and ethicists have spoken against the inhumane horrors of factory farming: "Does the Church really see the suffering of farm animals? Does it have any appreciation of what they have to endure in intensive farming—debeaking, castration, tail-docking without anesthetics, battery cages—to take only a few examples? . . . Has it really grasped that now, as never before, we have turned God's creatures into meat machines?"[96] Linzey develops a *theos*-rights approach to human treatment of nonhuman animals. He maintains that nonhuman animals have intrinsic rights and value because they belong to God, who finds that they have intrinsic value and worth. He suggested that as "we speak of animal rights we conceptualize what is objectively owed to animals as a matter of justice by virture of their Creator right."[97]

92. Miller, *Animal Ethics*, 153.

93. Barth, *Church Dogmatics* III/4, 354.

94. On factory farming, see Wennberg, *God, Humans, and Animals*, 232–39.

95. Gross, *The Question of the Animals and Religion*; Pachirat, *Every Twelve Seconds*.

96. Silva, "Religion and Factory Farming."

97. Linzey, *Christianity and the Rights of Animals*, 97. See a Catholic use and

Factory farming of nonhuman animals has led to outbreaks of disease, requiring intense antibiotic usage in food supplies and thus entering the food chain creating antibiotic resistance in human animals. Wennberg cites a study by Marian Dawkins indicating nonhuman animal suffering in factory farming: "1) the prevention of natural behaviors . . . 2) the presence of abnormal behavior, 3) associated health problems."[98] Nonhuman animal suffering in factory farming, even when kosher slaughter of nonhuman animals humanely, raises a red flag for Christians on their relationship to nonhuman animals and remaining consistent to an incarnational spirituality. Wennberg affirms, "Not to feel in the moral realm is tantamount to not seeing; it constitutes a form of moral blindness."[99]

For example, our human addiction to beef leads to three negative consequences: 1) 21 pounds of grain for every pound of beef—a wasteful use of food that could be used to feed the world's hungry; 2) Human addiction to beef has led to deforestation of the Amazon River Basin for grazing land for cattle-raising; 3) nonhuman animal confinement leads to the release of large amounts of methane waste into the atmosphere and the surrounding area aquifers, streams, and rivers. Methane release raises the atmosphere temperature forty times more than that of carbon. All of the above provide environmental objections to eating beef, along with modern concerns for human heart health and climate warming.

As a teenager, my ambivalence to nonhuman cruelty to calves for use for veal dishes led me to refuse ordering veal in restaurants. As I began to realize not only the cruelty of nonhuman animal slaughtered, I chose to eat less meat or eat lower on the food chain, poultry and fish. I find myself praying for the life of the nonhuman animal given at the meal. However, I am troubled that twenty-first century factory farming is the biggest source of nonhuman animal cruelty on this planet. There is the story that Anne Benvenuti narrates about the Dalai Lama witnessing the suffering of a chicken.[100] This gave him the courage to become a vegetarian. The Dalai Lama comments on his conversion to vegetarianism: "I have been particularly concerned with the sufferings of the chickens for many years. It was the death of a chicken that finally strengthened my resolve to become a vegetarian. These days, when I see a row of plucked

development of Linzey's notion of rights applied to factory farming: Kurzma, "A Catholic Response to Factory Farming."

98. Wennberg, *God, Humans, and Animals*, 238.

99. Ibid., 227.

100. Benvenuti, *Spirit Unleashed*, loc 3816–3826.

chickens hanging in the meat shop it hurts. I find it unacceptable that violence is the basis of our food habits."[101] Marc Bekoff, likewise, claims the Buddhist notion of compassion for his own vegetarian praxis: "The Golden rule applies to human animals, other animals, trees, plants, and even the earth itself."[102] Nature and the Earth do not belong to us, and they command respect by the fact or participating in God's image. This leads me into my discussion of the second influential factor in my discernment process, the Eucharist. Michael Norcott turns to the eucharist as the rite that sacramentally remembers and celebrates the death of Jesus on the cross and his resurrection: "Early Christian worship was organized around meals which excluded meat. It was a vegetarian worship."[103] The elements of early Christian eucharists show a variation of foods: bread and wine, fish, water, salt, yogurt, cheese, fruits, and vegetables.[104] What is excluded is from the eucharist meals in early Christian rituals is meat because it connected to the Temple sacrifice.[105] Northcott further adds, "In the eucharist, animals are no longer sacrificed or eaten, since sacrificial slaughter has come to an end on the cross of Christ."[106] The correlation of Jesus' death on the cross with the slaughter of the paschal lambs in John's Gospel, along with the Temple demonstration of Jesus in releasing the nonhuman animals caged for sale and Temple sacrifice, provide a dangerous memory of Jesus' Last Supper.

Jesus' rubric command at the Last Supper, "Do this in memory of me" speaks the invitation to compassion and nonviolence. The eating of consecrated bread and wine (or grape juice) provides an invitation of "wild grace" to end exclusion from God's table as an end to violence. As I celebrate and participate in the memories of Christ's life and death, I share consecrated bread and wine as pledge to eat life and peace, and to practice the grace of extravagant inclusion and abundant love as demonstrated by Jesus' table fellowship. This has expressed the mission of our church as practicing the open commensality of Jesus and radical inclusive love.

101. Dalai Lama, "Vegetarian Diet, Kindness to Animals," quoted in Benvenuti, ibid., 3816–3826.

102. Bekoff, *The Emotional Lives*, 164.

103. Norcott, "Eucharistic Eating," 240

104. McGowan, *Ascetic Eucharists*, 89–214.

105. Ibid., 60–67. There are hints of this issue in 1 Cor 8:1–8, where sacrificial meat to Greco-Roman idols at community meals is a divisive conflict.

106. Ibid., 238.

But there is an additional component to the eucharist when we consider Jesus' action in the Temple action in releasing the animals from their confinements, why he is arrested and crucifed embeds not only a political reason for death, and a correlation of his death on cross while the paschal lambs are slain for Passover. There is an interconnection of the Temple action and Jesus' death. The Anglican convert to Catholicism, John Cardinal Henry Newman, who in a sermon on Good Friday compared innocent nonhuman animals and their sufferings and death to those inflicted on Christ, the Lamb of God:

> Since the scripture compares (Christ) to this inoffensive and unprotected animal, we may without presumption or irreverence take this image (of the lamb) as a means of conveying to our minds the feelings which our Lord's suffering should excite within us. I mean consider how very horrible to read accounts which sometimes meet us of cruelty inflicted upon brute animals. For what was this but the very cruelty inflicted upon the Lord . . . Think then, my brethren, of your feelings at cruelty practiced on brute animals, and you will gain one sort of feeling which the history of Christ's cross and passion ought to excite you.[107]

Newman's Good Friday sermon correlates human cruelty to nonhuman animals and Christ on the cross, and this strikes an eucharist chord of my spirituality. The Lord's Supper ends animal sacrifice, but it did not end animal cruelty and violence. Christ's death in the eucharist proclaims that God loves life, and Christians anticipate no more human animal and nonhuman crucifixions. To eat the eucharist affirms our intentions not to participate in cruelty to animals, ending the shedding of blood, and further our dependence upon God's extravagant grace. Webb proposes,

> The Eucharist is connected to animal sacrifices in the sense that it puts an end to all sacrifices and places the economy of God's relationship to the world in the framework of grateful giving, not the shedding of blood. The remains of Jesus are inedible as body and blood because that body is resurrected and ubiquitous, intimately identified with all suffering flesh. Jesus' words, take this and eat, thus serve as a warning; they mean, do not eat—do not eat what can feel the same pain that I feel. As you

---

107. Quoted in: Linzey, *Animal Gospel*, 65.

eat your memories of me, eat life and peace, not violence and death.[108]

Webb also points out how food historian Margaret Visser's insights into the Lord's Supper. It is the act that Christians share as part of the body of Christ, and Visser calls eucharist a meal of peace, noting that meals of peace do not offer dead flesh:

> In it (the Eucharist), animals are not killed because one message of the Eucharist is that, for believers, it reenacts the conclusive sacrifice; neither human beings, nor animals need ever be immolated again, because the thing has been done . . . No animal or new death is needed, no bridges required: God enters directly.[109]

Visser notes that meat limits the number of participants while Webb astutely observes that meat eaters and non-meaters reflect class distinction. He notes that meat is the food of the wealthy and privileged classes.[110] This explains the social conflicts over meat sacrificed to idols at the community agape meals; there is class conflict over the eating of meat sacrificed between upper class and lower classes. The eucharist, ideally as the inclusive sharing of bread and wine, removes the communal strife over the sharing of sacrificial meat. We often forget that the temples in the ancient Greco-Roman world were not only places of sacrificing nonhuman animals to the divine, but they butchered the carcasses and roasted the meat sold. Some of the meat was reserved for the divine, others for the priests, and the remainder to the client. Sacrificial meat reflected a hierarchical system, and it seems contrary to the egalitarian ideal and radical inclusion practiced in Jesus' open commensality.

Stephen Webb has powerfully written on dietary pacificism and the eucharist. He raises a significant question on Christian eucharist:

> Could it be possible to argue that this meal is both literally and figuratively vegetarian, that is, that by remembering the suffering of Jesus in the context of the covenant of God with all of creation, it anticipates the total reign of God in a world of complete harmony, void of all strife and suffering? Is the Eucharist not only a meal in which suffering is remembered but also a meal in which pain is not inflicted in its preparation and in

---

108. Webb, On God and Dogs, loc, 2478.
109. Visser, The Rituals of Dinne, 36; quoted in Webb, Good Eating, 145.
110. See the discussion, Webb, ibid., 46–47.

which the abolition of all suffering is confidently hoped for and expected?[111]

In the Christian remembrance and celebration of the eucharist, God puts an end to nonhuman suffering and slaughter. It reveals God's wild grace of compassion and overcoming the consequences of violence in religious sacrifice. Early Christians seemed to feel that eating meat at the Lord's Supper was inappropriate with the death of Jesus as the Lamb of God and embody the ideals of God's green grace in the resurrection and the greening of the cross. Carol Adams has made the strongest case for a vegetarian eucharist: "A Christology of vegetarianism would affirm that no more crucifixions are necessary, and insist that animals, who are still being crucified, must be freed from the cross."[112] The eucharist is a nonviolent meal ending violence.

As ritual of Christ's presence, the Eucharist becomes a contradiction for the practice of violence (even though Christianities since Constantine have practiced imperial violence). I reminded the disturbing insight of contradiction of patriarchal justification of using Eucharist to sanctioning meat eating. Her observation is spiritually and emotionally troubling: "One cannot feed on grace and eat animals."[113] I understood this practically years before Adams writing in the context of the practice of compassion and nonviolence and the grace of the eucharist. God's grace and violence are incompatible in the dangerous memories of the eucharist, for it was ameal that established my non-violent practice. Adams suggests a starting location for reflection of Christians on meat eating:

> A Christology of vegetarianism would affirm that no more cru-
> cifixions are necessary, and insist that animals, who are still be
> crucified, must be freed from the cross . . . The suffering of ani-
> mals, our sacrificial lambs, does not bring about our redemption
> but further suffering, suffering from preventable disease related
> to eating animals, suffering environmental problems, suffering
> from inauthenticity that institutional violence promote . . .[114]

There is the question of two gospel images; The Last Supper as a Passover meal and the Lamb of God imagery. There is much scholarly debate on whether the Last Supper was even a Passover meal because of

111. Webb, *On God and Dogs,* loc 2463.

112. Adams, "Eating Grace," 156.

113 Ibid., 157.

114. Ibid., 156.

timing presented in the gospels. Christians in the first century definitely understood Jesus as the paschal lamb but equally understood that he also ended once and for all the sacrifice of animals (Heb 9:12).

Webb and Adams make a strong case for spiritual discernment on the eating of meat. When we are directly removed the sights of nonhuman slaughter in factory farms, we do not reflect this "meat" we are devouring was once a nonhuman animal, living and breathing, with desire to live, and possessing an inner emotional life. Daniel Miller ends his *Animal Ethics and Theology*, with thoughts that popular culture names as "meat, livestock, and crop," this places an ideological barrier between human animals and nonhuman animals: "They set up an artificial remoteness that hides the animals' physiological closeness, relationality, historic nearness to humans and human society."[115] They are our neighbors, and maybe we can live Jesus' Parable and become a Good Samaritan and restore ourselves through the eucharist as non-violence Christian, deeply incarnated and interrelated with all fleshy life.

Aaron Gross raises some substantial questions on factory farming practices:

> Is this the relationship we want to have over life? That anything goes, so long as somebody can profit from it? That is what our current law says, and it means that people who want to do terrible things—like force chickens to live in spaces the size of a legal size piece of paper, with chopped off beaks and genetics so messed up that their very physiology causes them to suffer—are protected by the law. This isn't the vision of the Good Shepherd we have in mind. If the shepherds of today extract profit for corporations at the expense of animal suffering, what kind of religious vision are we putting forth?[116]

Farm Forward helps religious communities go through a process of discernment on their relationship to nonhuman animals by understanding where their food comes from, the treatment of nonhuman animals in factory farming, and making descisions on the the types of ethical actions that they may want to take.[117] Food justice and Christian theological understanding of eating are issues too wide to cover in this volume. The key to food issues is to engage in personal and communal discernment

115. Miller, *Animal Ethics and Theology*, 168.

116. Aghapour, "What If Animals Believe in God?"

117. See the mission statement of Farm Forward: https://farmforward.com/mission/.

processes to raise the questions about our food production and eating and explore the possibilities of healthly production of food, just sharing of food, and the ethics of eating. How does God feel about this reckless actions of humanity directed against creatures that God loves and finds valuable? As pointed out earlier by ethologists and other champions of nonhuman animals earlier, we human animals share much in common with the emotional and inner lives of nonhuman animals. Anne Benvenuti offers some final words for reflection: "Love one little thing and you love the entire universe that holds it, as well as the essence from which it pours forth, and the pulse that beats in it, and that the breath that heaves it, and the awareness that connects it. Save one little thing and you save your entire soul."[118] Let that experience launch your ethical discernment.

118. Benvenuti, *Spirit Unleashed*, 3433.

9

Incarnational Spirituality:
Engaged Compassionate Action

*We will not save what we do not love. It is also true that we will neither
love nor save what we do not experience as sacred.*

—Thomas Merton[1]

Compassion is the radicalism of our time.

—Dalai Lama[2]

This chapter turns to ecological Christian, contemplative and actively
engaged with the Earth and all interrelated life. All the previous chapters lead to a profound greening of our embodied spirits, hearts and
minds to the reverence for life and the fight to protect what our God
loves and cherishes so much. Philippians 2:6–11 is a lens for Christian
interpretation of the Jesus' radical ministry of inclusive love and kenotic
compassion. George Ellis provides an inclusive definition of human life
congruent with notions of a kenotic Creator God, and self-sacrificing incarnate Christ: "*Kenosis*: a joyful, kind, and loving attitude that is willing

1. Merton, *When the Trees Say Nothing*, 18.

2. This saying of the Dalai Lama is now on a bumper sticker. http://www.northern-
sun.com/Compassion-Dalai-Lama-Bumper-Sticker-(7088).html.

to give up selfish desires and to make sacrifices on behalf of others for the common good and the glory of God, doing this in a generous and creative way, avoiding the pitfall of pride, guided and inspired by the love of God and the gift of grace."[3] Ellis' definition sets off alarm bells for Christian feminists who reject patriarchal notions of "self-emptying" as promoting a theology of female submission: "Sacrificial love is suspect because it is used as an ideological tool for the silencing of women."[4] Instead, the self-emptying of God in the Incarnation can be understood as freeing the deity and yourself from the andromorphic projections and female submission.[5] Sallie McFague offers her own definition of *kenosis*: "Kenosis is the recognition that restraint, openness, humility, respect for otherness, and even sacrifice (diminishment and death) are part of life if one assumes that individual well-being takes place within political and cosmic well-being."[6]

My Buddhist-Christian interpretation regards *kenosis* for Christians as self-emptying of ego-centeredness and a self understood in an ecological network of interrelatedness. McFague understands this network from her engagement with Buddhist notions of the emptiness of the self and the comprehension of a universal self.[7] Kenotic spirituality is an awareness of one's self in a web of interconnected selves; it re-orients self from the center of gravity to ecological awareness whereby we relate mindfully or contemplatively centered on the network of interrelatedness and committed to practice incarnational compassion.[8] Kenotic spirituality simply is living the compassionate dynamics of Christ's incarnation in everyday life. It often requires self-restraint and discipline for the sake of emotional solidarity and compassionate care for the poor and the Earth. Jesus lived self-emptying love in his ministry by embodying God's compassion, forgiveness, and non-violence love.

The Austrian theologian Karl Rahner writes, "God is the prodigal that squanders himself (Godself)."[9] Rahner compares God's self-emptying love in creation as "the prodigal that squanders." God's creation is a

3. Ellis, "Kenosis as Unifying Theme for Cosmology," 107.

4. Frascati-Lochhead, *Kenosis and Feminist Theology,* 161.

5. See feminist rejections of male usage of *kenosis*: Ibid., 149–210.

6. McFague, *Blessed Are the Consumers*, 144.

7. Ibid., 125–35.

8. Sasaki Roshi, *Buddha Is the Center of Gravity*.

9. Rahner, "Thoughts on the Theology of Christmas," 32.

prodigal outpouring of boundlessly extravagant and unconditional love through the incarnation of Christ and the Spirit. It refers to the squandering of God's space to make room for creation, the self-emptying love of Christ, not clinging to divinity, but humbly serving as a slave. Two aspects in the hymn in Philippians is self-emptying or a spaciousness and humility. Spaciousness is the mindful practice of making space within self for others, and this includes the other that is the incarnate Christ. Emptying oneself is the kenotic action of surrendering ego-centeredness to divine kenosis of interrelatedness within all creation. It is to deny oneself and take up the cross, sacrificial love that is willing to let go of one's center and find one's center in the interrelated network of other life. Letting go of our ego-centeredness is counterintuitive to our basic human nature of self grasping and craving.

The Dalai Lama understands this as "a radical reorientation from our habitual pre-occupation with self," and requires a "restraint, for "we cannot be loving and compassionate unless at the same time we curb our own harmful impulses and desires."[10] Christianity and Buddhism have a common language of compassion, and in Christian history God's compassionate love is grace. Compassion actively expresses an awareness of interconnectedness that makes us dangerous because we act in behalf of suffering life.

Sallie McFague used the word "wild space," "a space where one is available for deep change from the conventional model of living to another one."[11] She uses "wild space" to describe Francis of Assisi living voluntary poverty and later in her examination of the lives of John Woolman, Simone Weil, and Dorothy Day. McFague explores a "kenotic hagiography" of Christian saints to elaborate her understanding of kenotic living of compassionate care for the world. It is compassion unfolding in everyday action for the benefit of others. She wants to uncover how a person moves "from knowing the good to actually doing it."[12] This is what the contemplative movements in Christianity and Buddhism have

10. Quoted in McFague, *Blessed Are the Consumers*, 128. Dalai Lama, *Ethics for a New Millennium*, 24, 26.

11. McFague, *Blessed Are the Consumers*, xii. She later describes it as "a term anthropologists have used for the peculiar insight into the alternative ways of living of some people have. Often wild space occurs in those individuals who do not fit into conventions of their own cultures, due to the difference." Ibid. 47–48.

12. Ibid., 40.

described as "contemplative in action" or "mindful compassion in action." She grounds *kenosis* in "paying attention" to otherness.

Sallie McFague notes that there are four stages of development in the lives of the saints to move from becoming aware of "goodness" to engaging the world by doing goodness:

> First parables, voluntary poverty, and other forms of "wild space" open up the possibility of something different; the "bubble" of conventionality is burst so that one might contemplate another way of being in the world. Second, this awakening allows one to practice paying attention to others, focusing primarily on their material condition, their bodily needs. Third, this practice results in a much broader view of the self, one that involves loving neighbor as the self and thus calls for kenosis, sharing restraint, self-sacrifice, and limits, as the sense of self eventually becomes "universal." Finally, this worldview is relevant at both the personal and public level—the need for kenosis at the personal level (at least for the privileged) and restraint at the public level.[13]

McFague introduces us to hagiography or lives of the saints that often Catholics have appropriated their virtues for imitating. She notes that "saints are extreme, excessive, often "wild"; voluntary poverty appears to be a significant feature of these folks; they see things differently than the rest of us."[14] In his choice to live voluntarily poverty, Francis of Assisi, for example, was considered crazy by his family and extreme then, and now his voluntary poverty would disturb the modern materialist and consumptive imagination of many. David Matzko McCarthy writes about the impact of hagiography, "Saints are expected to transform us. They are expected to disturb the world with God."[15] In other words, Edith Wyschogrod argues that saints make statements with their bodies: "The saintly body acts as a signifier, as a carnal general that condenses and channels meaning, a signifier that expresses extremes of love, compassion, and generosity."[16] Saints communicate embodied value with their lives. McFague observes: "From the saints, we learn the meaning

13. Ibid.

14. Ibid.

15. McCarthy, "Desirous Saints," 307.

16. Wyschogrod, *Saints and Postmodernism*, 52. See McFague's discussion of saints in *Blessed Are the Consumers*, 127–29.

of 'altruism,' and we see it performed in a way that is both particular and more expowerfully expressed than an essay or ethics could possibly convey."[17]

McFague views kenotic spirituality beneficial for ecological praxis of incarnational compassion in action. This is embodied in the physicality of Jesus, his radical inclusive ministry and living out the challenges of compassion in an exclusive, patriarchal world dominated by empire and the religious-political theologies of holiness. Sallie McFague understands that an ecological Christology has two features: embodiment and inclusion.

> By bringing God into the realm of the body, of matter, nature is included within the divine reach. This inclusion is possible only if incarnation is understood in a broad, not narrow fashion: that is, if Jesus as the incarnate Logos, Wisdom, or Spirit of God is paradigmatic of what is evident everywhere else as well . . . Incarnational Christology means that salvation is neither solely human nor spiritual. It must be for the entire creation . . . Incarnational Christology says that God wants all of nature, human beings and all other entities, to enjoy well-being in body and spirit. Incarnational Christology, then, expands the ministry and death of Jesus, the model for Christians of "God with us" to envelop the entire universe.[18]

What McFague describes is an "incarnational inclusivity" that starts with the Big Bang and explodes the incarnated limits of God to include all matter, humanity and all beings, to the limits of the universe. God's incarnation is intimately and integrally involved and present within ourselves and the world. The energy that enlivens the universe is the self-emptying compassionate triune God, the risen Christ and the Spirit giving and receiving, interrelated with everything. "If the Incarnation is indeed our best window into the nature of God, then it makes sense that a kenotic Christology should lead us to a kenotic theism, in which the self-giving love shown in Christ is seen as central to God's very nature."[19] But the resurrection of Christ destroys the physical boundedness of the Incarnation simultaneously extends fleshliness of the Incarnation into the interconnections with human and non-human animal bodies, and the universe. The incarnation of Christ embodies the dynamics of compassionate love

17. Ibid., 127.

18. McFague, "An Ecological Christology," 37–38.

19. Evans. "Introduction," 16.

in a kenotic spirituality and practice: "*Kenosis*, then, is the gateway to mutual understanding, and beyond this, to an understanding sharing that is a consummation of relationship in union . . . By dispossession of self, we are able to absorb the amazing riches of others."[20] *Kenosis* allows us to participate in a universal communion of subjects.

Incarnational Compassion and Hospitality

In his book, *Virtues*, Leonardo Boff tells the myth of Baucis and Philemon from Ovid's *Metamorphoses*. They were an elderly couple deeply in love with each and lived with scant resources and in a run-down house. The gods—Jupiter and Mercury in disguise—visited a thousand houses but were turned away from each of them. The elderly couple, however, welcomed the disguised Gods into their thatched cottage, preparing the best meal that they could even if their resources were scant. They washed the feet of the strangers, and poured wine for the strangers. Each time the bowl was emptied they saw it become filled once more. In their generosity, they offered to give up their bed for the strangers. They asked the elderly couple to be guardians of the temple, and when they died, the Gods turned into two intertwining trees. Boff notes even today that tourists in Turkey reminded of the tale by two centennial trees intertwined: "Whoever welcomes a pilgrim, a foreigner, a poor person welcomes God. Whoever welcomes God, turns himself or herself into a temple of God. Whoever sees a stranger as part of his or her community inherits joyful immortality."[21] Boff observes that this hospitality to strangers, to make them feel at home, is incarnated in a Franciscan tradition to never allow a guest or guests to eat alone. The hosting brother or the superior brother of the convent, even if he ate, sits at table to make the guests feel at home. To welcome the stranger in hospitality is to realize our interrelatedness and inclusive solidarity with each other. Boff includes as the other or stranger the poor, indigenous peoples, peoples of other religions, and even the Earth. He remarks, "Hospitality toward a stranger involves openness, courage to face and overcome the strangeness that provokes fear, suspicion, disconnection, and even the rejection of the other."[22]

20. Raguin, *I Am Sending You*, 112.
21. Boff, *Virtues*, 42.
22. Ibid., 68.

Hospitality is making room or space for others and to welcome them as related, and it expresses incarnational compassion.

Jesus is the incarnate and compassionate face of God.[23] He invites us, "Be compassionate as Abba God is compassionate" (Luke 6:36). Compassion is also the merciful kindness of the Samaritan towards a stranger that is unexpected in most situations. The life of Christ has inspired many Christians throughout the centuries to care for the lame, deformed, broken-hearted, sick, dying and those who are in need. Henri Nouwen describes compassion:

> Compassion asks us to go where it hurts, to enter into the places of pain, to share in brokenness, fear, confusion, and anguish. Compassion challenges us to cry out with those in misery, to mourn with those who are lonely, to weep with those in tears. Compassion requires us to be weak with the weak, vulnerable with the vulnerable, and powerless with the powerless. Compassion means full immersion in the condition of being human (and all life: my corrective).[24]

For Nouwen, the hermeneutics of solidarity is based on a compassionate Christology that identifies Christ with the poor, marginalized, the vulnerable, and suffering. Both Leonardo Boff and Sallie McFague maintain a simultaneous dual perspective of compassionate care for the poor and the vulnerable Earth. Jesus' gospel tolerates no human boundaries that exclude, including barriers between human animals and nonhuman animals and other life. Compassion has the dimension of solidarity which comprehends that we are increasingly bound together as a global community and that we bear social and ecological responsibility for one another's well being. Empathetic solidarity moves *us/them* to *us/us* and to responsible action. Yet compassion has also a political and justice dimension as demonstrated Jesus finding himself at odds with the religious culture of exclusion and the political empire of domination. Maureen O'Connell affirms, "Compassion is not comfortable and private but rather dangerous and political . . . Compassion unleashes the interruptive and liberating power of contrast experience and hones our ability to feel, to imagine, and to enact alternatives to what is."[25] Through solidar-

23. Hellwig, *Jesus*; Sweeney, *The Suffering and Victorious Christ*; Borg, *Meeting Jesus*, 46–68.

24. Nouwen et al., *Compassion*, 4.

25. O'Connell, *Compassion*, 3, 51.

ity with the suffering, compassion helps us to understand how injustice feels, and it moves us beyond our heartbreak identification to action to alleviate suffering. O'Connell aptly notes the dynamics of compassion: "Compassion does not just alleviate suffering, but rather transforms it.[26] It first transforms us by divesting ourselves in our encounters with suffering and injustice and we experience what injustice might feel like. This dynamic is the dangerous memory of Jesus' life and ministry, his death and resurrection.

In other words, compassion is "contemplative compassion in action." McFague turns to Buddhists such as Thich Nhat Hanh and the Dalai Lama to further develop a notion of contemplative compassion while Leonardo Boff taps into the Franciscan contemplative traditions of compassion. Contemplative compassion in action is realizes the need to step back from any personal differences I may have with another human being and see that person as they are at their core, as another child of God, the Christ, and act in accordance. It is the ability to look past the details that create the illusion of separation between myself and another child of God or nonhuman animal life. Compassion remembers that no matter what differences another person and/or nonhuman animal have, there is an incarnational connectedness between us as neighbors. McFague writes: "The gradual development of a "universal self: as the line constituting one's concern (compassion or empathy) moves from a narrow focus on the ego (and one's nearest and dearest) to reach out further and further until there is no line left: even a caterpillar counts. The journey, rather than diminishing the self, increases its delight but, at the cost, of one's old egoistic model."[27] This universal self described by McFague, is an ecological self or kenotic self interrelated as part of the Earth's community of life. Contemplative practices enable practitioners to see the natural world and all life as God sees or what McFague has called seeing "with a loving gazing" or with the eyes of love." An ecologic ethic—living the virtues of hospitality, compassion, and co-living is to be mindful of our interrelatedness with each and all interconnections with the Earth. Mindful meditation with the Earth and other life produces such compassion that sees no boundary between one's self and others, and we are moved to do something alleviate a fellow creature of God is hurting—whether it is another species, a human, or the planet. CnB]emplation helps to see the

26. Ibid., 2.

27. McFague, *Blessed Are the Consumers*, xiii.

natural as "enchanted," as the site of God's reealing presence, and invites us to act lovingly.

Co-living

Leonardo Boff describes co-living: "Co-living allows for sitting together and to co-exist and exchange."[28] Co-living is contemplative compassion in action; it is what Sallie McFague describes as kenotic living with and towards others. It raises question how do we live together with compassionate care and hospitality. Ultimately, it raises the question, "why do we live together?" Boff gives a marvelous example that serves as living parable of kenotic spirituality on how to listen to the cries of the Earth and listen to the cries of the poor. In 1952, a group of the Little Sisters of Jesus traveled to the remote state of Mato Grasso, a jungle area in central Brazil. They heard that the Tapirape tribe faced extinction. Their unique way of life—co-living with the natural forests—would soon be lost to human history. The mission statement of the Little Sisters of Jesus reads as follows:[29]

> We believe that a truly contemplative life can be lived in the midst of the ordinary life of people around the world, simply sharing their day to day life, living conditions, work and dreams - as Jesus did at Nazareth. As our prayer becomes grounded in this ordinary life, as friendships grow with neighbors and co-workers, together we look for the face of God in the midst of the joys and struggles that arise. Not a passive approach, "presence" is what we learn from Jesus through the Incarnation. It is a dynamic way of simply placing oneself within situations in such a way that one's very life becomes rooted and dependent upon what happens there.[30]

By the time, the Little Sisters of Jesus arrived, the Tapirape's numbers were reduced from 1500 to 47 people because of war, disease brought by white Brazilians, who found no value in the tribe. The Sisters respectfully

28. Boff, *Virtues*, 121.

29. Charles de Foucauld was a French Catholic priest and missionary that went to live with Muslims in the Algerian desert in the early twentieth century. Charles de Foucauld's aim was not to directly convert the Muslim tribal folks but to live with them and share their differences together. Charles de Foucauld, 1856–1916. http://www.vatican.va/news_services/liturgy/saints/ns_lit_doc_20051113_de-foucauld_en.html.

30. Little Sisters of Jesus, http://www.rc.net/org/littlesisters/.

asked permission of the Tapirape to co-live with the tribe. They were welcomed to live in the communal hut, but they decided to live in a log cabin that they built with a chapel with their own hands. They lived contemplatively Jesus' gospel of love, making the Incarnate Christ present. They worked with the Tapirape to restore the orchards, enjoyed moments of food bounty and scarcity with the tribe.

The Little Sisters of Jesus lived the parable of the Good Samaritan for Boff; they practiced the compassion of God that Jesus spoke. The Sisters stripped themselves of their egos, their European prejudices and culture, to learn the ways of a different culture and religion of indigenous peoples. The Sisters perceived the Tapirape as their neighbor, taking Jesus' commandment of loving your neighbor as yourself. They practiced the virtues of co-living—love, compassionate care and respect for the other, listening and attentiveness to cultural differences, learning the language, and living as the Tapirape tribe lived with nature. But for the most part, they stood in solidarity with the tribe, learned about the ancestral grace of Tapirape living with the land. It is important to recognize as the Sisters co-lived with the Tapirape; they learned a land ethic on how to live close with nature. Within co-living, compassionate mutual learning takes place with respect for differences and living with differences, sharing other ways of life and sharing other people's struggles. Through co-living, the Sisters learned as much from the Tapirape as they demonstrated respect for the dignity of the tribe. And together they brought the tribe back from near extinction to life.

At the end of fifty years co-living with the Tapirape, not one member of the tribe converted to Christianity. From a missionary perspective of evangelism, the Sisters were a failure, but if we judge their mission as to co-live with the Earth and Tapirape, they were succesful. Co-living is the incarnational function of midwives who birth Christ through living the presence of Christ's love.[31] Boff describes his virtue of co-living and coexisting:

> Co-living and coexisting are "ways of being" that are encompassing and inclusive. To live is an outcome of life, of life taken in all complexities, of life shared with others, of coexisting with others and of sharing dynamically in others' lives, of sharing others' way-of-being, of sharing others' struggles, quests, defeats, and victories. It is within this co-living that real learning takes place, real learning as a collective effort for knowledge, as

31. Boff, *Virtues*, 35–115, 128–35.

a vision of the world, as values that guide life and as a utopia that
maintains the future open ended.[32]

The Little Sisters of Jesus preserved a part of indigenous human life that
can teach us so much about the ancestral grace of loving God by co-
living with nature and learning from the original peoples of the Earth.
We have lost our ancestral grace that God's divine presence companions
and cherishes all life on Earth. While the Sisters assisted the Tapirape to
flourish, the Tapirape gave them, the Little Sisters, the gift of learning to
lvie with the Earth.

Leonardo Boff frequently directs us to learn from the original peoples so that we once more might learn how to reconnect to the Earth.[33]
He approvingly quotes Brazilian champions of the indigenous—Orlando
and Claudio Villas-Boas: "But if we want to be rich, accumulate power,
and rule the Earth, there is no point in asking the native peoples. But
if we want to be happy, combine being human with being divine, integrate life and death, put the person in nature, connect work and leisure,
harmonize relations between generations, then listen to the indigenous
peoples. They have wise lessons to impart to us."[34] Boff underscores that
the indigenous peoples have an ancestral wisdom in their stories and
myths built on listening to the Earth; they are aware that "the Earth is
not a mere means of production but an extension of life and the body.
It is Pacha Mama, the Great Mother, who gives birth, feels, and envelops
all."[35] Thomas Berry, self-identified "geologian," reiterates that original
peoples had much to offer European settlers in North America: "The indigenous peoples of this continent tried to teach us the value of the land,
but unfortunately we could not understand them, blinded as were by our
dreams of manifest destiny. Instead we were scandalized, because they
insisted on living simply rather than working industriously. We desired
to teach them our ways, never thinking that they could teach us theirs."[36]
Like Boff, Berry appreciates the wisdom of indigenous peoples past and
present, and he finds that surviving indigenous cultures have preserved
elements of a wisdom tradition despite the ravages to the environment by
industrial cultures. These indigenous societies with sustainable ecologi-

32. Ibid., 135.

33. Boff, *Cry of the Earth.*

34. Ibid., loc. 2694.

35. Ibid., loc. 2733.

36. Berry, *The Sacred Universe,* loc. 2110.

cal values and wisdom may inform our efforts to recover a sense of sacred in nature.[37]

Huston Smith narrates the story of Oren Lyons of the Onondagan tribe, after completing college and asked a single question by his uncle: "Who are you?" His uncle rejected all answers and then finally answered: "Do you see that bluff over there? Oren, you are that bluff. And that giant pine on the other shore? Oren, you are that pine. And this water that supports this boat? You are this water."[38] Oren's uncle instructs him with a Zen-style answer of emptiness of self and identification with an interconnected "universal self." At the Parliament of World Religions Conference (2015), I had the opportunity to talk with a Lakota Chief and described how my church made the Earth a member of the congregation. He remarked, "You understand how the Earth Mother is part of the Lakota peoples." Thomas Berry observes reflectively, "As the years pass, it becomes ever clear that dialogue with native people here and throughout the world is urgently needed to provide the human community with models of a more integral human presence to the Earth."[39]

Congregational Kenosis

Incarnational kenosis is living compassionately for the Earth and other life. The Valley UCC church is an older, progressive Protestant congregation with Catholic spiritual leanings, facing the challenges of an aging population. Since we were commited to live Jesus' radical inclusive love and his compassion, we decided to include the Earth as a member of the congregation. This inclusion of the Earth began a transformational process, starting with replacing all the light bulbs with CFL(s) and later Led(s), then our outdoor water heater was replaced with a tankless water heat, recycling, creating a garden to tear asphalt to allow water into the water table, landscaping the new created garden from donations of members and non-members, and composting our food and plant remains.[40]

37. Finders, *Thomas Berry's Sacred Surround*, loc. 993–1039.

38. Smith, *The World's Religions*, 371.

39. Berry, *The Great Work*, 178.

40. For some practical advice on the transformation of a church/congregation, I suggest the following talks on YouTube by myself and Allis Druffel, Southern California Coordinator of California Interfaith Power & Light and myself: Shore-Goss, "Introduction: Falling in Love with God's Earth"; Shore-Goss, "State of the Earth," Part 1 & 2. Shore-Goss, "How to Get Started?"; Shore-Goss, "Greening Your Campus";

In 2009, we had the opportunity to investigate a twenty-year lease for ninety solar panels. The congregational vote was unanimous for the decision since it was a very good business decision by reducing our monthly electric bills by five to seven hundred dollars. Most churches are used heavily at night and on weekends while peak usage is Monday-Friday from 9 AM- 5 PM, peak usage times and higher rates. Thus, low usage during these peak moments could be sold back to the utility company while purchasing it during the evenings and weekends at lower rates.

Each year we took the green justice congregational diagnosi scale, first scoring nearly 80—being a great score. Over the years we have progressed until our congregational scored over 140. We held educational forums, screen videos on climate change, held discussion groups for input, and greened our preaching on regular basis and green our sacraments and rituals. We have attained over the years a carbon neutral footprint for the church and water judiciously our garden with deep watering and water saved from rain barrels that harvest nearly 100 gallons of water every two weeks in rain barrows form condensation runoffs from air conditioning. We joined California Interfaith Power and Light, and the church was awarded by CIPL a green Oscar for advocacy.[41] I have facilitated workshops on greening congregations for UCC annual conference meetings and for alumni days at Claremont School of Theology, providing resources for clergy and training folks within the UCC Southern California/Nevada Conference to green their congregations, and a workshop at the Parliament of World Religions (2015). The congregation has hosted what we have termed "solar nights" for other faith communities, residential housing, and local businesses on the merit and cost savings from the installation of solar panels. During the declared water drought, we offered water conservation workshops on reducing water usage and change green lawns to desert landscapes.

Individual lives as well as the congregational life have changed for kenotic living. I pass on petitions and email campaigns to Congress and the California legislature spread by California Interfaith Power and Light,

Shore-Goss, "Greening Your Campus, Part 2"; Allis Druffel, "Greening Congregations and IPL."

41. Hosenfeld, *Eco-Faith: Creating & Sustaining Green Congregations.* Two good diagnostic tools for congregations: Take the survey "Becoming a Green Justice Congregation," http://www.ucc.org/environmental-ministries/just-green-congregations. html; Interfaith Power & Light Use the congregational start-up kit: http://www.cool-congregations.org/start-up-kit/.

Green Peace, and various ecojustice groups. We became the first Creation Justice Congregation in the United Church of Christ.[42] I also found that LA Department of Power and Water was dragging hooking up the congregation's solar panels to the grid, and after four months, I decided to attend the LA meeting on the City Council hearings on rate hikes of electrical power. I attended with my clergy collar and embarrassed the General Manger and the Assistant General Manger, and we were hooked to the grid in four days.

With stress on the dual biblical preferential option for the poor and Earth, we processed ongoing interconnections between the poor and the homeless and the vulnerable impact upon nonhuman animals and climate processes. These two ministerial foci are important to the congregation and its spirituality. Sallie McFague comprehends kenosis: "Kenosis is the recognition of restraint, openness, humility, respect for otherness, and even sacrifice (diminishment and death) are part of life, if one assumes that individual well-being within political and cosmic well-being."[43] Wendell Berry observes about the restraint of limits in escapable in living with the Earth during the climate crisis; "It is more likely that we will have to live within our limits . . . or not live at all."[44]

Kenosis as "Reverence for Life"

Lynn White made a second suggestion of a remarkable figure in the twentieth century to model compassion upon: Albert Schweitzer, theologian, philosopher, musician, missionary, and medical doctor, and recipient of the Nobel Peace Prize in 1952. He spent most of life in rural Africa where he established a medical clinic for the poor. His missionary medical practice was grounded in his desire to be a disciple of Jesus, but his humanitarian compassion extended beyond to the poor and the sick, for it also included nonhuman animals that were sick or injured. His earlier encounters with Jain and Buddhist traditions of nonviolence (*ahimsa*) and compassion when he travelled to India, impacted his Christian praxis with a deep reverence and compassion for life. On a small steam ship on the Ogowe River, while making its way through a herd of hippopotamuses, Schweitzer describes a flash of illumination at the phrase of

42. UCC Creation Justice Church: http://www.ucc.org/creation_justice_churches/.
43. McFague, *Blessed Are the Consumers*, 144.
44. Berry, *The Unsettling of American Culture*, 92.

"reverence for life."[45] It was a moment of grace that shaped his philosophy and spirituality of life. While many authors describe him as a Christian, he was not typical. His philosophy of the reverence for life woven into his spirituality, influenced and shaped by his devotion to following Christ in discipleship and his praxis of a biophilic spirituality.

In his correspondence, Albert Schweitzer contextualizes his notion of reverence for life as grounded in Jesus: "The ethics of reverence for life is nothing but Jesus' great commandment to love—a commandment that is reached by thinking religion and thinking meet in the mysticism of belonging to God through love."[46] He argues that his praxis of reverence for life is greater than the verbal description. There is language of grace inclusive of the apophatic dimensions of experiencing life in his language. For Schweitzer, Jesus incarnates God's compassion extended to other life; it becomes universalized. Schweitzer writes, "The friend of nature is the man who feels himself inwardly united with everything that lives in nature, who shares in the fate of all creatures, helps them when he can in their pain and need, as far as possible avoids injuring or taking life."[47] In a sermon on Romans 14:7, he sounds very Buddhist in his description of compassion: "Wherever you see life—that is you! In everything you recognize yourself again . . . a compassionate sharing of experiences with all of life. I can do no other than to have compassion for all that us called life . . . We are ethical if we abandon our selfishness, if we surrender our estrangement toward other creatures, and share in and empathies with that from their experience which surrounds us."[48] Through compassion, a person breaks down the egocentric barriers with the suffering creature(s) and shares empathy. His biophilic spirituality overlaps the spiritual sensitivities of Francis of Assisi. He kept the windows closed at night to keep out insects harmed by candlelight. If he would see an earthworm on a road, Schweitzer would place the worm on grass. Such an ethical practice of compassionate care originates from a profound spirituality that includes meditative attention and compassionate love. Most criticism of Schweitzer's ethical praxis centers around his refusal to differentiate between life forms and provide ethical guidelines for evaluating between various life forms. The question for modern interpreters is whether one

45. Quoted in Barsam, *Reverence for Life*, ix.

46. Ibid., 23.

47. Ibid., 70.

48. Ibid., 71.

accepts the pro-life position of Schweitzer in its entirety or introduces a hierarchy of value of other life. Birch and Cobb criticize Schweitzer: "Judgments of value among species will have a subjective element, and similarity to human beings is likely to play a distorting role at times. But it does not follow that no generalizations are possible or that human beings will show greater wisdom in this area if they make decisions *ad hoc*. An adequate ethic reverence for life requires the development which Schweitzer refused to give it."[49] Schweitzer embraced his position of an ethical mysticism of a reverence for life precisely because it afforded no guidelines of creating choices between competing life forms and thus create a hierarchy. John Cobb and Charles Birch propose a three-fold valuation of life. 1) rocks, cells, and plants are at low rung, 2) with animals, increased complexity of the central nervous system and brain development and their increased emotional capacity provide a greater ethical claim upon human animals, 3) humanity at the highest summit of the tree of life because of our consciousness has the greatest demand for ethical attentiveness. They still introduce an anthropocentric hierarchy.

Jay McDaniel develops the schema of their life-centered ethic that attempts to unite a concern for individual animal life and the larger eco-system. His intent is to develop a life-supporting spirituality that proceeds from his premise of life-centered God. God's love is unlimited: "I mean love, 1) that is universal in scope, inclusive of all creatures with sentience and needs, and 2) that is infinitely tender, desirous of well-being of each sentient being for its own sake and cognizant of each being as an end in itself."[50] McDaniel attempts a creative synthesis of two approaches: the reverence for life of Albert Schweitzer, whom he considers the mentor of the animal rights movement and the land ethic of Aldo Leopold who promotes the welfare and integrity of the biotic community. Leopold recalls an incident in his youth in hunting wolves:

> We reached the old wolf in time to watch a fierce green fire dying in her eyes. I realized then, and have known ever since, that there was something new to me in those eyes—something known only to her and to the mountain. I was young then, and full of trigger-itch; I thought that because fewer wolves meant more deer, that no wolves would mean hunters' paradise. But

49. Birch and Cobb, *The Liberation of Life*, 149.

50. McDaniel, *Of God and Pelicans*, 21.

> after seeing the green fire die, I sensed that neither the wolf nor
> the mountain agreed with such a view.[51]

He looked into the eyes of the dying wolf he shot, realizing that neither the wolf nor the mountain approved his action. He empatheically adopted the view of thinking like the mountain. This fostered Leopolo's reverence for nature and all life. McDaniel envisions:

> The 'land ethic' of Aldo Leopold, which has been taken by many
> an environmentalist, needs to be complemented by 'life ethic" of
> Albert Schweitzer . . . The task instead is to synthesize aspects of
> each into a larger whole: into a life-centered ethic that responds
> both to the abuse of individual of animals under human subju-
> gation and to the degradation and to the degradation of larger
> biotic wholes, which are themselves habitats for countless living
> beings. Put differently, the task is to shift horizons in such a way
> that anthropocentrism with respect to individual animals and
> ecological wholes is eliminated. To eliminate anthropocentrism
> is to recognize the intrinsic value of life.[52]

McDaniel balances land ethic and life ethic, but still falls into anthropocentric hierarchies of giving greater value to more developed nonhuman animals on the tree of evolutionary life. He states directly, "The need for judgment on the basis of degree of value must be complemented by reverence for life . . ."[53] Creatures of lesser value than creatures of greater value are yet valuable to God: "For those interested in a biocentric Christianity, God must be conceived as loving all creatures on their own terms and for their own sake: the living cell, the mosquito, the pelican and the human being."[54] McDaniel turns to a biocentric spirituality that celebrates and reverences life on Earth, and appropriates Buddhist notions of emptiness, dependent origination (interbeing), and compassion into a hybrid Buddhist Christian biocentric practice. What attracts me to McDaniel's ecotheology, as well to McFague, is that he is one of the few Christian theologians to suggest that Christians engage in a daily spiritual practice of meditation/prayer with the Earth. He speaks about prayer poetically

51. Leopold, "Thinking Like A Mountain"; an excerpt from Aldo Leopold's *A Sand County Almanac*.

52. McDaniel, *With Roots and Wings*, 55, 60.

53. McDaniel, *Of God and Pelicans*, 84.

54. Ibid.

as "an inwardly felt lure offering grace sufficient to the moment."[55] A little later, he describes the purpose of silent prayer as "to hear God's prayer and God's presence."[56] He describes the contemplative in action or compassion in action ideal: "God's prayer is the called-for-action relative to the situation at hand. God's presence is the silence, the spacious freedom that merges in our inner lives when our chattering has subsided and we rest in the still point of the turning world."[57] There are two points I want to underscore here. The first is on-going daily contemplative practices—which include nature, our companion animals, forests or oceans, mountains and deserts can become important doorways to engage God in the midst of the natural world. Amidst our silent network of interrelations, our egos dissolve, and there is the pregnant now, transparent with God. We being to repair our relations to the Earth; we are repairing us Earth creatures and continue to repair human damage to the Earth community. Franciscan theologian Ilia Delia writes,

> Prayer is subversive and perhaps more subversive than science, for a person of prayer is one deeply rooted in the transformative power of God's love. Through prayer, we come to perceive the world in new ways. Prayer helps us to recognize that we humans (together with creation) have a capacity for self-transcendence.
>
> We are, in a sense, "wired for God." Prayer is that openness to God, or to use a modern term, "downloading" God into our hearts and minds. It is the breadth of the Spirit that nurtures the roots of our lives. It is prayer that can change the way that we go about in this creation because the Spirit creates a new heart within us and thus a new vision of the world.[58]

Contemplative prayer provides a venue for personal transformation that redefines the self as network of interrelated life and earthly processes. It leads to an incarnational conversion to the Earth, and this turning to the Earth does not exclude God but recognizes that the distant God is really embodied and incarnately present in the interrelated Earth and the universe. Another scientist, Christopher Uhl, describes the dynamics of mindfulness and doing something to awaken ourselves to action. He actually describes the contemplative in action ideal, the dynamics of

55. McDaniel, *With Roots and Wings*, 226.

56. Ibid., 229.

57. Ibid.

58. Delio et al, *Care for Creation*, 124.

incarnate compassion in action.[59] Such ongoing contemplative experience with God in the world forms and informs our spirituality to make difficult judgment calls between an ethics of the land and a reverence for life.

Eco-Contemplation and Wings of Change

One of the trajectories of the popularization of the Christian contemplative movement in the 1950s and 1960s can be traced to Thomas Merton at the Trappist monastery of Gethsemane. Merton wrote his books for Catholics and non-Catholics seeking silence and solitude from the busy life that was frenetic, experiencing change around sexuality and gender issues, the African-American civil rights movement, and the development of non-violent movement and the antiwar sentiment against the Vietnam war. Merton introduced me as a Catholic teenager to a contemplative vision of connecting with God and engaging in social justice finding God in the experience of non-Christians. Contemplative interconnections to social and environmental justice are now growing in popularity. The Buddhist-Christian monastic dialogue began with Thomas Merton, and it has opened both traditions to a greater familiarity with each others' practices and spiritualities. Many naturalists and wilderness conservations have discovered a contemplative awareness what it means to live, listen, and learn from nature. Mindful attentiveness has the focus of intense awareness and the playful capaciousness; it can grow deep roots and wings to fly the expanse of the skies. For example, Aldo Leopold writes,

> The song of a river is audible to the ear, but there is other music ... by no means audible to all. To hear a few notes of it you must first live here for a long time, and you must know the speech of hills and rivers. Then on a still night, when the campfire is low and the Pleiades have climbed over rimrocks, sit quietly and listen for a wolf to howl, and think hard of everything you have seen and tried to understand. Then you may hear it—a vast and pulsing harmony—its score inscribed on a thousand hills, its notes the lives and deaths of plants and animals, its rhythms spanning seconds and centuries.[60]

59. Uhl, *Developing Ecological Consciousness,* loc. 4536–4590.
60. Leopold, *A Sand County Almanac,* 149–50.

Leopold hears the voice of the river amidst the interconnected voices of nature, for he often exposes the web-like complexity of nature and how we human animals are part of that complex web of interbeing. Leopold often felt that conservationists were too shallow in their approaches to nature by just comprehending its individual worth with human economic interest rather than the worth found in a species or a tree itself. His synoptic vision resulted from his mental attentiveness to the particular voice and the symphony of blended voices in the web of nature. Mindful attentiveness is not a monopoly of religious contemplatives, but it is more universal than we imagine in folks who have deep aesthetic experiences of nature, whose passions are ignited to fight to preserve wilderness regions or particular species.

When I read Aldo Leopold, John Muir, Wendell Berry, or Rachel Carson and others, I recalled Teilhard's experience celebrating eucharist in the Gobi Desert without the elements of bread and wine, "The Mass of the Universe." Similarly, Rachel Carson brings Albert Schweitzer's spirituality and reverence for life into her writings: "The discipline of a (nature) writer is to learn to be still and listen to the subject has to tell him (her)."[61] Carson's books on the oceans or her prophetic book *Silent Spring* manifest how her inner life engages the outer world with a sense of reverence and expresses a spirituality of compassionate care. E. Marina Schauffler writes, "Ecological writers can be characterized as 'prospectors for revelation,' individuals who seek out numinous encounters and consciously sift through their experiences to locate valuable nuggets. This prospecting may become an enduring avocation so that crystalline moments collected like gems."[62] Schauffler contextualizes the revelatory experiences of ecological writers taking place in wilderness and domesticated settings—all communicating a sense of beauty, wonder, and belonging.

When we compare these revelatory moments of grace within nature of ecological writes, Thomas Berry's description of a natural epiphany in his youth of the "meadow across the creek," with spring lilies with white blossoms above thick grass, the singing of crickets, the woodlands in the distance, the sky and the clouds: "Yet as the years pass, this moment returns to me, and whenever I think about my basic life attitude and the whole trend of my mind and the causes to which I have given my efforts,

61. Brooks, *House of Life*, 2.

62. Schauffler, *Turning to the Earth*, 79.

I seem to come back to this moment and the impact it has on my feeling for what is real and worthwhile in life."[63] Berry uses his natural epiphany as the beginnings of his own ecological spirituality to contrast how alienated we have become:

> The difficulty is that with the rise of the modern sciences we began to think of the universe as a collection of objects rather than a communion of subjects . . . We have not only controlled the planet in much of its basic functioning of the natural world, but control has not always had beneficial consequences . . . We no longer hear the voice of the rivers, the mountains, or the seas. The trees and meadows are no longer intimate modes of spirit presence.[64]

One element of Berry's approach to the natural world is how his engagement with Buddhist notions of compassion and mindfulness shape his contemplative sensitivity to nature. For Berry, the only way to become a "life-enhancing species" is to re-orient ourselves to nature with wonder and compassion, and this is the only way humanity can lead us to develop a "wonder-filled intimacy with the planet."[65] There is strong overlap between Buddhist and Christian contemplative experiences. Compassion arises from the experience that everything is interrelated, we are all interconnected, we are all kin to everything in our lives.

Flashes of illumination or grace associated with a particular natural location does not recede in the lives of ecological writers, for they serve as impetus for the cultivation of compassionate connection with nature and the divine, a vocation to belonging and commitment of reciprocal responsibility and care. Thomas Berry consistently points to the necessity to hear the language of the divine with nature:

> The divine has ways of speaking that are not human ways. So too natural phenomena have ways of speaking that are not human language . . . To think that the various phenomena, such as stars do not speak to us is to break with natural systems . . . In early times, this break or separation between human language and the language of other natural phenomena was not evident. This sense of human/nonhuman language goes back to the fact that the divine communicates to us primarily through the languages

63. Berry, *The Great Work*, 13; see his description of the meadow on 12.

64. Ibid., 15–16.

65. Berry, *The Sacred Universe*, loc. 1759, 2013.

of the natural world. Not to hear the natural world is not to hear
the divine.[66]

This is a panentheist claim of ecological spirituality, similar to those of
Leonardo Boff and Sallie McFague, who comprehend the divine speaking
through the language of nature. It requires a meditative listening, a natural *lectio divina*, to pay reflectively attention and meditatively hear the
divine within the natural world. Berry asserts: "I have often said that the
wonder and beauty of the natural world is the only way we save ourselves.
Just now we are losing our world of meaning through our destruction of
the natural world wherein the divine speaks to us."[67]

We find similar meditative style language in Sallie McFague when
she proposes a simple rule for how Christians should love nature: "pay
attention to it." McFague defines what "attention" means with Simone
Weil's observation, "absolute attention is prayer."[68] She cogently argues
that we cannot love nature if we do not know nature. McFague turns
to nature writers to find conversion experiences in falling in love with
nature. She includes nature writers such as Annie Dillard and Joseph Wood
Krutch as well as Harvard biologist E.O. Wilson. For example, South-
west nature writer Joseph Krutch describes his conversion experience in
first encountering the desert: "Suddenly a new, undreamed world was
revealed. There was something so unexpected in the combination of bril-
liant sun and earth that my first reaction was delighted amusement."[69]
Nature writers discover a sense of wonder and "help us to see what we
otherwise might not notice at all by arresting our attention, making us
stop and take notice."[70] In a book length-letter to a Southern Baptist minister, Edward O. Wilson speaks of biophilia, "the inborn attraction to the
natural world."[71] He asks the pastor to promote more naturalists: "To be
a naturalist is not just an activity but an honorable state of mind. Those
who have expressed its value and protected living nature are among
America's heroes: John James Audubon, Henry David Thoreau, John
Muir, Theodore Roosevelt."[72]

66. Ibid., loc. 1710.

67. Ibid., loc. 1727.

68. McFague, *Super, Natural Christians*, 29.

69. Ibid., 152.

70. Ibid., 135.

71. Wilson, *The Creation*, 139.

72. Ibid., 140.

Nature writers find within the natural world or a particular locale an expansion of their enclosed self, pushing outwards into the natural world to find rootedness, interrelatedness, and an experience of wholeness. It is a heart-felt or conversion-style experience, often described as a mystical connection or a natural mysticism, but it is similar to the experiences of religious mystics. Such connections to the natural world are not lesser than the profound experiences of God by religious contemplatives.[73]

Rachel Carson recounts a formative epiphany in college:

> Years ago on a night when rain and wind bear against the windows of my college dormitory room, a line from (Tennyson's) "Locksley Hall'" burned itself into my mind—"For the mighty wind arises, roaring seaward, and I go." I can still remember my intense emotional response as that line spoke to something within me seeming to tell me that my own path led to the sea—which I have never seen—and that my own destiny was somehow linked with the sea. And so, as you know, it has been.[74]

Carson became a "biographer of the sea," detailing direct, personal appreciation of individual organisms as well as love for the Maine seacoast. Paul Brooks says, "She felt a spiritual as well as a physical closeness to the individual creatures about whom she wrote: a sense of identification that is an essential element in her literary style."[75] Carson later became a champion for human and non-human life in her final book *Silent Spring*.[76]

The point is that Christian passionate commitments must not presume a monopoly over of contemplative experience. Hildegard of Bingen looked for the primordial voice (*prima vox*), the greening or animating principle everywhere in the world and perceivable to anyone sensitive to become mindful of it.[77] Any human with focused attention and listening with great sensitivity to the natural world around them can discover the presence of God operative in the living world. The contemplative practice of silent attentiveness opens folks to a world of unimagined experience and connectedness to God's grace.[78] Contemplatives from a spiritual

73. Grey, *Sacred Longings*, 149–71; Fischer, *Loving Creation*.

74. Carson, *Always Rachel*, 59.

75. Brooks, Ibid., 7–8.

76. Sideris, "The Secular and Religious Sources of Rachel Carson's Sense of Wonder."

77. Hildegard, *Symphonia*, 126–27.

78. Some good resources: Christie, *The Blue Sapphire of the Mind*; Schauffler, *Turning to the Earth*; Fischer, *Loving Creation*; Highland, *Meditations of John Muir*.

ecology background, Christian and interfaith, can begin to share their experiences, their stories of grace and nature, and their passion for care of the earth and all life. This contemplative movement can build coalition and share a commitment to Earthcare. Working together brings a force for change rooted in the Incarnate Christ and ensouled Spirit during these perilous times.

But there are some good traditional sources of Christian spirituality that can be tapped for ecological composting or revitalizing our individual spiritualities as well as our communal spiritualities: Some of these sources ere Franciscan, Hildegard of Bingen, Ignatian and Teilhard, Buddhist, Matthew Fox, naturalist and indigenous traditions. Berry points to five Christian ecological models for living with the natural world:

1. Celtic spirituality

2. the Benedictine custodial model

3. the Franciscan of fraternal kinship

4. the fertility model of Hildegard of Bingen

5. the integral model of Teilhard de Chardin (Jesuit).[79]

Celtic Christianity is a blend of early Celtic Earth-centered traditions with Christian spirituality. Scottish theologian and Anglican priest John Maquarrie highlights how Celtic Christianity draws its focus to divine immanence in the natural world.

> Although it (Celtic spirituality) belongs to a culture that has almost vanished it fulfills in many respects the condition to which contemporary spirituality would have to conform. At the very centre of this type spirituality was an intense sense of presence. The Celt was very much a God-intoxicated man whose life was embraced on all sides by divine being. But his presence was always mediated through some finite, this-world-reality so that it would be difficult to imagine a spirituality more down to earth than this one. The sense of God's immanence in His creation was so strong in Celtic spirituality so as to amount sometimes to pantheism.[80]

79. Berry points out, "The celebration of creation in medieval Christianity retained its place. The natural world was exalted as continued modes of divine presence. We find expressions of this in forms of Celtic animism, in Benedictine stewardship liturgies, in the devotions of Hildegard of Bingen, in the fraternal prayer of Francis of Assisi." Berry, *The Christian Future*, 107.

80. Macquarrie, "Paths in Spirituality," 7.

Much of pre-Christian Celtic spirituality was assimilated into Celtic Christianity, and a perusal of Celtic prayers and theologies reveal a strong link with the sacramental nature theology of Orthodox Christianity. Celtic Christian spirituality finds God deep with the seasonal cycles, days of the week, in the streams and rivers, and forests. Imagine us as God intoxicated lovers ande defenders of the Earth![81]

Kenotic Lifestyle

The Green Patriarch Bartholomew speaks of asceticism, a communal attitude and practice that leads to respectful use and restraint of the fruits of the Earth. How we use and preserve material goods originates from love of God's Earth, community, and future generations. He invites us to learn generosity rather than giving up, reducing our expenditures of natural resources. This loving praxis of restraint replaces overconsumption with sacrifice, greed with generosity, and wastefulness with a spirit of sharing. Orthodox theologian John Chryssavgis writes, "The goal of asceticism is moderation, not repression. Its content is positive, not negative; it looks to service, not selfishness; to reconciliation, not renunciation."[82]

Similarly, James Nash speaks about practices and virtues of the Puritans, later Congregationalists, which included "thrift, moderation, frugality, sobriety, and diligence." Nash continues, "Ironically, the chief ecological virtues of modern environmental movement correspond with the virtues of classic Puritanism."[83] In a later article, Nash expands the notion of frugality to include also cost-effectiveness, efficient usage, and a material sufficiency.[84] Green discipleship includes the virtue of living with less to practice sustainability with the Earth: "Frugality is an earth-affirming and enriching norm that delights in the non- and less-consumptive joys of the mind and flesh, especially the enhanced lives for human communities and other creatures that only constrained consumption and production can make possible on a finite planet . . . Frugality minimizes harm to humans and other life forms, enabling thereby a

---

81. Some good sources: Joyce, *Celtic Christianity*; Newell, *The Book of Creation*; *Christ of the Celts.*

82. Chryssavgis, "A New Heaven and a New Earth," loc. 3263.

83. Nash, *Loving Nature*, 76–77.

84. s Nash, "On the Subversive Virtue: Frugality," 421.

greater thriving of all life.[85] Frugality like the word asceticism does not go over with consumerist-oriented people. . Richard Rohr calls for Franciscan notion of enoughness for living sustaianably: "to recognize that there is *enough to go around and meet everyone's need but not everyone's greed.*"[86] We might choose less to share more.

Sallie McFague asks "Is consumer life good for the planet?" Nonrenewable resources are finite, and they are expended at alarming rates. Taking the global footprint calculator quiz surprises folks with the calculations of the number of planets needed to sustain individual lifestyles.[87] The quiz is based on our choices of driving, air transportation, recycling, purchase, types of energy, and so. This raises the question civic engagement and green technologies employed. The aim of such a diagnostic is move individuals and organizations to attempt to move as closely as possible to a carbon neutral footprint. It can be achieved communally, but where the difficulty is the translation of such practices to reduce carbon footprints of individuals and families. It is out of love that we practice ecological restraint in consuming for the sake of our children, nephews and nieces, and grandchildren.

McFague raises a kenotic alternative: "Ecological economics is a human enterprise that seeks to maximize the optimal functioning of the planet's gifts and services for all."[88] She uses the metaphor of the household for the Planet and household rules: "take your share, clean up after yourself, and keep the house in good repair for others."[89] She shifts to positive language of human and planetary well-being and flourishing. She focuses on "wild space, a place to stand and to interpret one's culture from the outside."[90] Such a spatially countercultural location allows for us "to see differently, to imagine other possibilities, to pay attention to others."[91] It leads to grassroots change of lifestyles. She argues, "The practice of kenosis is a fundamentally different paradigm for living and acting in the world: one which we give up all forms of privilege whether these have to with economics or our reputation. Kenosis points to an

85. Ibid., 427.

86. Rohr, "Enoughness instead of never Enough."

87. Global Footprint Network, http://www.footprintnetwork.org/en/index.php/GFN/page/calculators/.

88. McFague, *Life Abundant*, 100.

89. McFague, *A New Climate*, 53.

90. McFague, *Blessed are the Consumers*, 85.

91. Ibid.

understanding of power as facilitating the well-being of other rather than control of these others; from the evolutionary level of give and take reciprocity, death before life, to the dynamic dance of self-giving love in the Trinity."[92] McFague invites us to imitate the saints, to live compassionately kenotic lives and practice compassionate action on personal and public levels. She espouses a counter space of action: "the way of extravagant generosity, of willed sacrifice for the vulnerable, of recognizing radical interdependence, of self-emptying."[93] She notes, "Kenosis is not sack cloth and ashes, depriving the self of all worldly good and pleasures for personal purification and salvation."[94] It is joyous and generous living, paying attention to the Earth and all life. She quotes Berry, "It is more likely that we will have either to live within our limits . . . or not all."[95] Ilia Delio and co-authors write about voluntary poverty,

> Conversion to poverty is conversion to justice . . . Once we realize our need for God, we begin to realize our need for others, including the created world. The grace of poverty is the grace of dependency, rendering us open and grateful for that enables us to explain the planet Earth. It is looking into the eyes of our neighbor and seeing there the light of God touching. It is touching the trees and the rocks and the Earth on which we stand and feeling the goodness of God.[96]

> Justice is right relationship, respecting in others inherent goodness that is uniquely theirs and loving the good that is in them. It is granting to others what rightfully belongs to them as creatures of God and sharing with others what is ours to share. Justice is the sister of the poverty.[97]

Many of the eco-theologians such as Leonardo Boff, Buddhists, the Green Patriarch Bartholomew, and Pope Francis call for variations of kenotic spirituality, self-emptying love, frugality over wastefulness and compassionate care for the flourishing and well-being of humanity and all life.

92. Ibid., 96.
93. Ibid., 137.
94. Ibid., 145.
95. Ibid., 148; Berry, *The Unsettling of America*, 94.
96. Delia et al., *Care for Creation*, 181.
97. Ibid.

Engaged Green Communities

In *Green Sisters*, Sarah McFarland Taylor points how out how Catholic religious imagination and green culture share a number of affinities. Catholic sacramental imagination and a deep incarnationalism create strong bonds with green American culture.[98] The more central that the incarnated Christ becomes, the more sacramental nature becomes to the focus of spiritual practice and a reverence of life. There was the example of Benedict of Nursia and his monastic rule that impacted western monasticism and its developments. Benedictine spirituality and subsequent monastic derivation of the Benedictine rule stood as countercultural critique of mainline culture. Benedictine spirituality derived from the rule has maintained a strong commitment to a specific geographical location through the vow of stability, stress on humility and frugality.[99] Stability is a commitment to a geographic location, not to deplete its resources but to look to ways to renew the fertility of the soil. Terrence Kardong writes about stability: "To really get to know and love a place a person must live there for a long time . . . (T)hose who live in a place are usually in the best position to know what is appropriate for that place . . ."[100] Working the land over -generations produces an intimate knowing of the land, a wisdom passed down to monastics each generation. Benedictine Abbott John Klassen expands upon the commitment to stability:

> It [stability] is a knowledge that will lead us to recognize the habitats that are necessary for different kinds of wildlife. It will draw us to learn something about the forest that was originally in a place, to review topography and soil and climate conditions, and reforest if necessary. It is an argument for "wildness," for resisting the temptation to create places where there is not tall grass, fallen trees, and piles of leaves for animals to dwell. This knowledge will change us and the kind of education we give to our students. As described above, nature itself has much to teach about human limits, the seasons of a person's life, the cycle of death and renewal and will be part of the educational process.[101]

98. Taylor, *Green Sisters,*45.

99. Abbott John Klassen, "The Rule of St. Benedict and Environmental Stewardship."

100. Kardong, "Ecological Resources in the Benedictine Rule," 167.

101. Ibid.

By focusing on the land, Benedictines learned how to connect to the wildlife, the grasses and trees, fields and seasons. Contemporary Benedictine spirituality attempts to stress sustainability of the land and the community. Thomas Berry understood the Benedictine monastic movement as a forerunner for environmental stewardship: "One of the great things Benedictines developed was the idea of that intellectual activity was associated with physical work, particularly work with the land . . . There was an emphasis on cultivation of the soil as well as learning about it."[102] With a stress on simplicity and reduction of waste, land spirituality stands in contrast to a consumerist and extractive relationship with the land. Each monastic receives a share of the land's fruits. Russell Butkus notes Benedictine countercultural lifestyle:

> Given the high degree of mobility in our culture, Benedict's teaching on stability of place would most likely be perceived as a countercultural (but necessary) palliative to our predicament of unsustainability but not nearly as countercultural or as difficult to achieve, as the Benedictine virtue of frugality. This strikes at the very core of our unsustainable way of life . . . The countercultural and perhaps subversive virtue of frugality is one of the most significant contributions the Benedictine tradition can make in our affluent society.[103]

Stability and simplicity form an ascetical stewardship of the land that does not overtax the land, rejoices in its fruitfulness, and co-lives respectfully with the land and creates a sustainable community. Benedicitne *lectio divina* creates actions for sustainable life with the Earth.

One of the examples is the Sisters of the Earth, an international network inspired by Thomas Berry and his writings. They are a network of Catholic religious women and women from other religious traditions dedicated to live in sustainable communities with the Earth. They are teachers, gardeners, artists, writers, workshop facilitators, retreat presenters and spiritual mentors, mothers, contemplatives and eco-activists. The Sisters are involved in the work healing the human spirit and its breach with the Earth and restoring the Earth's life support systems. John Carroll assesses the Sisters of the Earth network: "they represent one of the purest examples of life lived according to ecological principle, to sustainability principle . . . They also represent among the purest forms of

102. Didcoct, "Choosing Our Roots," 28.

103. Butkus, "Sustainability and the Benedictine Way"; quoted in Carroll, *Sustainability and Spirituality*, 112.

practice of life according to the teachings of Francis of Assisi, Teilhard de Chardin, Wendell Berry . . . and Thomas Berry."[104] Dominican Sister Miriam Therese MacGillis with Thomas Berry founded Genesis Farm in New Jersey in the early 1990s. The Sisters are Earth pioneers living into what Berry described as the EcoZoic age. Berry saw the potential power of uniting eco-feminism and monasticism: "If a women's religious congregation committed to the saving of the natural world was unthinkable in former centuries, it is now unthinkable that any women's congregation should not be committed as a primary concern and purpose to the saving of the natural world."[105] At the bi-annual conference they share such topics as sustainability, organic farming, conservation, seed saving, earth spirituality, Earth literacy, and ecojustice.[106] These communities are ecumenical and even interfaith, open to Asian and creation-centered spiritualities.[107] The Green Sisters of Green Mountain Monastery, The Thomas Berry Sanctuary. preserve the Benedictine spirituality of living with the land.[108]

Two non-monastic centers offer some periods for retreat for contemplative experience and eco-education are the Presbyterian Ghost Ranch in Taos (NM) and the Franciscan Center for Action and Contemplation (Albuquerque, NM) under the leadership of Richard Rohr.[109] Both include contemplative approaches but also link social justice with environmental justice. Both have strong ecumenical programming with strong eco-spiritual components. Ghost Ranch has a sustainable agricultural center demonstrating the possibility of sustainability and promotes the Presbyterian commitments to environmental justice. These centers assist people to connect with the beautiful landscapes in New Mexico and fall in love with nature and listen meditatively to the voice of nature and God. They plant seeds for the emergence of the Tree of Life.

104. Carroll, ibid., 53–54.

105. Ibid., 56. From Berry, "Religious Women as the Voice of the Earth."

106. "The Sisters of the Earth International," The Forum of Ecology and Religion at Yale, http://fore.yale.edu/religion/christianity/projects/sisters_earth/.

107. Ibid., 64–72.

108. See Taylor, Green Sisters, ch. 4.

109. Ghost Ranch, https://www.ghostranch.org/; also see Carroll, Sustainability and Spirituality, 156–58. Center for Action and Contemplation, https://cac.org/richard-rohr/richard-rohr-ofm/; Carroll, Sustainability and Spirituality, 160–61.

Interfaith Eco-Contemplative Movements

Contemplative movements have popularized in Christian, Buddhist, and interfaith circles, and some have moved further to connect meditation with engaged social action and climate change. There is a coalescing of religious and spiritual traditions creating the Earth Charter, the Charter of Compassion, and The Parliament of Word. The Earth Charter was quoted in the encyclical, *Laudato Si*, of Pope Francis: "Let ours be a time remembered for the awakening of a new reverence for life, a firm resolve to achieve sustainability, the quickening of the struggle for justice and peace, and the joyful celebration of life." The convergence of the spiritual compassion movements is a positive interfaith development offers a promising development, a sharing of resources and coalition building based on the Spirit of compassion.[110] In his book *Virtues*, Leonardo Boff starts his section on communality with a line from the Earth Charter: "Peace is created by right relationship with oneself, other persons, other cultures, other life, Earth and the larger which all are a part."[111] The Earth Charter represents an initial step in dividing off nature's fair share. It calls upon humanity to offer a treaty with the Earth and for the political will and solidarity of humanity to sign on.

The Charter for Compassion, founded by religious scholar Karen Armstrong and author of *Twelve Steps to a Compassionate Life*, has made impressive strides as a grassroots internet community and movement. Armstrong created a global community of compassion. Armstrong asserts, "we cannot confine our compassion to our own group; we must also reach out the same way to the stranger and the foreigner—even to the enemy."[112] The Charter of Compassion invites folks to join and embrace the compassion revolution:

> *The principle of compassion lies at the heart of all religious, ethical and spiritual traditions, calling us always to treat all others as we wish to be treated ourselves. Compassion impels us to work tirelessly to alleviate the suffering of our fellow creatures, to dethrone ourselves from the centre of our world and put another there, and to honor the inviolable sanctity of every single human being,*

110. Several good books on Compassion: Armstrong, *Twelve Steps to a Compassionate Life*; O'Connell, *Compassion*; Rogers, *Practicing Compassion*.

111. Boff, *Virtues*, 196; earthcharter.org/, *Earth Charter*.

112. Armstrong, *Twelve Steps to a Compassionate Life*, 143.

*treating everybody, without exception, with absolute justice, eq-
uity and respect.*[113]

Armstrong argues, "Mindfulness is a form of meditation that we perform as we go about our daily lives and is designed to give us more control over our minds so that we can reverse ingrained tendencies and cultivate new ones."[114] It can lead to compassion and ecological conversion. Armstrong proposes, "As we practice the Immeasurables, we are bound to become aware of the selfishness that impedes our compassionate outreach, balks at extending our friendship to an enemy."[115] Meditation practice leads to compassionate action, and it direct us to compassionate response to humanity's harm of other life and the Earth. The Charter for Compassion offers international connections for a compassionate revolution, crossing over the major world religions and creating a culture of religious intersectionality of compassionate action. Frank Rogers notes, "Acts of kindness also restore those looking from the sidelines. Compassion is contagious. Seeing a person care for another can inspire care within us as well."[116] Interfaith, ecological coalitions of contemplative traditions can lead to compassionate action and a groundswell for social justice and combating climate change.

Religions, fostering contemplative coalition for social change and work against climate change.[117] The convergence of contemplative movements towards social engagement and climate change is growing and a promising trend for hope. The Buddhist Center for the Contemplative Mind has focus training of social workers, justice activists, and green activists. The Center has developed an expansive program of training social justice people about the contemplative arts and how to integrate social and environmental justice into their contemplative practice.[118] The

---

113. Charter for Compassion: http://www.charterforcompassion.org/index.php/charter.

114. Armstrong, *Twelve Steps*, 106.

115. Ibid.,105. The Buddhist four immeasurables are *maîtri* (loving kindness), *karuna* (compassion), *mudita* (joy), and *upeksha* (equanimity). For Buddhist spirituality, they are stretched to the farthest corner of the world, inclusive of all creatures.

116. Rogers, *Practicing Compassion*, 109. Rogers gives a useful method for discerning a compassionate action. Ibid., 105–29.

117. Earth Charter, http://earthcharter.org/; The Charter of Compassion, http://www.charterforcompassion.org/; Parliament of World Religions.

118. Center for the Contemplative Mind in Society: Explore their trainings and programming: http://www.contemplativemind.org/archives/socialjustice

Garrison Institute promotes contemplation as a force of social change, for it "explores the intersection between contemplation and engaged action in the world, applying contemplative wisdom to social and environmental change."[119] Finally, the Franciscan priest Richard Rohr in his Center for Action and Contemplation promotes with daily email meditative teachings, training programs on Franciscan spirituality of "alternative orthodoxy"—"practices of contemplation and self-emptying, expressing itself in radical compassion, particularly for the socially marginalized."[120]

The last example I want to point out is Charlotte Congregational Church (United Church of Christ), which created a Contemplation and Social Action Committee. The mission of the committee is to "deepen and promote the Christian values of peace, justice, community, and reverence for creation by identifying social and environmental issues, stimulating study, dialogue and prayer, and inviting action."[121] Such formative model is a good trajectory to the evolution of ecological community. Imagine the possibilities: Training ourselves and environmentalist activists, disaffiliated youth and millennials concerned about climate church, and harnessing of the energy of the Spirit unleashed.

Contemplative Eco-Justice

There is no question that from the discussions in this chapter, I believe strongly in eco-justice actions for the Earth and protection of life on the planet. At the end of July 2015, I read on internet news services of thirteen Green Peace activists who rappelled off a bridge in Portland, Oregon, over the Columbia River to block Shell Company's icebreaker Fennica destined for the Arctic Ocean to begin drilling for oil. Other Green Peace activists attempted to block passage of the river channel. In October 2014, thousands of faith climate activists descended upon New York and the United Nations for the largest Climate Change March so far.[122] It included tens of thousands of faith activists from all the world religions, more than fifty thousand students participated, along with environmental groups,

119. Garrison Institute, http://www.garrisoninstitute.org/retreats-a-gatherings/contemplation-as-a-force-for-social-change/.

120. https://cac.org/richard-rohr/richard-rohr-ofm/.

121. http://www.charlotteucc.org/ - !casa-social-justice/cmao.

122. See Climate Change March Report of the Parliament of World Religions, https://www.parliamentofreligions.org/content/report-religions-earth-and-people%E2%80%99s-climate-march/.

climate scientists, and lovers of the Earth. Environmentalist and author Bill McKibben, Leonardo DiCaprio, artists, primatologist Jane Goodall, religious leaders, three US Democratic Senators, along with former Vice President Al Gore, and U.N. Secretary-General Ban Ki-moon. Over three hundred thousand rallied and marched for life and Earthcare.

Environmental Buddhist and eco-activist, Stephanie Kaza reports that Buddhist teachers are sought to provide meditational training for environmental activists: "Buddhist meditation instruction is perceived to be neutral training available for people of any faith or secular persuasion. It is generally not seen as proselytizing. Environmentalists who tend to reject organized religion and find spiritual fulfillment in the outdoors are open to Buddhist support for environmental aims."[123]

For example, as environmentalists attended a meditation retreat of Thich Nhat Hanh at Ojai, California, the environmentalists sparked several writings of Nhat Hanh on Earthcare, especially, his book *Love Letter to the Earth*.[124] Contemplative ecology is the place where environmental action meets contemplation, and this being fostered across interfaith traditions from the contemplative practices of Catholic, Orthodox Christians, and Quakers; to Earth-renewal practices of Judaism of the Shalom Center; contemplative environmentalism and transpersonal psychology and ecology. These are convergences of the Spirit, providing a matrix where contemplative and activists may meet, co-engage, and build bridges for Earth justice. Another example is JustFaith. Founder Jack Jezreel, founder of JustFaith, writes, "The world cannot be changed by love to become just unless we are changed by love to become whole, *but* we cannot be made whole without engaging in the work of making the world whole."[125] Personal, social, and ecological transformations are interconnected.

The 2015 Parliament of World Religions brought a convergence of academic, environmentalist organizations and indigenous peoples and people of all the world faiths together. Interfaith leaders at the Parliament voiced supported Pope Francis' historic climate change encyclical and his call to action before the US Congress and at the United Nations to care for the poor and the Earth.[126] Elizabeth Johnson concludes:

123. Kaza, "Greening of Buddhism: Promise and Perils," 200.

124. Ibid. Nhat Hanh, *Love Letter to the Earth*; Nhat Hanh, *The World We Have*.

125. Jezreel, "To Love Without Exception"; Jezreel, "Perfection," *Oneing*, vol 4, no. 1. See JustFaith: http://justfaith.org/about-us/history-mission/

126. See the reports of support: https://www.parliamentofreligions.org/tags/

Being converted to the earth in its hour of suffering place us in resonant cooperation with the deepest reality of creation, Creator Spirit. When we work with people and movements committed to cherishing the earth and opposing its plunder, we are participating in the Spirit's own political economy of life. Instead of living as thoughtless or g reedy exploiters we are empowered to become sisters and brothers, friends and lovers, gardeners and stewards, advocates and poets, priests and prophets, colleagues and fellow dancers, co-creators and children of the world that give us life. Too much has been lost. But the narrative memory of the dead, as always, has the capacity to bring a living future if we cooperate with the compassionate power of the Creator Spirit.[127]

climate-change

127. Johnson, *Women, Earth, and Creator Spirit*, loc. 587.

Epilogue

The Tree of Life

*A tree becomes sacred through recognition of the power it expresses.
This power may be manifested as the food, shelter, fuel, materials to
build boats, or medicine that the tree provides . . . Sacred trees have also
provided beauty, hope, comfort, and inspiration, nurturing and healing
the mental, emotional, and spiritual levels of our being. They are
symbols of life, abundance, creativity, generosity, permanence, energy,
and strength.*

—Nathaniel Altman[1]

*. . . you love all things that exist, and detest none of the things that you
have made . . .*

—Wisdom 11:24

*If we cannot conspire to heal our planet, our reason for being is called
into question.*

—Rev. John Dorhauer, President and General Minister
of the United Church of Christ[2]

1. Altman, *Sacred Trees*, 9.
2. http://www.macucc.org/environment

*Let ours be a time remembered for the awakening of a new reverence
for life, the firm resolve to achieve sustainability, the quickening of the
struggle for justice and peace, and the joyful celebration of life.*

—The Earth Charter

In *Spiritual Ecology*, Leslie Sponsel devotes his first chapter to trees, their
life-giving and interdependent connections to the production of oxygen,
water exchange system and pump, leaves fall and decompose, providing
compost for soil fertility. He observes,

> From the perspective of the systems approach of ecology, a
> single tree can contribute significantly to the environmental and
> biodiversity conservation. When a tree is considered sacred,
> and accordingly afforded special protection from harm, then
> it may help to conserve a multitude of other species and their
> symbioses as well as particular microclimates, microenviron-
> ments, and soil and water resources.[3]

Trees have been a central image throughout the book, from Gauguin's
image of Christ's cross as greening energy provides compost for the Tree
of Life. The Tree of Life becomes a central spiritual metaphor for my envisioning of eco-conversion and the building an ecological movement.
The Romans perverted the tree, making it an instrument of torture and
death, crucifying Christ. The Christ of the Earth has suffered physical
abuse and exploitation at human hands. The Earth body of Christ has
been mine-stripped, beaten and polluted, humiliated, despised, flogged
and bleeding from the wounds of living creatures, the death cries of
nonhuman animals and species beloved of the Creator. The Earth Body
carries her cross to Golgotha while the imperial troops await with the
vertical beam and spikes. Climate deniers jeer at the abuse with mocked
greed and deny climate change. We look to the Tree of Life in the Garden
for renewed hope.

I read James Lovelock's *The Revenge of Gaia* and E. O. Wilson's
The Creation. The last chapter of Lovelock's book took my breath away
as I read the clarity of his argument on climate changes within twenty
years. The escalating severe weather events, almost daily, confirm his dire
predictions that a tipping point has almost been reached in the Earth's

3. Sponsel *Spiritual Ecology*, 5.

equilibrium in regulating between hot and cold temperatures to support life. If the temperature of the Earth continues to rise, the Earth will be unable to sustain life comfortably. In the final chapter, Lovelock suggest, "One thing we can do to lessen the consequences of catastrophe is to write a guidebook for our survivors to help rebuild civilization without repeating too many of our mistakes."[4] He anticipates that human civilization will end this century, moving into an environmental Dark Ages. Lovelock suggests that such guidebook be an accurate account of our present and past knowledge of the environment for the survivors.

At the same time, E. O. Wilson wrote *The Creation: An Appeal to Save Life on Earth*; it is a letter of a biologist and naturalist, himself, to a Southern Baptist Pastor:

> The HUMAN HAMMER having fallen, the sixth mass extinction has begun. The spasm of permanent loss is expected, if it is not abated, to reach the end-of-Mesozoic level by the end of the century. We then what poets and scientists alike may choose to call the Eremozoic Era—the Age of Loneliness. We have it all on our own, and conscious of what was happening. God's will is not to blame.
>
> The first five spasms took ten million years on average to repair by natural evolution. A new ten- million-year slump is unacceptable. Humanity must make a decision, and make it right now: conserve Earth's natural heritage, or let future generations adjust to a biologically impoverished world. There is no way to weasel out of this choice.[5]

Wilson musters arguments to support his claim that the only way to save the diversity of life and become at peace with nature is to study biology. He understands every child is a potential naturalist. E. O. Wilson reaches out to religion, for religion and science are two powerful forces in the world and together, he believes, they can save creation. He calls for an "alliance for life."[6] We can align ourselves together for life since we share a common love for creation. Wilson, in another book, proposed Earth restoration projects to increase the share of Earth allotted space to nature. He recommends a 50/50 split: "Half the world for humanity, half for the

4. Lovelock, *The Revenge of Gaia*, 156.

5. Wilson, *The Creation*, 91.

6. Ibid., 165–67.

rest of life, to create a planet both self-sustaining and pleasant."[7] Can we create an alliance for life?"

Dreaming Green: Composting with the Earth

Many Christians and their churches have separated themselves from the soil community, the natural world, and the Earth. Our preaching, sacraments, worship, and compassionate outreach does not include the Earth. It does not care for the Earth because it is not a pressing issue. The Jesuit poet Gerard Manley Hopkins, however, wrote, "the just man justices; Keeps grace: that keeps all his goings graces; Acts in God's eye what in God's eye he is—Christ—For Christ plays in ten thousand places, Lovely in limbs, and lovely in eyes, not his."[8] For Hopkins and those converted to the Earthcare, the world is a communion of subjects. It is a vision and lifestyle of living interrelatedly, past and present into the future.

When we speak about the on-going presence of the Incarnation in the world, Christians find themselves focusing on the Spirit. The Spirit is the divine composter and draws us closer to Christ's Incarnation and embodiment with the Earth. We can never be too incarnational or too Earth-centered in our spirituality. The process of composting creates a nutrient-rich humus soil mix. Compost consists of organic waste recycled for fertilizing and introducing microscopic beneficial organisms for life. In many ways, the Holy Spirit composts our lives, recycles what is beneficial in our lives and spirit, connecting us with the Earth. The humus is used to fertilize plants in a garden. What I am suggesting by composting? Two elements need to be composted: God's Incarnation in Christ and our connection with the soil community of the Earth (Earth, the interconnected web of life). Elizabeth Johnson writes, "Deep Incarnation alerts Christians to the presence of Christ throughout the natural world. How tragic it is when human action shatters and destroys the flesh that the Word became."[9] This widens our spirituality to include Earth-connections of the cosmic Christ.

Mark Wallace recovers a traditional image of the Spirit as *vinculum caritatis* (bonds of love) that undermines our distinctions between humankind and otherkind by composting all living things into a "heap

7. Ibid., 163.

8. Hopkins, "As Kingfishers Catch Fire," in Lichtmann, *Poetry as Prayer,* 66.

9. Johnson, "Jesus and the Cosmos," 140.

of interconnected life forms."[10] The Spirit returns us to the Earth, our original soil community to become a mixture of spirit and Earth: Wallace writes,

> The Spirit's work threatens to tear apart the nature-indifferent *imago Dei* self-concept many prize as their birthright and replace it with an *imago muni* anthropology instead. Living on the borders of the postindustrial megamachine as a catalyst for disorienting change, the Spirit reminds us that as God's image we are earth creatures fashioned from the muck and mire of the soil . . . To dismantle the debilitating difference that separates humankind from otherkind—this is the Spirit's special work in a world teetering on the edge of ecological collapse. We can learn to understand the Spirit's ministry of biotic reconciliation by resensitizing ourselves to the double identity of the Spirit as a personal agent, on one hand, and inanimate force on the other.[11]

Composting our spiritual lives to the physical Earth and all other life, returns us to a profoundly incarnational spirituality of fleshly Word of interbeing. In many ways, both death cycles of nature and the death/resurrection of Christ conflate in a personal death to self-centeredness and rebirth of new ways of practicing a profound incarnational Earth spirituality of interbeing. Boff speaks of change of interbeing spirituality:

> Spirituality arises from an awareness of one's part and from the intuition of that every being and the whole universe itself are sustained and infused by a powerful loving force, the Abyss of all energy, the source of all being. One can sense the mysterious thread that connects and reconnects into cosmos and out of chaos. Spirituality inspires awe in us at the wonder of the universe and fill us with self-respect so that we might admire, enjoy, and celebrate all that is. So much of how we think must be changed until these new habits of thought are a given among us all.[12]

Have argued for eco-spirituality that is thoroughly Earth-centered, thus incarnational—humbly letting go of the self and exploring our networks of interconnectedness where we encounter the world as a communion of subjects. This communion of subjects is an ecological self, interconnected and interrelated to everything. Thich Nhat Hanh describes our change:

10. Wallace, *Fragments of the Spirit Nature*, 152.
11. Ibid., 152–53.
12. Boff, *Toward An Eco-Spirituality*, 14.

"We cannot just be by ourselves alone. We have to inter-be with every other thing."[13] Conversion to the Earth is a turning to the Earth and the community of life, but it is simultaneously a conversion to the Incarnate Christ, who is interwoven with all life and material reality. Leonardo Boff an eco-spirituality identified with the Earth:

> In terms of eco-spirituality, love leads us to identify ever more with the Earth . . .we must think ourselves as Earth, feel ourselves as Earth, love ourselves as Earth. Earth is the great living subject feeling, loving, thinking, and through us knowing that it thinks, loves, and feels. Love leads us to identify with the Earth in such a way we no longer need to become aware of these things, for they have become second nature. Then we can be the mountain, sea, air, road, tree, animal. We can be one with Christ, with the Spirit, and ultimately with God.[14]

This identification with the Earth incorporates the humus or soil community of the Earth into our lives and spirituality. We realize of our communion with the Earth as we become part of the body risen Tree of Life.

Thus, conversion is our response to the Incarnation's grace, God's self-bestowal of divine intimacy to us. The Incarnate Christ was in the big bang, the explosive expansion of the universe from a singularity to a cosmic history of fifteen billion years till the birth of Jesus, his ministry, death and resurrection. It is important for us to recognize the depth of composting in cosmic and evolutionary development. We compost the Earth and Incarnate Christ into our ecological spirituality. For example, Rev. Margaret Bullitt-Jonas, an Episcopal priest, writes about connecting to nature:

> I also began to connect with nature. I began to see that God loved not only my body, but also the whole 'body" of creation. My prayer began to change. It was like turning my pocket inside out; whereas once I found God merely in the silent inward contemplation, now God began showing up around me—in the pond, the rocks, the willow tree. If you spend an hour gazing at a willow tree, after a while it begins to disclose God.[15]

Rev. Bullitt-Jonas proposes a three-stage process of eco-conversion: creation, crucifixion, and resurrection. They are not necessarily

13. Naht Hanh, *Peace in Every Step*, 96.
14. Boff, *Cry of the Earth*, loc. 4308.
15. Bullitt-Jonas, "Conversion to Eco-Justice," 133.

chronological but spirally overlapping. The creation stage is where we discover the goodness of creation: God saw creation was good, and we experience delight in God's presence through the natural world. The crucifixion stage is the place of grief, sadness, and anger where we witness the human assault upon the natural world from mountain top harvesting for coal, ocean dead zones, extinction of species, human cruelty to nonhuman animals, pollution of the Earth, and climate change, We feel the pain of Christ crucified in the passion of the Earth and the poor. The many eco-organizations have weekly news briefs of the human assault and exploitation of the world.[16] The third stage is sharing Christ's resurrection on Easter. Jesus, God's Christ, is resurrected from the garden tomb of the Earth. Christ is raised as the Tree of Life and the Gardener who calls us to Easter hope and the vocation as gardeners to heal and care for the Earth and community of life. These three stages may converge simultaneously. Anger often becomes a holy anger for the natural world, exploited and trashed. We can become eco-contemplatives seeking Earth justice by living sustainably with the Earth, protesting the fracking of the fossil fuel corporations, envirnomental pollution, civic participation at municipal meetings examining how to pressure utilitiesto develop more energy renewable energy, or practicing sustainable living. We can witness the pain and anguish of the crucified Earth community, but also witness to Easter hope. Hope may be one of the greatest Christian gifts to eco-activists when the tipping of environmental degradation and climate change is moving rapidly towards catastrophe.

Dreaming Green II: Composting Church

The idea of composting churches may find resistance because of disincarantional theologies. Yet it is a fruitful process of communal spirituality and organic vitality. My own church has undergone composting with the Earth but as with the United Church of Christ. Church composting is the work of the Holy Spirit, throwing dead branches, leaves, and lawn clippings into a compost bin for the fertilization of new Earth-centered churches for the twenty-first century. Decaying is a grace opportunity to change forms and create a totally new organic movement. Composting is the vital power of the Spirit, growing new Earth-centered communities and the seeding of new ways learning and living on the Earth. New

16. Eco-penance, Delio et al., *Care for Creation*, 185–200.

sprouts will grow with decaying structures until the ecological church emerges and seeds new mode of celebrating the radical inclusive love of Jesus and incarnational dynamics predominate. The disaffiliated young and old have left institutional religion but not spirituality. The Incarnation has been institutionally undervalued or not valued sufficiently, and its potential for reforming Christianity has led to counter-measures and resistance against incarnational renewal. The greening of churches incarnational renewal and change. It will require the spiritual adaptability to incorporate Earth-centered practices to recover the incarnational dynamism of interbeing and compassionate action. It is, in fact, realizing our embodiment, our humus or soilness, a connection to the Earth, and the body of the cosmic, incarnated Christ.

One composting transition to the Earth is the Episcopal Church of the Woods, in Canterbury, New Hampshire, created by Rev. Steve Blackmer, as an ecumenical and interfaith community. Rev. Blackmer created a sacred space or church with 106 acres of forest and wetlands. There is no choice between building and mission to the Earth: "Church of the Woods is a place where the earth itself, rather than a building, is the bearer of sacredness; a place where people gather for contemplative practice in communion with each other and nature; a place where the church exists to serve a mission rather than the other way around; a place where people come together to learn, explore, and take action to transform themselves and renew the earth."[17] Its liturgy, events, and pilgrimage rituals include the care of the forest and wetlands acreage as sacred. It is clear that the Earth provides church space. The land and wildlife educate folks on connecting to God. Rev. A Rober Hirshfield, Bishop of the Diocese of New Hampshire, comments, "His (Blackmer's) congregation is made up of people who may or may not have been baptized into the name of Jesus, but who I believe are doing Jesus' work."[18] Another effective ministry is where churches grow food for the poor; for it reconnects churches to the soil while it expresses care for the poor and food justice.

Many denominations have nature camps for kids and congregants to connect with nature. Many of the UCC camps have ecological educational components of connecting kids and young adults to nature. Here the churches can seed what E. O. Wilson describes as future naturalists,

17. Church of the Woods, http://kairosearth.org/churchservices/open-house-at-church-of-the-woods/

18. Ian Wilson "Canterbury Church of the Woods to Connect with Higher Power through Nature."

or Earth-lovers. Pilgrim Firs Camp and Conference Center (WA) and Silverlake Conference Center (CT) are used for training wcojustice and ecological awareness.[19] The UCC Conferences of Massachusetts and Connecticut are the greenest of the UCC regional conferences due to its leaders committed to environmental justice. The conference websites list congregational ecological resources for churches to move to become more ecologically involved. Conference leaders, clergy, and laity bused in hundreds of church protesters into New York for the United Nations Climate March (2014).

Rev. Jim Anal, the Conference Minister and President of the UCC in Massachusetts, has asked the conference to allow him to dedicate twenty percent of his time to climate change. His leadership in environmental justice and advocacy, has been effective at the conference level in Massachusetts as well with other conferences of the UCC.[20] At General Synod 2013, he brought a historic resolution for the UCC to divest its pension investments from fossil fuel companies. In a public lecture at University of Redlands, Evironmentalist Bill McKibben and founder of 365.org pushed divestment from fossil fuel companies to pressure transition to renewable energies. In addition, there were two other resolutions adopted: opposing mountain top harvesting of coal and calling for carbon neutral church campuses by 2030. Furthermore, the UCC Cornerstone Fund offers low interest loans for churches to invest in solar panels to reduce their energy usage from fossil fuels. This is one small corner of the global Christian green movement that has composting energy creating green churches.

Another prophet, I admire, is Rev. Sally Bingham, Episcopalian Canon for the Environment of the Diocese of California, who founded Interfaith Power & Light, an interfaith movement for fighting climate change. The mission of Interfaith Power & Light is faithful care for Creation" by responding to global warming through the promotion of energy conservation, energy efficiency, and renewable energy."[21] Her commitment to the Earth had deep personal consequence of choosing to fight against climate or her marriage. Her prophetic leadership has contributed to great interfaith movement effecting the reduction of carbon

19. Pilgrim Firs, http://www.ucc.org/pilgrim-firs, SilverLake Conference Center, http://www.ucc.org/silver_lake_conference_center.

20. Jim Antal was arrested at the White House on Ash Wednesday against the Tar Sands pipeline demonstration: http://www.ucc.org/ucc-conference-minister.

21. See: Interfaith Power & Light, http://www.interfaithpowerandlight.org/about

emissions in local faith communities and faith advocacy at the state and federal governmental levels. My church was awarded a Green Oscar for advocacy by California Interfaith Power & Light.

A third prophet that I want to highlight is Matthew Fox—theologian, spiritual mentor, and founder of Wisdom University (formerly University of Creation Spirituality) and its degree programs that offer many Christians and interfaith folks opportunity to participate in classes and workshop for reclaiming the Earth as an incarnational center and to awaken people to the impending crisis of climate change.[22] Fox has been long-time theologian, author, and teacher of embodied, Earth-centered spirituality. He also has been an ecologically focused and interfaith in his theology since the 1980s and has been advocate for changing our relationship to Earth with climate change.[23] The strength of Fox's program is that it attracts a mix of various denominational and interfaith clergy, scientists, poets, laity, and artists.

One of the significant coalitions of many environmental faith groups is Blessed Tomorrow. It brings faith communities along with such leaders as Jim Walls, Founder of Sojourners and Mary Evelyn Tucker and John Grim, Directors of The Forum of Ecology and Religion at Yale, into an expanding coalition of green organizations and church leaders.[24] This is a significant step forward to the organization of the environmental movement. But absent are the voices of the Orthodox and Catholic Church. It still needs to become even more inclusive the theological academy, university scholars in Religious Studies, and seminaries training future clergy.

While adding solar panels to church buildings reduce your electric energy use, some churches make the error that they are then green churches. But there are many more actions that a church can do to reduce their carbon footprint.[25] There is ongoing education, discussion groups, training, and public advocacy needed. A concrete suggestion is to assign various folks to participate in green groups, such as Interfaith Power & Light, Green Peace, denominational groups, National Resources Defense Fund, Environmental Defense Fund, Sierra Club, Humane Society,

22. University of Creation Center Spirituality, http://matthewfox.org/about-matthew-fox/univ-of-creation-spirituality/

23. Fox, "Why Climate Change requires a spiritual rebirth," http://www.religionnews.com/2015/11/30/battling-climate-change-requires-spiritual-rebirth-commentary/

24. See http://blessedtomorrow.org/leaders.

25. See the suggestions in Hosenfeld, *Eco Faith.*

Ocean Conservancy, the Oxford Center for Animal Ethics, the Ecology and Religion Forum at Yale, and various conservation and animal rights groups. Prepare electronic summaries for monthly distribution for continual education of the congregation. I often write on ecological groups in our monthly church newsletter. But these are useful actions for communities, but what fuels Earthcare on sustainable basis is the eco-conversion and contemplative connection to the earth. That provides the impetus of love to fight for the Earth.

Seminaries and divinity schools are making more eco-theology courses available to students and, in some cases, continuing education of alumni. Some schools might add degrees in ecological ministry, inclusive of internships in conservationism, eco-contemplative arts, and green advocacy. We must train green Christians—theologians, laity, clergy—to engage, dialogue, and build bridges, as Edward O. Wilson has recommended, to climate scientists, university biologists and ethologists, other specialists in sustainability studies. Wilson proposes for an alliance for life between science and religion. Leonardo Boff understands this as a mutually beneficial alliance to move these forces in the world, not to save the world. He observes, "The problem is not so much to save the Earth but rather to change our relationship to it."[26]

Already there is a great body of eco-religious and eco-theological resources, books, articles, and online sources for sermons and liturgical worship from the Harvard Series of Ecology and Religion to the Yale Forum on Ecology and Religion.[27] Particular dioceses, conferences of churches, or regional networks need to invite green theologians, eco-activists, eco-contemplatives, naturalists, scientists, poets and artists, and political lobbyists, and representatives from ecological organizations to their annual or even national conferences for education purposes and trainings church folks in the skills to fully participate in the global green movements for eco-justice.

The kenotic church lives kenotically, that is, living interrelated and realizing the compassionate dynamics of care for the excluded, the poor, and the vulnerable. Through the practice of compassion, the community becomes the "church vulnerable." The church vulnerable identifies contemplatively Christ with the "least of my family" and practices an

26. Boff, *Towards An Eco-Spirituality*, 19.

27. Religions of the World and Ecology Book Series http://fore.yale.edu/publications/books/cswr/; The Forum of Religion and Ecology at Yale, http://fore.yale.edu/about-us/.

incarnational compassionate care for the least among humanity and other life. Irish theologian Diarmuid O'Murchu speaks eloquently about the dynamics of what I consider to be the church vulnerable:

> Gospel based compassion tolerates no outsiders. It is embraces and seeks to bring in all who are marginalized, oppressed, and excluded from empowering fellowship. It evokes a double response requiring a reawakened heart that knows it cannot withhold the just action that liberates and empowers. The transformation of the heart which might also be described as the contemplative gaze, asks us to go where it hurts, to enter into the places of pain, to share in brokenness, fear, confusion, and anguish. Compassion challenges us to cry out with those in misery, to mourn with those who are lonely, to weep with those in tears. Compassion requires us to be weak with the weak, vulnerable with the vulnerable, and powerless with the powerless.[28]

The ecological church is a church that identifies with the vulnerable, lives with the vulnerable whether they are poor or homeless, nonhuman animal or plant species at risk, or active harm to the environment or a bioregion. The ecological church has a responsibility to link the suffering of the poor from environmental degradation, the greed of the hundred or so individuals who own nearly fifty percent of the wealth of the planet.

Dreaming Green III: "An Alliance of Life"

In his book, *Blessed Unrest*, Paul Hawkins reports that globally more than a million organizations (perhaps up to two million) faith-based and many non-faith environmental organizations and movements, are working for "ecological sustainability and social justice."[29] This consists of various faith organizations, local and international, humanist, social justice and sustainability movements for NGOs, scientific networks and associations, sustainability and agricultural centers, academic centers, nonhuman animal sanctuaries, gardens, environmental centers, governmental agencies, wildlife preservation areas, and so on. Hawkins claims that we are now in the midst of one largest social movements in history with tens of millions people involved in grassroots levels to address changes to

---

28. O'Murchu, *Inclusivity*, loc. 618.

29. Hawkins, *Blessed Unrest*, 2.

climate and the biosphere. His solution is twofold. Hawkins claims love and compassion as he quotes David James Dunscan:

> When small things are done with love, it's not a flawed you or me who does them in love. I have no faith in any political party, left, right, or centrist. I have boundless faith in love. In keeping with this faith, the only spiritually responsible way I know to be a citizen, artist, or activist in these strange times is by giving little or no thought to 'great things' such as saving the planet, achieving world peace, or stopping neocon greed. Great things tend to be undoable things. Whereas small things lovingly done are always within our reach.[30]

Hawkins turns to the language of the Spirit with Dunscan's quotation. He calls it this response from the heart to heal the wounds within ourselves and offer salve to the wounds of the world. The next suggestion that Hawkins offers for ecologists is not to readily expect the social justice movement to take up the environmental cause but to join social justice movements to heal wounds to create a holistic movement to address the environmental crisis we face. Hawkins appears to be unaware of ecotheologies in the last two decades that have linked social justice and environmental justice and their interconnections. But his intuition is on target, for such a holistic perspective—the preferential option for the poor and the preferential option for vulnerable life espoused by Leonardo Boff, Sallie McFague, and Pope Francis and others—realizes the truth. Ecojustice is social justice, and social justice is ecojustice.

Edward O. Wilson's invitation to "An Alliance of Life" is nothing less than an invitation to a revolution of human life: a change of consumption patterns and relationship to the Earth. Leslie Sponsel suggests that a spirituality of revolutionary dissent is necessary. He quotes the former president of Czech Republic, Vaclav Havel:

> What could change the direction of today's civiization. It is my deep conviction that the only option for change is a change in the sphere of the spirit, in the sphere of the human conscience. It is not enough to invent new machines, new regulations, new institutions. We must develop a new understanding of the true purpose of our existence on Earth. Only by making such a fundamental shift will we be able to create new models of behavior and a new set of values for the planet.[31]

30. Ibid., 188. Dunscan, *God Laughs and Plays*, 118.

31. Havel, "Spirit of the Earth," *Resurgence*, November-December, 1990, 191, 30.

John Cobb's foundation of Pando Populus is the beginning of such an alliance. The movement draws its name from the "largest and oldest organism on the planet—a giant quaking aspen tree, spread over more than a hundred acres, thousands of years old, connected by a single root system."[32] The metaphor develops a beautiful metaphor for the Tree of Life, and the movement of philosophers, designers, educators, and community leaders is committed to create ecological civilization from grassroots level up. In my previous greening dreams, I claim that individual and institutional churches need to be composted with the Earth.

Earlier we observed how Leonardo Boff described humanity with the Earth metaphor,: "the human being is the Earth who walks." Or Sallie McFague states, Sallie McFague: "I am of the Earth." Incorporating the humus or soil of the Earth into our individual lives and communities of faith provides the soil for the Tree of Life. But Tree of Life drops leaves into the soil, transforming the leaves into humus, the dark and fertile soil, for the cycle and web of life. The Tree of Life pours its fleshliness and vital nutrients into the soil. It is soil and at the same time the vitality of the greening grace of God in the risen Christ and the green dynamism of the Spirit that inter-be(s) in us and with us and all life. The roots of the Tree of Life are planted in the Earth, and they are underground networking and circulating water and nutrients underground to bring fruit and green leaves on the tree. This Tree of Life energizes us to form "An Alliance of Life" with the greening grace (*viriditas*) of Christ, who is sacrifices his life on the cross against a lethal and oppressive Empire. The Tree of Life is all of us, Earth and life, and grows for all of us. We tap the green energy of the risen Christ to restore the garden Earth.

Quoted in Sponsel, *Spiritual Ecology*, 172.

32. Pando Populus, http://www.pandopopulus.com/.

Bibliography

Abbate, Michael. *Gardening Eden*. Colorado Springs: Water Brook, 2009.

Abram, David. *The Spell of the Sensuous: Perception and Language in a More than Human World*. New York: Vintage Books, 1997.

Adams, Carol J. "Eating Grace: Institutional Violence, Christianity, and Vegetarianism." In *Good News for Animals? Christian Approaches for Animal Well-Being*, edited by Charles Pinches and Jay, B. McDaniel. Ecology and Justice Series. 1993. Reprinted, Eugene, OR: Wipf & Stock, 2008.

Aghapour, Andrew. "What if Animals Believe in God?" *Religion Dispatches*, March 7, 2016. http://religiondispatches.org/what-if-animals-believe-in-god/?utm_source=Religion+Dispatches+Newsletter&utm_campaign=788014f40d-RD_Daily_Newsletter&utm_medium=email&utm_term=0_742d86f519-788014f40d-42427113/.

Altman, Nathaniel. *Sacred Trees*. San Francisco: Sierra Club Books, 1994.

Armstrong, Karen. *Twelve Steps to a Compassionate Life*. New York: Knopf, 2011.

Ayala, Francisco. "The Myth of Eve: Molecular Biology and Human Origin." *Science* 270 no. 5244, (1995) 1930–36.

Baker, Denise Kowakowski. *Julian of Norwich's Showings: From Vision to Book*. Princeton: Princeton University Press, 1994,

Barker, Margaret. "Adam as the High Priest of Creation." In *Creation: A Biblical Vision for the Environment*, 193–236. London: T. & T. Clark, 2010.

Barsam, Paul, and Ara Paul. *Reverence for Life: Albert Schweitzer's Great Contribution to Ethical Thought*. New York: Oxford University Press, 2008.

Barth, Karl. *Church Dogmatics*. Vol. III/1. Edinburgh, T. & T. Clark, 1958.

Birch, Charles. *Confronting the Future*. Melbourne: Penguin, 1993.

Bauckham, Richard. *The Bible and Ecology: Rediscovering the Community of Creation*. Waco, TX: Baylor University Press, 2010.

———. *Living with Other Creatures: Green Exegeses and Theology*. London: Paternoster, 2012.

Bekoff, Marc. *The Emotional Lives of Animals*. Novato, CA: New World Library, 2007.

———. *Rewilding Our Hearts: Building Pathways of Compassion and Coexistence*. Novato, CA: New World Library, 2014.

Bekoff, Marc, and Jessica Pierce. *Wild Justice: The Moral Lives of Animals*. Chicago: University of Chicago Press, 2009.

Benvenuti, Ann. *Spirit Unleashed: Reimagining Human Animal Relations*. Eugene, OR: Cascade Books, 2014.

Bingham, Sallie G. *Love God, Heal the Earth*. Pittsburgh: St. Lynn's Press, 2009.

Berry, Thomas. *The Christian Future and the Fate of the Earth*. Maryknoll, NY: Orbis, 2011.

———. *The Dream of the Earth*. San Francisco: Sierra Club Books, 1988.

———. *The Great Work: Our Way into the Future*. New York: Bell Tower, 1999.

———. "Religious Women as the Voice of the Earth." Unpublished paper.

———. *The Sacred Universe: Earth, Spirituality and Religion in the Twenty-First Century*. New York: Columbia University Press, 2009.

Berry, Wendell. *The Art of the Commonplace: The Agrarian Essays of Wendell* Berry. Edited by Norman Wirzba. Washington, DC: Counterpoimt, 2002.

———. *The Gift of the Good Land*. San Francisco: North Point, 1981.

———. *Jayber Crow*. Washington, DC: Counterpoint, 2000.

———. "A Native Hill." In *The Long-Legged House*, 1969. Washington, DC: Shoemaker & Hoard, 2004.

———. "Two Economies." From the World Wisdom online library: http://www.worldwisdom.com/public/library/default.aspx.

———. *The Unsettling of American Culture and Agriculture*. San Francisco: Sierra Club Books, 1977.

Birch, Charles, and John B. Cobb Jr. *The Liberation of Life: From the Cell to the Community*. Cambridge: Cambridge University Press, 1981.

Bond, L. Susan. *Trouble with Jesus: Women, Christology, and Preaching*. St. Louis: Chalice, 1999.

Boff, Leonardo. *Christianity in a Nutshell*. Translated by Phillip Berryman. Maryknoll, NY: Orbis, 2013.

———. *Cry of the Earth, Cry of the Poor*. Translated by Phillip Berryman. Maryknoll, NY: Orbis, 1997.

———. *Ecology and Liberation: A New Paradigm*. Translated by John Cumming. Maryknoll, NY: Orbis, 2014.

———. *Francis of Rome, Francis of Assisi: New Springtime of the Church*. Translated by Dinah Livingstone. Maryknoll, NY: Orbis, 2014.

———. *Holy Trinity, Perfect Community*. Translated by Phillip Berryman. Maryknoll, NY: Orbis, 2000.

———. *Liberating Grace*. Translated by John Drury. 1979. Reprinted, Eugene, OR: Wipf & Stock, 2005.

———. "The Path as Archetype." 09/12/2012. https://leonardoboff.wordpress.com/2012/12/09/THE-PATH-AS-ARCHETYPE/.

———. *Saint Francis: A Model for Human Liberation*. Translated by John W. Diercksmeier. New York: Crossroad, 1982.

———. *Toward An Eco-Spirituality: Church at the Crossroad*. Translated by Robert H. Hopke. New York: Crossroad, 2014.

———. *Virtues for Another Possible World*. Translated by Alexandre Guilherme. Eugene, OR: Cascade Books, 2011.

———. *When Theology Listens to the Poor*. Translated by Robert R. Barr. San Francisco: Harper & Row, 1988.

Borg, Marcus. *Jesus: A New Vision*. San Francisco: Harper & Row, 1987.

———. *Meeting Jesus Again for the First Time*. San Franciso: HarperSanFrancisco, 1995.

Bourgeault, Cynthia. *The Wisdom Jesus: Transforming Heart and Mind—a New Perspective on Christ and His Message.* Boston: Shambhala, 2011.

Bourma-Prediger, Steven. *For the Beauty of the Earth: A Christian Vision of Creation Care.* Grand Rapids: Baker, 2001.

———. *The Greening of Theology: The Ecological Models of Rosemary Radford Ruether, Joseph Sittler, and Jürgen Moltmann.* American Academy of Religion Academy Series 91. Atlanta: Scholars 1995.

Bredin, Mark. *The Ecology of the New Testament: Creation, Re-Creation, and the Environment.* Colorado Springs: Biblica, 2010.

Brooks, Paul. *House of Life: Rachel Carson at Work.* Boston: Houghton, 1972.

Brown, David. *Tradition and Inspiration: Revelation and Change.* Oxford: Oxford University Press, 1999.

Brown, Raymond E. *The Gospel of John.* Vol. 1. Garden City, NY: Doubleday, 1966.

Brueggemann, Walter. *Genesis.* Interpretation. Atlanta: John Knox, 2010.

Bruteau, Beatrice. "Eucharistic Ecology and Ecological Spirituality." *Cross Currents* 40 (1990–91) 499–514. http://www.crosscurrents.org/eucharist.htm.

Buchanan, Kathy. "New Zealand: Animal Welfare Recognizes Animals as Sentient Beings, Bans Cosmetic Testing." *Global Legal Monitor,* May 19, 2015. http://www.loc.gov/law/foreign-news/article/new-zealand-animal-welfare-legislation-recognizes-animals-as-sentient-bans-cosmetic-testing/.

Budiansky, Stephen. *The Covenant of the Wild: Why Wild Animals Chose Domestication.* New Haven: Yale University Press, 1999.

Bullitt-Jonas, Margaret. "Conversion to Eco-Justice." In *Claiming Earth as Common Ground: The Ecological Crisis through the Lens of Faith,* by Andrea Cohen-Kiener, 130–37. Woodstock, VT: SkyLight Paths, 2009.

Butkus, Russell. "Sustainability and the Benedictine Way: An Eco-Theological Analysis." Paper delivered at Perspectives Environment Conference, Atchison, Kansas, 1997.

Butler Bass, Diana. *Grounded: Finding God in the World, A Spiritual Revolution.* San Francisco: HarperOne, 2015.

Callicott, J. Baird. "Genesis and John Muir." In *Covenant for a New Creation Ethics: Religion and Public Policy,* edited by Carol S. Robb and Carl J. Casebolt, 107–40. Maryknoll, NY: Orbis, 1991.

Campolo, Tony, and Mary Albert Darling. *The God of Intimacy and Action: Reconnecting Ancient Spiritual Practices, Evangelism, and Justice.* San Francisco: Jossey-Bass, 2007.

Čapek, Karel. *The Gardener's Year.* Translated by Geoffrey Newsome. New York: Modern Library, 2002.

Carroll, John E. *Sustainability and Spirituality.* Albany: SUNY Press, 2004.

Carson, Rachel. *Always Rachel: The Letters of Rachel Carson and Dorothy Freeman, 1952–1964.* Edited by Martha Freeman. Boston: Beacon, 1995.

Chang, Paul Y. "Listening to the Listeners: A Study of the Parable of the Wicked Tenants, Mark 12:1–12." *Theological Forum* 66 (2011) 165–86. http://web.yonsei.ac.kr/paulchang/website/Research/final_wicked_tenants.pdf

Cheng, Patrick S. *Radical Love: An Introduction to Queer Theology.* New York: Seabury, 2011.

———. *From Sin to Amazing Grace: Discovering the Queer Christ.* New York: Seabury, 2012.

Chilton, Bruce. *Rabbi Jesus: An Intimate Biography.* New York: Doubleday, 2000.

Christie, Douglas, *The Blue Sapphire of the Mind: Notes for Contemplative Ecology*. New York: Oxford University Press. 2013.

Chryssavgis, John. "A New Heaven and a New Earth: Orthodox Christian Insights from Theology, Spirituality, and the Sacraments." In *God's Earth Is Sacred: Essays on Eco-Justice*, edited by Larry Rasmussen and Paul Santimire, 152–62. Washington, DC: National Council of Churches, 2011.

Clough, David. *On Animals*. Vol. 1, *Systematic Theology*. London: T. & T. Clark, 2012.

Clutton-Brock, Juliette. "Origins of the Dog: Domestication and Early History." In *The Domestic Dog: Its Evolution, Behavior, and Interactions with People*, edited by James Serpell, 7–20. Cambridge: Cambridge University Press, 2004.

Cobb, John. "All Things in Christ?" In *Animals on the Agenda*, edited by Andrew Linzey and Dorothy Yamamoto, 173–80. Chicago: University of Illinois Press, 1998.

Coloe, Mary L. "Creation in the Gospel of John." In *Creation Is Groaning: Biblical and Theological Perspectives*, edited by Mary L. Coloe, 1637–2065. Collegeville, MN: Liturgical, 2013.

Commission for Society and Social Affairs/Commission for International Church Affairs: *Climate Change: A Focal Point of Global, Intergenerational and Ecological Justice*. 2nd, updated edition, Bonn 2007.

Conradie, Ernest M. "What On Earth is Ecological Hermeneutics? Some Broad Parameters." In *Ecological Hermeneutics: Biblical, Historical, and Theological*, edited by David G. Horrell, et al., 295–314. New York: T. & T. Clark, 2010.

Craine, Renate. *Hildegard: Prophet of the Cosmic Christ*. Crossroad Spiritual Legacy Series. New York: Crossroad, 1997.

Crossan, John Dominic. *The Birth of Christianity: Discovering What Happened in the Years after the Execution of Jesus*. San Francisco: HarperSan Francisco, 1998.

———. *The Historical Jesus: The Life of a Mediterranean Jewish Peasant*. San Francisco: HarperSanFrancisco, 1991.

———. *Jesus: A Revolutionary Biography*. San Francisco: HarperSanFrancisco, 1994.

Cunningham, David, "The Way of All Flesh: Rethinking the Imago Dei." In *Creaturely Theology: On God, Humans, and Animals*, edited by Celia Deane-Drummond and David Clough, 100–120. London, SCM, 2009.

Dalai Lama. *Ethics for a New Millennium*. New York: Riverhead, 1999.

Daly, Gabriel. *Creation and Redemption*. Dublin: Gill & Macmillan, 1988.

Darragh, Neil. *At Home in the Earth*. Auckland: Ascent, 2000.

Delio, Ilia. *Christ in Evolution*. Maryknoll, NY: Orbis, 2008.

———. *Compassion: Living in the Spirit of St. Francis*. Cincinnati: St. Anthony Messenger Press, 2011.

———. *The Emergent Christ: Exploring the Meaning of Catholic in an Evolutionary Universe*. Maryknoll, NY: Orbis, 2011.

———. *A Franciscan View of Creation: Leaning to Live in a Sacramental World*. Vol. 2. St. Bonaventure, NY: Franciscan Institute, 2003.

———. *From Teilhard to Omega: Co-Creating an Unfinished Universe*. Maryknoll, NY: Orbis, 2014.

———. "Revisiting the Franciscan Doctrine of Christ." *Theological Studies* 64 (2003) 3–23. http://web.sbu.edu/friedsam/ereserve/coughlin_reserve/Delio_4.pdf.

———. *The Unbearable Wholeness of Being: God, Evolution, and the Power of Love*. Maryknoll, NY: Orbis, 2013.

Delio, Ilia et al. *Care for Creation: A Franciscan Spirituality of the Earth*. Cincinnati: St. Anthony Messenger Press, 2008.

Didcoct, Betty. "Choosing Our Roots: Traditional Christian Attitudes Offer Problems and Promise for Healing the Earth, an Interview with Thomas Berry." *Context* (Winter 1984). http://www.context.org/iclib/ico8/berry/.

Dodd, C. H. *The Parables of the Kingdom*. Rev. ed. New York: Scribner, 1961.

Doming, Daryl P., with Monika Hellwig. *Original Selfishness: Original Sin and Evil in the Light of Evolution*. Burlington, VT: Ashgate, 2005.

Dowd, Michael. *Earthspirit: A Handbook for Nurturing Ecological Christianity*. Mystic, CT: Twenty-Third Publications, 1991.

Doyle, Eric. "'The Canticle of Brother Sun' and the Value of Nature." In *Franciscan Theology of the Environment: An Introductory Reader*, edited by Dawn M. Nothwehr, 155–74. Quincy, IL: Franciscan Press, 2002.

Drob, Sanford L. *Kabbalah and Postmodernism: A Dialogue*. Studies in Judaism 3. New York: Lang, 2009.

Druffel, Allis. "Greening Congregations and IPL." https://www.youtube.com/watch?v=j9lnEfp_9hA.

Dubois, Rene. *The Wooing of the Earth: New Perspectives: Man's Use of Nature*. New York: Scribner, 1980.

Duncan, David James. *God Laughs and Plays*. Great Barrington, MA: Triad, 2006.

Dunkerly, Roderic. *Beyond the Gospels*. Harmondsworth, UK: Penguin, 1957.

Dunn, James D. G. *Jesus Remembered*. Grand Rapids: Eerdmans, 2003.

Dyck, Sally, and Sarah Ehrman. *A Hopeful Earth: Faith, Science and the Message of Jesus*. Nashville: Abingdon, 2010.

Earth Bible Team. "Guiding Ecojustice Principles." In *Readings From the Perspective of Earth*, 38–53. Earth Bible 1. Cleveland: Pilgrim Press, 2000.

Eaton, Heather. "Ecofeminist Contributions to Ecological Hermeneutics." In *Readings from the Perspective of the Earth*, edited by Norman C. Habel, 54–71. Cleveland: Pilgrim, 2000.

Echlin, Edward P. *Climate and Christ: A Prophetic Alternative,* Dublin, Columban Press, 2011.

———. *The Cosmic Circle: Jesus and Ecology*. Dublin: Columban Press, 2004.

———. *Earth Spirituality: Jesus at the Centre*. New Alresford: James, 1999.

Edwards, Denis. *Breath of Life: A Theology of Creator Spirit*. Maryknoll, NY: Orbis, 2004.

———. *Ecology at the Heart of Faith: The Change of Heart that Leads to a New Way of Living on Earth*. Maryknoll, NY: Orbis, 2007.

———. "Foreword." In Ilia Delio, Keith Douglass Warner, and Pamela Wood, *Care for Creation: A Franciscan Spirituality of the Earth*. Cincinnati: St. Anthony's Messenger Press, 2007.

———. *The God of Evolution: A Trinitarian Theology*. New York: Paulist, 1999.

———. *How God Acts: Creation, Redemption, and Special Divine Action*. Minneapolis: Fortress, 2010.

———. *Jesus and the Cosmos*. Mahwah, NJ: Paulist, 1991.

———. *Jesus the Wisdom of God: An Ecological Theology*. Ecology and Justice. 1995. Reprinted, Eugene, OR: Wipf & Stock, 2005.

———. "The Redemption of Animals in an Incarnational Theology." In *Creaturely Theology: On God, Humans, and Animals*, edited by Celia Deane-Drummond and David Clough, 81—99. London, SCM, 2009.

————. *Partaking of God: Trinity, Evolution, and Ecology*. Collegeville, MN: Liturgical, 2014.

Ellis, George F. R., "Kenosis as Unifying Theme for Cosmology." In *The Work of Love, Creation as Kenosis*, 106–28. Grand Rapids: Eerdmans, 2001.

Erickson, Jacob. "The Apophatic Animal: Toward a Negative Zootheological Imago Dei." In *Divinanimality: Animal Theory, Creaturely Theology*, edited by Stephen D. Moore, 88–99. New York: Fordham University Press, 2014.

Evans, C. Stephen. "Introduction: Understanding Jesus the Christ as Human and Divine." *Exploring Kenotic Christology, The Self-Emptying God*, 1–24. New York: Oxford University Press, 2006.

————. "Kenotic Theology and the Nature of God." In *Exploring Kenotic Christology: The Self-Emptying God*, 190–217. New York: Oxford University Press, 2006.

Frascati-Lochhead, Marta. *Kenosis and Feminist Theology: The Challenge of Gianni Vatttimo*. McGill Studies in the History of Religions. Albany: SUNY Press, 1998.

Finders, Tim. *Thomas Berry's Sacred Surround: An Introduction to his Thought and Spirituality*. Petaluma, CA: Two Rock, 2011.

Fischer, Kathleen. *Loving Creation: Christian Spirituality, Earth-Centered and Just*. New York: Paulist, 2009.

Freyne, Sean. *Jesus, a Jewish Galilean: A New Reading of the Jesus-Story*. London: T. & T. Clark, 2004.

Fowler, Robert Booth. *The Greening of Protestant Thought*. Chapel Hill: University of North Carolina Press, 1995.

Fox, Matthew. *The Coming of the Cosmic Christ*. San Francisco: Harper & Row, 1988.

————. *Confessions: The Making of Post-Denominational Priest*. New York: Harper-Collins, 1996.

————. *Creativity: Where the Divine and the Human Meet*. New York: Putnam, 2002.

————. "Finding the Divine Everywhere." *Foundations*, March 25, 2014. http://thecosmicmass.com/finding-the-divine-everywhere/.

————. *Living Questions*. http://livingthequestionsonline.com/2013/02/18/jesus-never-heard-of-original-sin/.

————. *Original Blessing*. Santa Fe, NM: Bear & Co., 1983.

————. *Sins of the Spirit, Blessings of the Earth*. New York: Harmony, 1999.

————. "The Vision of the Cosmic Mass." http://thecosmicmass.com/the-vision/.

————. "Why Climate Change Requires a Spiritual Rebirth." Religion News Service, Nov. 30, 2015. http://www.religionnews.com/2015/11/30/battling-climate-change-requires-spiritual-rebirth-commentary/.

Fox, Matthew, and Marc Andrus. *The Visionary Stations of the Cosmic Christ*. Kion: Yamaguchi, 2016.

Gadamer, Hans-Georg. *Truth and Method*. Translation revised by Joel Weinsheimer and Donald G. Marshall. Continuum Impact. New York: Continuum, 2004.

Garcia-Rivera, Alejandro. *The Garden of God: A Theological Cosmology*. Minneapolis: Fortress, 2009.

Gary, William. "Wisdom Christology in the New Testament: Its Scope and Relevance." *Theology*, 89 (1986) 448–59.

Glacken, Clarence. *Traces on the Rhodian Shore: Nature and Culture in Western Thought from Ancient Times to the End of the Eighteenth Century*. Berkeley: University of California Press, 1967.

Goodall, Jane. *Reason for Hope: A Spiritual Journey*. New York: Kadokawa Shoten, 1999.

————. "Primate Spirituality." In The Encyclopedia of Religion and Nature, edited by E. B Taylor, 1304–5. New York: Continuum, 2005.

Goss, Robert. *Jesus Acted Up: A Gay and Lesbian Manifesto*. San Francisco: HarperSanFrancisco, 1994.

Gottlieb, Roger, ed. "Introduction." In *This Sacred Earth: Religion, Nature and Environment*. London: Routledge, 1996.

Gregersen, Niels Henrik. "The Cross of Christ in an Evolutionary World." *Dialog: Journal of Theology* 40 (2001) 192–207.

————. "Laws of Physics, Principles of Self-Organization, and Natural Capacities: On Explaining Self-Organizing World." In *Creation, Law, and Probability*, edited by Fraser Watts, 81–100. Minneapolis: Fortress, 2009.

————, ed. *Incarnation: On the Scope and Depth of Christology*. Minneapolis: Fortress, 2015.

"The Extended Body of Christ: Three Dimensions of Deep Incarnation." in *Incarnation: On the Scope and Depth of Christology*, edited by Niels Henrik Gregersen, 225–251. Minneapolis: Fortress, 2015

Grey, Mary C., *Sacred Longings: The Ecological Spirit and Global Culture*. Minneapolis: Fortress, 2004.

Gross, Aaron S., "The Question of the Creature: Animals, Theology, and Levinas' Dog." In *Creaturely Theology: On God, Humans and Other Animals*, edited by Celia Deane-Drummond and David Clough, 121–37. London, SCM, 2009.

————. *The Question of Animal and Religion: Theoretical Stakes, Practical Implications*. New York: Columbia University Press, 2015.

Gurney, Dorothy Francis. "God's Garden." In *Poems*. London: Country Life, 1913.

Gutierrez, Gustavo. *A Theology of Liberation: History, Politics, and Salvation*. Maryknoll, NY: Orbis 1971. Reprinted, 1986.

Gutierrez, Gustavo, and Gerhard Ludwig Muller. *On the Side of the Poor: The Theology of Liberation*. Maryknoll, NY: Orbis, 2010.

Gutting, Gary. "Modern Cosmology versus God's Creation." *New York Times*, June 15, 2014. http://opinionator.blogs.nytimes.com/2014/06/15/modern-cosmology-versus-gods-creation/?_r=0/.

Habel, Norman C., ed. *The Earth Story in the Psalms and the Prophets*. Cleveland: Pilgrim, 2001.

————. "Introducing Ecological Hermeneutics." In *Exploring Ecological Hermeneutics*, edited by Norman C. Habel and Peter Trudinger, 1–8. Atlanta: Society of Biblical Literature, 2008.

————. "Introducing the Earth Bible." In *Readings from the Perspective of the Earth*, edited by Norman C. Habel, 25–54. Cleveland: Pilgrim, 2000.

————. *Rainbow of Mysteries: Meeting the Sacred in Nature*. Kelowna, BC: CopperHouse, 2012.

Habel, Norman C., and Vicky Balabanski. *The Earth Story in New Testament*. Cleveland: Pilgrim, 2002.

Habel, Norman C., and Shirley Wurst. *The Earth Story in Genesis*. Cleveland: Pilgrim, 2000.

————. *The Earth Story in Wisdom Traditions*. Cleveland: Pilgrim, 2001.

Habel, Norman C. et al. *The Season of Creation: A Preaching Commentary*. Minneapolis: Fortress, 2011.

Hall, Douglas John. *Imaging God: Dominion as Stewardship*. Grand Rapids: Eerdmans, 1986.

———. *The Steward: A Biblical Symbol Come of Age*. Grand Rapids: Eerdmans, 1990.

———. "Stewardship as a Human Vocation." *Stewardship of Life* (September 7, 2010) http://www.stewardshipoflife.org/2010/09/stewardship-as-a-human-vocation/

Hammerton-Kelly, Robert G. *The Gospel and the Sacred, the Poetics of Violence*. Minneapolis: Fortress, 1994.

Hare, Brian, and Vanessa Woods. "We Didn't Domesticate Dogs, They Domesticated Us: Scientists argue that friendly wolves sought out humans." *National Geographic*, http://news.nationalgeographic.com/news/2013/03/130302-dog-domestic-evolution-science-wolf-wolves-human/

Hargrove, E. C. "Introduction." In *Religion and Environmental Crisis*. Edited by E. C. Hargrove. Athens: University of Georgia Press, 1986.

Hart, John, *Sacramental Commons: Christian Ecological Ethics*. New York: Rowman & Littlefield, 2006.

Hatch, Stephen K., *The Contemplative John Muir: Spiritual Quotation from the Great American Naturalist*. Amazon Digital Services, 2012.

Hathway, Mark, and Leonardo Boff. *The Tao of Liberation: Exploring the Ecology of Transformation*. Maryknoll, NY: Orbis, 2009.

Haught, John. *Christianity and Science: Toward a Theology of Nature*. Theology in Global Perspective Series. Maryknoll, NY: Orbis, 2007.

Hawkins, Paul. *Blessed Unrest: How the Largest Social Movement in History is Restoring Grace, Justice, and Beauty to the World*. New York: Penguin, 2008.

Healy, Kim Coleman. "Christ the Gardener: Labors of Redemption." *Parabola* 26/1 (2001) 73–79.

Hellwig, Monika. *Jesus: The Compassion of God: New Perspectives on the Tradition of Christianity*. Theology and Life Series 9. Wilmington, DE: Glazier, 1983.

Hiebert, Theodore. "The Human Vocation: Origins and Transformations." In *Christianity and Ecology: Seeking the Well-being of Earth and Humans*, edited by Dieter T. Hessel and Rosemary Radford Ruether, 135–54. Relgions of the World and Ecology. Cambridge: Harvard University Press, 2000.

Hildegard of Bingen. *Smyposia: A Critical Edition of the Symphonia Armonie Celestium Revelationum*. Translated and edited by Barbara Newman. Ithaca, NY: Cornell University Press, 1988.

Hillel, Daniel. *Out of the Earth: Civilization and the Life of the Soil*. Berkeley: University of California Press, 1992.

Highland, Chris. *Meditations of John Muir: Nature's Temple*. Birmingham, AL: Wilderness Press, 2001.

Hines, Michael J., and Kenneth R. Hines. "Sacrament of Creation." In *Franciscan Theology of the Environment: An Introductory Reader*, edited by Dawn M. Nothwehr, 345–60. Quincy, IL: Franciscan Press, 2002.

Hobgood-Oster, Laura. *A Dog's History of the World*. Dallas: Baylor University Press, 2014.

Horan, Daniel P. "The Franciscan Character of *Laudato Si*." *America*, June 18, 2015. http://americamagazine.org/issue/franciscan-character-laudato-si/.

Horrel, David G., Cheryl Hunt, and Christopher Southgate. *Greening Paul: Rereading the Apostle in a Time of Ecological Crisis*. Waco, TX: Baylor University Press, 2010.

Horsley, Richard. *Jesus and The Spiral of Violence: Popular Jewish Resistance in Roman Palestine*. Minneapolis: Fortress, 1993.

Hosenfeld, Charlene. *EcoFaith: Creating & Sustaining Green Congregations*. Cleveland: Pilgrim, 2009.

Jenkins, Willis. *Ecologies of Grace: Environmental Ethics and Christian Theology*. New York: Oxford University Press, 2008.

———. "After Lynn White: Religious Ethics and Environmental Problems." *Journal of Religious Ethics* 37 (2009) 283–309.

Jezreel, Jack. "To Love without Exception," "Perfection." *Oneing* 4.1, Center for Action and Contemplation: 2016, 52.

Johnson, Elizabeth. *Ask the Beasts: Darwin and the God of Love*. London: Bloomsbury, 2014.

———. *Consider Jesus: Waves of Renewal in Christology*. New York: Crossroad, 1990.

———. "Jesus and the Cosmos: Soundings in Deep Christology." In *Incarnation: On the Scope and Depth of Christology*, edited by Niels Henrik Gregersen, 133–156. Minneapolis: Fortress.

———. "Jesus, the Wisdom of God." *EThL* 61 (1985) 261–94.

———. *She Who Is: The Mystery of God in Feminist Theological Discourse*. New York: Crossroad, 1992.

———. *Women, Earth and Creator Spirit*. Mahwah, NJ: Paulist, 1993.

Joyce, Timothy. *Celtic Christianity: A Sacred Tradition, A Vision of Hope*. Maryknoll, NY: Orbis, 1998.

Kahl, Brigette. "Fratricide and Ecocide: Rereading Genesis 2–4." In *Earth Habitant Ecojustice and the Church's Response*, edited by Dieter Hessel and Larry Rasmussen, 53–70. Minneapolis: Fortress, 2000.

Kardong, Terrence. "Ecological Resources in the Benedictine Rule." In *Embracing Earth: Catholic Approaches to Ecology*. Maryknoll, NY: Orbis, 1994.

Karkakaien, Veli-Matti. *Pneumatology: The Holy Spirit in Ecumenical, International, and Contextual Perspective*, Grand Rapids: Baker Academic, 2002.

Kaza, Stephanie. *The Attentive Heart: Conversations with Trees*. New York: Fawcett, 1993.

———. "The Greening of Buddhism: Promise and Perils." In *The Oxford Handbook of Religion and Ecology*, edited by Roger Gottlieb, 184–206. New York: Oxford University Press, 2006.

———. *Mindfully Green: A Personal and Spiritual Guide to Whole Earth Thinking*: Boston: Shambhala, 2011.

Keating, Daniel A. *Deification and Grace*. Ave Maria, FL: Sapienta, 2007.

Keen, Sam. "Original Blessing, Not Original Sin: Matthew Fox and Creation Spirituality." 1989.   http://www.abuddhistlibrary.com/Buddhism/H%20-%20World%20 Religions%20and%20Poetry/World%20Religions/Christianity/Various%20 Topics/Original%20Blessing/Original%20oblessing.rtf/.

Keller, Catherine. *From a Broken Web: Separation, Sexism, and Self*. Boston: Beacon, 1986.

Kelly, Tony. *Bread of God: Nurturing A Eucharistic Imagination*, Liguori, MO: Ligouri, 2001.

Kiley, Matthew T. "A Spiritual Democracy of All God's Creatures: Ecotheology and the Animals of Lynn White, Jr." In *Divinanimality: Animal Theory, Creaturely Theology*, edited by Stephen D. Moore, 241–60. New York: Fordham University Press, 2014.

Kinsley, David. *Ecology and Religion: Ecological Spirituality in Cross-Cultural Perspective.* Englewood Cliffs, NJ: Prentice Hall, 1995.

Klassen, Abbott John. "The Rule of St. Benedict and Environmental Stewardship." https://www.csbsju.edu/sju-sustainability/about-us/benedictine-stewardship/values/klassen.

Korsmeyer, Jerry D. *Evolution and Eden: Original Sin and Contemporary Science.* New York: Paulist, 1998.

Kraybill, Donald B. *The Upside-Down Kingdom.* 25th ann. ed. Scottsdale, PA: Herald Press, 2003.

Kujawa-Holbrook, Sheryyl A. *Hildegard of Bingen: Essential Writings of a Christian Mystic—Annotated & Explained.* Woodstock, NY: Skylight Paths, 2015.

Kurlansky, Mark. *Nonviolence: The History of a Dangerous Idea.* New York: Modern Library Reprint, 2008.

Kurzma, Andrew. "A Catholic Response to Factory Farming." *Glossalalia* 2.2 (June 2010) 17–34.

Leclerc, Eloi. *The Canticle of the Creatures: Symbols of Union: An Analysis of St. Francis of Assisi.* Chicago: Franciscan Herald, 1977.

Lee, Bryan Jeongguk. *Celebrating God's Cosmic Perichoresis: The Eschatological Panentheism of Jürgen Moltmann as Resource for an Ecological Christian Worship.* Eugene, OR, Pickwick Publications, 2011.

Leopold, Aldo. *County Almanac, And Sketches Here and There.* New York: Oxford University Press, 1949.

———. "Thinking Like A Mountain: Wolves and Deforestation." http://www.eco-action.org/dt/thinking.html/.

Lichtmann, Maria. *Poetry as Prayer, Gerard Manley Hopkins.* Boston: Pauline, 2002.

Linzey, Andrew. *Animal Gospel.* Louisville: Westminster John Knox, 1999.

———. *Christianity and the Rights of Animals.* New York: Crossroad, 1987.

———, ed. *Creatures of the Same God: Explorations in Animal Theology.* Winchester, UK: Winchester University Press, 2009.

———. "Is Christianity Irredeemably Speciesist?" In *Animals on the Agenda: Questions about Animals for Theology and Ethics.* London: SCM, 1998.

———. *Why Animals Suffering Matters: Philosophy, Theology, and Practical Ethics.* New York: Oxford University Press, 2013.

Loader, William. "Good News—for the Earth? Reflections on Mark 1:1–15." In *The Earth Story in the New Testament*, edited by Norman Habel and Vicky Balanbanski, 28–43. Earth Bible Series 5. Cleveland: Pilgrim, 2002.

Lovelock, James. *The Revenge of Gaia: Earth's Climate Crisis and the Fate of Humanity.* New York: Basic Books 2007.

Loy, David R., *The World Is Made Up of Stories.* Boston: Wisdom, 2010.

Macquarrie, John. "Paths in Spirituality." In *Irish Spirituality*, edited by Michael Maher. Dublin: Veritas, 1985.

Matzko McCarthy, David. "Desirous Saints." In *Queer Theology: Rethinking the Western Body*, edited by Gerard Loughlin, 305–12. Malden, MA: Blackwell, 2007.

Maudlin, Timothy. *The Philosophy of Physics, Time and Space.* Princeton: Princeton University Press, 2012.

McAfee, Gene. "Ecology and Biblical Studies." In *Theology for Earth Community: A Field Guide*, edited by Dieter T. Hessel, 31–44. Ecology and Justice Series. 1996. Reprinted, Eugene, OR: Wipf & Stock, 2003.

McDaniel, Jay B. "Can Animal Suffering Be Reconciled with Belief?" In *Animals on the Agenda*, edited by Andrew Linzey and Dorothy Yamamoto, 161–70. Chicago: University of Illinois Press, 1998.

———. *Earth, Sky, Gods, and Mortals: Developing an Ecological Spirituality*. 1990. Reprinted, Eugene, OR: Wipf & Stock, 1990.

———. *Of God and Pelicans: A Theology of Reverence for Life*. Louisville: Westminster John Knox Press, 1989.

———. *With Roots and Wings: Christianity in an Age of Ecology and Dialogue*. Maryknoll, NY: Orbis, 1995.

McDonagh, Sean. *Greening the Christian Millennium*. Dublin: Dominican Publications, 2000.

———. *Passion for the Earth: The Christian Vocation to promote Justice, Peace, and the Integrity of Creation*. Maryknoll, NY: Orbis, 1994.

McDonnell, Kilian. *The Baptism of Jesus in the Jordan: the Trinitarian and Cosmic Order of Salvation*. Collegeville, MN: Liturgical, 1996.

McFague, Sallie. *Blessed are the Consumers: Climate Change and the Practice of Restraint*. Minneapolis: Fortress, 2012.

———. *The Body of God: An Ecological Theology*. Minneapolis: Fortress, 1993.

———. *Collected Readings*. Edited by David B. Lott. Minneapolis: Fortress, 2013.

———. "An Ecological Christology: Does Christianity Have It?." In *Christianity and Ecology: Seeking the Well-Being of Earth and Humanity*, edited by Dieter T. Hessel and Rosemary Radford Ruether, 29–45. Cambridge: Harvard University Press, 2000.

———. "The Church Is Ecological." In *Many Marks of the Church*, edited by William Madges and Michael Daley, 120–128. New London, CT: Twenty-Third Publications, 2006.

———. *Models of God: Theology for an Ecological Nuclear Age*. Philadelphia, Fortress, 1988.

———. *A New Climate for Theology: God, the World, and Global Warming*. Minneapolis: Fortress, 2007.

———. *Super, Natural Christians: How We Should Love Nature*. Minneapolis: Fortress, 1997.

McGowan, Andrew. *Ascetic Eucharists: Food and Drink in Early Christian Ritual Meals*. New York: Oxford University Press, 1999.

McGrath, Alister E., *Christian Theology: As Introduction*, Oxford: Blackwell, 1994.

McIntosh, Mark, *Mystical Theology: The integrity of Spirituality and Theology*. Oxford: Blackwell, 1998.

McLellan, William L (Scotty). "Resisting Religion, Spreading Love." In *Christian Dissent for the 21st Century*, edited by Michael G. Long, 62–69. Maryknoll, NY: Orbis, 2008.

Merchant, Carolyn. *The Death of Nature: Women, Ecology, and Scientific Revolution*. San Francisco: HarperSanFrancisco, 1989.

———. *Reinventing Eden: The Fate if Nature in Western Culture*. 2nd ed. New York: Routledge, 2013.

Meir, John P. *A Marginal Jew: Rethinking the Historical Jesus*. Vol. 1. Anchor Bible Reference Library. New York: Doubleday, 1991.

Merton, Thomas. *When the Trees Say Nothing: Writings on Nature*. Edited by Kathleen Deignan. Notre Dame, IN: Sorin, 2003.

Mesters, Carlos. *Eden: Golden Age or Goad to Action*. Maryknoll, NY: Orbis, 1974,

Miller, Daniel K., *Animal Ethics and Theology: The Lens of the Good Samaritan*. New York: Routledge, 2012.

Miller, Michael Miller, "Why Are Brazil's Environmentalists Being Murdered?" *Washington Post*, August 27, 2015. https://www.washingtonpost.com/news/morning-mix/wp/2015/08/27/why-are-brazils-environmentalists-being-murdered/

Moltmann, Jürgen. *The Coming of God: Christian Eschatology*. Translated by Margaret Kohl. Minneapolis: Fortress, 2004.

———. *Ethics of Hope*. Translated by Margaret Kohl. Minneapolis: Fortress, 2012.

———. *God in Creation: A New Theology of Creation and the Spirit of God*. Minneapolis: Fortress, 1993.

———. *The Trinity and the Kingdom of God: The Divine Doctrine of God*. Translated by Margaret Kohl. London: SCM, 1981.

———. *The Way of Jesus Christ: Christology in Messianic Dimensions*. San Francisco: Harper, 1990.

Moss, Cynthia. *Elephant Memories: Thirteen Years in the Life of an Elephant Family*. Chicago: University of Chicago Press, 2000.

Mulhodland, Seamus. "Christ: The Haeccitas of God." In *Franciscan Theology of the Environment: An Introductory Reader*, edited by Dawn M. Nothwehr, 305–12. Quincy, IL, Franciscan Press.

Muir, John, *A Thousand Mile Walk to the Gulf*. Edited by William Frederich Bade. New York: Houghton Mifflin, 1916.

———. "My First Summer in the Sierra." Part II, *The Atlantic*, February, 1911. http://www.theatlantic.com/past/docs/unbound/flashbks/muir/muirfeb.htm;

———. *My First Summer in the Sierra*. Boston: Houghton Mifflin,1988.

Murtagh, Thomas. "St. Francis and Ecology." In *Franciscan Theology of the Environment: An Introductory Reader*, edited by Dawon M. Nothwehr. Quincy, IL: Franciscan Press, 2002.

Hanh, Thich Nhat. *Living Buddha, Living Christ*. New York: Riverside, 1995.

———. *Love Letter to the Earth*, Berkeley: Parrallax, 2013.

———. *Peace Is Every Step: The Path of Mindfulness in Everyday Life*. New York: Bantam, 1991.

———. *The Sun My Heart: From Mindfullness to Insight Meditation*. Berkeley, Parallax, 1988.

———. *The World We Have: A Buddhist Approach to Peace and Ecology*. Berkeley: Parallax, 2008.

Nash, James A. *Loving Nature: Ecological Integrity and Christian Responsibility*. Nashville: Abingdon, 1991.

———. On the Subversive Virtue: Frugality," *Ethics of Consumption: The Good Life, Justice, and Global Stewardship*, edited by David A. Crocker and Toby Linden, 416–36. Lanham, MD: Rowman & Littlefield, 1998.

Nash, Roderick, *The Rights of Nature: A History of Environmental Ethics*, Madison, University of Wisconsin Press, 1989.

Nelson, Richard. *The Island Within*. New York: Random House, 1989.

Newell, J. Phillip. *The Book of Creation: An Introduction to Celtic Spirituality*, Mahwah, Paulist Press, 1999.

———. *Christ of the Celts: The Healing of Creation*. San Francisco, Jossey-Bass, 2008.

Newsom, Carol. "Common Ground: An Ecological Reading of Genesis 2–3." In *The Earth Story in Genesis*, edited by Norman Habel and Shirley Wurst, 60–72. Sheffield, Sheffield Academic Press/The Pilgrim Press, 200.

Neyrey, Jerome H., "Reader's Guide to Clean/Unclean, Pure/Polluted, and Holy/Profane: The Idea and System of Purity." https://www3.nd.edu/~jneyrey1/purity.html;

———. "A Symbolic Approach to Mark 7." https://www3.nd.edu/~jneyrey1/symbolic.html/.

Nolan, Albert. *Jesus Before Christianity*. 25th anniv. ed. Maryknoll, NY: Orbis, 2002.

Norcott, Michael S. "Eucharistic Eating and Why Many Early Christians Preferred Fish." In *Eating and Believing*, edited by David Grumett and Rachel Muers. London: T. & T. Clark, 2008, chapter 16.

Nouwen, Henri J. M., Donald P. McNeill, Douglas A. Morrison. *Compassion: A Reflection on Christian Life*. New York: Image, 1982.

Osborne, Kenan R., "Incarnation, Individuality, and Diversity: How Does Christ Reveal the Unique Vale of Each Person and Thing?" In *Franciscan Theology of the Environment: An Introductory Reader*, edited by Dawn M. Nothwehr, 295–309. Quincy, IL: Franciscan Press, 2002.

Oakman, Douglas E. *Jesus and the Economic Questions of His Day*. Studies in Bible and Early Christianity 8. Lewiston, NY: Mellen, 1986.

O'Collins, Gerald. "Word, Spirit, and Wisdom in the Universe: A Biblical ad Theological Reflection." In *Incarnation: On the Scope and Depth of Christology*, edited by Niels Henrik Gregersen, 59–78. Minneapolis. Fortress, 2015.

O'Connell, Maureen. *Compassion: Loving Our Neighbor in an Age of Globalization*. Maryknoll, NY: Orbis, 2009.

O'Donnell, Hugh, *Eucharist and the Living Earth: Care for the Earth and the Celebration of Eucharist*. Rev. ed. Dublin: Columba, 2012.

O'Murchu, Diarmuid. *Christianity's Dangerous Memory: A Rediscovery of the Revolutionary Jesus*. New York: Crossroad, 2011.

———. *Inclusivity: A Gospel Imperative*. Maryknoll, NY: Orbis, 2015.

———. *Jesus in the Power of Poetry: A New Voice for Gospel Truth*. New York: Crossroad, 2009.

Page, Nick. *The Wrong Messiah: The Real Story of Jesus of Nazareth*. London: Hodder & Stoughton, 2012.

Pachirat, Timothy. *Every Twelve Seconds: Industrialized Slaughter and the Politics of Sight*. New Haven: Yale University Press, 2011.

Pagels, Elaine. *Adam, Eve, and The Serpent: Sex and Politics in Early Christianity*. New York: Vintage, 2011.

Palmer, Clare. "Stewardship: A Case Study in Environmental Ethics." In *The Earth Beneath: A Critical Guide to Green Theology*, edited by Ian Ball, Clare Palmer, and John Reader. London: SPCK, 1992.

Pannikar, Raimundo. *Christophany: The Fullness of Man*. Maryknoll, NY: Orbis, 2004.

———. *The Unknown Christ of Hinduism: Towards an Ecumenical Christophany*. Maryknoll, NY: Orbis, 1981.

Patriarch Batholomew. *Cosmic Grace, Humble Prayer: The Ecological Vision of the Green Patriarch Bartholomew I*. Edited by John Chryssavgis. Grand Rapids: Eerdmans, 2003.

Patterson, Stephen J. *Beyond the Passion: Rethinking the Death and Life of Jesus*. Minneapolis: Fortress, 2004.

———. *The God of Jesus: The Historical Jesus and the Search for Meaning*. Harrisburg, PA: Trinity, 1988.

Peet, Richard, and Michael Watts, *Liberation Ecologies: Environment, Development, Social Movements*. New York: Routledge, 199.

Perenyi, Eleanor. *Green Thoughts: A Writer in the Garden*. New York: Random: 1981.

Polkinghorne, John. *Science and Religion in the Quest of Truth*. New Haven: Yale University Press, 2012.

———, ed. *The Work of Love: Creation as Kenosis*. Grand Rapids: Eerdmans, 2001.

Primavesi, Anne. *Cultivating Unity within the Biodiversity of God*. Salem, OR: Polebridge, 2011.

———. *Gaia and Climate Change: A Theology of Gift Events*. New York: Routledge, 2009.

Profit, James, "Spiritual Exercises and Ecology." http://www.sjweb.info/sjs/pjold/pj_show.cfm?pubtextid=2831.

Queen, Christopher S. "Introduction." In *Engaged Buddhism in the West*, edited by Christopher S. Queen, 1–34. Boston: Wisdom, 2000.

Radford Rosemary Ruether. *Gaia &God: An Ecofeminist Theology of Earth Healing*. San Francisco: HarperSanFrancisco, 1992.

Raguin, Yves, *I am Sending You (John 20:21): Spirituality of the Missioner*. Manila: East Asian Pastoral Institute, 1973.

Rahner, Karl. "The Economic Trinity Is the Immanent Trinity and Vice Versa." In *Theological Investigations IV: More Recent Writings*. New York, Crossroad, 1973.

———. *Foundations of Christian Faith: An Introduction to the Idea of Christianity*. Translated by William V. Dych. New York: Crossroad, 1978.

———. *On the Theology of Death*. Translated by Charles H. Henkey. New York: Herder & Herder, 1961.

———. "Thoughts on the Theology of Christmas." In *Theological Investigations III: The Theology of the Spiritual Life*. New York: Seabury, 1974.

———. "The Specific Character of the Christian Concept of God." *Theological Investigations XXI: Science and Christian Faith*. New York: Crossroad, 1988.

Rasmussen, Larry L. "The Church's Mission to Society." In *Christianity and Ecology*, edited by Dieter T. Hessel and Rosemary Radford Ruether, 516–27. Cambridge: Harvard University Press, 2000.

———. *Earth Community, Earth Ethics*. Ecology and Justice Series. Maryknoll, NY: Orbis, 1996.

Rigby, Kate. "Animal Calls." In *Divinanimality: Animal Theory, Creaturely Theology*, edited by Stephen Moore, 116–33. New York: Fordham University Press, 2014.

Risik, Mariusz. "Discovering the Secrets of God's Garden: Resurrection as New Creation (Gen. 2:4b—3:24; Jn. 20:1–8)." *Studium Biblicum Franciscanum: Liber Annus* 58 (2007).

Rivera, Marya. *Poetics of the Flesh*. Durham: Duke University Press, 2015.

Robinson, Timothy H. (2013) "Sanctified Waters: Toward a Baptismal Ethic of Creation Care." *Leaven* 21/3 (2013). http://digitalcommons.pepperdine.edu/leaven/vol21/iss3/10

Rogers, Frank. *Practicing Compassion*. Nashville: Fresh Air, 2015.

Rohr, Richard. "Creation as the Body of God." *Spiritual Ecology: The Cry of the Earth*, edited by Llewellyn Vaughan-Lee, 239–48. Point Reyes, CA: Golden Sufi Center, 2013.

———. "Incarnation: God Is Not Out There." *Daily Meditation*, Sunday, January 10, 2016.

———. "Enoughness Instead of Never Enough." Daily Meditation, Friday, February 19, 2016.

Root, Gerald. *C.S. Lewis as an Advocate for Animals.* Published by the Humane Society of the United States, http://www.humanesociety.org/about/departments/faith/cs_lewis_narnia_gerald_root.html

Rudy, Kathy. *Loving Animals: Towards a New Animal Advocacy.* Minneapolis: University of Minnesota Press, 2011.

Russell, Robert. *Time in Eternity: Pannenberg, Physics, and Eschatology in Creative Mutual Action*, Notre Dame, IN: University of Notre Dame Press, 2012.

Sanguin, Bruce. *Darwin, Divinity, and the Dance of the Cosmos: An Ecological Christianity.* Kelowna, BC: CopperHouse, 2007.

Santmire, H. Paul, *Nature Reborn: The Ecological and Cosmic Promise of Christian Theology and the Sciences.* Minneapolis: Fortress, 2000.

Sasaki Roshi, Joshu. *Buddha Is the Center of Gravity.* San Cristobal, NM: Lama Foundation, 1974.

Schade, Leah D. *Creation-Crisis Preaching: Ecology, Theology, and the Pulpit.* St. Louis: Chalice, 2015.

Schauffler, E. Marina. *Turning to the Earth: Stories of Ecological Conversion.* Charlottesville: University of Virginia Press, 2003.

Schillebeeckx, Edward. *Christ: The Experience of Jesus as Lord.* Translated by John Bowden. New York: Crossroad, 1983.

Scott, Bernard Brandon. *Re-Imagine the World: An Introduction to the Parables of Jesus.* Santa Rosa, CA: Polebridge, 2001.

Schüssler Fiorenza, Elisabeth. *Jesus, Miriam's Child, Sophia's Prophet: Critical Issues in Feminist Theology.* New York: Continuum, 1994.

———. *In Memory of Her: A Feminist Theological Reconstruction of Christian Origins.* 10th ann. ed. New York: Crossroad, 2002.

Scully, Matthew. *Dominion: The Power of Man, the Suffering of Animals, and the Call to Mercy.* New York: St. Martin's, 2002.

Sears, Robert T., and Joseph A. Bracken. *Self-Emptying Love: The Spiritual Exercises and the Environment.* Eugene, OR: Cascade Books, 2006.

Seidenberg, David Mevorach. *Kabbalah and Ecology: God's Image in the More-Than-Human World.* New York: Cambridge University Press, 2015.

Shaw, George Bernard. *The Adventures of the Black Girl in Her Search for God.* Dodd, Mead, 1933.

Shore-Goss, Robert E. "Easter Is the Source of Our Green Faith." http://www.mischievousspiritandtheology.com/category/ecology/easter/.

———. "Greening Your Campus." https://www.youtube.com/watch?v=TPuCEr1lClQ.

———. "Greening Your Campus, Part 2." https://www.youtube.com/watch?v=FXODDBieD6I

———. "How to Get Started?" https://www.youtube.com/watch?v=H5nES106AJA.

———. "Introduction: Falling in Love with God's Earth." https://www.youtube.com/watch?v=deOVqVEGvo8.

———. "State of the Earth." Part 1 & 2. https://www.youtube.com/watch?v=
ExLSvJXWjlQ; https://www.youtube.com/watch?v=-e2oOB2sqrA.

Sideris, Lisa. "The Secular and Religious Sources of Rachel Carson's Sense of Wonder."
In *Rachael Carson: Legacy and Challenge*, Lisa H. Sideris and Kathleen Dean
Moore, eds., 232–50. Albany: State University of New York Press. http://indiana.
edu/~relstud/assets/docs/Sideris_rachel_carson_sense_of_wonder.pdf.

Silva, Jose. "Religion and Factory Farming: A Briefing of Compassion in World
Farming." 2015. https://www.ciwf.org.uk/media/7425967/compassion-2015-
religious-views-on-factory-farming.pdf/.

Sittler, Joseph A. "Called to Unity." *Ecumenical Review* 14 (1962) 177–87. http://www.
augie.edu/pub/values/sittler.pdf.

———. *Essays on Nature and Grace*. Philadelphia: Fortress, 1972.

———. *Gravity and Grace: Reflections and Provocations*. Minneapolis: Fortress, 2004.

Simmons, Ernest L. *The Entangled Trinity: Quantum Physics and Theology*. Minneapolis:
Fortress, 2014.

Slobodchikoff, Con. *Chasing Doctor Dolittle: Learning the Language of Animals*. New
York: St. Martin's, 2012.

Smith, Huston. *The World's Religions*. San Francisco: HarperSanFrancisco, 1991.

Southgate, Christopher. *The Groaning of Creation: God, Evolution, and the Problem of
Evil*. Louisville: Westminster John Knox, 2008.

Spencer, Daniel. *Gay and Gaia: Ethics, Ecology, and the Erotic*. Cleveland: Pilgrim, 1996.

Sponsel, Leslie E. *Spiritual Ecology: A Quiet Revolution*. Santa Barbara: Praeger, 2012.

Stark, Rodney. *Cities of God: The Real Story of How Christianity Became an Urban Movement and Conquered Rome*. New York: HarperOne, 2007.

Stewart, Benjamin M. *A Watered Garden: Christian Worship and Earth's Ecology*. Worship Matters. Minneapolis: Augsburg Fortress, 2014.

Stone, Ken. "The Dogs of Exodus and the Question of the Animal." In *Divinanimality:
Animal Theory, Creaturely Theology*, edited by Stephen D. Moore, 36–50. New
York: Fordham University Press, 2014.

Sweeney, Douglas. *The Suffering and Victorious Christ: Towards a Compassionate Christology*. Grand Rapids: Baker Academic, 2013.

Swimme, Brian. *The Universe is a Green Dragon*. Santa Fe, NM: Bear & Co., 1984.

Swimme, Brian, and Thomas Berry. *The Universe Story: From the Primordial Flaring
Forth to the Ecozoic Era—A Celebration of the Unfolding of the Cosmos*. New York:
HarperOne, 1994.

Swimme, Brian, and Mary Evelyn Tucker. *Journey of the Universe*. New Haven: Yale
University Press, 2011.

Taylor, Sarah McFarland. *Green Sisters*. Cambridge: Harvard University Press, 2007.

Tawney, R. H., *Religion and the Rise of Capitalism*. New York: New American Library,
1962.

Teilhard de Chardin, Pierre. *Hymn of the Universe*. New York: Harper & Row, 1981.

Theokritoff, Elizabeth. *Living in God's Creation: Orthodox Perspectives on Ecology*.
Crestwood, NY: St. Vladimir's Seminary Press, 2009.

Theokritoff, George. "The Cosmology of the Eucharist." In *Toward an Ecology of
Transfiguration: Orthodox Christian Perspectives on Environment, Nature, and
Creation*, 131–35. New York: Fordham University Press, 2009.

Torjessen, Karen J., *When Women Were Priests: Women's Leadership in Early Church,
and the Scandal of Their Subordination in the Rise of Christianity*. San Francisco:
HarperSanFrancisco, 1995.

Torrance, Thomas F. *The Christian Doctrine of God; One Being Three Persons*. Edinburgh T. & T. Clark, 1996.

Uhl, Christopher. *Developing Ecological Consciousness: The End of Separation*. 2nd ed. New York: Rowman & Littlefield, 2013.

Vaughan-Lee, Llwewlyn, *Spiritual Ecology: The Cry of the Earth*. Point Reyes, CA: Golden Sufi Center, 2013.

Visser, Margaret, *The Rituals of Dinner: The Origins, Evolution, Eccentricities, and Meaning of Table Manners*. New York: Penguin, 1992.

Waal, Frans B. M. de. *Are We Smart Enough to Know How Smart Animals Are?* New York: Norton, 2016.

———. *The Bonobo and the Atheist: In Search of Humanism Among the Primates*. New York: Norton, 2013.

Waetjen, Herman C. *A Reordering of Power: A Socio-Political Reading of Mark's Gospel*. 1989. Reprinted, Eugene, OR: Wipf & Stock, 2014.

Wallace, Mark I. *Finding God in the Singing River*. Minneapolis: Fortress, 2005.

———. *Fragments of the Spirit: Nature, Violence, and the Renewal of Creation*. Harrisburg, PA: Trinity, 2002.

———. *Green Christianity: Five Ways to a Sustainable Future*. Minneapolis: Fortress, 2010.

———. "The Green Face of God: Christianity in an Age of Ecocide." *CrossCurrents* 50 (2000) 310–31. http://www.crosscurrents.org/wallacefoo.htm.

———. "The Wounded Spirit as the Basis for Hope in an Age of Radical Ecology." In *Christianity and Ecology: Seeking the Well-Being of Earth and Humanity*, edited by Dieter T. Hessel and Rosemary Radford Ruether, 51–72. Cambridge: Harvard University Press, 2000.

Warner, Keith D. "Get Him out the Birdbath: What Does It Mean to Have a Patron Saint of Ecology." In *Franciscan Theology of the Environment*, edited by Dawn M. Nothwehr, 361–76. Quincy, IL: Franciscan Press, 2002.

Webb, Stephen H. *Good Eating: The Christian Practice of Everyday Life*. Grand Rapids: Brazos, 2001.

———. *On God and Dogs: A Christian Theology of Compassion for Animals*. New York: Oxford University Press, 1998

Wennberg. Robert N. *God, Humans, and Animals: An Invitation to Enlarge Our Moral Universe*. Grand Rapids: Eerdmans, 2003.

Westermann, Claus. *Creation*. Translated by John J. Scullion. Philadelphia: Fortress, 1974.

———. *Genesis 1–11*. Translated by John J. Scullion. Continental Commentaries. Minneapolis: Augsburg, 1984.

White, Lynn, Jr. "Continuing the Conversation." In *Western Man and Environmental Ethics*, edited by Ian Barbour. Reading, MA: Longman Higher Education,1973.

———. "The Future of Compassion." *Ecumenical Review* 30 (April 1978) 100–109.

———. "The Historical Roots of Our Ecologic Crisis." *Science* 155 (March 10, 1967) 1203–7.

———. "Snakes, Nests, and Icons: Some Observations on Theology and Ecology." *Anticipation: Christian Social Thought in Future Perspective*, 10, February 1972,

Whitney, Elspeth. "Lynn White Jr." In *Encyclopedia of Religion and Nature*, edited by Bron Taylor, 2:1735–36. New York: Continuum, 2005.

Wilder, Amos N. *Early Christian Rhetoric: The Language of the Gospel.* 1964. Reprinted, Eugene, OR: Wipf & Stock, 2014.

Wilkinson, Katherine K. *Between God & Green: How Evangelicals are Cultivating a Middle Ground on Climate Change.* New York: Oxford University Press, 2011.

Williams, Patricia A. *Doing without Adam and Eve: Sociobiology and Original Sin.* Minneapolis: Fortress, 2001.

Wills, Garry. *What Jesus Meant.* New York: Viking, 2006.

Wilson, A. N. *Jesus: A Life.* New York: Norton, 1992.

Wilson, E. O. *The Creation: An Appeal to Save Life on Earth.* New York: Norton, 2006.

———. *The Future of Life.* New York: Knopf, 2002.

Wilson, Ian. "Canterbury Church of the Woods to Connect with Higher Power through Nature." *Concord Monitor,* June 27, 2014. http://www.concordmonitor.com/home/12491175-95/canterburys-church-of-the-woods-connects-with-higher-power-through-nature

Wintz, Jack. *Will I See My Dog in Heaven?* Brewster, MA: Paraclete, 2009.

Wirzba, Norman. *Food and Faith: A Theology of Eating.* New York: Cambridge University of Press, 2011.

———. *From Nature to Creation: A Christian Vision for Understanding and Loving Our World.* Grand Rapids: Baker Academic, 2015.

———. *The Paradise of God: Renewing Religion in an Ecological Age.* New York: Oxford University Press, 2003.

Wolfhart, Graziela. "Liberation Theology and Ecological Concerns: Leonardo Boff and the Call of Mother Earth." October 11, 2012. http://iglesiadescalza.blogspot.com/2012/10/liberation-theology-and-ecological.html/.

Wooden, Cindy. "Pope Francis Explains Why He Chose St. Francis of Assisi's Name." *Catholic News Service,* March 17, 2013, http://www.thecatholictelegraph.com/pope-francis-explains-why-he-chose-st-francis-of-assisis-name/13243/.

Worster, Donald. *A Passion for Nature: The Life of John Muir.* New York: Oxford University Press, 2008.

Wright, N. T. *The Challenge of Jesus: Rediscovering Who Jesus Was and Is.* Downers Grove, IL: InterVarsity, 1999.

———. *Surprised by Hope.* London, SPCK, 2004.

Wurst, Shirley. "'Beloved, Come Back to Me': Ground's Theme Song in Genesis 3?" In *The Earth's Story in Genesis,* edited by Norman Habel and Shirley Wurst, 87–104. Cleveland: Pilgrim, 2001.

Wyschogrod, Edith. *Saints and Postmodernism: Revisioning Moral Philosophy.* Chicago: University of Chicago Press, 1990.

Zizioulas, John. *Being as Communion: Studies in Personhood and the Church.* Crestwood, NY: St. Vladimir's Seminary Press, 1993.

———. "Preserving God's Creation: Three Lectures on Theology and Ecology." *King's Theological Review* 12.1 (1989) 1–5.